From the Civil War to the Apocalypse

Postmodern History and American Fiction

Timothy Parrish

University of Massachusetts Press

Amherst

Copyright © 2008 by
University of Massachusetts Press
All rights reserved
Printed in the United States of America
LC 2007024294
ISBN 978-1-55849-627-9 (paper); 626-2 (library cloth)
Designed by Richard Hendel
Set in Quadraat and The Serif types by dix! Digital Prepress, Inc.
Printed and bound by The Maple-Vail Book Manufacturing Group

Library of Congress Cataloging-in-Publication Data
Parrish, Timothy, 1964–
   From the Civil War to the apocalypse :
postmodern history and American fiction / Timothy Parrish.
       p.   cm.
   Includes bibliographical references and index.
   ISBN 978-1-55849-627-9 (pbk. : alk. paper) —
ISBN 978-1-55849-626-2 (alk. paper)
   1. American literature—20th century—History and criticism.
2. History in literature.   3. Literature and history—United States—
History—20th century.   4. Postmodernism (Literature)   I. Title.
   PS228.H57P37   2007
   813.009'3582—dc22

                                                 2007024294

British Library Cataloguing in Publication data are available.

LIBBY

Contents

Acknowledgments

This book first began to take material form while I was teaching, year after year, sections of American Fiction 4400 at the University of North Texas. Its arguments were worked out during hundreds of hours of class discussions with the brilliant and inquisitive students there, whose passion for what they read continually inspired my own. I hope that they will recognize in this book a version of what we shared and that they will accept it as my offering to them for what they gave me and for what I cannot repay.

I first read Joan Didion when I was an undergraduate under the severe instruction of Victoria Aarons. Thomas Pynchon's work I met through that Pynchonesque medium, John David Brantley. I wish that John could read this. Over twenty years ago, Char Miller somehow found space to let me think that it was possible to lose myself in Faulkner's sense of time. Once there, one never leaves, and, as you may see, Vicki and Char, some of this book was spoken by me to you (or by you to me) in the offices and halls of Northrup and Chapman during that not quite lost time.

Ross Posnock's continued support of my work and career has been invaluable. Brian Evenson, David Gillota, Robert Lawson-Rodriguez, Jocelyn Moore, Tim Murray, Cindy Phillips, Mark Wiebe, and Brett Zalkan kept me company with their intelligence and moral support. Great readers they are, every one.

In ways too opaque to specify, I have been helped by the example of Neil Easterbrook, who embodies, I think, what Plato's ideal of a colleague must be. Thanks, too, to David Vanderwerken for his immense knowledge of all things Faulkner and his ability to steer one over freezing roads and through icy conditions.

Very close to the time this book went to press I presented a version of the last chapter to the English Department at Florida State University. Their keen questions provoked me to rethink and, I hope, improve the rhetoric of my argument. Thanks especially to Ralph Berry, Leigh Edwards, Andrew Epstein, David Kirby, Jim O'Rourke, Diane Roberts, and Dan Vitkus.

Clark Dougan once again has made working with the University of Massachusetts Press a pleasure. Carol Betsch and Joan Vidal helped tremendously in preparing the manuscript for publication. Texas Christian University students Amy Milakovic and John Wood also read and corrected early versions of the manuscript.

While I was writing this book, my son, Matthew, asked me where language came from. Before I could try to answer he speculated that weapons perhaps came before words and in any case weapons must have made possible the invention of language. I felt that I was chasing Matthew's insight while reading and writing much of this book. I cannot wait until he reads *Blood Meridian*. About that same time, my daughter, Samantha, hid her brother's globe (our family orrery) in his closet. This allowed her to inform the family that the whole world now resided in Matthew's closet and that if Matthew were to seek the world, he would find himself already discovering it in that hidden quadrant of his room. She will love *Don Quixote*.

When I seek the world, as I only seem to do again and again in my favorite books, I find always Matthew, Samantha, and my cherished wife and partner, Elizabeth, to whom I dedicate this book and who must know that its lines are animated by her beautiful, loving presence.

Part of the Introduction appeared as "Texas Schoolbook: The History Lessons of Don DeLillo's *Libra*," *Clio* 30.1 (2000): 1–31, and is reprinted with permission. An early version of chapter 1 was published as "Faulkner's *Absalom, Absalom!* The True History of the South," *Prospects* 29 (2004): 1–39, and is reprinted with permission. A portion of what became chapter 5 appeared in "After Henry Adams: Rewriting History in Joan Didion's *Democracy*," *Critique* 47.2 (2006): 167–84, (c) 2006 by the Helen Dwight Reid Educational Foundation, published by Heldref Publications, 1319 18th Street, NW, Washington, DC 20036–1802 (www.heldref.org), reprinted by permission. Another portion of chapter 5 appeared as "From Hoover's F.B.I. to Eisenstein's *Unterwelt*: Don DeLillo Writes the Postmodern Novel," *MFS: Modern Fiction Studies* 45.3 (Fall 1999): 696–723, published by Johns Hopkins University Press, and is reprinted with permission.

From the Civil War to the Apocalypse

Introduction
When Fiction Became History

We historians must somehow get ourselves to the point where we no longer feel that if we cannot refute contemporary skepticism—or if, in some moment of inexcusable weakness, we allow ourselves to be seduced by the likes of Henry Adams or William Faulkner (not to mention the white-haired archfiend himself, holed up somewhere in Paris, writing yet another treatise on death and deconstruction)—then all is lost, history will slide into fiction.
—David Harlan

I

This book addresses the claims of recent postmodern theory that history works as fiction does. I will not be arguing that a postmodern understanding of history means that history is dead (or hopelessly relativistic). Ordinarily, one assumes that novelists offer "versions" of history—they make readers think or rethink what history means. Historians, in contrast, seem to offer the real thing—history by itself and separate from one's contemplation of it. The basic premise that theorists such as Hayden White and Linda Hutcheon have advanced is that history is a narrative art, or practice, and thus must be understood as one would any form of narrative representation. History, from this critical perspective, has no inherent meaning and can never be a straight-forward recounting of the facts. The "facts" of history matter only insofar as they are part of a narrative that controls and manipulates their meaning. That the Battle of Hastings took place in 1066 is itself insignificant without a story that explains why and to whom this "fact" matters. Recognizing that history, like fiction, is a form of representation does not turn history into something that is untrue or merely fantastic. History is inevitably a story, one that is well or not so well told, and thus is always, in its deepest sense, a way of perceiving the world that is also a fight to make the world over as one wants it to be.

From the Civil War to the Apocalypse is about narrative authority in the postmodern age. What historical narrative is, who masters it, who distributes it, who receives it, and who controls it are questions that consume each of the authors I discuss. This book engages American history at key points that remain significant because they remain unresolved. The authors examined plot a discontinuous line that goes from the demarcation of the Mason–Dixon Line in the 1760s to the expansion of the United States borders after the Mexican War in the 1840s, through the Civil War and the African American Diaspora that followed Reconstruction, through the J. Edgar Hoover years of the Cold War and Vietnam. The book ends by looking beyond the post-9/11 world to a time when history still exists but America does not. What survives a reading of these novels is the sense that writers who are otherwise identified as multicultural or postmodern share the view that nothing matters more than history and a belief in its possibilities.

Although the practice of history may be contingent and subject to the restrictions that narrative demands, the belief in history as something that transcends one's own time and place cannot be argued or "critiqued" away. Thus, what postmodern theorists of history have failed to emphasize is how since modernism novelists have been not only critiquing history as a practice but also practicing history by writing, or making, it themselves. Novels such as William Faulkner's Absalom, Absalom! (1936) or Cormac McCarthy's Blood Meridian (1985) compel their readers to accept their narratives as true in the same ways that historians expect their readers to accept their narratives as true. These authors write history as a form of fiction. The novelist historians that I will be discussing tell us that history is always a form of social action and as such obligates its readers either to accept its call to action as true or fight its claims. One resists the truth of a given history not only by labeling it as false but also by writing, or enacting, a counterhistory in narrative form. Toni Morrison, for instance, responds to William Faulkner not so much as a rival novelist but as a skeptical historian. Her frequent claims that her work speaks to and for African Americans testify to the extent that she wants to be read as as a historian and not only as a novelist. Her work consistently portrays slavery as an ongoing fact that continues to dominate American life through the twentieth century, and it does so by countering directly the powerful history that Faulkner offers in Absalom, Absalom!

As Morrison's African American revision of Faulkner suggests, the postmodernist critique of history cannot be separated from the rise of multiculturalism. Postmodernism and multiculturalism are often linked because both challenge the authority of what Jean-Francois Lyotard refers to as metanarratives. "Can we," Lyotard asks, "continue to organize the events which crowd in upon us from the human and nonhuman worlds with the help of the Idea of a universal history of humanity?" (qtd. in Rorty, *Objectivity* 212) Lyotard's implied answer is no, since a multiplicity of irreconcilable cultural differences would seem to make any universalist claim to history impossible. In Europe the critique of a universal history of humanity since World War II is in part a response to Adolf Hitler's catastrophic metanarrative of the Third Reich. In the United States the rise of multiculturalism, sometimes referred to as identity politics, has constituted a counterattack on the tradition of American exceptionalism that understands American history as a single coherent story of a people progressing ever forward toward a social heaven on earth. Multiculturalism argues not only for an American society of diverse peoples but also an American history that is at odds with itself because no point of view exists that fairly encompasses the experience of all Americans (African Americans, Native Americans, Anglo Americans, Chinese Americans, and Hispanic Americans, among others).[1]

Taken collectively, the authors I examine destroy the presumption that "American" history is a coherent story of a single people committed to equal treatment for all. For these authors, any coherence in "American" history resides in the success of a handful of white people commandeering the nation's (and, since the twentieth century, the world's) resources for the benefit of a few who call themselves "Americans" and pretend to act in the name of those whom they exploit. This story is appallingly coherent and is known as the history of the "United States," or, to call it what it has become, the history of the United States Empire. It begins in the sixteenth century with the European appropriation of the wealth and the people of Africa, North America, and South America and continues to the present day, most obviously, in the Middle East. The authors I examine, however, focus not on U.S. imperialism abroad but on U.S. imperialism at home. To them, there is no America, per se, only the United States and the often horrific acts it commits in the name of "Americans." Faulkner's *Absalom, Absalom!* is emblematic of this stance since it speaks for people whose homes have been invaded and destroyed by United States forces. Nor does *Absalom* try to reconstruct out of the ruins of its history some better America, some new "city on the hill." Rather, it assures surviving white Southerners that the South was not lost during the United States Civil

War and implies that the South can rise again because it has never been finally defeated. We, the novel says, need not surrender permanently to the U.S. Empire. Thus, ironically, Faulkner's novel asserts a kind of racism consistent with that of United States history but nonetheless still refuses to acknowledge the appropriation of Southern history by the United States except as a form of conquest that they (Southerners) deny to this day. Although Morrison's *Beloved* portrays *Absalom*'s racism as pernicious to its chosen people, African Americans and their descendants, it does not dispute *Absalom*'s contention that United States history is imperialist and morally untenable. Nor do DeLillo, Didion, Johnson, McCarthy or Pynchon dispute this contention. To each of them, American history has deconstructed into competing fragments that cannot made be whole except through what would be totalitarian acts of oppression. For Faulkner, Johnson, and Morrison, writing histories that refuse to be called American is a first step toward claiming one's history as something other than what the United States had made it.

Regarding the claim that *Absalom* advances a Confederate history opposed to the reality of U.S. history, one may object that everyone knows that the South lost the Civil War to the North and the result had two objective, verifiable consequences: the freeing of the slaves and the consolidation of the United States as an incipient world power. Yet, as Morrison shows, the slaves may have been freed but their descendants were never integrated into the affluence of United States society. Nor have most of the Southern white descendants been assimilated into the prosperity of the Unites States Empire since the Southern states continue to suffer the highest levels of poverty and lowest levels of education in the United States. U.S. power abroad has not and does not translate into social equality at home. Thus, within the overarching and fundamentally imperialist history that goes under the name of "United States," there exist "alternative histories," stories of peoples who may be called "Americans" but who construct histories about themselves in opposition to so-called United States history. These histories reject United States history as it is taught in most public schools and presented in the mainstream media. Instead of American exceptionalism as usual, they offer faith—in the most profound sense of the word—in histories that many Americans— including the author of this book—cannot accept as their own.

In the postmodern era, the belief in history and its importance remains paramount. What is often dismissed as identity politics should more properly be understood as a battle to claim authority over the present, which means, for the combatants, the truth of the past. From this perspective, history, rather than identity, is the common ground of postmodern writers. Yet there is a sense—and this is crucial to understand—that the postmodern histories I discuss are not obviously postmodern at all. They are not skeptical toward narrative's capacity to convey truth. They believe narrative is truth. They are not—in John Barth's famous phrase—"lost in the funhouse," and they should be distinguished from the "aesthetic" postmodernism associated with Barth, Donald Barthelme, Robert Coover, William Gaddis, or William Gass. Where Gass and Barthelme, say, practice linguistic skepticism as a mode of perceiving that never gets beyond itself, Morrison and Johnson write to affirm a version of communal truth that its practitioners, or believers, assume to be transcendent and enduring. To the extent that they expose the incoherence of so-called "American" history, they may reveal to some readers, often despite their intentions, the contingency of truth—that truth is never whole but always seen from a particular, and thus fallible, point of view. Except for Morrison's response to Faulkner and, arguably, McCarthy's response to the issues Faulkner and Morrison raise, however, the authors I discuss are not talking to each other. They speak not to outsiders, or interested third parties, but to those who share their story and know its truth as a matter of faith. Taking each history on its own terms, they focus on truth and belief in ways distinctively un-postmodern, since none of the historians I present are concerned about "the truth" of any history except their own. They care only about having the moral authority to claim, for their people, the present as the consequence of "our" shared past. In this respect, they imagine a reality that is not postmodernist in orientation but governed by the beliefs they assert to be true, regardless of what those outside their community might contend.

These authors give the lie to the premise that a critique of history's narrative suppositions somehow effaces history altogether. In this attitude they run counter to the dominant concerns of the most influential literary critic of postmodernism, Linda Hutcheon. Of literary critics, Hutcheon has been the most persuasive in showing that in postmodernist fiction "history does not exist except as text" (*Poetics* 16). Hutcheon terms fiction that emphasizes the textuality of history *historiographic metafiction*. In novels such as E. L. Doctorow's *Ragtime* (1975) or John Fowles's *A Maggot* (1985), according to Hutcheon, "the narrativization of past events is not hidden; the events no longer seem to speak for themselves, but are shown to be consciously composed into a narrative, whose constructed—not found—order is imposed upon them, often overtly by a narrating figure" (*Politics* 63). Of course the broader point is not merely that fiction renders history as something invented but that the practice of history even by historians always requires narrative invention to be accepted as true. Hutcheon's arguments cannot account for how a particular critique of a previous history may itself become a type of history that a new audience perceives as true. The point is not quite that history is fiction, or that fiction eliminates claims of history, but that we should treat some types of fiction as we do history. To demystify history, however, is not the same as to do away with history or with people's need to believe in it. As we will see when we discuss Johnson's *Fiskadoro*, history is impossible without faith. History's "facts" are always secondary to the faith that binds them together into a story people believe to be true.

By discussing how postmodern fiction demystifies history, Hutcheon, in effect, inscribes the dividing line between the two genres. Once we see how malleable is the line between history and fiction in the postmodern era, though, we can also see how pervasive and vital the ability to shape reality through narrative is. The consequences of this insight for understanding the importance of the postmodern novel are enormous since it suggests that the postmodern novel is not a trivial, overaestheticized response to modernism limited to appreciation by elite, mostly academic, audiences. Rather, the post-modern novel engages with and even establishes the models for how political and social meaning has been shaped since the Cold War. As we shall see, post-modernist writers such as Don DeLillo or Joan Didion understand the success of such figures as J. Edgar Hoover or Ronald Reagan in terms of their ability to script or be scripted by narrative artists who recognize that history is its most powerful—its most true—when it is rendered as fiction. The postmod-ern novel is the arena not only where old-fashioned history is critiqued but also where one can watch history being made (and remade). Beyond offering another critique of history or its possibilities, the most powerful postmodern writers go beyond what Hutcheon stakes out for them because they aspire in their writing to the narrative status that was once accorded to history.

Historian David Harlan calls history's traditional appeal "one of our primary forms of moral reflection," while also noting that most "literary critics tend to leave the room when anyone starts talking about ethical criti-cism" (*Degradation* 213, 155). Postmodernist fiction is often accused of being relativistic. If everything is a text, then what can ever be true? Works such as Morrison's *Beloved* (1987) or Didion's *Democracy* (1984) unsettle readers' confidence in what they perceive to be true, not because they play narrative games that are as old as *Don Quixote* (1605, 1615) but because they ask in as challenging a form as possible who is the we who is reading this text and who benefits from calling this story but not that story moral or true? These works do not promote relativism, in my view, except for those readers who reject their premises and their conclusions. Rather, the novelists I discuss seem to accept that if one wants one's history to be accepted as true, one has to fight for that truth with whatever verbal strategies one can employ. To the criticism that postmodern fiction surrenders its claim to truth, one might respond with words from William James's essay "Is Life Worth Living?" James asserts, "If this life not be a real fight, in which something is eternally gained for the universe by success, it is no better than a game of private theatricals from which one may withdraw at will. But it feels like a fight" (61). In other words, each of us fights for the truth and hopes that the universe, or our portion of it, gains something from what we take and make to be "our" history. The possibility that one's belief may not be objectively true or one's fight not demonstrably winnable will not prevent one from acting according to what one believes. The postmodernist historians I discuss disagree about what American history is or has been, but they all agree with James that one can never withdraw from Hstory—even if History is in practice only histories that, taken together, seem to be a mere succession of staged theatricals.

Any historian, even if a novelist, must believe the history told is true. Novelists who practice history seem easy to dismiss precisely because their arguments come with a generic disclaimer—they are "fiction." Yet why should a novelist's interpretation of history be less true than a historian's version of history that—as it must—elicits the objections of other historians? Historians argue about the past—about whether the American Civil War was fought over the question of slavery or over a "states rights" interpretation of the U.S. Constitution. The Civil War is a "fact" of American history, but what it means to present-day Americans cannot be proved, but only claimed. Collecting so-called objective facts and arranging them into well-constructed narratives does not compel a reader to assent to their "truth." Belief alone can achieve that state of truth. From this perspective, the "truth" of any given history requires what James called "a will to believe" on the part of those who understand their lives to be a part of the history that is being told, made, and fought for. To argue this point of view is to say that history is never only a story about the past but is also a groping toward the future—a search for an entryway to that which has not yet happened and therefore something that must be imagined.

The works I discuss run from the high modernism of Faulkner to the post-postmodernism of Denis Johnson. They function as histories because they involve not only a creative recounting of a particular past but also a fight to define the present in terms of a livable future. In important ways Faulkner initiates the historicist-narrative critique that Hutcheon would label as postmodernist. Each of the books is centrally concerned with the question of history as a practice and a type of belief. Each takes as a premise the idea that history in its most powerful form enacts a will to power that has nothing to do with objectivity or getting the facts straight. Professional historians, by contrast, do not usually understand themselves to be speaking from any point of view broader than their own professional presentation of a specifically defined subject. Moreover, most—with the crucial exception of popular narrative historians—do not understand themselves to be speaking to or for anyone except other professional historians. Understandably and correctly, they do not see deception to be an explicit or implicit part of what they do.

In *Beyond the Great Story* (1995), Robert Berkhofer gives a definitive account of how postmodernist theory has challenged the foundations of historical inquiry.[2] His concise formulation is: "Postmodernist theory questions what history can be, both as a real past and as a discourse about it. Historians disagree about how best to meet the challenge" (1). Given that postmodernism denies the assumptions that have governed the discipline since the nineteenth century, one can understand why historians have not rushed to confront its implications. Berkhofer explains that as "the crisis of representation raised by late modernist and structuralist theorists" became "first 'a linguistic turn'" and then took "'interpretative' and 'rhetorical turns,'" the "strict separation of objectivity and subjectivity, whether as fact versus value or empiricism versus moral advocacy" led to the unhinging of the "received viewpoint grounding the social sciences" (3, 1). Thus, "the linguistic and rhetorical turns seemed to collapse all reality into its representation, all history into its text [textualization]" (110).

On this account, the linguistic turn kept turning until—as Lyotard also suggests—it cut the cables that anchored all of the humanities to the idea that they preserved some essence of being human that could be traced to the beginning of known history. White has been the most prominent voice to translate the implications of the linguistic turn to the practice of history, but the influence of his work has been limited mostly to English departments. Linking White to William James, Harlan comments that White "adopted an explicitly present-minded stance toward the past" that meant the "past was teeming with as yet unavailable meanings" and was thus a "source of imaginative possibilities rather than causal explanations" (qtd. in Harlan, *Degradation* 108). If nothing can be known outside a text that has not already been constituted by the text itself, then does it not follow that "history" itself is merely a text, an endless play of signifiers whose meaning cannot be arrested except arbitrarily? White even points to Jacob Burckhardt as an example of a nineteenth-century historian who had "abandoned the dream of telling the truth about the past by means of telling a story because he had long since abandoned the belief that history has any *inherent* meaning or significance" (qtd. in Harlan, *Degradation* 108).[3] One can perhaps see this turn more clearly with White, though, than with Burckhardt (although one of Burckhardt's students, Friedrich Nietzsche, certainly saw the turn with him). As Berkhofer argues, the discipline of history, with its nearly two-century-old belief in concrete facts and "true" narratives confirmed by rigorous methodologies, has, among the human sciences, been the most resistant to the insights of postmodernism.

Meanwhile, what happened with the "linguistic turn" in English departments is well documented. Instead of understanding novels and poems to be precisely constructed artifacts that conveyed intended, knowable meanings to sympathetic and well-trained readers, academic readers came to understand works of literature as exercises in writing that communicated an endless play of potential—but never fixed—meanings. The celebration of writing (*écriture*) replaced the celebration of writers. Inspired by the brilliant philosopher of language Jacques Derrida, the ruling premise of literary studies became the phrase "nothing outside of the text." Following the implications of the critique of language first offered by Ferdinand de Saussure, Derrida saw that words, or signifiers, can have meaning only in the context of, or in relationship to, other signifiers. A text, then, is merely a chain of different signifiers among which there is an ongoing and never-ending play of differences, what Derrida calls "différance," or the play among signifiers that makes signification, or meaning (or interpretation), possible. On this account, the meaning of any given text is made by the reader as much as by the author, or encoder, and any one interpretation is subject to the variety of conflicting interpretations that other readers may locate within the text.This orientation not only does away with the intention of the author, and therefore the idea that the text has a specific meaning that can be known and communicated, but also seems to make a search for truth (at best) an irrelevant concern. As Richard Rorty has argued:

> When philosophers like Derrida say things like "there is nothing outside the text" they are not making theoretical remarks, remarks backed up by epistemological or semantic arguments. Rather, they are saying, cryptically and aphoristically, that a certain framework of interconnected ideas—truth as correspondence, language as picture, language as imitation—ought to be abandoned. They are not, however, claiming to have discovered the real nature of truth or language or literature. Rather, they are saying that the very notion of discovering the nature of such things is part of the intellectual framework that we must abandon—part of what Heidegger calls "the metaphysics of presence," or "the onto-theological tradition." (*Consequences* 140)

Although Derridean theory caused anxiety because it challenged the belief that within a given literary work there inhered a quality of timeless greatness, it encouraged new and ingenious readings of texts that often revitalized the discipline. In the case of the New Historicism, literary scholars such as Stephen Greenblatt and Walter Benn Michaels succeeded in blurring the boundary between literary context and historical context. However, for historians, such a blurring is inherently problematic. A belief in what Rorty calls a "certain framework of ideas" within which inheres a knowable truth, or related truths, that can be communicated intact from generation to generation, is what most historians understand history and its study to offer. As Berkhofer suggests, for historians "reducing the past to its textualization denies the ability of historians to know the past as such" (14). As Peter Gay asserts, "The objects of the historian's inquiry are precisely that, objects, out there in a real and single past. Historical controversy in no way compromises their ontological integrity" (qtd. in Berkhofer 48).[4]

In an almost offhanded remark, Rorty nicely suggests how the linguistic turn has changed the way many conceive historical practice. He observes that "for Derrida, writing always leads to more writing, and more, and still more—just as history does not lead to Absolute Knowledge or the Final

Struggle, but more history, and more, and still more" (*Consequences* 94). Yet, as Gay's remark suggests, many historians would say that history does stop, in the sense that the past can be distinguished from the present. To Gay, history can never simply be endless redescription of what happened. To so characterize the practice of history, as Rorty does, contradicts two basic premises that, according to F. R. Ankersmit, historians have shared since at least the nineteenth century: first, that "the historical text is considered 'transparent' with regard to underlying historical reality," and, second, that the historical text is "transparent with regard to the historian's judgment of the relevant part of the past" (qtd. in Berkhofer 28). As Jenkins explains, some historians continue to believe that there is both an "upper case," or metanarrative history, on one hand, and a "lower case," or academic history, on the other. The latter is a localized version of the former. A lower-case history that may involve a narrow subject such as "labor movements during the American teens" takes its meaning from the understanding that it exists within a larger, upper-case history that tells the story of "America's quest for freedom from the Pilgrims to the present." It is in this context that Berkhofer astutely defines the practice of history in terms of its telling "a Great Story" that can allow contradictory perspectives because everything in the Great Story exists in the context of "one Great Past" (46). Berkhofer concludes that history cannot change "once the Past is past, no matter what histories are written," and thus "a plurality of interpretations in practice never implies a plurality of (hi)stories, let alone a plurality of past" (47, 49). Thus, as Berkhofer explains, "a Great Story provides a device for embedding partial (hi)stories in their larger context in order to show their significance." Yet, on this view, despite various kinds of methodological claims that historians may employ, history remains fundamentally narrative in its orientation, which means that history is subject to the same kinds of critiques as any other kind of narrative practice.

In the afterword to his controversial *Dead Certainties* (1992), the historian Simon Schama expresses his exasperation with his peers for their failure to confront the types of arguments that Berkhofer and Jenkins acknowledge:

> Even in the most austere scholarly report from the archives, the inventive faculty—selecting, pruning, editing, commenting, interpreting, and delivering judgments—is in full play. This is not a naively relativist position that insists that the lived past is *nothing* more than an artificially designed

text.... But it does accept the rather banal axiom that claims for historical knowledge must always be fatally circumscribed by the character and
prejudices of the narrator. (322)

As Schama notes, even sober "reports" from laboratories, archival libraries,
and field interviews depend on the ability of the recorder to transform the
"facts" he finds into a plausible narrative. Schama's point is that relying on
the truth of the archives and primary sources to confirm the truth of one's
history—an article of faith for historians since Leopold von Ranke first es-
poused it in the nineteenth century—ignores that there is simply no objective way to interconnect the facts that one finds. As White argues, historians
persist in their "reluctance to consider historical narratives as what they most
manifestly are: verbal fictions, the contents of which are as much *invented*
as *found* and the forms of which have more in common with their counterparts in literature than they have with those in the sciences" (*Tropics* 82). In
a postmodern context, history can no longer be considered "a groundable
(epistemological/ontological) discourse, and we are left in a condition allowing or necessitating only ungroundable temporal stylizations in *infinitum*" (2).
Jenkins concludes, "Put simply, we are the *source* of whatever the past means
for us" (14).

To historians trained to believe in objectivity as a goal and in the idea that
history is an object that can be known, such a view can only mean that history
is not a discipline of secure, shared knowledge but the ongoing perpetuation
of a kind of monstrous relativism.[5] Responding to postmodern critiques of
history, Richard J. Evans argues against the relativist implications of postmodern theory by saying that "the theory of history is too important a matter
to be left to the theoreticians" (*In Defense* 12). In a very useful chapter called "A
History of History," Evans shows how historians have continually reframed
their understanding of their own practices in response to discoveries from
other disciplines. Modern history began, in his view, when Ranke applied
the lesson of nineteenth-century philology to the writing of historical narrative. In 1903 the Regius Professor of Modern History (Cambridge), J. B. Bury,
declared, "history is a science, no less and no more and thus 'not a branch
of literature'" (qtd. in Evans, *In Defense* 19). After World War I, "the triumph
of modernism in art, music and literature increased this sense of disorientation among historians" (25). Once Albert Einstein's theories were accepted
as workable, the discipline of history was suddenly a part of "an intellectual

climate in which it was thought the 'aspect of things' changed with the position of the observer" (26). That is, even before "the linguistic turn" had been explicitly formulated, Evans tells us, historians were already trying to resist the implication of Benedetto Croce's famous phrase "All history is contemporary history" (26).

Historians are compelled to defend their discipline against postmodernist invaders because these outsiders seem to have found the methodology that makes the practice of a professional historian superfluous. Noting that postmodernist theory "potentially seems to shake the very foundations of our enterprise," the historian William Cronon asks, "If our choice of narratives reflects only our power to impose a preferred vision of reality on a past that cannot resist us, then what is left of history?" (qtd. in Berkhofer 50). To Jenkins, the fits of existential agony that have afflicted so many historians in the wake of the linguistic turn are, to say the least, misplaced and should be understood as "just a part of the flawed experiment of modernity" (204). Jenkins, like Rorty and Harlan, sees the postmodern challenge to history as an unambiguous "good thing," explaining that "the optimum conditions for the creation of and sustaining of history now lie behind us, and that we should now forget such configurations and embrace a non-historicizing postmodernism" (9). Yet, as Evans's defense also suggests, to call for the end of history is not the same thing as ending it. Jenkins's emancipatory call "to forget history and ethics altogether" is itself subject to a type of postmodernist critique. Jenkins says, "Perhaps we are now under conditions where we can live our lives within new ways of timing time which do not refer to a past tense" (2). Who is the "we" to whom Jenkins refers, and why should his version of what is or is not history be my or your version of history? Is history not always about the competing claims of particular groups of people who claim to know each other through a particular story that they share? If so, can history ever be forgotten? Would it not be better to say that history is never forgotten (or even proved untrue) so much as it is *rewritten*?

Even the conservative Evans finds much to admire in postmodern approaches to history when he discusses examples of postmodern history rather than postmodern theory about history.[6] Evans acknowledges that postmodernism "has shifted the emphasis in historical writing" from the "socio-scientific to literary models" (216). If so, then postmodernism has brought history full circle back to Ranke's attempt to ground history as an objective discipline in the nineteenth century. Ranke's famous formulation was to present history as "wie es eigentlich gewesen" (qtd. in Evans 14)—usually translated as "what actually happened," although Evans prefers the translation "how it essentially was" (14). Ranke argues that the past cannot be seen in terms of the present and therefore one's view of the past depends on primary sources that have to be examined scrupulously to eliminate any forgeries that might compromise one's account. If one stuck to the record, and the record were authenticated, then the interconnections one drew between documents would be objectively true. As we have seen, a postmodern account would nevertheless object that no fact, however true, could exist except within a narrative that makes use of that fact to tell a particular a story. Ranke's methodology denied this premise. Ironically, as Evans relates, Ranke "was converted to history by the shock of discovering that [Walter] Scott's novel *Quentin Dunward* was historically inaccurate. He determined therefore that he would apply the methods he had learned as a philologist to the study of historical texts in order to make such inaccuracies impossible in the future" (14). If you read novels for facts, then you will indeed become confused. The point, however, is that history concerns arguing not about facts but about the narratives within which those facts are contained. It may be that a set of agreed-upon facts can help to refute a historical hoax, such as the "Hitler Diaries," but no amount of facts was able to prevent Hitler from killing millions of Jews. Unfortunately, that required a narrative in which millions of people could believe.[7]

III

Claims of history that are limited to verifiable facts can be understood as true only in the contexts that assert them. Such claims are narrow and by definition academic. By contrast, narratives whose scope provides their appeal suffer little from a few missing facts as long as the story they tell seems plausible. That Ranke, the founder of the objective, scientifically based school of history writing, could be confused into thinking a novel that he was reading was in fact a "true" historical account suggests how difficult it is for any definition of history to subdue narrative's power to overwhelm facts in favor of belief. For many Americans, history is a form of communal memory and not necessarily to be found in books at all. Certainly, for most Americans, history is not what academics write for other academics. If history is to be found in books, it will be sought in books that are far removed from the kinds of intellectual debates I have been rehearsing but that are perhaps not far from having the kind of appeal that Sir Walter Scott held for nineteenth-century readers. Popular works of American history such as Walter Isaacson's *Benjamin Franklin* (2003), Joseph Ellis's *Founding Brothers* (2000), or David McCullough's *John Adams* (2001) are read by hundreds of thousand of Americans, and their message is reinforced on television networks such as C-Span and the History Channel. Such works appear blissfully unaware that the authenticity of narrative history has been challenged from any postmodern theoretical perspective. They understand history in terms of legendary, quasi-mythical figures (usually the "Founding Fathers") who are associated with the origins of the nation. Readers enjoy such books because they propose an uncomplicated relationship between past and present; they read them as stories that happen to be true. As Richard Hofstatder observed in 1968, "Americans seem to conceive of their history within a very shallow time span, in which one age is very much like another, in which the Founding Fathers become timeless oracles, to be consulted for wisdom on perplexing current problems" (*Progressive* 5–6). Such books perpetually promise that the past is something that is easily knowable and that the present is a diminished, but happier, version of the past.

One should dismiss neither the authors of these books nor their readers as having a simplistic notion of history, though. As Berkhofer observes, the fact that even academic "historians assume in practice a Great Story (and therefore a Great Past) as the larger or largest context of their subject matter is poignantly demonstrated in the quest of American historians for a synthetic principle to tie the United States experience together" (40). In *Telling the Truth about American History* (1994), the academic historians Joyce Appleby, Lynn Hunt, and Margaret Jacob argue that "a comprehensive national history" is "a cultural imperative" for renewing the integrity of education in the United States (Harlan, *Degradation* 100). Harlan, by contrast—commenting that in the wake of the 1960s, with the proliferation of histories that do not assume that they must be integrated, this quest has been decisively splintered—notes "the sheer impossibility of such a thing" (101). As Berkhofer and Harlan both observe, the postmodernist attack on narrative objectivity coincides with the rise of multiculturalism within the academy and in the public national discourse (Berkhofer 25). Just as postmodern theory attacks the idea of an objective history, multiculturalism attacks the idea that American history can be contained within a single national story. Best-selling histories that retell the bravery and uncommon wisdom of the Founding Fathers arguably serve to resist the troubling implications of the social revolt that the 1960s released.

The Founding Fathers (or Brothers) type of history that so dominates the best-seller lists not only commits the postmodern fallacy of concealing the perspective of the historian but also points to a vision of America that is compelling to the extent that it offers a type of fantasy consistent with what used to be called historical fiction. Such works pretend to educate Americans about their past, but they actually work to insulate their audience from both the past and its relation to the present. Their appeal is that they never confront how American history has progressed beyond and diverged from its retrospective idyllic beginnings. In the guise of offering instruction, they offer endless entertainment, attracting serial readers, or consumers, in such high numbers. If, as Harlan argues, historians in the 1970s "turned to the social sciences for guidance" hoping for the "holy grail of objective knowledge vouchsafed through the institution of established procedure," contemporary popular historians have been working over the genre of nineteenth-century realist fiction and marketing it as history.

In the context of the postmodern critique of history, the continuing appeal of Founding Fathers–style American history is worth considering because it suggests that what continues to make history coherent as a genre is not a particular intellectual methodology. Rather, history endures as a belief system that obligates its adherents to particular practices. The fact that neither a conventional academic historian (such as Hollinger) nor a postmodernist critic of history (such as Jenkins) would accept Isaacson's biography of Benjamin Franklin as a useful model for understanding history matters less than the fact that there is a considerable audience that does. From this perspective, it is not just that postmodernist critiques of history have failed to transform the practice of history departments in ways that they have other disciplines; it is that history as a genre and as a popular practice has still not come to terms with the narrative insights of the great modernist masters such as Virginia Woolf, James Joyce, and Marcel Proust.

We know who the great premodernist historians of American history are: Francis Parkman, George Bancroft, and Henry Adams. Who are the great historians after modernism? Who is the Joyce or Proust of historical narrative? Jenkins, Berkhofer, and Harlan agree that the practice of history is yet to be changed by the linguistic turn. "Despite the fears of [Bryan] Palmer, [Gertrude] Himmelfarb, and others," Berkhofer writes, "few books of Anglophone historians have exemplified in practice the possibilities of the linguistic and other turns for writing histories." He adds, "The few books and articles that have supposedly practiced deconstruction or followed the linguistic or rhetorical turns look more like old history in how they approach their subject, present their findings, or represent the past than the challenges would seem to imply or demand" (25). At best, what has changed is how we think about history, the sense that history can never be objective and nonideological. Rorty flatly states, "I do not think that there is a non-ideological way of telling a country's story. Calling a story 'mythical' or 'ideological' would be meaningful only if such stories could be contrasted with an 'objective' story" (*Achieving* 11). Thus, when Jenkins, Berkhofer, and Harlan wonder what a postmodernist history might actually look like, it may be that the answer is more obvious than they think. Indeed, my claim throughout is that postmodernist histories have already been written and are being written by novelists.

We can see the crucially historicist perspective of these postmodern novel-histories when we contrast them with the popular "realist" histories that are their most obvious rivals. Relying on novelistic devices, popular histories gratify readers' desire for a linear narrative that promises the past can be reliably joined to both the present and a comfortable future. I call these best-selling histories "realist" histories because they attract their readers through the skillful manipulation of assumptions and narrative devices that we ordinarily associate with the nineteenth-century realist novel. "It is a hot summer morning in 1804," writes Ellis at the outset of *Founding Brothers*. "Aaron Burr and Alexander Hamilton are being rowed in separate boats across the Hudson River for an appointment on the plains of Weehawken. The water is eerily calm and the air thick with a heavy mist" (19). These writers understand that their readers enjoy their histories not only because they tell a story that pleases them but also because they understand that story to be their own. The histories they tell also conform to the ideological tradition of nineteenth-century historians such as Parkman and Bancroft (although they may be less troubling than the accounts of Parkman, who at least reported the British use of smallpox as a weapon in the French and Indian War).[8]

Untroubled by such theorists of historical narrative as Georg Lukács, Kenneth Burke, or Walter Benjamin—let alone White, Derrida, or Lyotard—these writers work hard to portray the story of the Founding Fathers not as the beginning but as the *end point* of American history. During an interview broadcast on C-Span, Isaacson told a television audience how he conceived the structure of his popular life of Benjamin Franklin. He said that any history or biography must be told chronologically, from birth to death, for that was how the life of Jesus Christ was told and what better model could a biographer-historian follow than the life of Christ? Isaacson's remark suggests a number of contradicory observations. First, as a historian, Isaacson believes that a single person's story can represent the story of a multitude. The material conditions of a given society—its kinship structures, mercantile practices, religious differences—matter less than the premise that a person's success in life may become an uncomplicated representation of how masses of others live their lives. Second, Isaacson's perspective assumes an omniscient, unifying point of view that treats questions (such as slavery, women's rights, and the extermination of Native Americans in the name of progress) as unessential. It is not just that he looks to the eighteenth century to define America; he wants to pretend that America is still living in the eighteenth century. That is the pleasant fiction, the willing suspension of disbelief, embedded in his understanding of history.

In this context, consider also David McCullough's best-selling work *John Adams*, in which John and Abigail Adams become the protagonists of a nineteenth-century novel. Their story is unadorned triumph with little room for acts of moral ambiguity. A realist novel presented as history, *John Adams* allows the reader to participate in the vicarious thrill that fiction provides—to join the Adamses on their destined march to sublime moral grandeur. As a retro-realist novel, McCullough's *John Adams* is timeless, an America for all times and for all Americans. The reader's perspective on these pilgrims' progress is rendered through the familiar device of third-person objective authorial omniscience. Yet, because this narrative is labelled "history" rather than "fiction," the author's objectivity is not taken as a pleasant narrative game but the honest-to-goodness truth. And of course this device of "truth" makes the narrative even more pleasureable to read. It also encourages one to overlook how Adams's Founding Father status is the narrative given that excuses all troubling questions about his life and legacy. Adams's controversial acts (his defense of the British men who killed Crispus Attucks, the first black "American" victim of the Revolutionary War) and controversial stances (his support of the Alien and Sedition Act) can be seen as exciting yet nonthreatening plot elements that have no real relevance to contemporary U.S. society. Just as realist novels encourage the reader to believe in the reality of their representation, so do realist histories conceal from the reader the possiblity that their history is a distortion of "the facts" they pretend to serve.[9] The narrator of history, like the narrator of fiction, may be unreliable, but to acknowledge this possibility means violating (effacing) the genre one presumes to enact. Popular histories from works by Parson Weems to works by David McCullough recall Hofstatder's charge in *The American Political Tradition* (1948) that the practice of American history is too often a type of consumption rather than an attempt at critical inquiry. Hofstadter writes:

> Historical novels, fictionalized autobiographies, collections of pictures and cartoons, books on American regions and rivers, have poured forth to satisfy a ravenous appetite for Americana. This quest for the American past is carried on *in a spirit of sentimental appreciation rather than critical analysis*. An awareness of history is always a part of any culturally alert national life; but I believe that what underlies this overpowering nostalgia of the last fifteen years is a keen feeling of insecurity. . . . American history, presenting itself as a rich and rewarding spectacle, a succession of well-fulfilled promises, induces a desire to enjoy, not to analyze and act. The most common vision of national life, in its fondness for the panoramic backward glance, has been that of the observation-car platform. (xxxiii–xxxiv)

Most best-selling histories betray no understanding that their realistic narrative model has been a museum piece since James Joyce. As White and Jameson both suggest in different contexts, prior to modernism the genres of history and fiction and fictional narrative moved in step with one another. By the nineteenth century, the practice of history was becoming increasingly professionalized as historians began to worry about how their work seemed to overlap with the work of fiction writers. Late-nineteenth-century historians such as Alexis de Tocqueville and Johann Huizinga then began self-consciously to develop strategies that distanced the practice of history from the practice of novel-like narrative.[10] "History has a double face," says White, "a scientific one and an artistic one. That's what makes it interesting. You're always facing in two directions. But the historians don't know that, because since the nineteenth century they have been taught that they must keep their literary and poetic effects out of their writing" ("Interview" 97). Despite the turn toward the objectivity of science, the practice of history was still shadowed by the form of the novel. Indeed, distinguishing history from fiction has since its beginning been problematic. As White notes, "Historiography in the West arises against the background of a distinctively literary (or rather 'fictional') discourse which itself took shape against even more archaic discourse of myth" (44). White's argument is confirmed by inverse logic when we recall that the novel emerged as a distinctive genre in part by associating its form with that of history. Thus, what Miguel de Cervantes gives us in the "history" of Don Quixote, and what Laurence Sterne gives us in the "history" of Tristram Shandy, and what Daniel Defoe gives us in the "history" of Robinson Crusoe are heroes whose identity is clearly the invention of ingenious fiction makers. Yet, because these fictions implicate the reader directly in their narratives of possibility, they force the reader to question the distinction that seems to separate the "fictional" text from the "real" world. The reader after all imhabits both worlds simulataneously. Like the eighteenth-century novel, "the eighteenth century historical imagination was," in the words of Jenkins, "ironic. 'It' knew that the past could be read in innumerable ways; that what appeared to be done up in one instance could be undone in another; that numerous reversals, unintended consequences and umpteen ironies could never be straightened out" (129).

In the nineteenth century, as history writing was becoming more self-consciously objective, the novel likewise continued to insist on its "reality" and did so most forcefully through the pretense of the omniscient narrator. The playful narrators of the works of Sterne, Henry Fielding, and even Jane Austen gave way to the seemingly disinterested narrators of the works of Stendhal, Honoré de Balzac, and George Eliot. Now "realist" authors left less room for the critical involvement of the reader in their works and thus seemed to insist more forcefully that their fictions were real.[11] Like their historian counterparts, the great nineteenth-century realist novelists wanted the reader to pretend that what he or she was reading was true but not told. One thinks of Henry James's famous complaint in the realist manifesto "The Art of Fiction" that Anthony Trollope compromised the veracity of his illusion by intruding his authorial voice upon the story. The "realists" then gave way to the "naturalists," who incorporated into their novels insights from scientific studies and whose work often attempted to prove a particular thesis about character or society (Theodore Dreiser, Frank Norris, Émile Zola, and Edmond and Jules Goncourt).

The revolutionary narrative impact that modernism had on realism and naturalism is well documented. What is less understood, though, is how modernism also radically changed the meaning, practice, and even the possibility of history. To Berkhofer, "the modernist paradigm" for historians meant that "historians sought in their writing and teaching to combine intuitive insights with rigorous empiricism, generalizations and abstractions with concrete and specific facts, arguments and analysis with story-telling, interpretative understanding with logical explanation, creative organization with objective reporting, impartiality and detachment with moral judgment and advocacy" (11–12). Yet, according to Berkhofer, "this reconciliation between art and science" proved impossible in the wake of criticisms of "philosophers, literary theorists, and social scientists" (12). From the perspective of narrative practice, though, modernist literature made the historian's modernist paradigm untenable. Literary modernism elevated consciousness, or perspective, as a narrative problem to be solved. Another way of putting this is to say that modernism's essential insight about narrative, when applied to historical writing, is that the historian is part of the story and thus narrative objectivity is impossible. As we shall see, *Absalom, Absalom!* is the definitive expression of this insight in American modernism.

The expectation that through narrative one can transcend previous forms and write history as if it were a consequence of a single gifted person's artistic vision (Proust or Joyce) was both the hope of modernism and, ultimately, the dream it could not quite sustain. Faulkner's account of how he wrote *The Sound and the Fury* (1925) is emblematic of the process by which drive for aesthetic autonomy becomes instead a concession to the contingency of narrative. The novel begins with the radical subjectivity of the idiot, Benjamin, and then moves through the poetic self-absorption of Quentin and the bigoted selfishness of Jason, before concluding with the perspective of Dilsey, the African American witness to the dissolution of the Compson family. Famously, Faulkner described the process as four different instances of narrative failure. Consequently, the novel dramatizes a process of recognition where the lasting insight is that the kind of autonomous individual subjectivity celebrated by Isaacson, among others, is insufficient to tell a true history. Once a writer puts the narrator into the narrative as a perceiving actor, the possibility for an uncomplicated relationship with the story that is being told is no longer possible. As we will see in Chapter 5, this insight prompted Henry Adams to experiment with writing his autobiography in the third person, an effort that ultimately led Adams to doubt the efficacy of history writing as a truth-telling enterprise.

The hallmark of antirealist (modernist and postmodernist) writing is to turn narrative back into itself in a way that makes the telling of any story epistemologically problematic.[12] Modernist works make the act of telling the story part of the story being told, either by involving the narrator in the story as a participant or by turning the protagonist's thoughts into the action of the story. The great modernists did not so much destroy previous narrative forms, or even historical consciousness, though, as make their own specific narratives the ground of knowledge, however conflicted. Contradictory narrative strategies and voices provided the friction that propelled James Joyce's *Ulysses* (1922) and Faulkner's *Absalom, Absalom!* (1936), even if the works seemed to point to a single artist-god who was inventing these narratives above and beyond the work's enactment. The modernists thus initiated a narrative practice that foregrounded perspective as a narrative problem to be solved. How to tell what you cannot fully know? How can you know what cannot be fully told? This sense that narrative itself made possible and was a bar to the telling of stories became the hallmark of postmodern writing. As we have seen with the linguistic turn, once objects, or facts, are understood in terms of how they are being told or described in a particular narrative, the truth status of any assertion becomes problematic.

Postmodernist fiction, even more so than modernist fiction, has been concerned with dramatizing this insight as the given of any narrative act. Emblematic postmodernist works such as Pynchon's *Gravity's Rainbow* (1973), John Fowles's *The French Lieutenant's Woman*, and John Barth's *Lost in the Funhouse* (1969) could be adduced as examples of this practice, but I would like to turn instead to Don DeLillo's *Libra* (1988) because perhaps no other postmodernist novel has so transparently and brilliantly dramatized the effect of the modernist narrative revolution on the practice of history. This novel about the unresolved allegations regarding the assassination of John F. Kennedy does not address the kinds of multicultural conflicts that are found in the works of Faulkner, Morrison, Pynchon, and Johnson. *Libra* may or may not, as I believe *Absalom* or *Beloved* do, itself constitute a history. What *Libra* certainly enacts, though, is how in the postmodern era modernist questions about epistemology have been translated, brought to ground, so to speak, into arguments about the nature of history and historical possibility. For even as DeLillo critiques those who would presume to know history in a premodernist sense, he does not deny the possibility of history as much as he defends it as the human practice that is most worth pursuing and preserving. In the end, the reader, not the author, must determine who or what force killed Kennedy and thus how any history progresses from a conclusion that can only be a premise for another story.

IV

Libra portrays the historian who cannot come to terms with a narrative situation that cannot be explained by the facts alone, but requires an act of narrative imagination to be made true. It examines how governments, rather than professional historians, have consolidated the modernist critique of historical narrative and incorporated it into their own strategies of social control. For DeLillo, the recognition that the narrative practices of history and fiction cannot be separated means that whoever tells the most compelling story to the largest number of people will control history. Emphasizing the narrative component of history means recognizing that telling history always involves a kind of will to narrative power. For modernists such as Joyce or Proust, this narrative will to power expressed itself as the triumph of the artist through the complexity of his narrative strategies. In the postmodern era, by contrast, the most effective artists are those who control what we might call the means of historical representation. These figures are not artists working separate from the concerns of society but those who, using the media and other forms of information dissemination and control, conceal their work within bureaucracies (Foucault would call them technologies) that have enormous power to shape the narratives of what Americans understand reality (political and social) to be. Such artists who can still be identified as modernist in orientation are likely to be CIA agents and advertising campaigners. The death of the author so often invoked in discussions of postmodernity is replaced, in DeLillo's work, by the triumph of multiple, often simultaneous, narrative practices that are controlled usually by the government or its secret representatives. For this reason, the ostensible subject of the novel—Lee Harvey Oswald and what led him to his alleged assassination of the president—is not as important as the narrative forces that Oswald can neither discern nor control. In Libra, DeLillo rewrites Franz Kafka's The Trial or The Castle as if its protagonist were not Joseph K or K but the state machinery of repression and obfuscation that torments, yet also defines, K.

Libra enriches Hutcheon's notion of "historiographic metafiction" by suggesting that the narrative advances associated with modernism have been appropriated not just by the corporate national media but also by the U.S. government. Since the time of J. Edgar Hoover, who began his tenure with the FBI during the modernist era, the U.S. government has been in the business of inventing history and subjecting its citizens to acceptable roles in its ongoing plot. Celebrating the postmodern triumph of fiction over history,

Jenkins asks, "Why not now forget history and live in imaginaries without it?" (132). *Libra*'s powerful answer is that those who are unaware of the dangers of making fiction equivalent to history are themselves most subject to the most dangerous kinds of lies: those that are passed off as truth by a government whose power largely rests in its ability to employ postmodernist narrative strategies to disenfranchise audiences who naïvely continue to believe that realism is a viable narrative form in a postmodern world. DeLillo's choice of subject—the Kennedy assassination and the ongoing arguments about "what really happened"—is revealing. Kennedy's death—unlike, say, Adams's or Franklin's—is so problematic that it has not yet been successfully trans-formed into hagiography. This is because its climax is so difficult to identify: Is the climax the life that led up to the assassination? Is it the assassination itself? Or—and this is the postmodern question—is the climax the fact that we cannot yet say what his story means because we do not and indeed cannot know what actually occurred? Is the climax our recognition that there can be no climax? In any case, the narrative possibilities that emerge from the event are endless in a way that a book that celebrates the Founding Fathers can-not be.

On the face of it, the Kennedy assassination has so many of the story-line elements that should make for best-selling historical narrative. It has two doubled heroes: an ambitious poor boy—a version of Dreiser's Clyde Griffith—whose fate is paired with the charismatic President whom he will one day attempt to kill. The plot promises moral scope, fast-paced action, and a resolution that remains shocking even though already known. Yet DeLillo portrays the Kennedy assassination in none of these terms; rather, he sees it as the coming to historical consciousness of an entire generation, and virtu-ally every sentence is reflected through DeLillo's recognition that each reader has a contradictory interpretation about what the story means. As such, not once does *Libra*—or *Texas Schoolbook*, as DeLillo first titled it—let the reader forget that one is always inheriting a history that one cannot completely write or control. If the book's protagonist, Oswald, tries and fails to be the author of his own story, then so does the novel's official historian, Nicholas Branch, fail to plot the meaning of Oswald's life as a history. The novel is less interested in revealing who killed Kennedy, or why, than in showing how any given event is unknowable except through an act of narrative belief. From this perspective, the fiction writer's version of the Kennedy assassination is likely to be more compelling and even believable than that of any given historian who claims to possess championing objectivity and thus the key to the end of the story.

In his postscript to Libra, DeLillo expressly identifies his narrative as a work of fiction and not history. DeLillo reinforces this distinction in part because he believes that because fiction need not be beholden to facts, it can render a more believable account of a historical event whose details can never be fully known. He also wants to warn away critics who would criticize the book for not being true in a factual sense. A novel writer perhaps should not have to insist on this distinction, but the fact that DeLillo does so reveals the extent to which history and fiction have become confused after modernism. As critics have been quick to point out, the novel presents history "as a text," since it includes as a part of its aesthetic the textualized—one almost wants to say compromised—sense of history that has come to characterize postmodernity (Kronick 109). Peter Knight argues that DeLillo's portrayal of this cultural phenomenon, an exercise in cultural paranoia, "is ultimately experienced as a loss of consciousness, a fall into a postmodern sense of epistemological—and social—fragmentation" (813–14). It should be stressed—and this is crucial—that DeLillo is not saying that there is no such thing as history or that history is merely a fiction. As he himself asserted in a 1991 interview, the work is an attempt "to drive through common memory and common history to fiction" (DeCurtis 288). The "common memory and common history" that his novel works toward is one in which we do not agree on any fact except the death of Kennedy. If, for DeLillo, the Kennedy assassination marks the point at which Americans began to express what Lyotard would term "incredulity toward metanarratives," then that incredulity is the shared context in which we now understand and write both history and fiction. If DeLillo recognizes that a shared sense of indeterminacy undermines the idea that Americans share a common history that each American can claim as his or her own, then he also recognizes this insight to be a necessary condition for writing histories that are less naïve about their assumptions or the stories they tell.[13]

Libra invokes the paranoid narrative conspiracy theories that have proliferated since the Kennedy assassination and then yokes them to a high modernist sensibility. The great modernist novels often work like puzzles, where solving the text's problems transforms the reader into being a kind of double for the author who created them. One thinks of Joyce imagining his perfect reader as one who never slept and spent one's entire life deciphering Finnegan's

Wake (1939). When DeLillo has Branch call *The Warren Commission Report* "the megaton novel James Joyce would have written if he'd moved to Iowa City and lived to be a hundred" (181), he intimates that properly telling the story of the Kennedy assassination would require a writer of Joyce's imagination and mastery. Yet even Joyce could not control a narrative that was perpetually being written by multiple authors all under the same title—that is how DeLillo represents the Kennedy assassination. *Libra*'s singular achievement is that it displaces modernist narrative complexity into the world outside the text and then denies the artist the ability to remaster, or recontain, those narrative energies within a single text that can be controlled by a single author and a compliant ideal reader. In *Libra*, the artist manqué is not a novelist but a historian, Nicholas Branch, who has been asked by the CIA to write the definitive history of Kennedy's assassination. Branch is the "official" artist who would control the story, but, like a would-be popular historian, he relies too much on old nineteenth-century narrative models that make it impossible for him to complete his task. Ultimately, there are too many versions, too many rival narrators, and too many ingenious readers for Branch to succeed. He wishes that his history could follow the conventional realist model, where the view of Oswald as the protagonist would control the story, but he finds that narrative possibilities proliferate faster than Branch can control them within a story. Kennedy's presumed murder by Oswald would be the climax and end of that story. Such a single, plausible linear narrative is centered on the assumption that one's character is always coherent and knowable. By the end of *Libra*, the reader understands that the historian with his essentially premodernist methods for organizing the world can no longer explain the world he confronts.

DeLillo does not think that the Kennedy assassination can be known except as the expression of a particular and therefore limited narrative purpose. Its lessons require a different kind of writer than Branch, and, implicitly, that writer is the novelist (in this case, DeLillo). To Harlan's question—what would a postmodernist history look like?—DeLillo answers that it would look like a postmodern novel (210). Yet *Libra* does not perform the kind of technical narrative mastery that is associated with Joyce. In DeLillo's novel the dislocations—the "difficulty"—associated with reading a work of high modernism are attributed to reality itself. Some critics have mistakenly confused DeLillo the novelist with the historian he portrays. Paul Civello says that Branch "comes to represent the impossibility of the objective observer and, by extension, of the experimental novelist" (54). Actually, Branch fails where

DeLillo succeeds. DeLillo, not Branch, assimilates the various histories, films, medical examinations, situation reenactments, into a coherent story. Branch cannot write, "because the data keeps coming in. Because new lives enter the record all the time. The past is changing as he writes" (DeLillo, *Libra* 301). Where once modernism was castigated for its difficulty and its tendency to appeal only to highly aesthetic, cultural elite, *Libra* tells us that since at least 1963 the only place that a reader may feel secure from modernist "difficulty" is in works by conventional historians. They, not Joyce, and certainly not the other authors studied in this book, are the ones writing from and creating a world apart. *Libra* portrays how the tendencies—radical uncertainty and narrative instability—that are said to mark the so-called postmodern era should be understood as normalization of the dominating political and cultural style.

In attributing to the U.S. government the power to create through fiction the vision of reality that the public accepts as historical truth, *Libra* portrays how modernist traditional understandings of history and fiction have traded places. Accordingly, DeLillo's CIA does not collect facts; it distributes different narratives that the public will one day accept as true. Working from the assumption that "the deeper the ambiguity, the more we believe," the narratives the CIA constructs always assume "there is another level, another secret, a way in which the heart breeds a deception so mysterious and complex it can only be taken for a deeper kind of truth" (260). DeLillo and the Agency both prize intricate narratives that highlight their contingent status. Each narrative maker enjoys using multiple narrators who are implicated in surprising ways in the action of their narrative. The actors involved in the construction of these narratives do not expect to create an ultimate truth so much as they expect to preserve the possibility of narrative coherence. When CIA operative Win Everett devises a plot meant to result in the near assassination of John F. Kennedy and the real assassination of Fidel Castro, he structures the plan so that its full ambiguity will be registered: "He would not consider the plan a success if the uncovering of its successive layers did not reveal the CIA's schemes, his own schemes in some cases to assassinate Fidel Castro. This was the little surprise he was keeping for the end. It was his personal contribution to an informed public" (53). His plot is a "modernist" one, and, other than DeLillo, he is the most sophisticated plotter in the novel. However, Everett will not be able to control his plot any better than Branch or Oswald can, but he differs from them in that he accepts multiple, contingent narratives as part of his narrative premise. For the CIA, the tendency of a narrative to deconstruct or be deconstructed only means that as intentions change so can stories and even agents in them. For DeLillo, this narrative tendency becomes an end unto itself insofar as it reveals the capacity of the U.S. government to transform the indeterminacy of historical narrative into insidious cultural and political games that may or may not result in the assassination of a president or, by analogy, the destruction of the World Trade Center.[14]

In *Libra*, all would-be history makers must plot their acts within a world after modernism, a world in which their plots collide with other narrative possibilities in unexpected ways. Hoping to reopen the covert war on Cuba by staging a fake assassination of the president, Everett's plan depends on finding an assassin to be the patsy of the operation—someone who can be blamed for the fiasco but who does not know the role he plays in Everett's story. Everett "would put someone together, build an identity, a skein of persuasion and habit, ever so subtle" (78). "His gunman would appear behind a strip of scenic gauze. You have to leave them with coincidence, lingering mystery. This is what makes it real" (147). As if on cue, Oswald walks right into Everett's plot. Oswald has no "true" identity in the linear, realist sense. In fact, it is Oswald's belief in his own ability to make history as he wills it to be that makes him the narrative's patsy. Unlike Joyce or DeLillo and more like the realist historian, Everett cannot construct a historical narrative that is not subject to textual intervention by others. Seeking "the bodily frame [he] might use to extend [his] fiction out into the world," Everett finds that the world responds with counterfictions—that his plot can be moved forward but not authored.

In fact, no author of plots in *Libra* has true control over the stories he plots except DeLillo. Even Oswald becomes a version of Branch's dilemma as a historian in that the story he wants to write cannot be written the way he wants to write it. Repeatedly, DeLillo dramatizes Oswald's inability to transform himself into language—into a linear, coherent story in which he is subject and author. As a youth, Oswald wants to write stories about the blind in order to understand their world. As an exile in the Soviet Union, he wants "to write short stories about American life." Portraying Oswald as a failed writer before he becomes a misplaced assassin, DeLillo implies that Oswald finds himself an assassin precisely because he cannot implement his vision of the world effectively through language. He wants to be a hero, but the narrative requires a patsy: a symbolic actor whose role is to conceal the complexity of other plots. He goes from being a writer of a plot he cannot complete to being an actor in a plot he did not write. His symbolic function is to conceal history's intractable fictitiousness.

DeLillo's Oswald represents the postmodern fragmentation of self and culture into a series of mutually conflicting yet nonetheless coincident plots. In this context, DeLillo's depiction of Oswald as a failed maker of narratives takes on special resonance. *Libra's* most compelling image of Oswald is not that of Oswald taking aim at the President with his rifle; it is that of Oswald struggling to find the words that will articulate his historical vision. This is Oswald writing his "Historic Diary":

> Even as he printed the words, he imagined people reading them, people moved by his loneliness and disappointment, even by his wretched spelling, the childish mess of composition. Let them see the struggle and humiliation, the effort he had to exert a single sentence.... Always the pain, the pain of composition. He could not find order in the little field of symbols. They were in the hazy distance. He could not see clearly the picture that is called a word. A word is also the picture of a word. He saw spaces, incomplete features, and tried to guess at the rest.... He watched sentences deteriorate, powerless to make them right. The nature of things was to be elusive. Things slipped through his perceptions. He could not get a grip on the runaway world. (211)

In this passage, DeLillo, the superior constructor of historical narrative, strips bare Oswald's pretension to the invention and control of his own historical narrative. When DeLillo attributes to Oswald the desire to flaunt his failure as a writer, it is an almost wistful attempt to recover Oswald's narrative prior to his objectification: "Let them see the struggle and humiliation, the effort he had to exert a single sentence." This portrayal of history writing contrasts with Ellis's *Founding Brothers*, who "seem so mythically heroic, in part, because they knew we would be listening and watching" (18). Oswald's inability to control his language predicts his inability to control how the meaning of the event that makes his diary truly "historic"—the assassination—will be interpreted. In a brilliant depiction, DeLillo portrays Oswald's death as the moment at which he becomes objectified by history's view of him. In death, he becomes, as it were, his own double. DeLillo filters the image of this horrible self-transformation through the lens of Oswald watching himself be murdered on television. "He could see himself shot as the camera caught it. Through the pain he watched T.V.... Through the pain, through the losing of sensation except where it hurt, Lee watched himself react to the auguring heat of the bullet" (439). Instead of being the actor who killed Kennedy and changed history, in this instant Oswald becomes, like the rest of us, a viewer, passively watching the spectacle of his transformation from killer to victim. Framed as a television viewer, the reader witnesses live history beamed on television, rendered "true" by its being televised. For his part, Oswald knows only his botched authorship of an assassination that, in DeLillo's version, as perhaps in real history, has been effaced.

DeLillo underscores how "history" in this moment becomes something we can witness but cannot know or perhaps even tell. As if he were some kind of television director or engineer, DeLillo runs Oswald's murder over and over—as has in fact occurred over the past forty years—until the original intention of Oswald's act is lost in the viewer's inability to comprehend any meaning other than poor Oswald's dissolution as a living, knowing self. Beryl Parmenter sees that

> there was something in Oswald's face, a glance at the camera before he was shot, that put him here in the audience, among the rest of us, sleepless in our homes—a glance, a way of telling us that he knows who we are and how we feel, that he has brought our perceptions and interpretations into his sense of the crime. . . . He is outside the moment, watching the rest of us. (447)

Oswald enters history as an image that can be detached from the event he would create. Rather than identifying with the loner who made history and achieved a moment of fame, we connect with Oswald as a self divided from his original act. Ordinarily, the phrase "outside the moment" would suggest that Oswald had achieved a kind of transcendence. What occurs here for Oswald, though, is that he is removed from the history that he himself is making. He no longer belongs to himself or to a version of history he can recognize; rather, he belongs to the camera and those watching the camera. Parmenter wonders, "Why do they keep running it, over and over?" while watching, over and over, Oswald's death (446). In an instant, Oswald's story is fragmented into multiple stories and narrative possibilities. The proliferation of self he must witness in his death enacts the proliferation of historical perspectives that consume his story after his death. The audience, like Oswald, has been doubled, and we too have been removed from the factuality of the event. But what happened? And who can say?

Here DeLillo portrays Oswald's death as a moment of pure individual modernist alienation as it morphs into a postmodern understanding of history. Oswald's death is not his own, since it also defines the viewer's relationship to the other viewers watching with him or her. Through Oswald's mediated death, DeLillo portrays the transformation of history understood from a single perspective that unites an audience as a single collective will to history understood as a form of communal fragmentation that inevitably leaves multiple narratives with conflicting and often hostile audiences (or communities) to fight over what is "true." Oswald's disintegration embodies the disintegration of the viewing audience into separate and rival conspiracy theorists. Twenty-five years later, the novel's representative historian is no closer to being able to tell what happened than Oswald was as he died or than Parmenter was as she watched him die. *Libra* reimagines Oswald's story from Oswald's perspective not to tell a revisionist history but to reveal how futile his dream of controlling history is. As DeLillo says repeatedly, Oswald's dream is to lose his identity within history. This, in fact, what DeLillo has happen to him—but not in the way that Oswald envisions. In *Libra*, history belongs not to the individual but to those forces that cause a particular event to take on a multiplicity of meanings and interpretations. DeLillo's account of Oswald's death reinforces the significance of Kennedy's death having been captured on film (the so-called Zapruder film). Accordingly, DeLillo actually portrays Oswald's death via the television camera and Kennedy's death via Abraham Zapruder's film lens (400). A piece of accidental film footage is the mechanism that will allow amateur historians, such as DeLillo, to construct their versions of history. These alternative historians will create proliferating narratives about Kennedy's assassination that will not cohere except as the general history of a shared skepticism about the efficacy of any history not sanctioned by personal affirmation. In a 1991 interview, DeLillo proposed that *Libra*'s "fiction rescues history from its confusions. [Fiction] provides the balance we don't experience in our daily lives. So the novel which is within history can also operate outside it—correcting, clearing up and, perhaps most important of all, finding rhythms and symmetries we don't find elsewhere" (DeCurtis). If, in the end, the role DeLillo assigns to fiction is the one usually assigned to history, then DeLillo's lesson seems to be that in the postmodern era only the novelist and the readers who affirm the truth the novelist relates can say what really happened and thus what is happening now.

V

In raising the question of how to reorient the practice of history in the wake of the linguistic turn, Harlan argues that we should follow Rorty's exhortation to "spend less time trying to reconstruct historical contexts and more time trying to assemble genealogies of predecessors" (Harlan, *Degradation* 155). In other words, history only matters insofar as it situates its believers within their present. Like Rorty, Harlan says that such a claim does not mean that history no longer has a moral imperative because history can never be anything other than a narrative that makes an argument about how and why things are as they seem to be. Rather, what this postmodernist orientation toward history offers is "the possibility that we could go all the way with contemporary theory and come out the other end with a reinvigorated but nevertheless traditional vision of history, that is, history as a form of moral reflection" (*Degradation* 210). As Harlan helpfully says, "It is the stories that sustain us, not the truth claims made on their behalf" (211). Similarly, Toews questions the "expressions of apocalyptic fear of the end of history" as overdetermined and asserts that "in spite of the relative autonomy of cultural meaning, human subjects still make and remake worlds of meaning in which they are suspended, and insist that these worlds are not creations *ex nihilo* but responses to, and shapings of, changing worlds of experience ultimately irreducible to the linguistic form in which they appear" (Berkhofer 17). But, as Berkhofer notes, "moving beyond normal history" is easier to talk about than to do (281–82).

Among those who discuss these issues, perhaps no question is asked more often and answered less convincingly than the one that such critiques seem to demand: what would a postmodern history look like? Too many historians see history in terms of the wall between it and other forms of narrative. In an *American Quarterly* issue devoted to Berkhofer's work, Betsy Erkkila notes:

> Literature and history is still a well-defended site of intra- and interdisciplinary wars. The intellectual stakes are very high: both sides fear the threat posed by poststructuralist theory to traditional notions of authorship, experience, writing, and representation. But whereas some literary critics fear that the "historical turn" will pollute the purity of literature and thus the primarily linguistic and aesthetic grounds of the literary profession, some historians fear that the "linguistic turn" will erode the objective and factual grounds of the historical profession by turning facts into fiction, and history into pure textuality. (359)

Another view to this argument, as Rorty might say, is that usable examples of postmodern history are visible if only we open our eyes. History is not so much something to be achieved as it is something to be sought: it is an act of definition that requires continuing acts of self-invention or cultural invention. Fiction may be the form through which history is rendered, but belief is the source of its continuing vitality. If so, can history's claim to know the past ever be truly forgotten and only at best reframed as the past we choose to know? From this perspective, a truly postmodern history has two functions. First, it is a critique of history as revealed; it is "objective truth" in precisely the ways that Hutcheon attributes to historiographic metafiction. This means that some novels are as involved with and enlightening about the question of history as some histories are. Second, history only works as a practice that binds a group to a particular story. As Harlan observes, history "is the stories that interest and sustain us, not the truth claims made on their behalf" (*Degradation* 212). Or, as a narrator remarks in DeLillo's *Underworld* (1997), history is longing on a large scale. This claim, in a "postmodern" novel, suggests that the collective will that makes history known to others cannot be changed by postmodernism. Postmodernism may make academic historians anxious not because it is hard to read but because it calls into question at every turn the practice (if not the necessity) of history.

In *Libra*, fiction is a way to history—the medium through which history is known and preserved as something worth knowing. The novel thus tells us about the specific history of the Kennedy assassination as it points us toward the practice of history that characterizes American literature since Faulkner. What happens when we give American history over to some of the greatest American novelists of the twentieth century? Along with being compelling examples of how narrative history is practiced in the postmodern era, together they offer, as it were, a history of the history of America in the twentieth century. Four of the authors—DeLillo, Johnson, McCarthy, and Morrison—wrote works that are included in the much-discussed 2006 list compiled by the *New York Times Book Review* of the single best American novel written in the last twenty-five years. Morrison's *Beloved* was accorded the honor of being the best book; DeLillo's *Underworld* and McCarthy's *Blood Meridian* were the first runners-up. That Pynchon's extraordinary but perhaps less accessible *Mason & Dixon* was not recognized is a surprising oversight but perhaps understandable given that *Gravity's Rainbow* (1973) has so often been discussed as the one successor to Joyce's *Ulysses* (1922). Moreover, since part of Pynchon's achievement has been to translate the narrative techniques of Joyce to the problems of historical inquiry, one can argue that Pynchon is the preeminent postmodern novelist-as-historian.

The *New York Times Book Review* list, like the novels that I analyze here, testifies to the degree to which fiction in the postmodern era has become the primary medium for arguing about what history is and which version of American history is true. The works on the *Times* list share a preoccupation with history both as a subject for storytelling and as practice for creating meaning. Insofar as history is about making sense of a community's perception of what binds its members together as a people, each novel on this list, I would argue, seeks to provide the text that would bind its reader to a communally verifiable shared past and hoped-for future. What may be most striking about the list, other than the superb writing it identifies, is how divergent and contradictory the histories represented and thus audiences implied by these novels actually are. African American readers who see in *Beloved* or in Edward P. Jones's *The Known World* (2003) their own communal history from the time of the slave ship to today will find little to see of themselves in John Updike's genteel Protestant "Rabbit" sage or Philip Roth's Jewish American version of post–World War II American history. Nor are readers of Roth or Updike likely to be comfortable with either DeLillo's skeptical, paranoid version of American history or McCarthy's brutal compression of American history into an endless cycle of violence.

Some readers may wonder why the recent work of Roth (who has six books on the *Times* list!) is not addressed in this study. The reason is that Roth's works, with the arguable exception of *American Pastoral* (1997), celebrate and confirm the kind of mainstream exceptionalist American history that is practiced by such modern-day Parson Weemses as David McCollough.[15] Roth's *Plot Against America* or even his celebrated American Trilogy are "historical" without either engaging in history as a practice or functioning as a communal call to arms. As such, they neither challenge received versions of American history nor practice it as anything other than as a kind of belated cultural affirmation of the triumph that American history is so often said to be. *American Pastoral* (1997) is "oppositional" only in that it questions the long-term efficacy of social protest in the 1960s. The novel treats Nixon's impeachment as the logical and necessary end to the 1960s. It also advocates a kind of "tribal" view of history that is partially in keeping with the works of Toni Morrison or Leslie Marmon Silko. However, unlike *Song of Solomon* (1977) or *Almanac of the Dead* (1991), it is less clear about whether challenges raised against the American Empire could sustain alternative histories worth preserving. Thus, in his counterfactual *Plot*, for instance, Roth imagines what might have happened had the anti-Semitic, Hitler-friendly Charles Lindbergh been elected president in 1940 instead of Franklin Delano Roosevelt (FDR). With such a premise many readers might expect a skeptical engagement with the practice of American history since Hitler. The novel does powerfully portray the sense of fear and impending oppression American Jews experience when Lindbergh initiates a government program meant to assimilate immigrant Jews to American values. The novel also makes credible the historical possibility of Jews being subjected to pogroms on American soil. In these moments, *Plot* verges on becoming the kind of tribal narrative that *Beloved* or Leslie Marmon Silko's *Almanac of the Dead* can be said to be. Yet, after daring to suggest that American Chirstains are just the right elected leader away from having their inner Nazis truly represented in Washington, Roth twists his novel so that history-as-we-know-it-to-have-always-been wins. FDR is returned to his rightful place as president and the optimistic course of post–World War II America is safe to be celebrated. In this context, the America that allows Updike's Harry Angstrom to become rich and successful does not seem that different from the America that allows JewishAmerican Philip Roth to become a prize-winning American writer who assures literate American readers that fascism, in the words of Sinclair Lewis, "can't happen here."

Between them, Roth and Updike are responsible for ten of the twenty-five novels on the *Times* list. Their ubiquity, I would suggest, attests to their ability to seem "historical" without truly threatening their audiences' sense of history as a rational process of upward mobility for all Americans. Roth, who writes from an avowedly Jewish American perspective, is arguably the postmodernist as narcissist par excellence, and the fact that his fiction is about Jews (and not WASPs) is due to the historical accident of being born Jewish rather than the historical necessity of being true to the premises of Jewish history. Roth's novels, like Updike's novels, do not seek to challenge or remake the history that they portray. Their protagonists's success—their rise in society—is portrayed as happily, typically American. They are not threatened by history, as DeLillo's Oswald or Morrison's Sethe is, because history exists for them merely as the necessary background for their own self-apotheosis. To the extent that Roth's narratives employ postmodern narrative devices that encourage the reader to question the authenticity of any self or culture, they do so mostly to subject the persona of the protagonist to an endlessly self-gratifing self-scrutiny. The self is endless impersonation, Roth likes to say, and this stance seems to make Roth's work definitively postmodern. Yet as postmodern as they may seem to be, Roth's heroes are worthy successors to the American individualist tradition of Ralph Waldo Emerson, Walt Whitman, and Ralph Ellison, and for this reason one should not be surprised to see him and Updike, literary and seemingly cultural rivals, dominating this list.

Unlike Roth or Updike, the authors I examine all share the recognition that after modernism Americans seem to be left with fragmented subjectivities at odds with mainstream ("official") American society and its politics. Their fictions each identify communities (rather than atomistic individuals) that are at odds with traditional presentations of American history that are represented by both popular historians such as Ellis, McCullough, and Isaacson and academic historians such as Appleby, Hunt, and Jacob. Their histories are also political attacks on what they take to be the status quo of American history. Unlike the authors I discuss, Roth, Updike and conventionally popular American historians are unwilling to designate "U.S. history" as a term that signifies a brutal (and brutally successful) type of imperialism. Historians such as McCullough portray "U.S. history" not as the systematic usurpation of other peoples' property and resources (cultural and material) but as "the triumph of American liberty," or some such phrase. McCullough is the perfect example of what Gore Vidal often calls "the court historian." According to Vidal, most American historians are employed to justify the status quo of the U.S. Empire. To be a tenured American university historian, Vidal implies, is to work for the Empire.

No author I discuss can be accused of being a court historian. Arguably, the beginning point of my discussion, *Absalom, Absalom!*, is a court history—of the South. It also happens to be the paradigmatic instance of the modernist turn within history that refuses the consolations of individual alienation in favor of communal identification. It is a critique of history as a viable narrative practice and a celebration of history as a form of belief to be cherished. In so doing, it challenges the kind of U.S. history that so-called objective historians tell in order to justify "the triumph of American liberty." Readers have traditionally praised how Faulkner's narrative deconstructs of the notion of race in order to portray a society doomed by its reliance on a terrible misperception about the nature of humanity. My reading of *Absalom*, however, argues that we have praised Faulkner's modernist narrative genius only to miss what particular historical vision his narrative actually champions. On my reading *Absalom*'s goal is not to create a world open to an interpretation contrary to its implied historian's (Quentin's) truth; rather, it urges its reader (who is not Quentin) to accept the South that was suppoeedly destroyed by the Civil War as a still-living entity whose pre–Civil War aims have not yet been abandoned and continue to unite many Americans in their view of themselves and their future. Faulkner does not memorialize the South; instead, he creates a narrative of its living appeal. Its basic message is defiantly secessionist. As I argue, Quentin kills himself at the conclusion of *Absalom, Absalom!* not out of despair at being stranded from history but in order to memorialize the communal identity that, by going to school in the North, he has been unable to leave behind. Quentin's death is not so much a refusal of the past and its meaning as it is a surrender of Quentin's individualized identity to that past, a literal merging with history that is also the ongoing present. *Absalom*'s history resonates to this day as "a rebel yell," an eloquent, tragic refusal of U.S. history that most Americans outside the South are taught to be believe is true. Thus, *Absalom* establishes a frame for seeing how traditional exceptionalist American history cannot be reconciled with the many counter-American histories that are so powerfully enacted, though from different perspectives, by the other authors in this study.

Some readers may be surprised to find Thomas Pynchon linked closely with Toni Morrison and thus, by implication, Faulkner. From sharply divergent perspectives, Pynchon, Morrison, and Faulkner agree that the Civil War is the recurring terminus of American history. They further share the understanding that since modernism, fiction has become the critical genre for understanding how history is made. Each understands history first and foremost to be a practice, not an end, one that identifies and promotes a type of ongoing communal identity creation. They are not writing merely "historical" fiction because historical fiction is a genre that assumes a clear distinction between history and fiction. Their characters are invented, but their stories achieve their deepest meaning only if they are taken as "true" rather than "invented." Each author implies that the narrative being written transcends a notion of authorship: it is the lasting record of a specific community's past. Each author suggests that American history has generally been a dangerous fiction centered on the idea that all Americans are equal before the law and share the same possibilities for communal creation. Instead of a society dedicated to the well-being of each of its members, U.S history has been bent on disenfranchising the vulnerable in the name of a spurious equality (the exploitation of African slaves and the near extermination of the Native American people are only the most obvious examples). Pynchon, unlike Morrison, treats this situation with a mixture of despair and humor. Although he wants to believe that an audience exists who will reverse the course of U.S. history so that it truly lives up to its professed ideals, ultimately his *Mason & Dixon* is the history of an experiment in democracy that was doomed to fail from the beginning: a record of lost and vanished belief. Morrison too rejects typical American history as anything other than a form of colonialism; yet, surprisingly, she is more optimistic than Pynchon, Didion, or DeLillo.

All of the writers I discuss employ postmodern narrative strategies that challenge an easy belief in the possibility of a coherent narrative. If Faulkner, Morrison, McCarthy, and Johnson believe that a coherent narrative, or history, is possible they do so because they imagine that the can speak for and to an audience that shares their biases. Significantly, Pynchon, DeLillo, and Didion are especially concerned with the confluence of government, media, and technology and how it has altered the way we perceive and receive history. They are more suspicious that coherent narratives are possible except as a form of mass media brainwashing. Their true audience might be the one that DeLillo's *Libra* defines: readers who are collectively alienated from a mainstream American history that they can no longer believe in or affirm. Interested in narrative as a form of technology and technology as a form of narrative, their true subject is the mutability of narrative authority in the postmodern age, and thus they are more concerned with a cultural situation in which narrative and therefore history are understood to be invented. The other writers I discuss imagine that their narratives can, in effect, destroy all rival narratives, whereas Pynchon, Didion, and DeLillo are more typically postmodern in exploring the ways contradictory narratives impinge on one another. Recognizing, for instance, that seemingly fact-based discourses such as the president's inaugural address or the news printed in the *New York Times* depend as much on the narrative techniques of fiction as any novel that they may write, these authors explore how easily something as presumably "true" as history, or the news, can be manipulated in a supposedly democratic society for the benefit of a very few. Their skepticism about realist, linear narratives is a part of their recognition that, as Tony Tanner says of *Gravity's Rainbow*, no context exists in which a viewer or reader may "move comfortably from some ideal 'emptiness' of meaning to a satisfying fullness" but must instead become "involved in a process in which any perception can precipitate a new confusion, and an apparent clarification turn into a prelude for further difficulties" (*American Mystery* 70). At the same time, these writers see their works as hopelessly implicated in the same networks of history (or historical representation) that they would oppose. They know that they write as marginalized historians who are recording and their audience is anyone, presnt or future, who may wish to understand and even redress how the most optimistic premises of American history were distorted and destroyed by forces that were only pretending to act in the name of equality and justice.

Chapter 2 takes up McCarthy's *Blood Meridian* (1985). McCarthy's novel reframes the debates about slavery, freedom, and community that link Faulkner and Morrison as the story of the European conquest of the New World. Beginning as a kind of strange *Huckleberry Finn*, the novel leads the reader to the American wilderness in order to suggest that, despite far-flung cities, roads, and air-conditioning systems, Americans will never conquer the territories that they have "lit out for" and claimed. *Blood Meridian* would contain within its frame all subsequent histories of American, written and unwritten. It is the first and last book of American history, demolishing all others. For McCarthy, the typical moral questions concerning slavery and freedom are merely small, incidental components of a much greater story. The book returns the reader to the origins of America that are located in the initial confrontation between European and non-European. McCarthy suggests that American history can never transcend the violence of that encounter and that Americans are doomed to repeat that violence until our history is ended. At that point, *Blood Meridian* might be said to echo *Absalom, Absalom!* *Blood Meridian* does not imagine that a historical perspective alternative to the one set in motion by the European Conquest is possible. Our fate as Americans is to destroy ourselves and likely the environment that sustains us. Americans will know their history only as it ends.

In Chapter 3 I discuss how Toni Morrison's *Beloved* and *Song of Solomon* oppose the history that Faulkner's *Absalom, Absalom!* presents as true. Morrison not only canonizes Faulkner's work as a type of history rather than fiction but she also gives the lie to misguided claims that history in the postmodern era is irrelevant or unknowable except as identity politics. I contrast Morrison's powerful defense of history with Michaels's analysis of Morrison as a kind of accidental instance of what Francis Fukuyama has called "the end of history" (qtd. in Michaels, *Shape* 19). Whereas Michaels dismisses Morrison's purpose in *Beloved* as merely "the production of that paradigmatically identitarian emotion, 'pride,'" I argue that Morrison privileges history over identity (78). As I argue, it is Michaels's view, not Morrison's, that is engaged in a particularly vicious game of identity politics, since his reading denies Morrison the ground for claiming her history at all.

Chapter 4 turns to Pynchon's stunning re-creation of late-eighteenth-century America on the eve of its initiation into "official" history as a sovereign nation. Pynchon's title, *Mason & Dixon* (1997), alludes to the Civil War without ever dramatizing it in the novel. Pynchon invites the reader to create the historical narrative that connects the events of the novel to subsequent American reality. Like contemporary best-selling historians, whom he parodies, Pynchon returns to the time of the Founding Fathers and presumes to tell a cozy, familiar tale about the birth of the nation. The historian's voice in this novel speaks to the past and the future simultaneously in a quixotic attempt to link its narrative voice to everyone—Indians, blacks, and whites—who would (or did) oppose the ongoing creation of what became the American empire. Ultimately, Pynchon presents a critique of history and its reliance on slavery and the oppression of minority "others" that complements and extends Morrison's critique of Faulkner. More than other writers I discuss, though, Pynchon makes the difference between fiction and history the subject of his narrative. The joke at the heart of his novel is the ironic recognition that if history could be distinguished from fiction, then *Mason & Dixon* could be read only as an enjoyable, though erudite, novel full of entertaining anachronisms. But U.S. history is not a joke but a harrowing trajectory of global mass murder and dispossession. In this regard, *Mason & Dixon* is a conventional history in that it persuasively shows American history to be the inevitable consequence of the union between the New Science of the seventeenth century and the European will to conquest that was brought on by its need to identify and dominate world markets. The novel is an exercise in fantasy only in that it asks its readers to imagine an America different from the one that rules today.

Didion's *Democracy* and DeLillo's *Underworld* are the focus of Chapter 5. "Call me the author," Didion says (16). Her assertion, which is also an invitation, is an attempt to gain control of the story she is telling. *Democracy* is fragmented, however, and so is her narrative. Didion tries to write from within a mainstream American celebration of democracy and its possibilities, but she finds her point of view is endlessly co-opted and debased by the very forces her history would oppose. What should be a straightforward story about the devastating effects of U.S. imperialism in the twentieth century becomes, instead, a reflection of the impossibility of being able to tell this history to an audience who would wish it otherwise. Didion's dilemma is not, as Hutcheon might suggest, that history does not exist or that it cannot be told. Rather, her dilemma is that she cannot control or counteract the narrative mechanisms by which histories in the postmodern age are produced and packaged for easy consumption by the American public. As Didion stresses, Democracy is a novel because it is failed history. Its authorizing voice is that of Henry Adams, the historian who first questioned the efficacy of writing history in the modernist era. I contrast the Adams–Didion perspective with the history writer as modernist master that DeLillo's Underworld portrays in the figure of J. Edgar Hoover. Hoover's success is a direct consequence of his mastery of narrative strategies that are ordinarily associated with modernism. Together, Underworld and Democracy reveal how these unlikely past masters of (post)modernism—advertising consultants, politicians, FBI heads, and CIA operatives—employ their technical narrative know-how against the interests of citizens who, for the most part, can only helplessly collaborate with that which is destroying them.

Johnson's extraordinary Fiskadoro (1985) reminds us that history is inseparable from myth. One could call Fiskadoro the great post-9/11 novel were it not for the fact that it was published sixteen years before 9/11. Written in an eerily prophetic voice that uses the Koran as its model, Fiskadoro imagines a post-America future under a ruling authority that is, apparently, Muslim. Johnson's foretold future is both postmodern and multicultural; it exists in a postnuclear holocaust world that no longer knows or remembers American history. It communicates to its reader the uncanny recognition that U.S. history is near its end as America is dispersed into a variety of global conflicts that it is powerless to control. Fiskadoro imagines how a fragmented American history can be rendered whole again only through the submission of the reader's identity to a single divine narrative authority. Its narrative wisdom is that you the reader will die and be reborn into a history that is no longer America or American. In this way, Fiskadoro alone among the books I examine can be said to unify the discontinuous histories that From the Civil War to the Apocalypse traces.

Absalom, Absalom!
William Faulkner's True
History of the South

A Tallahassee Museum on Friday rejected a request by the local chapter of the Sons of Confederate Veterans to remove an exhibit the group considers disrespectful of the Confederate flag. The group, which has 56 members locally and about 1,500 statewide, asked the Mary Brogan Museum of Art and Science to remove "The Proper Way to Hang a Southern Flag" by John Sims. The work depicts a Confederate battle flag being lynched from a 13-foot-high wooden gallows. The request was made by Bob Hurst, commander of the Talllahassee camp of the Sons of Confederate Veterans. Mr. Hurst said the exhibit violated a Florida law that makes it illegal to "mutilate, deface, defile or contemptuously abuse" the Confederate flag.
—Christine Jordan Sexton, "Southern Group Protests a Depiction of the Confederate Flag," *New York Times*, March 17, 2007

I

In *Beyond the Great Story*, Robert Berkhofer observes, "In all histories as productions we may separate the text as a form of discourse from the meaning or message of the discourse" (77). Yet the central achievement of William Faulkner's *Absalom, Absalom!* is to deny that such separation is possible. As we saw in the Introduction, the practice of history since Leopold von Ranke has largely depended on making a hard distinction between "the past as past" and the present as something separate from the past. To many historians, this understanding means that the past is an object that can be known and about which uncontroversial claims can be made. Since the linguistic turn, however, this distinction no longer seems so evident. As Berkhofer asks, "To what extent can historians combine the two meanings of history as actually past and modern representation raised by late modernist and structuralist theorists?

What if a realist theory of the correspondence between history as written and the actual past is abandoned for a constructionist view of history as representation?" (3). Berkhofer acknowledges that postmodernist novelists, rather than historians, may provide the clues for understanding how history can continue despite its demystification as object (3). As the great achievement of American modernism, Faulkner's novel provides a pivotal text for understanding how the nineteenth-century realist conventions that generally underpin the genre of historical narrative were destroyed by the narrative innovations of modernism.

Absalom is both a critique of history and an affirmation of its inevitable constructedness. Absalom anticipates the postmodern fiction that Linda Hutcheon labels as "historiographic metafiction" but only to suggest that a powerful critique of history is likely to become history itself. Absalom is not a postmodernist text, but its narrative stance is one of extreme skepticism toward the notion that the past can ever be understood as an object separate from its telling. As Carolyn Porter notes, Quentin Compson's "very endeavor to secure and maintain a detached perspective on history by imposing narrative coherence on it leads inexorably to Quentin's participation in it" (Seeing 49). The novel consists of multiple tellings by multiple narrators of the same basic story: the rise and fall of Thomas Sutpen and his story's meaning for the community of Jefferson, Mississippi. If history were merely an object and true for all time, then the narrators need never have been compelled to tell and retell their story in different versions. Indeed, this collective "will to believe" in a history that might redeem its tellers is the engine that drives the book's multiple narratives. At every narrative turn, the novel conceals the implications of each previous critique of history by replacing it with a new history that its tellers want to believe is true.

Throughout Absalom, Quentin is confronted with the same dilemma that has troubled historians since the linguistic turn: how does one rescue the truth of the past from the deceptive narrative within which the past must be encased? Consider this semiotic definition of history, or hi/story, by A. J. Greiman and J. Courtes:

By hi/story is understood a semantic universe considered as an object of knowledge, the intelligibility of which, postulated a priori, is based on a diachronic articulation of its elements. In this sense, "history" can be considered as a semiotic system as object (or as a set of semiotic systems taken prior to their analysis) the approach of which is determined beforehand by certain postulates.

1. Hi/story (as story) corresponds, on the other hand, to the narration or to the description of actions the veridictory of which status is not fixed (they can be past and "real," imaginary or even un-decidable). From this viewpoint, hi/story is to be considered narrative discourse. (qtd. in Berkhofer 13)

To experience history as the first premise means never getting to the second premise. By the logic of the first premise, history is first a past that is either known or mandated as true by agreed-upon postulates. There is no need to argue about the past because no one experiences a discrepancy between then and now. On the second premise, history is not only a past but is also something that is *told*. The past becomes something else—discourse, narrative, or maybe a new set of postulates taken as true. *Absalom* collapses these two premises into one recurring act. In *Absalom*, the past becomes what is being told, but each telling seems to divide the teller from the tale that he wants to believe is the truth.

The fact that *Absalom* offers a powerful version of history as a kind of generic problem has been recognized by literary critics, if not historians, since its publication. Cleanth Brooks, likely the most forceful reader of *Absalom* before Toni Morrison, observes that the novel might be understood as "a persuasive commentary upon the thesis that much of 'history' is really a kind of imaginative construction" (qtd. in Warren, *Faulkner* 196). Following Brooks, Richard Poirier claims, "The attempt to create history is both the story of Sutpen and, with a difference, the conscious effort of Quentin as narrator of that story" ("'Strange Gods'" 2). Neither Brooks nor Poirier, nor anyone else who has addressed the subject, has pursued the implications of this claim by suggesting that *Absalom, Absalom!* should be read as if it actually were history.[1] Yet the audience that Faulkner invokes is indeed imagined to do precisely that. Hugh Kenner once observed that with *Absalom, Absalom!* the "ideal listener is not the ideal listener the communal storyteller supposes" (qtd. in Brodhead 72). Kenner's crucial point, largely overlooked, was that Faulkner employs modernist narrative techniques to tell a story that is essentially local, or Southern, and whose implied audience has little interest in modernist storytelling. Because a crucial division exists between how Faulkner tells his story and the story that he tells, Faulkner's brilliant modernist narrative strategies conceal the retrograde Southern history that is at its core. Even a critic as perceptive as Porter, who admires Brooks's reading above all others, insists that the novel is about "Faulkner's America" rather than about how Faulkner's America is implicated within a particular version of Southern history. I argue, by contrast, that when Faulkner's narrative strategy implicates the percipient with what is perceived, as Porter shows, Faulkner is not writing fiction only to explore an epistemological or aesthetic dilemma concerning the nature of seeing. Rather, he implicates the reader within a historical perspective not clearly reconcilable with that of post–Civil War United States.[2] As we shall see, Absalom's coded history tells white Southerners not to burn their Confederate money because the South is not dead yet. Only the Union is. If, as James Baldwin once observed of Faulkner, "it is apparently very difficult to be at once a Southerner and an American," then Absalom proves the impossibility of reconciling these two identities (212).

Because Absalom so ingeniously blurs the line between fiction and history, it may seduce the reader into believing that what is being presented is merely a brilliant act of storytelling rather than a case for justifying the present as the logical continuation of a civilization that was once founded on slavery. More insidiously than Margaret Mitchell's Gone with the Wind (which, like Absalom, was published in 1936), Absalom does not try to seal off the present from the past; rather, it tries to create the future as an ongoing version of a past that most Americans want to think is as long gone as Scarlett O'Hara's Tara. Historians such as Saul Cornell, who worry that "some variants of liberal pluralism might justify excluding the voices of those opposed to tolerance" and that "postmodern liberalism provides an anemic justification for such a policy" (354), can find all the confirmation they require happening already in Faulkner's modernist novel. What makes the novel both exhilarating and threatening as a narrative act is that it explicitly implicates the reader in the narrators' uncertainty about what they are telling. Faulkner asserts narrative power over his reader by doing something we now associate with postmodernist critiques of history: he has his is narrators define history as a set of conflicting propositions rather than as a listing of coherent "facts." In Absalom, strictly speaking, there is no such thing as a "fact," and this recognition may make one think it is a fiction and thus its reactionary history is harmless playacting. However, an easy distinction between history (facts) and fiction (narrative invention) is precisely what Absalom suggests cannot be sustained.

Consider the following "facts" that the novel presents. In one chapter, the reader learns that Charles Bon died wearing a locket around his neck that contained a picture of Judith Sutpen. In another chapter, the reader learns that Bon died wearing a locket that contained a picture of his octoroon wife and child. In one chapter, Bon is wounded in battle and then cared for by Henry Sutpen. In another, we are told that Henry was the one wounded and then cared for by Bon. None of these "facts" is more or less "true" than the rest of them; there is no way for the narrators, let alone the reader, to verify each "fact" is true. In *Absalom*, the facts contradict themselves, not in essence but because the narrators of these facts differ. Since there is no way for the narrators to know with certainty that the facts they posit are true, their relationship to the stories they tell are wholly provisional. The facts matter only to the extent that they are necessary to the story the narrator is telling.

Critics versed in postmodern theory have of course identified the method of narrative discontinuity Faulkner's narrative seems to embrace. John Duvall says that the novel's progression of narrative plots "moves us away from modernism's obsessive questioning ... and toward an eerie uncertainty about exactly what kind of world is being imagined" (Duvall and Abadie, *Faulkner* ix). Commenting on the moment in Chapter 8 when Shreve McCannon and Quentin abandon a straightforward concern with facts and instead begin to invent alternative narrative possibilities in order to make the story that is most persuasive to them, Brian McHale similarly notes that they "reach the limit of their knowledge of the Sutpen murder-mystery; nevertheless they go on, beyond reconstruction into pure speculation. The signs of the narrative act fall away, and with them all question of authority and reliability" (*Postmodernist* 10). As I have suggested, Shreve and Quentin's response keys the reader's response since the reader too must deal with how contradictory facts and outright speculations line up and must, if necessary, ignore the inconsistencies that seem irrelevant. Not surprisingly, *Absalom* has produced an impressive critical industry concerned with identifying which character knew what, when, and how. Although the narrative seems to demand this laborious critical debriefing, it is unclear that arguing over whether Compson did or did not know about Bon's "true" racial identity is essential to understanding the novel, since the most important effect of such questions is to make the reader into yet another version of Quentin and Shreve. Yet whether one aligns one's reading with Brooks's timeline of events or some other, no reader can assert his or her "history" of the "facts" of the novel as true or right except as an act of belief.

There is no way to know Bon's true identity, just as there is no argument except a racial argument that can justify Henry or Quentin's repudiation of Bon.

Yet postmodern theories of narrative, helpful as they are, are not what is required for us to see how Absalom, Absalom! blurs the generic line between history and fiction. As long as the reader cannot stand outside the narrative, the reader is obligated to assent to the version of history that Quentin represents as true. Obviously, one can dismiss as racist Quentin's premise about Bon's identity and even say that Faulkner's great work demonstrates the insanity of making claims of history or identity solely on race. Readers who reject identifying with Quentin would also reject the history that he represents—these readers are perhaps the most anxious to see the book only as a fiction, because most of them, presumably, do sympathize with Quentin's plight and the narrative power that portrays it. Nonetheless, the novel tells a communal history. To the characters telling the story, the story they tell is not fiction. Faulkner aligns the perspective of his narrators with that of the reader to ensure that the communal history created by the characters extends beyond the narrative frame to the reader.[3] This strategy creates the division that Kenner identifies between sophisticated modernist readers who know that they are reading a multilayered novel and the people about whom Faulkner writes who do not need to read Absalom because they already know and share the true story. If the novel did not present itself as a history, then the critical concerns expressed by McHale or Duvall would be rather beside the point, since one might very well ask: what is the art of fiction but the purest form of speculation?

My reading of Absalom goes against the grain of Faulkner readers who have wanted to see Absalom as repudiating both slavery and the racism on which it is based. Such readers have wanted to say with Molly Hite that by the end of the work "not only have its claims to gentility, civility, and innocence been exposed as hypocrisies, but its defining condition of racial separation is from its founding moment a lie" (76). Seen as a fiction, Absalom, Absalom! does offer a harrowing account of the folly of racism. As a history, though, its views on racism are more ambiguous than this reading admits. Walter Benn Michaels says of The Sound and the Fury, the companion novel to Absalom, that it enacts a kind of racialist logic endemic to the great modernist American texts. "The alternative to being a Jew in The Sound and the Fury," Michaels suggests, "is being an American" (Our America 9). Absalom does not fit Michaels's general argument that American modernist novels "must be understood as deeply committed to the nativist project of racializing the American" because Faulkner presents the American South as hopelessly racially mixed (13).[4] As *Absalom* shows, Faulkner was never interested in either Jews or Americans as much as Southerners, some white and some black. Thus, *Absalom* offers a national history (Southern) that stands in opposition to United States history since the Civil War.

The local story that *Absalom* celebrates and mourns is the not-quite-lost order of the antebellum South. It does not point its reader to the future; rather, it asks its truest reader to die (or fight) rather than move on from the Civil War. Yet because the book has generated so many brilliant "literary" readings (those by Brooks, Robert Penn Warren, John T. Irwin, Donald M. Kartiganer, and Porter, to name but a few), it has become increasingly difficult to see the "history" that the narrative serves.[5] Of the post-Porter readings, Richard Godden's comes closest, because he specifically connects Sutpen's story to the continuing twentieth-century obsession by white male Southerners to repress—on every social and political level—the rise of African Americans.[6] Contemporary readers of *Absalom* were more alive to the argument about a specific history being made in novel than subsequent readers have been. Philip Rahv's 1936 review characterized the novel in terms of "the classic avowal and exhortation of the peculiar trauma induced by the heritage of the Confederate South," noting that Faulkner's implied authorial stance excluded non-Southerners from an understanding of this trauma (285).[7] In 1941, Delmore Schwartz observed that "the conflict between the idea of the Old South and the progressive actuality of the New South had brought Faulkner to the extreme where he can only seize his values, which are those of the idea of the old South, by imagining them being violated by the most hideous crimes" (285). In *Absalom*, the violation of the ideal of the Old South that Faulkner cherished is portrayed in Henry Sutpen's murder of Charles Bon and Quentin's impending self-murder. For both the novel's characters and its readers, the key event in the narrative is the mysterious murder of Bon by Sutpen in 1865, just as the Civil War is about to end. Most readers, following the lead of Quentin and Shreve, assume that Henry murders Bon due to his brother's (presumed) black blood, an action that becomes emblematic of the inevitable fall not only of the house of Sutpen but of the South as well. On this view, the South is doomed because it built its house on the false distinction of race. Yet this perspective is not Quentin's perspective, and it is probably not Faulkner's either.

One reason that critics and readers may now have difficulty recognizing what Rahv and Schwartz saw so clearly is that *Absalom*'s modernist narrative remains alive, while its history—the nostalgic airs of Civil War gallantry and slavery-ridden Negroes—seems to have become discredited. Yet even if we say that *Absalom* links the antebellum South's end to the moral inadequacy of its reliance on slavery, we in effect assent to Faulkner's picturesque history of the South. Such a view, however inevitable it may seem, ignores the true historical cause of the South's demise since the South did not fall because people with black blood were murdered any more than it fell because it suffered collectively from the "curse" of slavery. The South fell because the North compelled it to fall by war and thereby forced it to abdicate the practice of slavery. Contrary to the logic of *Absalom*, the South fell due to an act of violence that was committed from without, not from within. Abraham Lincoln said the nation was a house divided, but in *Absalom*, the divided house belongs to the South alone. The counter–United States history that *Absalom* enacts is the affirmation that the South, not the North, has been the engineer of its own destiny. As history, *Absalom* resolutely denies the truth of Lincoln's Gettysburg Address, in particular its assertion of this "new nation, conceived in liberty, and dedicated to the proposition that all men are created equal" (536). Quentin's South, however, falls from within rather than from without. Henry and Bon are both sons of Sutpen, and their conflict, fraternal and incestuous, is what Quentin cannot escape. Although *Absalom*'s Civil War is not America's Civil War, the general American tendency to think of the Civil War in terms of brother fighting against brother prepares the reader to accept *Absalom*'s sustaining, apocryphal premise without protest.

The genius of Faulkner's book as history is the extent to which it confines readers to arguing about Bon's true racial identity and thus perpetuates a misunderstanding of the "conflict" of Faulkner's South as one about violence between family members committed to the same social order rather than as one about violence between family members committed to opposed social orders. From an American (as opposed to a Southern) perspective, the Civil War is also understood to have pitted brother against brother. Yet this formulation should only highlight the contradiction that its racism conceals. As Kartiganer has best pointed out, Bon's black blood, fictional or not, drives Quentin's version of the story, since, without that premise, the story is, to Quentin, illogical. By following Quentin to the grave, where this story only seems to lie, we have missed how Faulkner's great achievement is not to have written a detective story with any number of solutions to the crime at its center but to have rewritten Southern history—and, by implication, American history—from a perspective that makes the Civil War irrelevant. While focusing on what really did or did not happen, most readers fail to recognize the premise that Faulkner has forced them to accept: that however one understands the South, the Civil War is at best only an incidental anecdote and certainly not the climax of its history. Moreover, from the perspective of Faulkner's South, the North—the United States—does not really exist at all. By making the reader assent to the premise that the Quentin–Shreve version is the one that best narrates the events of the novel, Faulkner also causes the reader to assent to the particular history that the unreconstructed post–Civil War South would most like to believe. This point has been insufficiently recognized, perhaps because it seems so problematic, even embarrassing, to suggest that Faulkner was at heart not an American writer (any more than, during the Civil War, Robert E. Lee was an American general).[8] In making this argument, I am not suggesting that *Absalom* is not a novel or that its achievement as a work of art is dubious because it offers a version of history untenable to most readers. Rather, I am trying to take seriously what happens when we understand history to be narrative and when fiction acquires the power of history over both our understanding of the past and our experience of the present.

II

Faulkner's characters are compulsive storytellers—historians before the age of professionalization—who want to preserve the present as past. Not only do they share a region, or a sense of place; they also share the sense that time belongs to them. This sense of time means that their past is their only subject and thus that every word they speak is a form of history making. The communal history that Faulkner creates is not a kind of genealogical oral history passed from one generation to the next—this perspective implies change, even if only in the form of errors of transmission. Rather, in keeping with his emphasis on presenting a retrograde history, Faulkner situates his characters in a single historical moment. The opening page of *Absalom* establishes a time frame for the novel that really does not ever change.

> From a little after two o'clock until almost sundown of the long still hot weary dead September afternoon they sat in what Miss Coldfield still called the office because her father had called it that—a dim hot airless room with the blinds all closed and fastened for forty-three summers because when she was a girl someone had believed that light and moving air carried heat

and that dark was always cooler, and which (as the sun shone fuller and
fuller on that side of the house) became latticed with yellow slashes full of
dust motes which Quentin thought of as being flecks of the dead old dried
paint itself blown inward from the scaling blinds as wind might have blown
them. (3)

Faulkner's sentence makes the summer of 1909 coincident with the summer of
1863 and every summer in between. By the end of the paragraph, the timeless
time will move back to include 1833, the year of Sutpen's arrival. It is in keeping with Faulkner's famous assertion to Malcolm Cowley that his ambition
was to compress the world into a single sentence, not because of its length, or
the action it portrays, but because it assumes a moment of time that contains
within it all potential narrative acts, past and future. By the end of the novel,
Quentin's narrative will take place at Harvard and he will sit freezing in a cold
room unlike this one, but the time that he lives in is the same, and one may
even question whether he has really left Rosa Coldfield's company at all. In the
opening-page passage, not only does light mostly fail to enter the "hot airless"
room but so too does the passing of time that the appearance of light is supposed to signal. The room has not changed since Rosa's father's self-imposed
death by starvation. It is "still called the office because her father had called
it that," because as long as Rosa lives, and perhaps even after she dies, the
room will continue to be her father's. Rosa is a servant to the room and to her
idea of it as a memory that is also the present. Dust, not moving light, is the
material presence of time and is precious to her because its remains do not
change.

Rosa's servitude to the room typifies how characters in *Absalom* understand
time and their relation to it: time advances only to stand still. Rosa is encased
in this room, in this time, as she is "embattled in virginity" (4). She strives to
live in a state of purity, unmolested and therefore unchanged by the passing of
time. For Rosa, the old forms must prevail, and her identity consists in being
subjected to the prior identity of someone else. In Rosa's case, this person is
her father, against whom she has rebelled but whose presence in her life she
cannot overthrow. Her virginity testifies to this failure, as does the fact that she
still lives in his office inside his house. The closed room is a figure for Rosa's
barren womb. She is enthralled before her own helplessness, which she can
express only as outrage, although she is not really outraged. It is likely that
she is happy, since even her outrage can only testify to her submission to the

authority of the past lives that dominate her: those of Sutpen, her sister, her nephew and nieces, and most especially her father.

In a kind of inversion of Andrew Marvell's "To His Coy Mistress," Rosa has summoned Quentin to sit with her, in effect inviting Quentin to join her in the tomb where the object of their shared love, which is their history, remains. Ever the gentleman, Quentin will join her for the last time when the novel ends. Her invitation to Quentin initiates the chain of events—the discovery of Henry, the burning of Sutpen's mansion, Quentin's suicide—that will bind the two in death in 1909. Rosa takes advantage of Quentin's chivalry, because she wants to make another, more significant, date with him. This six-hour (or more) tête-à-tête is foreplay for that decisive, even fatal, encounter. As Mr. Compson tells Quentin "She will need someone to go with her—a man, a gentleman, yet one still young enough to do what she wants" (8). Readers, following Shreve's lead, often suggest that Quentin's narrative is different from Rosa's, but insofar as Quentin shares the time that Rosa's room encloses, their stories are not very different. They are both already dead.

The long sentence begun in the previous quotation opens as if it were a straightforward third-person omniscient perspective but then shifts to being represented as "Quentin's thought." As the paragraph continues, the reader's view of Rosa is spliced with Quentin's perception of her. A shocking intimacy between them is established as Rosa's "embattled virginity" is encased in Quentin's mind (a critical formulation that cannot help but be pregnant with allusion to readers of *The Sound and the Fury*). Readers of *Absalom* will not know Rosa's full narrative until Chapter 5, but by the time we receive it, we experience it as something that has already happened in Quentin's mind. Rosa's narrative cannot be effectively distinguished from Quentin's reception of it. So Rosa and Quentin, Faulkner's two permanent virgins, sit together in Rosa's father's study, almost as if they were lovers holding hands, as one tells the other the story of how the ruin of the South and of her life are one and the same. Rosa chooses Quentin because he is to her family, which means, crucially, that he is a part of her story—"his very body was an empty hall echoing with sonorous defeated names; he was not a being, an entity, he was a commonwealth" (7). On the other hand, to be outside their narrative frame is to be outside the story: not to exist. This perspective explains why the North, the "United States," has no place in *Absalom, Absalom!* In the second half of the novel, Quentin and Shreve will make up versions of the Sutpen story unknown and unimaginable to Rosa, but Quentin will be unable to invent his way out of this initial intimacy with Rosa. Rosa's "latticed room" and Quentin's "empty hall" are perfectly joined; together they inhabit a tomb, the very destination that together they seek and where they will speak perfectly and forever the "long silence of not-people talking in notlanguage" (5).

The third sentence of Chapter 2 begins with Quentin listening to the sound of the church bells ringing, knowing that the bells are making the same sound they made that Sunday morning in 1833 when "the stranger" Thomas Sutpen arrived at the Holton House (23). A sentence that begins with Quentin "listening" ends with the sudden, unexpected appearance of Thomas Sutpen. It is not only as if Sutpen himself has risen from his forty-year death to appear before a startled Quentin on the front gallery of his parents' house but also that even in 1909 Sutpen's arrival, and not the arrival of the Northern invaders, remains as startling as it is inescapable. What is remarkable, though, is not just how Faulkner makes 1909 and 1833 part of the same seemingly timeless time but also that, for Quentin and Rosa, Sutpen's arrival actually marks the beginning of historical time. Their entire narrative, or history, is a failed attempt to eradicate not only Sutpen and the history he seems to bring but also the instant that they become conscious of themselves as a community with a specific history. Neither Quentin nor Rosa can assimilate an event that happened fifty-eight years before Quentin's birth, because the community has never surrendered its desire to deny that Sutpen's story is also its story; to the community, if Sutpen had never arrived, then the community need not have been doomed. Once Sutpen arrives, though, he moves among the members of the community like a breath, a contagion they cannot escape: "the stranger's name went back and forth among the places of business and of idleness and among the residences in steady strophe and antistrophe: *Sutpen. Sutpen. Sutpen. Sutpen*" (24). These words seem to attach themselves to the wind that blows through the town, but they are actually the product of Quentin's reflection, suggesting how, for Quentin, the arrival of Sutpen coincides with the imminent death of the community as it has known (or not known) itself.

Quentin and Rosa share the ability to seek the past as a suitor or as an intended would. Rosa's voice is "not ceasing but vanishing" (5), and Quentin speaks to himself in the "long silence of notpeople talking in notlanguage" because their identities have been merged with that of Sutpen, or the history that he represents to them. Each of the characters returns to the moment of Sutpen's arrival because it marks *their own birth into time* (5). For Quentin and Rosa, to be born into time is also to identify your death. The telling of their story and the conclusion of their story exist as if in the same moment. One might even say that Quentin's suicide is superfluous, since it makes literal the symbolic death that he and Rosa (and his father) tell and retell for the entire narrative. Prior to Sutpen's entry, Jefferson has no essence except as something that Sutpen despoils. If *Absalom*'s communal history seems to involve an act of making by tellers and listeners, it is also one in which its tellers presume themselves to be the passive recipients of a history they are powerless to change and can only, helplessly, join. Important to Faulkner's conception of history is the fact that Quentin and Rosa are both virgins whose virginity reinforces, if not defines, their roles within the family. Quentin is Brother Quentin and Rosa is Aunt Rosa. If they are ultimately the caretakers and preservers of their communal history, then their job is to keep that history pure of outside influence. In a work rife with implied incest, Aunt Rosa and Brother Quentin are arguably more closely paired than any other two characters, including whatever combination of Henry/Bon/Judith one cares to name. Each experiences Sutpen's entry into their community as a violation. Each wants to believe that without Sutpen's arrival the arcadia that was Jefferson would still remain intact.

In theological terms, the act that is their narrative becomes possible only in a fallen world, the world that the reader inherits and that *Absalom* struggles to replace with its glorification of the past. Quentin and Rosa do not want to live in a future that abolishes the old order, as they understand it. Once they identify a moment when history begins, they can only retell the stories of their own deaths. In *The Sound and the Fury*, Quentin breaks his watch in a futile attempt to release himself from the burden of time. In that novel, Quentin's failure to escape time is almost entirely psychological and connected to his doomed relationship with his sister. In *Absalom, Absalom!* Quentin's failure is a consequence of becoming a historian who is unable to shape his subject so that the present may be different from the past—he must act out his role as the "commonwealth" for the stories that his father and Rosa tell him about Sutpen. Rosa's voice will sound until it vanishes, just as Quentin will be imprisoned forever within the house of Sutpen even if he literally dies in Cambridge's Charles River. They live and die perpetually within the moment in which their arcadia is destroyed.

Quentin and Rosa's obsession with Sutpen is also their obsession with their falling into history, or death. They see him in terms of his unstoppable, epic drive. An intruder becomes the county's biggest landowner. His "single unflagging effort" is required precisely because he arrives with "a name nobody ever heard before" (9). Like the later Faulkner character Flem Snopes, who also takes over Jefferson, Sutpen is described as a kind of mechanical wonder. He is to his biographers not a person but some machine-like principle that they are powerless to stop. The irony is that their descriptions of Sutpen are as mechanical and as abstract as Sutpen is said to be. To have a name is to have a place within their society, and to have a place within their society is also to know that you are never allowed to leave it. In a well-known passage, Judith defines how the Southerner's sense of ingrained place can be suffocating to the point of self-annihilation:

> Because you make so little impression, you see. You get born and you try this and you don't know why only you keep on trying it and you are born at the same time with a lot of other people, all mixed up with them, like trying to, having to, move your arms and legs with strings only the same strings are hitched to all the other arms and legs and the others all trying and they don't know why either except that the strings are all in one another's way like five or six people all trying to make a rug on the same loom only each one wants to weave his own pattern into the rug; and it can't matter, you know that, or the Ones that set up the loom would have arranged it a little better, and yet it must matter because you keep on trying or having to keep on trying and then all of a sudden it's all over and all you have is a block of stone with scratches on it provided there was someone to remember to have the marble scratched and set up or had time to, and it rains on it and the sun shines on it and after a while they don't even remember the name and what the scratches were trying to tell, and it doesn't matter. (100–101)

Judith speaks as one whose name always belongs to another. She is the daughter of Thomas Sutpen, or the sister of Henry Sutpen, or the fiancée of Charles Bon. It is, for her, a terrible irony that Henry's murder of Bon denies her the status of being known as Bon's widow. In Faulkner's novels, Southern women experience more keenly than Southern men the bonds of place—the bonds that dictate that you are known only in terms of how you relate, or are related, to someone else. However, sons are also subject to fathers, and both Quentin and his father must live up to the imposing legacy left by General Compson. You are known by your relationship not only to the living but also to the dead. Judith speaks of needing the living to mark your memory when you are dead; otherwise, it will be as if you never existed at all. Judith's fear is misplaced, because it is actually the dead who give the living both their identity and their history. Sutpen has neither a name nor a history, because he has no dead in town to claim him. We see here the logic that must exclude Sutpen: you cannot be here, one of us, unless you were always here and one of us. Quentin and Rosa are the insiders. They own the story and thus would own Sutpen. Yet Sutpen usurps their story, and that usurpation becomes, against their wishes, their community's history.

Rosa and Quentin accept the logical impossibility of the community's "purity" but they also share Judith's anger at being denied an identity that is truly their own. Rosa and Quentin are bound not only by their virginity but also by their submission to their fathers, even though neither believes that the father has earned his or her respect. Quentin's father is a cynical, self-hating nihilist who, judging from his account of Sutpen's wedding in Chapter 2, hates his townspeople almost as much as he hates Sutpen. Certainly, his stance during *The Sound and the Fury* is calculated to nullify the meaning of every potential event, and Quentin's suicide in that novel can be seen as the logical expression of his father's nihilism. We know Rosa's father only through others' representations of him, but Rosa's decision to write poetry memorializing the Confederate dead at the very moment that her father was killing himself to protest the war suggests that she would kill him herself if only she could. She also hates him for bringing Sutpen into their family. Yet she lives the rest of her life in his house, maintains "his" study, and never stops being his daughter, his creation. Theoretically, Rosa and Quentin might sympathize with Sutpen's status as an outsider within the community. Sutpen would seem to give them an opportunity to rebel against their predetermined identity. This stance would require them to violate their predetermined roles as defenders of the community, regardless of cost or logic, but this they cannot do. It is not even a possibility except as one reads Judith's remarks as a version of one character speaking the unspeakable for the other characters (which it surely is).

Rosa, Quentin, and even Quentin's father are themselves the creations of their community, and their outrage at Sutpen expresses their acceptance of their condition. They lack the terrible rage of Judith that allows her to speak out against its system of identity formation. Rosa is a Coldfield, and Quentin is a Compson. Their names give them standing, and together they think they own Sutpen's story more fully than he does himself. Rosa's father allowed Sutpen into the community, and Quentin's grandfather was Sutpen's only friend. Together they feel culpable in the eyes of the community because their families sponsored Sutpen's success in Jefferson. Sutpen outrages the community because he makes its stories his story. In his actions, he seems to speak aloud what they would keep silent: the fact that slavery, not honor, is the basis of their "honorable" society. In addition to his "design," with its "wild niggers," its French architect, and his need for a wife, Sutpen gives the town its most significant and fatal gift other than chattel slavery: a history. The war is a cataclysmic event in the community, not exactly because it threatens its members' Way of Life but because it forces them to acknowledge that Sutpen is *one of them*. Understanding this point gives these words of Rosa's their iconic and ironic power: "But that our cause, our very life and future and hopes and past pride, should have been thrown into the balance with men like that to buttress it—men with valor and strength but without pity or honor. Is it any wonder that Heaven saw fit to let us lose?" (13). Notice that Rosa's "cause" is not specifically the right to keep slaves but more abstractly the right to define who counts as one of us and who does not. With this logic, the South can assure itself that the war was not about slavery or about having fewer soldiers and no mechanized industry and no money. Rather, the war was heaven's just punishment for allowing outsiders into its midst.

In the first paragraph of *Absalom*, Quentin thinks about how this "demon" Sutpen "*came out of nowhere and without warning upon the land with a band of strange niggers and built a plantation—(Tore violently a plantation, Miss Rosa Coldfield says)—tore violently*" (5). It is possible to attribute the "demonizing" of Sutpen to the hysterical spinster rage of Rosa or to the mockery of Shreve. All of *Absalom*'s narrators, however, are intent on distancing themselves from Sutpen, even if they agree that he was courageous during the war. Quentin's father and Rosa (and Cleanth Brooks) harp on Sutpen's vulgarity and lack of breeding. Rosa's mantra, words she uses repeatedly to keep her tale going, is this: "He wasn't a gentleman. He wasn't even a gentleman." Worse, he came with "a name which nobody ever heard before" (9). Quentin's father says that after one visit to Jefferson Sutpen was "a public enemy" (33). He characterizes Sutpen's rise to become "the single biggest landowner and cotton-planter in the county" as having been achieved by "the same tactics with which he had built his house—the same singleminded unflagging effort and utter disregard of how his actions which the town could see might look" (56). When Sutpen tells his life story to General Compson, his speech is represented as stilted and improper. To those who tell his story, he remains white trash born in West Virginia, even if, as the novel is told, the community can never really know Sutpen's origins. To accept Sutpen as an outsider is to limit one's view to the most local form of history possible—it is to do as Quentin and Rosa do and to accept the constructed, highly artificial values of their community as "real" or "true." Actually, Sutpen is the incarnation of the system that they represent. He dramatizes, in his own singular person, the story of their own beginnings. W. J. Cash's classic study *The Mind of the South* (1941), published five years after *Absalom*, demonstrates that the Cavalier myth was pretty much that—a myth. The gentleman planter, to the extent that he existed, had no need to leave Virginia because he already had everything he wanted. Those who moved west and south were by definition not of the "Quality," except perhaps as second or third sons. Virginia-style plantations moved west and south, but the process was so rapid that the plantation and the frontier existed side by side and often on the same ground. In the mid-nineteenth century, the newly established planter class might claim to be gentry, but sweat stains were still on their shirts, and their lines of succession had not yet been established.

In this historical context, Sutpen's story is fairly typical. In the nineteenth century, Mississippi was a frontier state, and it was "settled" largely through the efforts of slaves and later the cruelly misnamed "freedmen." As Melvin Backman has noted, Sutpen himself seems to represent the process by which the frontier gave way to a plantation society (121–29). Sutpen is born into a frontier society in what would become West Virginia (this point is significant because this region would not secede from the Union), but he moved east, against his desire, to a plantation society. The defining event for Sutpen, often recounted, occurs when, in his childhood, a black slave refuses him entry into a white man's mansion and sends him around back. Prior to that moment, Sutpen did not know that the world was hierarchical and his place was at the bottom, below even the slaves. Initially, he wants to seek revenge against the "balloon faced nigger" who denies him entry, by doing as his father did when similarly challenged (Sutpen's father attacked a black man to assert his authority as a white man). Unlike his father, Sutpen later recognizes that this is the only power available to a man of his station, and he rejects it. However, he does not reject the social system that defines him as one below "niggers." He is no class warrior. Sutpen seeks to acquire the power that the white man who owns the mansion has. Unlike Huck Finn, Sutpen will not light out for the territory in order to escape the moral taint of slavery. Sutpen instead wants to re-create the system that humiliated him, only this time he will be on top. The fact that he fails is underscored by the irony that he is murdered by Wash Jones, a version of the fated life he tried to escape. Sutpen's ambition is both remarkably imitative and shrewd. Short of leaving the South and becoming Lincoln, William Lloyd Garrison, or Grant, Sutpen can only make even the slight he suffered by becoming the plantation owner with a back door at his own big house.

Edouard Glissant's extraordinary study of Faulkner, *Faulkner, Mississippi*, perfectly expresses the narrative and historical moment that Quentin and Rosa inhabit and that Faulkner's history, despite the death of characters, communicates as still being alive:

> When Faulkner was writing, what he put at risk was the supreme institution of this Southern community. He questioned its very legitimacy, its original establishment, its Genesis, its irrefutable source. All his works are shaped by an unsurpassable *a priori*, a question putting everything in vertigo: how to explain the "beginnings" of the South—this monopoly of the land by the Whites from Europe, actually from nowhere, all of them (in the writing) prone to violence? . . . [H]ow can one understand, or at least envision, the South's "damnation"? Is it connected to the South's dark entanglement with slavery, inextricable from its roots and its tormented history? (21)

Glissant suggests that "to these basic, primordial questions the work [of Faulkner] makes no reply" and thus "the inconceivable and impossible situation of the country (its failure to respond to these basic questions) has become an absolute" (21). Neither Rosa nor Quentin can answer Glissant's penetrating questions, because they have no interest in knowing what the answer might be. These questions comprise the given of Faulkner's work only because he writes to repress them from his, or our, characters' full consciousness. Quentin and Rosa are aware that the land is cursed, but they attribute that curse not so much to the historical choices that their ancestors made and that they have inherited but to a single force: the one they name Sutpen.

Faulkner's "Genealogy" to the novel says that Quentin was born in 1891 and died in 1910. One may claim that in a defining way both Quentin and Rosa were born in 1833, the year that Sutpen entered Jefferson, but their devout belief is that time did not exist in Jefferson before Sutpen's arrival. Rosa, perhaps more obviously that Quentin, represents the South's desire to believe that it is a country separate from the North and that whatever evil befell it was brought from the outside. Thus, Sutpen is forever "a stranger," one whose every act, even bringing slaves, inspires the town's disbelieving outrage. Brooks notes, though, that what makes Sutpen distinctive in the matter of race is that he fights with his slaves ("History" 189). What makes Sutpen potent as a symbol of authority for even Rosa and Quentin is that his personal history implies that he earned his right to be a slaveholder by putting down a slave rebellion in Haiti, just as he reconfirms his superior status to his slaves when he battles them all over again on his plantation in Mississippi. As Godden has noted, Sutpen's suppression of the Haitian slave revolt in 1827 is historically anachronistic, since by then Toussant L'Ouverture's revolt had occurred and Haiti no longer had slaves. However, Sutpen's mastery of slaves and his intimate relationship to them is what matters here. As Godden argues, "In Sutpen's slaves Faulkner creates an anomalous archaism; they are historically free and yet doubly constrained, by a fiction (*Absalom, Absalom!*) and by a counter-revolutionary violence (Sutpen's) that is necessary to the workings of the plantation system.[9] If, as Godden suggests, Sutpen's physical contact with his male slaves works "to enact the pre-emptive counter-revolution, crucial to the authority of his class," then the intimacy of this contact also predicts his conjugal congress with his female slaves. Sutpen suppresses the slaves; yet, from the town's point of view, he is also strangely intimate with them. Through Sutpen, Jefferson must confront, or try not to confront, its own intimate involvement with what Faulkner at one point calls "the nigger in the woodpile."

Before Sutpen's arrival, the townspeople are unaware that collectively they were part of a specifically patterned social design—that they constituted a place in the world and that, as such, the place they understood as theirs might differ from other places. After Sutpen arrives, his "design" is pressed upon the community members, and they are obliged to accept Sutpen's design as if it were theirs. It is important to understand that their consciousness of slavery as something that occurs within their community happens as if simultaneously with Sutpen's arrival. They suffer a belated awakening into a consciousness of slavery as a moral problem that defines them on to Sutpen. To allay and perhaps even eradicate this suffering, they attribute slavery's origins to Sutpen's design. This fortunate denial allows them to believe slavery began elsewhere, simply because slavery is something they inherited and not something they created. The crime they eventually identify, besides their fall into time, is not so much Sutpen bringing chattel slavery but his bringing with him the fate of having "mixed" with the slaves. Rosa never knows that Sutpen came to her community to escape his fear that he had fathered a child who is part black. Alternately in love with Bon and with Sutpen, Rosa cannot suspect that she desires a man with black blood. Had she known Sutpen's full story, she would have had to confront the true origins of her desire and the community that contained it. Quentin, by contrast, knows or surmises Sutpen's past, because his grandfather has told him. It is unclear whether Quentin's father actually knows. (Quentin tells Shreve that his father does know, but if so this knowledge does not affect Quentin's father's interpretation of Sutpen.) Certainly, the community that viewed Sutpen as a "wanted man," is like Rosa and cannot know.

For Quentin, though, Sutpen's Haitian marriage means that to the extent that Sutpen's story is also their story, the existence and memory of Sutpen threatens the sanctity of the community's vision of itself. Keeping the community safe from dishonor is the main objective Absalom's history serves, and this means denying that the taint of slavery, with its attendant miscegenation, touches them. Although Quentin's life must conclude with the history that he relates, he dies, like Rosa, a virgin, which means in some essential sense that neither he nor she can be guilty of the same crime as Sutpen. They can transcend Sutpen's fate only by evading his fate. That is, if Sutpen's ultimate failure was his inability to create his empire as something that can be passed on, generation by generation, into the unending future, then Absalom will preserve the past as narrative into an unending future that does not have to include either Quentin or Rosa except as remembered tellers of the history they served and for which they died. Likewise, the tragedy that Absalom, Absalom! relates is not that of a society doomed by an unredeemable sin so much as a fall caused by the failure of the South to replicate its order through the generations. This failure is not the consequence of slavery or even of the North's invasion but is the direct result of the original sin of miscegenation. To preserve, or restore, the separate sanctity of the races, as Rosa and Quentin have done, would destroy Sutpen's legacy and enable the South to rise again.

Much is made by Quentin and Shreve of Sutpen's "innocence," by which they mean that he can pursue his design without regard to how he is being perceived. It also means that he can allow his Haitian wife to keep the majority of their wealth and believe that he does not dishonor her by leaving their marriage. Sutpen's "innocence" is best expressed, though, by his unwavering faith in his design. He never doubts that he will be squared with the past if only he can become the authority that once snubbed him. He does realize his ambition—twice—only to see it crumble both times. Sutpen's most perfect realization of his ambition, though, is precisely in his indifference to the prospect that by becoming the plantation gentleman, he perpetuates the very system that humiliated him as a child. In this respect, Sutpen's "innocence" is what permits his success, and it is that aspect about him that most exactly mirrors the community that he joins. What the community cannot see in itself it sees in Sutpen. When the war comes, Rosa's "cause" becomes indistinguishable from Sutpen's. His crime—that he brought history—becomes the property of the community, and it falls on Quentin to purge it. Thus, Sutpen comes to Jefferson and weaves the community into his design. The war, not his first marriage, unravels Sutpen's design and with it the townspeople's sense of their own innocence. If the creation of Sutpen's design is something they had at first resented and defied, then its destruction belongs to all of them. Sutpen's initial desire was never to rob Indians, or become a slaveholder, or take over a white community; it was *to square his life with the past.* For Quentin, if not for Rosa, this is what Sutpen can never do, and this failure is what he and his community are doomed to repeat. Their continued obsession with his meaning dramatizes their continued enslavement to the history that he represents. In the attempt to take over Sutpen's story, they assume his original burden. Eventually Quentin's suicide will stand as a tribute to a past that requires no act of expiation, only a memorial.

To argue, as Glissant does, that the unspoken given of Faulkner's fiction is that the South's origin is mixed up with slavery is to begin to suggest that we can no longer (provisionally or retrospectively) accept a view of the South as a separate land with a history unto itself. Yet, as Faulkner well knew, to separate the history of the South from the history of the North is to deny that the sin of slavery is one that even the victorious North inherits. Indeed, one strategy of *Absalom* is to associate the sin of slavery with its presumed eradicators. Certainly, Brooks assigns it this role when he argues that Sutpen represents not the fall of the South so much as the epitome of Northern mechanization, what he calls the "the secularized Puritan" ("History" 191). Sutpen is a version of the automatic man D. H. Lawrence satirized in the figure of Benjamin Franklin.[10] Brooks's argument is telling because it suggests how Southerners of Faulkner's time would resist the proposition that Sutpen's rise and fall embodies the rise and fall of the South. Brooks, like Quentin and Rosa, does not want to confront how the South was created, defined, and ultimately destroyed by its adherence to slavery. Reading Faulkner through Glissant (a Caribbean writer who sees his region as part of the same colonial story that Faulkner tells), we might see Sutpen as the embodiment of the historical process by which the New World was conquered and enslaved by Europeans and their descendants. Yet what Glissant suggests is that Faulkner's work is defined by a kind of American Southern exceptionalism that would remove it from a specifically postcolonial context. Sutpen may be a New World exploiter, but his story resonates for Americans because it excuses Quentin and the Southern nobility from being responsible for the very historical situation from which they profited. Sutpen does not invent the slave caste system; he only copies it.

Reading *Absalom* as the definitive history of the American South, one would think that slavery was a lamentable practice forced on the white South, as later Americans might see slavery only as an invention of the English or as another imperial outrage perpetrated by King George III. In this version, Southerners are actually more noble than Northerners, because Quentin and those he represents can acknowledge miscegenation as a sin that involved the exploitation of an entire caste of people—as Ike McCaslin does in Faulkner's "The Bear," from *Go Down, Moses*, and as Quentin does not do in *Absalom*—but they cannot be blamed for creating a society where miscegenation must be seen as a violation against society and history. Northerners, by contrast, say that slaves were exploited but accept no responsibility for this exploitation or how they benefited (and continue to this day to benefit) from it. From this perspective, Sutpen's story—and his peculiar innocence that Brooks identifies—is indeed an inexorably American one that leads to the War between the States. The war was fought not to end slavery (because who cares that some people who happened to be black were born slaves) but for the right of each side to claim innocence regarding the history of slavery. When Lee surrendered to Grant, the North did not actually win the right to declare slavery's demise (as Morrison also shows in *Beloved*). Rather, the North won the right to blame the South—for as long as America lasts—for slavery having ever been an "American" practice at all. With their victory came the right to declare Lincoln as the Great Emancipator and the North as the keeper of the ideals of the American Revolution. (That the post-1964 Republican Party claims to be the party of Lincoln but preserves its power by enacting policies designed to disenfranchise African Americans suggests how purely symbolic this triumphant version of post–Civil War American history is.) It would fall to Southerners, black and white, to accept responsibility for telling the true history of slavery and to enact the recognition that slavery exacted a cost America can never make square.

Until Lincoln and his war intervene, Sutpen might well be associated with self-made "American" heroes such as Benjamin Franklin or Jay Gatsby. What makes Sutpen's story irredeemably different from other American success

stories is that it depends on the existence of slaves rather than on a crafty almanac or some Daisy. This fact, however, concerns neither Sutpen—except
insofar as he needs to acquire slaves in order to achieve what he refers to as
his "design"—nor his historians. To them, as to Sutpen, his saga is first and
last about *family*, about dynastic succession. Without slaves, however, not only
would Sutpen be denied his status as lord of the manor but also there would
be no reason for an outside agent (Lincoln) to intervene in his story, unless he
came to remove Sutpen, just as Sutpen came to remove the Indians. With the
War between the States, though, Sutpen need not be seen as the outsider who
brought time to Jefferson; he can be seen, potentially, as the one who defended
and preserved Jefferson against armed legions of irrational outsiders. This
shift in Sutpen's significance to the tellers of his story does not quite happen,
however. Whereas in the war Sutpen is concerned with defending the estate he
has built, Rosa and Quentin understand the threat to their community as coming not from without (Lincoln) but from within (Bon). Thus, once the Civil
War intervenes, Sutpen and his tellers are allied only in the sense that from
different perspectives and for different reasons they all work to contain the
threat that Sutpen's unacknowledged black son posed. Race, not Lincoln or
even slavery, is the serpent in their garden.

    Absalom says race matters more than slavery because although Quentin and
Shreve determine that Bon is part black, they never worry that he is not a slave.
The threat he poses, not named by the characters, is that of a "black" South-
ern gentleman, arguably the most gracious Southern gentleman in the book.
Faulkner has a potential slave, Bon, fight heroically for the South because
Faulkner recognizes, even if most readers disagree with him, that any intrusion
into the history of the American South by any outside party, particularly the
American North, is unwanted, unnecessary, and completely beside the point.
He thus indulges in the happiest of Southern fantasies: that one of the bravest,
even one of the most noble, fighters for the southern cause should in fact have
been a slave. Faulkner's irony less suggests Bon's essential humanity, though
it certainly suggests it, than the communion shared by those who fought. Do
not exceed your place, as Sutpen does and as Bon threatens to do, and the nation can be preserved. Yet the blood mixture of slave and master, as prevalent
in Faulkner's work as it was in the South, is what makes Bon unfit to succeed
Sutpen. No one in the narrative, not even Shreve, questions this assumption.
Thus, none of the characters, and this is most especially true of Sutpen, sees
the Civil War as either a conclusion to or even a necessary adjunct to the his-

tory they are telling. Indeed, Sutpen's willingness to fight bravely in a war that, morally, is largely irrelevant to the South (except as a matter of defense and honor) is what makes Sutpen a hero despite his historians' reservations about his origins and questionable courting practices. For Sutpen and his historians, the Civil War is a strange parenthetical that merely sidetracks his/their story: its only significance is that it provides a field for Sutpen to prove his bravery and for his true heir to eliminate his false heir.

Whatever slavery has wrought, whatever miscegenation has wrought, Quentin's story says, it is "our" story to be dealt with in "our" ways. When Quentin first visits Rosa, he mistakenly thinks that Rosa wants to explain "why God let us lose the War" (6). But the whys and wherefores of the War are as irrelevant to Rosa and Quentin as they are to Faulkner: only preserving what remains matters. Although Rosa describes the War as a "holocaust," she does so because she understands it to be something done by men to men to prevent her from ever having the chance to marry. Quentin, too, cares little about the War as a historical event. Rather, it is a convenient theater for pursuing the destinies of the Sutpens. He mostly wants to know why Henry killed Bon. Even the reader inclined to understand Sutpen's story as a version of the rise and fall of the South is likely to become more concerned with Bon's murder than with the true "historical" reasons for the destruction of Sutpen's empire, because the multiple narratives of the novel all hinge on that story. Once Quentin and Shreve convince themselves that solving the mystery of Bon's murder is the key to understanding their history, they have succeeded in making the reader forget a point that should be obvious and should severely compromise the power of their narratives. That is, *Sutpen could never have regained his exalted place, or achieved again his design, even if the murder had not taken place.* Their belief that he can (or might) renew his empire testifies to their desire to continue the world that existed before the War—before they fell into time. After the war ends, slavery is abolished; the plantations are removed to the realm of myth. What cannot be removed to myth, though, is the shade of the dead black Southern gentleman. Sutpen dies; Bon, symbolically, does not. Quentin fears not only Bon's resurrection but also his redemption. After the war and Sutpen's demise, the narrative pointedly concerns itself with the decline of Bon's line into madness—a story that is much preferable to Southerners (such as Quentin) than the ones that will be told (as we shall see in Chapter 2) by "Faulkner's children," to use Ralph Ellison's self-defining phrase, referring to post-Faulkner black authors.[11]

Thus, with the war lost, Sutpen, ironically, becomes at last a kind of hero to his narrators: his quest is to restore, however impossibly, a true (white) patrimonial succession. At this point Sutpen becomes an integral part of and not an intruder in his community's story, and Quentin's narrative may now concentrate on the terrible purity of their shared fate. Sutpen is killed by one of the lower orders, someone who, like Sutpen as a youth, is below the slaves on the social order. (Clytemnestra will not let Wash inside Sutpen's house.) His death, described as if he were being killed by father time, gives him a kind of tragic grandeur, one that is realized when his younger son kills his older son. Yet to be a *tragic hero* is also to be expelled from one's community. Oedipus exiled himself in order to save Thebes from the plague that his corruption had engendered. Quentin and Rosa would exile Sutpen, too, but only if they could also erase the history-through-miscegenation that Sutpen leaves behind. However, once Sutpen's story becomes the sons' story, a series of virtually unanswerable questions emerges: Is Bon black? This is the most ominous question, but there are many others that must be asked as well: Is Bon really going to marry his sister? Does his morganatic marriage jeopardize this prospect? Will Henry prevent the marriage because Bon is part black or because Bon is Judith's half brother? Will Sutpen prevent the wedding by acknowledging Bon as his son? Does Bon know he is Sutpen's son? Does Bon know he is black? Raising and answering these questions drives the narrative that Quentin and Shreve concoct in Chapter 8 of the novel. As nearly everyone agrees, their sympathy lies with the sons against the father. Henry is thus willing to let Bon marry Judith (which Judith thinks is largely irrelevant) against their father's wishes as long as he thinks Bon is white. Once Shreve and Quentin decide that Bon is black, though, the story must end, since this history will abide no sequel that comes from miscegenation. Henry kills "the nigger who is going to marry [his] sister," and for all practical purposes the history that Quentin has been pursuing, first with Rosa and his father and now with Shreve, stops.

What makes this ending so extraordinary is that Bon's blackness is wholly provisional. Yet, for Quentin (and Shreve), this is the one "fact" in the story that cannot be treated as conditional or subject to another narrative version. Bon is black because that detail alone makes Sutpen's history comprehensible to Shreve and Quentin. What other reason could there be for Sutpen's abandonment of his plantation in Haiti? Why else would Henry kill his sister's highly desirable suitor who also happens to be his closest friend? Henry might kill Bon, if he is their brother, to protect Judith. This rationale explains why the murder occurred but not why the murder is possible—it does not explain why Sutpen left a legitimate male heir in Haiti. Bon may die for his "blackness," but Bon's blackness rescues Quentin's history from having to acknowledge (in any sustained way) the crime of slavery. In this history, Bon's "blackness" is quarantined from the blackness that made other people slaves. Bon's "blackness" is a matter that concerns family members only. Remember, there are two families in *Absalom*: the Sutpens and the narrators of the Sutpen story. There are no black people in the story who are not Sutpens, and, therefore, there is no authentic black voice to protest either the fact of slavery or its representation in the saga. Ironically, Clytemnestra is the de facto caretaker of the Sutpen history, the one who burns it rather than have outsiders know about it. Bon's descendants wear their blackness as the family curse (or wear the family curse as their blackness), and the last surviving Sutpen, Jim Bond, is portrayed as a howling idiot. He will tell no tales either.

One can argue whether Henry's murder of Bon is *noble* because he protects the honor of his sister, is *tragic* because he is the unwitting executor of his father's flawed design, or is *morally indefensible* because he kills his brother due to his color. From a literary perspective, this third line of reasoning, best expressed by Kartiganer, is the only one that is acceptable, because it justifies *Absalom* as a work of art that is not tied only to the mandates of history. The other two paradigms, however, accept Bon's blackness as true and, in so doing, most effectively treat *Absalom* as a narrative that functions as history functions. The consequence of such logic (or longing) is most evident in the work of Brooks, who more than any other critic has worked to prove that Bon's blackness can be verified as a "fact." [12] His readings also rather startlingly embody the process by which the reader becomes one with what is being read—the process by which the reader falls with Quentin into history. Returning to the question of Bon's identity again and again over the years, Brooks tried to answer every claim that has been made about the impossibility of determining Bon's true racial identity. For Brooks, Quentin knows because Henry told him on that 1909 evening when Quentin and Rosa went to Sutpen's mansion. Answering Hershel Parker's assertion that if Quentin was able to ascertain Bon's secret, it was because he recognized the "Sutpen face" in the visage of his descendant Jim Bond, Brooks counters with the claim that, in the exchange between Henry and Quentin, "we have been given only a fragment of the conversation and that Quentin found a solution to the riddle in something he *heard*" (*William, Toward* 325). Brooks then argues that if readers will only speak aloud this exchange, they will see that there is plenty of time for Henry to have told Quentin what Faulkner himself will not repeat. It is hard to say which is more astounding: the image of the paragon of New Criticism adducing evidence that is not written in the text in order to make his argument or the image of him reading *Absalom* aloud over and over until he imagines in the interval of his readings that he hears the words that his interpretation needs. Yet the image of Brooks reading *Absalom* aloud is not as idiosyncratic as it may at first appear, since it provides the perfect example of a reader becoming literally—and piously—a version of Quentin and Shreve as storytellers. From Faulkner's perspective, Parker's position is really no different from that of Brook, since each has surrendered to an aesthetic tactic that obligates readers to perpetuate *as truth* the presumably fictional history that they merely read.

Brooks doubles an already doubled scene into a state of endless regression, since his view is caught in the same reflection that endlessly mirrors Quentin and Henry as versions of the other. His identification with Quentin's belief that Henry killed Bon because he was black cannot be more complete. When Henry says, "I killed the nigger who was going to marry 'our' sister," he provides a rationale for a historical vision that requires no further explanation—one that Quentin and Brooks both endorse. Incest can be forgiven, but miscegenation cannot. At no point does Brooks object to the inadequacy of a race-based justification for the murder. Indeed, Brooks, like most subsequent commentators, will only call the story "tragic." Brooks writes, "For Faulkner, the tragic flaw of the South was harboring chattel slavery, yet the slaveholders, and in general the soldiers of the Confederacy, the majority of whom were not slaveholders at all, were essentially brave and worthy men. That was why, for Faulkner, the collapse of the Old South was authentically tragic" (*William, Toward* 272). One is uncertain what Brooks means by "tragedy" in this context. Brooks *wants* to say that *Absalom* displaces history with tragedy; actually, *Absalom* appropriates the lineaments of tragedy to dress up the history it enacts. The Civil War does not quite provide tragic knowledge for its losers, only suffering and perhaps a resolve—borne out by segregationist Strom Thurmond's run for president seventy-five years later on a segregationist ticket—that, when it comes to questions of race, they will not repeat the mistakes of the past. From the perspective of the United States history, though, *the Civil War saved the Union.* From the Southern perspective, *Absalom*'s tragic knowledge can consist only of recognizing how the practice of slavery became a necessary condition for the white community's claim to tragic splendor. Preserving this tragic splendor for future Southerners and their allies is *Absalom*'s greatest achievement as a history.

Readers who accept *Absalom*'s implied historical vision see that slavery was never truly a social problem or even a matter for civil protest. It was certainly nothing to go to war over. In *Absalom*, the only person who objects to the war is Rosa's father, a kind of abolitionist-pacifist who regards slavery and war as morally indefensible. Mr. Compson renders him a Puritan moral zealot, but it is likely that Coldfield adopts these positions to expiate his guilt for aligning his family with Sutpen's. When the war comes, he removes himself from the community and dies. From the community's perspective, he has taken an almost honorable position, because he does not give comfort to the enemy. Moreover, to be outside the community is to be dead; thus, by withdrawing to the attic to die, he merely formalizes his separation from the community. Although Coldfield gives Sutpen a place in the community by allowing Sutpen to marry his daughter, he also becomes a vehicle for the community to distance itself further from its association with Sutpen's "wild niggers." Brooks shrewdly, and I believe correctly, suggests that Coldfield is the perfect complement to and enabler of Sutpen's design. Like Coldfield's atheism, Sutpen's commitment to a "secularized society" is appropriate for one "who does not believe in Jehovah" ("History" 187, 193). Brooks's need to link Coldfield with Sutpen and thus dismiss him is as virulent as any of Rosa's so-called demonizing: "Mr. Coldfield denounces secession, closes his store, and finally nails himself up in the attic of his house, where he spends the last three years of his life. No more than Sutpen is he a coward; like Sutpen, too, his scheme of humor is abstract and mechanical." Brooks sees "no reason to quarrel with the motive Mr. Coldfield assigns for Mr. Coldfield's objection to the Civil War: a Puritan objection to waste in any form whatsoever" (190). In this formulation, it is impossible to tell whether Coldfield is a coward for denouncing secession or for helping to make Sutpen's rise possible. It is clear that Brooks, like Rosa and the Compsons, wishes that Jefferson could secede from the tyranny of Sutpen—then maybe the North would fight Sutpen and leave the rest of the South in God-worshipping peace. On Brooks's reading, one may object to Sutpen, as Coldfield clearly does, but one may not object to the South's involvement in the War. Certainly, the book addresses no audience who would have a different reading of the book than that of Brooks.

The book's most intractable narrative dilemma is in telling Quentin's story in such a way that even an outsider, someone who is not a white Southerner, can be made to assent to its retrograde history without necessarily knowing that such assent is being given. In this way, Faulkner wants his sophisticated non-Southern reader to fall into history's endless present with Quentin and to experience this fall as art. Such a fall resembles the Aristotelian notion of catharsis, and recognizing Quentin's "tragedy," rather than his affirmation of a communal way of seeing the past, becomes the means for safely distancing one's reading of the book from one's interpretation of the book. If the North, or the United States, has interest in a story known only by Southerners such as Quentin, his father, and Aunt Rosa, then someone must be found who will tell it to other interested strangers as "we" (Quentin et al.) would tell it. Faulkner's ultimate solution, provided by the frame of *Absalom* itself, is the invention of Shreve, who is an Outsider and, crucially, not an American. Again, *Absalom* cannot acknowledge the entity, which conquered the South, and so the reader's proxy cannot be a post–Civil War American. Shreve inherits, through Quentin, the history that the South wants to tell about itself, the history that the South wants to be told about itself after it has passed. That Quentin speaks to a Canadian is telling. Faulkner will not allow Quentin's story to become the property of the invaders. Although his use of Shreve as a narrative device seems to open the narrative to an audience outside the South, the real effect is to underscore how *irrelevant* specifically Yankee readers are to the story being told.

Quentin's assumption, though, is that when he dies, history ends. History goes with him to the grave but his wish is that it will not change after he is gone. Implicitly, Shreve is the narrative device that allows the reader to imagine that he or she can know the story at all, since *Absalom* aspires to a "purer" form of history than the device of Shreve can allow. Ideally, it would make a perfect, unbreakable loop connecting tellers to the actors in the tale: notpeople forever speaking the notlanguage that they all share. This is what Quentin experiences with Rosa and his father, and he somehow shares this ability with Shreve as well. More explicitly than the Rosa–Quentin narrative, the Shreve–Quentin narrative is presented as if it comes from a joined consciousness. The reader cannot always tell who is speaking and who is listening, and even Quentin sometimes does not care to make a distinction between "his" tale and the one that Shreve thinks he tells at Quentin's prompting. The climax to Shreve–Quentin's story occurs when Quentin meets Henry in the book's final chapter. Just as Shreve and Quentin seem to have become one teller, so Quentin and Henry merge into one as they address each other in sentences that form an unending palindrome: the implication is that Quentin, having become a version of Henry, can never transcend the historical moment that Henry occupies.[13] The broader implication is that this meeting creates a black hole into which the entire narrative disappears: it eerily evokes Quentin's eventual suicide. How can Quentin, or his story, progress when he (and the reader) sees that Quentin and Henry are versions of each other? Outsiders such as Shreve (who may or may not have heard of the encounter) who happen upon this strange historical drama with its inverted identities and time-imprisoned souls need not fall into the narrative hole with the tellers of the tale. Either the reader joins them in the sense of believing in a dead past as a living possibility, or the reader affirms the tragic results that befall its protagonists. This endlessly repeating recognition scene, between Henry and Quentin, doubled again by Quentin and Shreve in telling it as one voice, conveys powerfully a tacit acceptance by either (only seemingly opposed) implied readers that the white South need not move past the historical moment that *Absalom* memorializes.

To those who cannot share either Henry's or Quentin's history, to "Americans" who are outside their perspective but nonetheless inherit the events that made it, *Absalom, Absalom!* puts the reader at odds with his or her own history. Our only defense, one that deceives, is aesthetic appreciation. One may marvel at how cunningly *Absalom* portrays history as an invention and even a form of seduction. To the skeptical reader, not obligated to understand the text as the story of a fallen world, Bon's blackness, the fact that for Quentin doomed him and his civilization, is contingent, not final. Had the narrators accepted Bon's blackness as provisional and therefore subject to new understandings, Quentin and his people would not have been doomed to die (and live dying) in the past. This fact they enshrine, though, as the one "truth" that their history cannot replace but must preserve. Even if we distinguish Faulkner from Quentin, for instance, by saying that Faulkner is critiquing Quentin's failure to transcend Henry's murder of Bon, we must still acknowledge that the question that Faulkner intentionally left unanswered is what to do with this blackness once it is no longer seen as an immutable truth. That is, how will (or do) black people fit in the American history that has absorbed Quentin's history? Arguably, the crucial distinction between American history and southern history—whether or not slavery was an unjust practice that needed to be ended immediately—conceals the possibility that American history has vanquished the South only to preserve as "true" the kind of representation of black people that *Absalom* offers. Certainly, at the time that the Civil War was fought, the question of what to do with the freed slaves had not been answered. As

W. E. B. DuBois reminded his readers in *The Souls of Black Folk* (1903), General John Fremont's freeing of the slaves early in the war caused a serious political problem for Lincoln. That "problem" was that the suddenly freed slaves were uncertain about where to go, but even greater was their liberators' dismay about what to do with them. Faulkner did not have the answer and—given that a disproportionate percentage of prisoners in the United States today are African American men—one can say that *the question has yet to be adequately answered* or even persuasively asked.

According to Philip Weinstein, "To read *Absalom* is thus to undergo a racial recognition that moves into tragic recognition" (40, 55). If the reader experiences "tragic recognition," it is only because writers other than Faulkner, most likely African American writers, have taught the reader to interpret Faulkner's characters from critical contexts that Faulkner's work implies but does not provide. Perhaps the most unlikely fantasy that *Absalom* perpetrates, one that powerful Southern readers such as Brooks or Warren would never question, is the belief that the freed slaves and their descendants, left to their own devices, would actually be committed to preserving their relationship to the old order.[14] Warren praises the fact that even Faulkner's "Negro" characters may "exemplify traditional virtues" attributed to strong white characters ("Faulkner" 256). Warren gives what would become the classic defense for Faulkner's treatment of black characters, one used by Irving Howe and even Ralph Ellison: "What Faulkner does is to make the character transcend his sufferings *qua* Negro to emerge not as Negro but as man, that is, beyond complexion and ethnic considerations" (263). Warren adds that for Faulkner, "the final story is never one of social injustice, however important that element may be, but of an existential struggle against fate, for identity, a demonstration of the human will to assert itself" (263). Warren shrewdly transforms Faulkner from a social critic who offers a particular form of Southern history into an artist who speaks for everyone, even slavery-bound "Negroes." By this logic, it makes perfect sense for Warren to ask, "From the social perspective of a French, Italian, or Japanese reader, what difference does [the Negro question] make?" (263–64). My claim here is not only that Southern readers such as Warren or Brooks treat Faulkner's work as literature separate from history but also that they excuse the historical vision that Faulkner endorses.

More radically, in *Absalom, Absalom!* Faulkner situates the historical prospects of his black characters within the same historical moment that his white characters cannot escape.[15] Yet this fantasy is commonplace for white

Southerners of Faulkner's generation for whom "the War Between the States," as Blyden Jackson notes, "was still very much alive" and who lived at a time when there existed "a white man's concordat, both of action and of thought, regarding Negroes that it was virtually worth a white Mississippian's life not to embrace with all his mind and heart" (58). Faulkner was not a typical white Mississippian (he published an essay entitled "If I Were a Negro" and suggested that segregation hurt white as well as black students). Still, it is hard to argue with Alice Walker's charge that "unlike Leo Tolstoy, Faulkner was not prepared to struggle to change the society he was born in" (qtd. in Werner 41). Thadious Davis, who gives perhaps the most brilliant reading of race in *Absalom*, argues that Faulkner offers "a marginal pulling away from the myths of southern experience." Where white Southern writers usually said, in effect, "Look at what the black man has done to me," Faulkner's Quentin comes close to saying "See what I have done to myself" (T. Davis 105). Yet, as Davis acknowledges, Faulkner presents this possibility "obliquely," and it is "one that Quentin cannot thoroughly absorb" (105). In the 1950s, when—under pressure from the Civil Rights movement—Quentin's creator famously advised the black population "to go slow" in the quest for integration, Baldwin mocked Faulkner's presumption that "white Southerners, left to their own devices, will realize that their own social structure looks silly to the rest of the world and correct it of their own accord" (209).

Over the years, many sympathetic observers have tried to rewrite Faulkner's statements to appear more palatable to liberal, integrationist views. In particular, these readers have been preoccupied with explaining away Faulkner's boast—which was really a logical extension of Thurmond's 1948 Dixiecrat platform a few years earlier—that in a contest between the federal government and Mississippi, he would fight for Mississippi "even if it meant going out to the street and shooting Negroes." [16] Baldwin, however, insisted that with this claim Faulkner "never before more concretely expressed what it means to be a Southerner" (211). Faulkner's fiction did not sympathize with white Southerners who would shoot "Negroes" in the street, but it did not move much beyond the lost static social order mourned by *Absalom*. [17] In *Light in August*, Cinthy, the beloved slave of the Hightower family, meets the end of the war and the prospect of her freedom with these words: "Free? What's freedom done except git Marse Gail killed and made a bigger fool outen Pawmp den even de Lawd Hisself could do? Free? Don't talk ter me erbout freedom" (*Novels* 752). Her stance, from Faulkner's perspective, is heroic. She justifies the old order rather than take a place in the new one. The new order where blacks are free is perilous—too perilous for representation in Faulkner's work. The episode with Cinthy uses the voice of the African American to justify the pre–Civil War world. It points to a sense of dislocation and alienation within African American identity but refuses to explore it.

In *Absalom* Clytemnestra, Sutpen's black daughter, does not merely inhabit her father-master's house; she becomes its custodian, and burns it from memory. To say that the slave Clytemnestra—who, once freed, will not leave the family who enslaved her—acts with honor is also to say that the practice of slavery did not prevent Faulkner's fictional slaves from expressing the virtues that Faulkner most admired. From the perspective of history rather than fiction, slavery is an issue in *Absalom* only for those readers who want to be part of a society where slavery does not exist. Both Brooks and Weinstein, for instance, underscore the fact that Faulkner portrays Clytemnestra as Sutpen's daughter, albeit black, acknowledging that for a white man to have a black daugher is as least socially anomalous (Weinstein) and at worst socially pernicious (Brooks). More than her half-sister, Judith, or even Rosa, Clytemnestra is caretaker of the Sutpens and their legacy. Both as a Sutpen and as a slave, she presides (if that is the right word) over their inheritance. In her dual role as slave–sister, she sees to it that Judith's death is properly commemorated by making sure that the inscription on her tombstone is paid for. She cares for the prodigal Henry when he returns. Thus, when she burns down the Sutpen mansion, there is no way to tell whether she does so as a former slave or as a daughter. She repeats the role that Dilsey plays in *The Sound and the Fury*: she gives form and order to the affairs of white folks. Being a sister and daughter does not erase her blackness; yet her blackness does not abolish her family ties either. On the other hand, her family ties confine her to the social death of being black. Hence, her story must end with the death of the last white Sutpen.[18]

To place Clytemnestra's story in a postbellum framework—to carry it beyond 1865 through 1936, through 1962 (the year of Faulkner's death), and through today—the reader must violate the implied narrative and historical frame of *Absalom*. In this context, Faulkner's famous dictum that "the past is never past" implies not only the omnipresence of memory in the formation of identity but also a wish that the future will never come. I do not want to belabor the point, but that future was one that made possible a fully enfranchised African American presence in Southern life. As I will argue in Chapter 2, *Absalom* remained unchallenged in American literature as the definitive treatment of the South, the Civil War, and its aftermath until Toni Morrison's *Beloved* (1987) in effect imagined a future for Clytemnestra.[19] "If a house burns down," Sethe explains, "its gone, but the place—the picture of it—stays, and not just in my rememory, but out there, in the world" (36). Symbolically, the house that Sethe speaks of here is the same one that burns down in *Absalom*, just as *Beloved* is a "rememory" of *Absalom*. Morrison's version of Faulkner's novel, though, attempts to abolish Faulkner's work (as history) and render it harmless (as art). Ironically, because Morrison and Baldwin see from a historical perspective that is different from the one that Faulkner endorses, they are able to read him *aesthetically*. Note how Morrison's reading differs from that of Brooks. For Brooks, Henry's ultimate role in the novel is to bear indisputable evidence that Bon was black and thus Henry had to kill him to preserve his sister's honor. For Morrison, Faulkner's refusal to imagine an African American future different from the South's "tragic" end is a remarkable aesthetic acheivement put into the service of a dubious history. Her point is not only that Faulkner's work looks different when seen from an African American perspective but also that *Absalom, Absalom!* is so effective—magnificent, really—in denying that a specifically African American version of Southern history is even imaginable. A lasting consequence of Faulkner's achievement as a historian of the South has been to ennoble Southern history as a story that belongs to whites and their descendants. White readers who are not Southerners and who may not understand themselves to be "secret sharers" with Faulkner's vision of a living, unreconstructed South nonetheless become part of Faulkner's implied audience. Having accepted "the nobility" or "the tragedy" of Faulkner's history, but not being African American, white admirers of Faulkner have not had and have not looked for a perspective from which to criticize the history that *Abaslom* endorses. And these sons and daughters of Shreve—he who mockingly asserts that one day he and Quentin will be the descendants of African king—will not know or sympathize with Clytie's people to the extent that even Quentin does.

Faulkner ends the novel by having Shreve ask Quentin why he hates the South and having Quentin respond, famously, "I don't I don't I don't hate the South." He thus cunningly allows the reader to join Shreve in pretending to be Quentin's interpreter. "Of course Quentin hates the South," readers have generally thought, because why else does he kill himself shortly after the climactic telling of the Sutpen family history? According to Faulkner's letters, Quentin kills himself over Caddy.[20] However, as the living incarnation of white Southern history, Quentin's final gesture enacts the Southern desire to deny the "progress" of United States history through an act of self-consumption so complete that it also abolishes any implied future beyond his own death. "Dig in; hold on; don't give in to any future promised by outsiders," this logic implores. In the map that Faulkner drew to accompany the text to *Absalom, Absalom!* he famously referred to himself as sole owner and proprietor of Yoknapatawpha County. Faulkner's work likewise takes possession of Southern history and everything contained by it. Faulkner's property includes the slaves, their descendants, and their stories. When Rosa summons Quentin to hear her story and asks him to accompany her to Sutpen's mansion, she suggests that someday he might "enter the literary profession" and that he "will remember this and write about it." Quentin is no writer, though; he is mostly a listener. The bells ring in 1909, and Quentin hears them as the sound accompanying Sutpen's arrival in 1833. Faulkner probably echoes Marcel Proust's famous madeleine here as the bells' sound triggers for Quentin an involuntary memory—not self exactly but history. But this is not a memory that truly belongs to Quentin alone—it has been passed down to him by the dead and the near dead.

At the beginning of *Absalom*, Quentin imagines himself dividing into "two separate Quentins," just as his section in *The Sound and the Fury* begins with him trying to escape his shadow. With his death, Quentin escapes his shadow; he freezes time and history at the point where it stopped for him and his community, when the Quentin of 1909 chooses to become one with "the deep South dead since 1865" (4). As long as the South can exist as a communal dream in perfect harmony with itself, Quentin would have it continue. Thus, he kills himself to join his community and, by extension, to break with Shreve, who is in the story as an outsider who sets the boundaries of the community. As long as *Absalom, Absalom!* is read, the otherwise fleeting dream of Quentin's community can be said to be real—or to be made real. This dream, obviously, cannot abide outsiders except as mute and sympathetic witnesses. The very fact that Quentin tells his community's history to someone who is not of it indicates that the story he tells is, to Quentin, complete.

George Santayana famously said that those who do not know their past are doomed to repeat it. *Absalom* revises Santayana to say that repeating the past is the only way that one can know one's past. Jean-Paul Sartre was right to suggest that in Faulkner's best work one discerns that there is no future. Faulkner's aesthetic of the eternal present was not the creation of an untutored barbarian American existentialist, however; it was the creation of a white Southern American gentleman fiercely loyal to a South the North thought it had defeated. Perhaps the most telling criticism of *Absalom* still belongs to Warren, who, maybe more shrewdly than he realized, compared the novel to Homer's *Iliad*, with the U.S. Army as the Greeks and the vanquished Southerners as the Trojans. Warren meant to suggest that *Absalom* must be read as art. Yet, before the *Iliad* was poetry, it was experienced as history. In Faulkner's *Iliad* the invaders are never explicitly included in the telling of the story: Quentin speaks from the dead, as a Trojan speaking to and for other Trojans: "I am older at twenty than a lot of people who have died," Quentin says at the end, tired of his poem (301). Quentin kills himself and in his death becomes the object that his history dreams of being. Only Bond, the so-called howling idiot "nigger," and Shreve, an outsider, remain. But Faulkner has not given Bond the gift of telling. Read as a kind of modernist epic poem, *Absalom, Absalom!* might be seen as a beautiful artifact that preserves the annihilation of a history that its later readers can never have truly known. As history, *Absalom* lives even if its principal teller does not, and its greatest accomplishment for Union or Northern readers is to deceive them into believing the fiction that slavery. (and its consequences) belong to the South alone. Given that the Trojans need not and cannot experience the *Iliad*—since they must live and know the story as the defeated, as the dead, and thus, by definition, they are excluded from the telling of the story—they must look to shore their ruins and build again their Troy. Brooks is one such Trojan who lived beyond Quentin or Faulkner, continuing to dream and live the Southern world before it came to be known as fallen. Others live on today in the White House, the halls of Congress, and in many governors' mansions. From Troy fallen did not Rome rise?

III

In December 2002, Senate Majority Leader Trent Lott attended the one hundredth birthday celebration of South Carolina Senator Strom Thurmond and said something he had said many times before: that the nation "wouldn't have had all these problems over all these years" had Thurmond been elected president in 1948.[21] Lott's words sparked a national controversy that did not die down until he resigned his position as majority leader. To many, Lott's speech invoked the memory of a battle that had presumably been abandoned—the fight to preserve an America that was uncorrupted by the pretense to social equality. In fact, though, Lott's words hearkened back to a time before 1948, before 1876—the year that federal troops were removed from the South—before even the Civil War. His words speak to whichever mythical date one cares to identify as the climax of the white Southern dream to have a separate country that would be "free" to define its identity as distinct from that of the United States of America. In his own defense, Lott said that he was only paying tribute to a distinguished man who had lived for one hundred years and that his words meant no harm. Lott was pilloried by Republicans and Democrats, but in one sense he was right: the controversy was startling, not because of what Lott said but because of how (for a moment) his comments unexpectedly injected a genuine historical consciousness into the ordinary discussion of U.S. politics and usually disposable current events. That is (for a moment), Americans could see how un-unified American history has been and remains. Just as Lott was defending himself from a fury that he could never quite believe was going to unseat him, Americans were able to awaken, uncharacteristically and briefly, to the Faulknerian insight that "the past is never truly past." [22]

Reporters of the Lott controversy, apparently surprised to learn that Lott's words were part of a consistent pattern of speech (not inconsistent with being a prominent senator from the South), dutifully unearthed both Lott's previous tributes to Thurmond and accounts of Thurmond's 1948 bid for president. Many Americans were perhaps amazed to learn that as recently as the "greatest generation," a compelling presidential candidate had based his campaign on a "states' rights" platform that declared, "All the laws of Washington and all the bayonets of the Army cannot force the Negro into our homes, into our schools, our churches and our places of recreation and amusement" and then transformed that stance into thirty-eight electoral votes.[23] Those who were surprised were no doubt reassured when commentators pointed out that closer scrutiny of Thurmond's subsequent record revealed him to be an example of how the South had changed in the past half century. They noted, for instance, that Thurmond, unlike Lott, had voted to make the birthday of Martin Luther King Jr. a national holiday. Thus, the tribute, which Lott insisted brought pleasure to the old man whenever he heard it, cost Lott his place in the Senate at the same time that it initiated an informal reconsideration of Thurmond as an extraordinary example of white Southern toleration and progress since the time of the Civil Rights movement. Any ironic delight that some observers may have felt in seeing Lott hoisted on his own racial petard was most likely lost in the recognition that, as far as the national conversation was concerned, removing Lott from his post also closed down further discussion of the very real history that his words brought to conscious national life. Yet elevating Thurmond's "progressive" record at the expense of Lott's "reactionary" record, however absurd, effectively reinscribes the circumstances that made Lott's familiar words "a surprise" to so many, since doing so represses the recognition that Lott's words were, in fact, disturbingly ordinary and provide the unspoken subtext of virtually all contemporary discussions of American history and race.

As Carolyn Porter aptly comments, "Faulkner's voice may at times sound like God's, but in *Absalom, Absalom!* he uses it not to escape the nightmare of history, but to demonstrate that no escape is possible" (*Seeing* 302). Understanding the history that *Absalom* both serves and perpetuates is crucial if we are to understand that "controversies" such as the Lott–Thurmond episode are actually part of an ongoing North–South, Union–Confederacy battle that continues to this day.[24] Poetically and powerfully, *Absalom* provides the unspoken context to Lott's joke: the Civil War is not over, because "we" never joined "our" history to "yours."

Cormac McCarthy's *Blood Meridian* The First and Last Book of America

... wherein the hearts and enterprise of one small nation have been swallowed up and carried off by another.
—Cormac McCarthy, *Blood Meridian*

I

In Cormac McCarthy's *Blood Meridian*, fictional and historical characters intertwine within a story that describes U.S. imperial expansion as a "heliotropic plague" tending westward through cycles of death and destruction extending into a future that includes but is not contained by contemporary American reality. One cannot say precisely whether the novel is about the true nineteenth-century historical events that it describes or about the nature of history itself. *Blood Meridian* may seem at first an exemplary postmodern text because it seems to deny what Robert Berkhofer calls "the primary premise of the historical profession: the separation of history as the past from history as writing about that past," which would then deny "the ability of historians to know the past as such" (14). Yet despite its postmodern elements, *Blood Meridian* cannot be solely understood from within the postmodern perspective of seeming "to collapse all reality into its representation, all history into text(ualization)s" (11). Although the novel does "expose the nature of all representations for what they patently are: socially based discursive constructions," it is distinctively a-Derridean in its insistence that nature, or the things of nature, have an equivalence with human constructions (10). *Blood Meridian* also suggests that there has always been one way for humans to know the past: in terms of what Rene Girard calls a universal "will to violence" that humans codify as history. *Blood Meridian* does not insist that we know the past merely as the expression of our own contemporary interpretative or ideological perspective, although it tacitly acknowledges the prevalence of this view. According to *Blood Meridian*, history may be no more than different representations from differing points of view at different times, but it is the collision of these representations as forms of violence that makes them knowable to us as history.

History as a subject for inquiry is ordinarily divided into different epochs with different peoples who do (or have done) different things based on different assumptions about what is right and wrong. Insofar as these previous peoples have left records of what they have thought and done, later historians, through their own judgments of right and wrong, can endeavor to know these previous peoples. As we shall see, the novel's dominant character, the judge Holden, is a kind of historian who collects historical specimens, records them in his journal, and then destroys the original artifacts. If the past can be destroyed from within the perspective of the present, the novel suggests, this also means that the past has existed and might be known. For his part, the judge believes not only that history can be known but also that the past can be witness to the time through the future's apprehension of the past. This insight is not terribly comforting, however, since rather than question the possibility of knowing history as such, the book challenges history's significance as a form of human perception. For McCarthy, history is possibly the only means by and through which humans know themselves in a manner that can be communicated to others, but its insights obligate us to a kind of necessary form of collective self-deception about what is possible to know about humans' interaction with the world. In *Blood Meridian*, history can be known, but humans cannot necessarily know themselves through history. In this respect, the novel is neither postmodern nor premodern. It is instead an assertion about why history allows no progress and an astonishing attempt to create a narrative context that would contain within it the history of the world as it has been known and, paradoxically, not known.

Blood Meridian is surely an extraordinary novel—Harold Bloom calls it arguably the ultimate novel in American literature—and in the twenty years since it has been published, the novel has generated a number of compelling readings.[1] McCarthy has aptly said, "The ugly fact is that books are made out of books" (qtd. in D. Phillips 20). Among the books that the discerning reader may find in *Blood Meridian* are works by Homer, Herman Melville, William Faulkner, Joseph Conrad, James Joyce, William James, Friedrich Nietzsche, Martin Heidegger, and even the *Beowulf* author.[2] The range of influence that is suggested here indicates the extent to which McCarthy's novel addresses more than a local moment of, say, American history or postmodern theory. If David

Holloway says that McCarthy generally presents "the idea of history" in terms of "a now absent or inaccessible category" (65), then many other readers have said that, more than reject history as a knowable category, he engages specific, localized arguments about what *American* history can be said to be and how others have gotten American history wrong. Adam Parkes argues that "in showing the connections of a performative version of identity with the larger project of creating an American nation," *Blood Meridian* "suggests that the script of American history remains open to rewriting" (120). Neil Campbell comments that "what is being revised in McCarthy is a whole tradition of historiography, like Frederick Jackson Turner's," and thus McCarthy creates "a fictional landscape" for exploring "acts of imperialism and conquest so often omitted from more conventional historical accounts" (217–18). Others see McCarthy confronting a myth of the West or Manifest Destiny.[3] Sara Spurgeon argues that "the novel functions on the level of mythmaking and national fantasy as an American origin story" (75). Through the judge the novel portrays "the violent birth of a national symbolic that has made heroes out of scalphunters and Indian killers and constructed the near extinction of the buffalo and massive deforestation as symbols of triumph and mastery" (98). Steven Shaviro likewise argues that the novel "explode[s] the American dream of manifest destiny, of racial domination and endless imperial expansion," but he cautions that "the orgies of violence that punctuate *Blood Meridian*" do not "serve any comprehensible purpose" (144, 147). Shaviro's warning accurately registers the critical consensus that *Blood Meridian* defies interpretation altogether.

The most challenging reading of *Blood Meridian* so far comes from Dana Phillips. His essay is worth considering in detail because it articulates so well how the novel challenges readers' assumptions about what literature or history can be said to mean. According to Phillips, "The novel does not attempt to engage history, to explore the psyches of the characters and explain the meaning of the events it describes" (23).[4] Instead, *Blood Meridian* surrenders only a kind of "optical democracy" (the phrase comes from the novel) because it posits an equivalence between people and things (McCarthy 247).[5] Against Vereen Bell's argument that the novel opposes things to people as competitive forces, Phillips says, "Human beings and the natural world do not figure as antagonists" but constitute "parts of the same continuum and are constantly described by McCarthy as such" (32).[6] As evidence for this claim, Phillip adduces two typical sentences from the novel: "Above all else they appeared wholly at venture, primal, provisional, devoid of order. Like beings provoked out of the absolute rock and set nameless and at no remove from their own loomings to wander ravenous and doomed and mute as gorgons shambling the brutal wastes of Gondwanaland in a time before nomenclature was and each was all" (qtd. in D. Phillips 39). "For McCarthy," Phillips notes, "the history of the West is natural history" and thus of "processes by which these forces evolve into forces to which we give names [that] are not our own" (39). Thus, the novel portrays action with "no inner reality" through a narrative voice that is "omniscient, but there seems to be no knower providing us with the knowledge that it imparts" (40, 28). This "lack of human implication," Phillips concludes, is "*Blood Meridian*'s most disturbing feature" (33).

Positing an equivalence between things and people suggests that what people think does not matter. But there is a difference between being a rock and being a human—a human cannot think him- or herself into a rock, even if a human can imagine that his or her importance is, in the cosmic scheme of things, equal to that of a rock. By framing *Blood Meridian* as a "historical novel" that denies its own premise because it presents "character not as self" but as "something written," Phillips misses the fact that the novel aspires not to be "historical" but to be a portrayal of History as a narrative possibility (25). Phillips is closest to the novel's premise when he notes that in *Blood Meridian* "violence and death, it would seem, are the more or less objective truths of all human experience" (24). In *Blood Meridian*, the primal given of existence is violence. McCarthy portrays violence not as transcendent but as transhistorical. The novel recalls Girard's argument that civilization is the means through which humans transform a kind of primitive will to violence into social structures that can contain, if not eradicate, our human will to violence. Girard notes that "only violence can put an end to violence, and that is why violence is self-propagating" (26). A single murder may threaten an entire community, because revenge for the prior crime must be exacted. Without a way to persuade the family or friends of the victim to refrain from retaliating (thus jeopardizing their honor), the killing cannot stop, logically, until the desire for revenge is sated and everyone is dead. Civilization, with its elaborate laws and codes of punishment and compensation, is the mechanism for meeting blood not with blood but some compensatory symbolic act that stands in for murder-revenge. McCarthy once remarked that there is "no such thing as life without bloodshed" (qtd. in Parkes 104). From McCarthy's perspective, it is not just that events portrayed in the novel expose American history as the expression of a particular ideology or culture but also that ideological and cultural conflict are forms that violence takes on or inhabits. Violence and culture are coextensive.

Blood Meridian offers no particular moral and thus asserts that history yields no final truth; there is no Judgment Day on which God will assign every one and every act its "true" reward. As Girard observes, "Men always find it distasteful to admit that the 'reasons' on both sides of a dispute are equally valid—which is to say that *violence operates without reason*" (46). Yet the book does acknowledge that humans want to believe that in history inheres moral purpose and that history is therefore constitutive of social systems and how they work. Without the ordering that historical narrative supplies, humans would have no way of confronting the empty violence and the violent emptiness in which all human actions take shape. In *Blood Meridian* humans wage war against other humans, against things, and against nature. Alliances among humans can be formed but are never kept. *Blood Meridian* is an expression of existence as an ongoing, total war, and it addresses the reader with a narrative voice whose subject position is basically impossible to locate.[7] Thus, Phillips is right to say that plot may not matter in the novel, but he is wrong to assume that from this observation it follows that actions do not matter either. The actions that McCarthy depicts are expressions of self and communal knowledge—for the characters and for the reader. In one sense, the characters are merely the expression of this primal violence that animates his actions within the universe. Were it not for these acts of violence, there would be no way for any one of us to claim (rightly or wrongly) who she or he is or who we are.

This involuntary will to violence clothes itself always in historical guise. That is to say, Americans can claim that they are conquering the continent to promote freedom, to fulfill its Manifest Destiny, or even as a chance to lay down thousands of miles of railroad tracks just to see whether they can make trains work and run on time. McCarthy is not saying that with a different ideology there would be no killing; he is saying that the only way that we can know ourselves is through the acts of violence that are committed in the name of history. *Blood Meridian* reveals how so-called "identity politics" is really a postmodern-era name for identifying how different claims of different histories are colliding with each other. In the history of America that *Blood Meridian* implies, each expression of history or identity is itself a blind and dumb expression of a kind of will to violence that is asserted in the name of a given group's so-called identity: African American, Native American, American, Mexican, Spanish, English, French, Catholic, Protestant, Anasazi, whoever. For McCarthy, the "historical" reasons why a group of people commits some violent act are less important than the recognition that a belief in history as the true story about the destiny of a given people requires groups to assert their identity and thus their history through acts of violence. From this perspective, *Blood Meridian* frames the identity politics of multiculturalism as a kind of ongoing violence or war that has been inevitable since the founding of the United States. The novel's specific subject, however, may be provisionally defined as the collision between the New World (America) and the Old World (Europe) that began in the fifteenth century and continues, with proliferating subdivisions, to this day. This original violent collision between Indians and Europeans interests McCarthy because it reveals a rare encounter between different historical epochs. We who read the novel are living in the epoch that emerged, or is emerging, from this initial encounter. At war in the novel are people from radically different civilizations with radically different conceptions of time and space, yet—as far as *Blood Meridian* is concerned—they may as well be the Trojans and the Achaeans finding each other again in the endless war that is the *Iliad*. If history, and thus civilization, is but the continuation of an eternal violence by different names, then *Blood Meridian* implies both the beginning and the end to human history, and its true concern is with its own status as the book that binds the world together.

    Blood Meridian depicts American history as a series of violent encounters and ultimately unsuccessful attempts to establish a history other than the murderous one implied when the "civilized" Europeans enslaved or eradicated the "savages" they encountered. The book implicates in its story every American, living and dead. As I have suggested, though, it would be misleading to classify *Blood Meridian* as a conventional historical novel, because the events that the novel draws on are incidental to its actual narrative. It is as if the narrative exists prior to the events that are portrayed within it, and thus, whatever happens, real or imagined, is a consequence of that preexisting narrative. The "true" historical figures in the book—John Joel Glanton, the judge, Trias—are merely props for McCarthy's portrayal of history as the eternal return of violence. In part because *Blood Meridian* encompasses all of American literature and absorbs other major American works as a small part of its narrative frame, it makes these works (even *Moby-Dick* [1851]) seem puny and quaint by comparison.

Consider how much of American literature—works by Ralph Waldo Emerson, Henry David Thoreau, Herman Melville, Mark Twain, William Faulkner, Ralph Ellison, and Toni Morrison—has been concerned with addressing slavery as a stain on the nation's history and a moral wrong that generations of Americans must eradicate to be true to America's presumptively liberal origins. In *Blood Meridian*, however, the moral question of slavery is acknowledged only to be dismissed as irrelevant. The subject of slavery appears early in the novel when the character known as "the kid" takes shelter in a hermit's hut. He asks the hermit how he came to live in such a desolate country. The hermit responds, "I was a slaver, don't care to tell it. Made good money. I never did get caught. Just got sick of it. Sick of niggers" (18). The Civil War is still twelve years away but there is no hint that the hermit's former trade will divide the country in war. Bringing slaves into the country is just a job—a lucrative one for the daring. The fact that he does not care to tell his story may seem to suggest an uneasiness about his former occupation. The hermit's next act, however, casts doubt on this view. He displays for the kid's contemplation "some man's heart, dried and blackened" (18). The gesture introduces a persistent theme of the novel: the habit of the living preserving for their own use the body parts of the dead. Later, the kid will wear, as a penitent seeking God's grace would wear a cross, a scapular of blackened human ears. "You give two hundred dollars for it?" the kid asks of the former slave's heart. "I did," the hermit answers, "for that was the price they put on the black son of a bitch it hung inside of" (18). A history of slavery is contained in the hermit's remark: people trade other people for profit, and they demonize the people they trade in order to justify their practice. The expression "son of a bitch" conveys a grudging recognition that the black man possessed a will opposed to the hermit's will, but what matters finally is who has possession of whom and who gets to name the meaning of that possession.

Neither Faulkner nor Morrison would disagree with this observation. For Morrison, the hermit might represent the inherent evil of slavery and the need to resurrect (by invention) the murdered slave's perspective in order to counteract the continuing consequences of the hermit's act. For Faulkner, it is obviously wrong for a human to own another human, just as it is wrong for humans to own land. For either writer, the hermit might be said to hold a physical emblem of his corrupt soul. If the reader recognizes the failure of moral vision embedded in the slaver's acts, then perhaps a better history can result from this recognition. In *Blood Meridian*, however, acts exist prior to any telling of them and have a meaning that we cannot imagine (or historicize) away. The novel seeks no mitigating explanations for acts that have been committed and thus refuses to mythologize slavery as an experience singular to or constitutive of American history.

Blood Meridian suggests that when Americans relate the history of how we came to be who we are, we always speak as slavers of one kind or another. No history is free of the will to moral justification, but that will does not make a history true, because in the end nothing does or can. The novel defines American history as the consequence of the following premise: "not again in all the world's turning will there be terrains so wild and barbarous to try whether the stuff of creation may be shaped to man's will or whether his own heart is not another kind of clay" (5). When the former slaver holds a heart in his hand as if it were only ever a chunk of clay, he gives one answer to this proposition. Late in the book, the judge offers another response, when he tells the kid, "Your heart's desire is to be told some mystery. The mystery is that there is no mystery" (252). If American history is truly exceptional, says McCarthy, its exceptionalism consists in its unmatched opportunity to destroy worlds in the name of making one that it names as itself. In this respect, Blood Meridian portrays the American will to innocence that masks its underlying and more fundamental will to violence.

II

The novel builds what plot it has out of a relatively unsung but still decisive period in American history—the aftermath of the U.S. war against Mexico and the drive of the United States to become an imperial power during the middle of the nineteenth century. The action focuses on a group of "vicious looking humans" that the narrator identifes as the "scalphunters," who travel across the recently acquired "American" territory—and across territory still belonging to Mexico—on their way to San Diego. Often, their killing is socially sanctioned. A Mexican town hires them to remove so-called hostile Indians from the environment. Eventually the sanction turns against the sanctioners and killing is done for its own sake, as when the scalphunters slaughter the citizens who had previously hired them to slaughter the Indians, who were seen by the town, wrongly it turns out, as the principal threat to their community. As the scalphunters make their way across Texas toward California, their circle of violence expands to include everyone, regardless of race or community affiliation. Ultimately, the act of killing supersedes the reason for killing. As they realize themselves not so vaguely westward, the scalphunters' progress is shadowed by "pilgrims," or pioneers, many of whom are part of the California gold rush. These goldseekers, as it were, are described as "bleeding westward like some heliotropic plague," and it is implied that their motivation for moving westward differs little from that of the scalphunters. Both seek some form of conquest that involves the subjugation of others. When the scalphunters reach San Diego, they disguise themselves as "Indians" and kill goldseeking American "pilgrims" as they killed Indians and Mexicans before. This incident echoes Twain's famous description in *Roughing It* (1872) of Mormons who dressed up as Indians before massacring white American "pioneers." In Twain's version, one might be tempted to think about how Americans have appropriated the "savage" identities of "Indians" to shield themselves from the horror of their acts. In McCarthy's account, however, there is no way to shield imagined doer or reader from the knowledge that the act of killing has become its own justification.

Contrasting *Blood Meridian* with a typical recent work of revisionist history, Jane Tompkins's *West of Everything* (1992), one can see how quaint much politically correct revisionist history can be. For Tompkins, the American West can be found in dime novels and Saturday afternoon westerns—a pop culture West that has been with us since whites began to "settle" east of the Mississippi river. Tompkins's popular West clashes with what she sees at the Plains Indian Museum in Wyoming, and its artifacts that preserve examples of horrific violence. Finding the experience to be "incomprehensible" (194), Tompkins admits:

> I had expected that [the museum] would show me how life in nature ought to be lived: not the mindless destruction of nineteenth century America but an ideal form of communion with animals and the land. What the museum seemed to say instead was that cannibalism was universal.... [T]here was no such thing as the life lived in harmony with nature. It was bloodshed and killing, an unending cycle, over and over again, and no one could escape. (190)

Instead of asking how the dime-store versions of the West constituted another version of westward expansion, Tompkins identifies all acts of sustenance through violence as "cannibalism." Although meant to demonstrate solidarity with indigenous peoples, her word choice unwittingly reveals Tompkins's own participation in the history that she condemns, since cannibalism, as a concept, did not originate in the Americas but, like smallpox, was carried to America by western Europeans. Early European explorers came to the New World and saw cannibalism everywhere—even where it was not—because it represented their deepest cultural anxiety.[8] If the old, European anxiety was that cannibals violated sacred "human" taboos by eating one another, the revisionist fears that in the end Europeans and their descendants ate the cannibals. The point is not that western Europeans did not inflict genocidal violence on indigenous peoples; the point is that Blood Meridian shows that American historians cannot move beyond the original, primal scene that American history itself, whether understood to be revisionist or prerevisionist, seeks to supplant.

As the one who possesses the slave's heart, McCarthy's hermit also possesses the story about that heart; consequently, he is afforded the small pleasure of being able to moralize. The hermit cautions that separating claims of self-interest from claims of justice is an impossible task. He remarks, "The way of the transgressor is hard. God made this world, but he didn't make it to suit everybody, did he?" But who is the transgressor, and what does being the transgressor mean? Is the hermit the transgressor because as a slaver he violated God's code? Or is the transgressor someone who violates the rules of society in order to follow God's will? The hermit preaches:

> A man's at odds to know his mind cause his mind is aught he has to know it with. He can know his heart, but he dont want to. Rightly so. Best not to look in there. It aint the heart of a creature that is bound in the way that God has set for it. You can find meanness in the least of creatures, but when God made man the devil was at his elbow. A creature that can do anything. Make a machine. And make a machine to run a machine. And evil that can run itself a thousand years, no need to extend it. (19)

The advice that we should not look into our hearts is basically what Nietzsche found in the Greek tragedies. As Nietzsche notes in The Birth of Tragedy (1887), this is the knowledge that Silenus offered to Midas; it is the wisdom that Oedipus refused and thereby had to discover for himself. Also, if the devil was at God's elbow when "man" was made, then "man" is equal parts God and the devil. The machine that can run itself a thousand years predicts the civilization whose cause the kid will advance when he clears "the aborigines" from its path. The machine to run the machine will be a version of the American empire. But, as Blood Meridian shows, even imperialist Americans are not really running the machine; they just think they are.

Manifest Destiny is the name that nineteenth-century Americans created to pay tribute to the unstoppable "progress" of a superior technology sanctioned by a superior god. *Blood Meridian*, however, tells our national story as if the Christian "god" holds no higher status than the Indian (pagan) gods that the Christian god is presumed to have replaced. When a band of Comanches massacres a troop of former U.S. soldiers, leaving their disfigured remains horribly displayed to the eye of the sun and random travelers, a character contemplating the sight comments, "damn if they aint about a caution to the Christians" (56). In *Blood Meridian* Americans and Mexicans are merely two groups among many fighting to gain sovereignty over the land. The Christian-Americans' history is no more true or valid than anyone else's history. Retrospectively, Manifest Destiny may seem true because the Christians have silenced the ability of the other histories to be told, just as the slaver is represented as having possession over the life story of the man whose heart he now owns. *Blood Meridian* is likewise a caution to the Christians, because it suggests that once we remove the Christian leavening from American history, we will see only a version of what the hermit describes. God protects neither our acts nor our selves; it is the name that we invoke in order to shield from ourselves those places where, in the words of the hermit, it is best not to look after we have acted.

The novel's opening sentence addresses the reader and gives a command: "See the child" (3). This beginning literally fixes the reader to the kid and alerts the reader that she or he should be ready to confirm or reject any judgment that any other character might make of the kid in the course of the novel. It also invites the reader to join the kid's journey as a judge of his actions, although the hermit warns against this presumption. The designation *child* identifies the kid as an innocent, yet a few lines down we learn that at fourteen "in him broods already a taste for mindless violence" (3). The kid's taste for mindless violence does not displace his innocence; his innocence protects his will to violence. In New Orleans, "he lives in a room above a courtyard tavern and he comes down at night like some fairy book beast to fight with the sailors." Why and whom the kid fights does not matter; only *that* he fights matters. Nonetheless, "the child's face is curiously untouched behind the scars" (4). The narrative calls attention to the kid's face: "all history present in that visage, the child the father of the man" (3). McCarthy evokes William Wordsworth's famous line not to suggest the kid's uncommon appreciation of rainbows but to suggest how the kid's future acts as a man are committed as if by a child.[9] Throughout, the child's face remains behind the scars because experience marks his face but not his soul.

The kid is the bodily form that manifests history's unending cycle of violence. His birth signals apocalypse as he is born the night of the Leonids meteor shower in 1833. "God how the stars did fall," his father says. The sky staved in by stars eerily suggests that he arrives here from another world with the aim of destroying this one. As it happens, the kid's birth brings his mother's death. "The mother dead these fourteen years did incubate in her own bosom the creature who would carry her off" (3). From the moment of his birth, this "creature" is a killer (his blamelessness in his mother's death is irrelevant by the novel's logic). Ordinarily, one is born into something—a family, a social context, a history. Whatever ordinary history the kid might be said to inherit, however, is consumed by his birth. The phrase "did incubate in her...the creature who would carry her off" conveys the possibility that the mother was creating within her not so much a child as the act, which would destroy her body. The child is, and his life will become the embodiment of that act. His innocence comes from the fact that his past has been murdered in the form of his mother. The kid's father is a teacher who "quotes from poets whose names are now lost" (3). These lost poets' words echo from a history no longer pertinent. The father's knowledge is not passed along to the kid, who remains illiterate and ignorant, an intellectual orphan. When the kid runs away from home at age fourteen, he completes the act implied by his birth in that he enters the world completely divested of his origins. Mother, father, and the "sister in this world that he will not see again" are all removed from him and never mentioned again in the narrative. Their existence matters only as a past from which his consciousness has been removed.

McCarthy compresses the first sixteen years of the kid's life into three extraordinary pages. The kid "wanders west as far as Memphis," and then "a year later he is in Saint Louis" (4). He catches a flatboat to New Orleans, where he fights the sailors every night, before he makes his way over to Nacogdoches, Texas, where in 1849 his history begins again. It is appropriate that, as one who is seemingly shedding his history, his origins, this representative American should move west into a region that, to the European, is without history. What brings the kid west is the compulsion neither to make a home for himself nor to convert the region to the virtues of Christian civilization. His progress merely expresses his will to violence and his need to express it.

"See the child," we are told, and as we watch the kid advance west, we watch a version of ourselves, a version of "America," as we go in search of the violent encounters that will create America as a nation, as a new incarnation of what European descendants will call their American civilization.

What moral can be derived from someone whose defining trait is his "taste for mindless violence" and the opportunities to express it? A reader of Mark Twain or Charles Dickens might expect that the kid will somehow be redeemed. In the nineteenth-century English novel (in the novels of Charles Dickens, George Eliot, William Thackeray, or Charlotte Brontë), a protagonist's status as an orphan usually indicates his or her condition as one who is chosen, one whose fate is not to be corrupted by society.[10] Huckleberry Finn, for instance, struggles to escape not only his father but also the God-fearing, slaveholding society whose moral code defines his every act and thought. Huck's decision to help Jim go free is the ultimate act of betrayal to his society. Huck knows this and is prepared to go to hell as a fitting punishment for what he has done. Huck lights out for the territory because to be true to his act, he can no longer live in the society that would consign him to hell. The reader identifies with Huck because he or she self-consciously rejects the society's moral code. To the reader, the territory that Huck lights out for is the world where the reader lives—the morally more just future world implied by Huck's gesture.

In *Blood Meridian* no society exists for the kid to accept or reject; rather, the reader constitutes the society that determines what role the kid has played in the history of the novel. See the child; see yourself. The reader will want to see the kid redeemed, because otherwise the reader is implicated in a history that is very different from the one he or she has been taught to celebrate. If the kid is not understood to be removed from the novel's many murders, then the reader becomes an accomplice to the crimes that the kid witnesses and engages in while riding with the scalphunters—the telling of which takes up most of the novel. On this reading, the kid merely pretends to go along with the acts of figures who are more powerful in order to save his life, but by the end of the novel, when the consequences of the acts that were committed are being measured, the kid denies his "true" involvement with the scalphunters. He stands up to the clearly "evil" figure of the work, Judge Holden, whom the kid identifies as the true culprit responsible for the "crimes" the book depicts. If the kid is right and the events of the novel belong to the judge alone, then the kid's acts can be understood as separate from those of the judge.

In the nineteenth-century bildungsroman that McCarthy parodies, the protagonist is the plot. His or her acts compose the novel; the other characters exist to further the protagonist's story. In *Blood Meridian*, the kid is not the shaper or maker of his story. Rather, his acts are part of a context of action that he himself cannot understand and that many readers may not recognize, especially if they are looking to find a moral that the book has no intention of offering them. From the outset, the kid's significance is chiefly negative. He is blank. It is not just that his story remains to be written but that he is erasing it as he goes along. His only character trait is his impulse to violence. His acts only express his character. Other than their expression, the acts have no obvious narrative significance except what either we the readers or, arguably, the judge assigns to them. "I take it ye lost your way," the hermit says when he meets the kid. "No, I went right to it," the kid responds (17). Other than the path that he cuts to oblivion through his actions, the kid's way is unmarked and unknown. The kid is history's subject and will belong to whomever or whatever can best script him.

Thus, when robbers leave the kid without a mount, a gun, or clothes, he is "recruited" to join a renegade branch of the U.S. Army. The recruiter introduces himself to the kid as one who is "white and christian" (28). The mission the kid is asked to join is also "white and christian." Ignoring the peace treaty that has recently concluded the United States' War with Mexico, the group of men the kid first joins intend to finish the job that the U.S. government failed to complete: to turn all of Mexico into United States territory. The logic is as obvious as that of the name given to the company commander: Captain White. Here White justifies to the kid his self-appointed mission:

> What we are dealing with [i]s a race of degenerates. A mongrel race, little better than niggers. There is no government in Mexico. Hell, there's no God in Mexico. We are dealing with a people *manifestly* incapable of governing themselves. And do you know what happens with people who cannot govern themselves? That's right. Others come in to govern for them. . . . And we will be the ones to divide the spoils. (34, emphasis mine)

White speaks in the language of Manifest Destiny: The land is ours for the taking because the people already on it—Indians and Mexicans—do not know what to do with it. Given that there is neither God nor government in Mexico, what choice do we have as Christians but to help them? However, given that "whiteness" is not a trait that can be acquired, Captain White actually justifies a kind of genocide (at best slavery) in the name of Christian democratic rule.

Where the kid has a taste for mindless violence, White has a taste for mindless conquest. The encounter may endear the kid to the reader because the kid does not share White's organized mania. To the extent that the kid can be said to have a view, it is one of disinterested contempt. When asked if he is ready to go to Mexico, the kid responds, "I aint lost nothin down there" (29). Later, when the kid sees Captain White's head perfectly preserved in a glass jar, he dryly remarks, " he aint no kin to me" (70). The kid agrees to ride with White because without White's supplies he would not survive. (Join the marines; see the world.) The difference between them is that White's action is the logical extension of what the United States government already did and would continue to do—arguably to this day. If White's speech seems cartoonish, it is because we think that we are removed from his historical moment. His language would not be out of place in nineteenth-century newspapers or meetings of Congress. McCarthy allows us to laugh at White's preposterous bigotry but implies that our derision is comfortable only to the extent that men like White cleared the territory for our moral view. This is a moment in the novel where the reader easily sympathizes with the kid, because he is so clearly the tool of something that neither the reader nor the kid can quite sanction. The larger point, though, is that just as the kid's resistance does not prevent him from joining White, neither can the American reader easily dismiss American history as something that other "white Christians" have fashioned in their (our) own self-image.

We meet Captain White on page 29, and he is dead by page 54. McCarthy kills White quickly because *Blood Meridian*'s canvas is much broader than the figure of White can suggest and actually points to a time prior to the Europeans' arrival in the New World. White's intentions not only embody nineteenth-century American imperialism but also replay in almost comic form the European dream of building itself again in virgin America. White's fate is to be captured by neither the U.S. nor the Mexican armies but to be killed by "a legion of horribles" who are "howling in a barbarous tongue" and who come at White's Christians "from a hell more horrible yet than the land of christian reckoning" (52–53). The image of the slaughter is unsurpassed in any writing that takes the conquest of America as its subject:

> You could hear above the pounding of the unshod hooves the piping of the quena, flutes made from human bone . . . [and] there arose a fabled horde of mounted lancers and archers bearing shields bedight with bits of broken

mirrorglass that cast a thousand unpieced suns against the eyes of their enemies... wardrobed out of a fevered dream with the skins of animals and silk finery and pieces of uniform still tracked with the blood of prior owners, coats of slain dragoons, frogged and braided cavalry jackets, one in a stovepipe hat and one with an umbrella and one in white stockings and a bloodstained wedding veil and some in headgear of cranefeathers or rawhide helmets that bore the horns of bull or buffalo and one in a pigeontailed coat worn backwards and otherwise naked and one in the armor of a Spanish conquistador, the breastplate and pauldrons deeply dented with old blows of mace or sabre done in another country by men whose very bones were dust and many with their braids spliced up with the hair of other beasts until they trailed upon the ground and their horses' ears and tails worked with bits of brightly colored cloth and one whose horse's whole head was painted crimson red and all the horsemen's faces gaudy and grotesque with daubings like a company of mounted clowns, death hilarious. (52–53)

Written in the second person, the narrative puts the reader at the scene of his own destruction. What "you" see is at once unimaginable and also a version of yourself. This battle is not about winning Mexico or settling the West. It is an ancient battle even if this version of it goes back only four hundred years or so. Who the warriors are and which side, or history, they represent is not clear. The attacking Comanches have bedecked themselves in the lineaments of the white men's history since the white men "discovered" the New World. In listing the items that have been transformed into war costumes, the narrative builds to the dramatic revelation of "the armor of a Spanish conquistador, the breastplate and pauldrons deeply dented with old blows of mace or sabre done in another country." The Spanish, led by the Italian Christopher Columbus, came to the New World, conquered the Aztecs in Mexico and the Incas in South America. American armies completed the Spaniards' work in North America. White can see neither how he is of a piece with the dented armor nor how he has become a sacrificial lamb to an older, prior historical process. As the breastplate from the conquistador implies, the wars of Europe have been continued in the New World by warriors whom the original maker of the armor could never have imagined. White is another Don Quixote trying to make the resisting world into what he dreams to be true.

Initially, this "legion of horribles" seems absolutely Other to White and the American reader. But descriptions such as the "bloodstained wedding veil" and "their braids spliced up with the hair of other beasts" suggest that a union of identities is taking place. McCarthy's Comanches have braided more than animal hair to themselves—their history is being braided to that of the Europeans they unhorse. McCarthy portrays the Comanches as a version of the white men's projection of themselves. In this scene, perhaps the most crucial of *Blood Meridian*, White's gang neither triumphs over the savages nor slays the savages so that future generations may feel guilty about it. Neither heroic conquerors nor martyred dead, White's men are merely killed by better warriors who are dressed as versions of themselves. McCarthy thus presents American history as something that is not really about itself or what "we" claim for it. Thus, to the extent that as White understands his purpose to be specifically *American*, he is annihilated. Rather, he is a warrior among other warriors, and he could be known in or from any time. In other words, in *Blood Meridian* "history" is not fulfilled merely by "becoming American" and thus cannot truly be described as a national history. If one becomes American in this novel, one does so only by annihilating one's self as European. The Comanches thus occupy dual roles as warriors and cultural historians. In this reading, the Comanches would not just be wearing the costumes of their Anglo-Saxon enemies; they would have usurped their identities as well. But this perspective cannot be quite right either, since neither the reader nor any of White's company can know what the Comanches perceive as they slay these "unhorsed Saxons." To White and the reader, the Comanches may seem completely Other; actually, they have no identifiable identity except as the reflection of the white men's nightmare. Their "fevered dream" is in fact the psychic landscape on which the drama of American identity is continually fought even to this day. As the Comanches ride down upon White and his men "bedight with mirrors," they literally vanquish the white men by blinding them with their own projected self-images as conquerors. In the process, the Comanches compel their vanquished in the moment of their death to see their whole history in the New World as white men—from the time of the conquistadors to the moment that they die as Americans. Thus, the Americans die not only as soldiers but also as white men who have become the last Europeans forever given over to the image of what they most feared: the "savage Indian."

This "savage" encounter marks the originary moment of American history. Histories informed by the European perspective have been unable to recover a moment prior to this one and have in fact only replayed it endlessly. American "history" is ultimately the communal recollection of the earliest battle known and then the line of battles that the knowers can connect to that original one. White's troop may think that they are being destroyed by someone else's history when in fact they succumb, as they must, to their own. Although it occurs early in the novel, the slaughter of White's troops represents a crucial narrative end point. Even though the reader knows that the forces that White represents eventually "won" the West, the power of the scene derives from the feeling that Europeans and their history on this continent end with this battle. As a history of the Conquest of the New World, *Blood Meridian* dramatizes the fact that, from this moment, something Other from European history remains to haunt those who would establish the beginning of America as coincident with the Europeans' arrival in the New World. In this scene we see how the Spaniards' armor has been refitted for different kinds of battles that will create different kinds of histories from those that were imagined when it was first forged. Francisco Coronado is as dead as White, and both have been sacrificed to commemorate a forced and bloody union between two worlds, pre-Columbian versus European—again, see the bloodstained wedding veil. In *Blood Meridian* the unhorsed Saxons are joined to a prior, non-European history, and their deaths are but notes in an ancient song of war. Warring bodies have always traded costumes, and the Comanches' armor pays tribute to this fact (think of Hector wearing Achilles' armor as Achilles kills him), as do the flutes made out of human bones that they play. In *Blood Meridian*, the "savages" thus consummate the marriage between New and Old World when they fall "upon the dying and sodomized them with loud cries to their fellows" (254). The Saxons' remains will be absorbed into their conquerors' battle gear, and together they will ride on as a version of Glanton's scalphunters, the group that the kid joins after being the sole survivor of this battle.

Blood Meridian suggests that the Europeans have in some basic sense been destroyed by their encounter with the "savages" of their dreams. Richard Rodriguez suggests the sense of historical dislocation that *Blood Meridian* conveys in his brilliant essay "India." Rodriguez notes that the textbook story of American history is linear; it begins in Europe and moves one direction only: west. Looking for India, Europeans instead "discovered" America. In the European version of America's beginning, Rodriguez observes, "Indians" were passive entities subject to European desires; thus, "Indians" could be so easily misnamed. In contrast, Europeans represented themselves as the actors, doers, and fulfillers of destiny and the makers of history. "Had the world been flat," Rodriguez suggests, "then the European would have been as great a victor over history as he has portrayed himself to be" because "then the European could have traveled outward toward innocence" (7). What the European could not know, what he could not see through his telescope peering westward, was the eye that was already watching him, expecting him, waiting for him. Rodriguez replaces the traditional linear European version of history with this circular view circumscribed by the "Indian" eye. By this view, the Europeans conquer nothing; rather, they are absorbed into something else, something "other" than themselves.[11]

From this perspective, the "Americans" who eventually conquer the "savages" and claim the West as their possession do so as "Indians," not as Europeans. Even "American" histories have been unable to transcend the knowledge of this first encounter. The history of the European conquest of America is as old as human memory and no more unique than any memories that have been scratched into rock or forgotten. The massacre of Captain White's gang represents an ethos of violent transformation endemic to the creation of Americans and their history. America, if it can be said to exist at all in this novel, exists only as a kind of projection of the white man's inadequate understanding of the "savages" he could not replace but only copy. Consequently, the warring "Indians" enact the American idea that violent transformation is an essential component of White's—of any American's—character and can be seized from White in the same the way that he took it from others.

In this way, *Blood Meridian* offers a reading of American history that is also a reflection on our own multicultural moment. *Blood Meridian* shows not only that American history—however we define it—has been created out of inevitably murderous encounters such as the ones that this book depicts but also that the American present is itself a constellation of analogously murderous encounters. *Blood Meridian* says that Americans cannot retrospectively erase, or seal off, acts such as killing "Indian savages" or maintaining African slaves in order to fulfill the story that is American history. No mere writing of history can erase the obdurate facts of those murdered and enslaved dead. Confronting the past as intractable, *Blood Meridian* also suggests that the confluence of these older tribal histories into "an American" history is what makes American history "exceptional." This perspective suggests why Richard Rorty and Walter Benn Michaels are, as we shall see, wrong to dismiss as mere identity politics the work of Leslie Marmon Silko or Toni Morrison. Rather, their work expresses a view of history as a symbolic will to violence in its deepest, most enduring sense.[12] Underestimating the power of their point of view most likely will only increase the vehemence and potentially the violence with which it will be expressed. Arguments about so-called multiculturalism, then, are not irrelevant or unimportant to understanding American history; they are the inevitable expression of the violent encounter between New World and Old World that Blood Meridian stages into perpetuity. All of us—African Americans, Native Americans, American Americans—are peculiar New World creations who continue to know ourselves through staged violent encounters with Others whom we (whoever we may be) fear but can never possess. Addressing not only the past but the future of American history, the account of the unhorsed Saxons' death in Blood Meridian foreshadows the time when Americans will no longer be primarily white or Christian and when American history can no longer celebrate or mourn the death of the "Indians" (or the emancipation from slavery) as integral to its story.

Rodriguez's figure of the "eye" suggests a narrative to American history that informs our actions but escapes our consciousness. Because Americans see their history as something that they have created by acting on others, they cannot imagine the ways in which "others" have acted on them. In ways that most American readers are likely to experience as a form of disorientation, Rodriguez and McCarthy both ask us to see American history passively—as a fluid entity that consists of actions that have been absorbed into something (and somebody) else—rather than solely as a collection of actions done unto something (and somebody) else. Americans have not so much become the "Indians" as they have become one with the force that would destroy the "Indians" and themselves. In a limited sense, the kid is the "Indian eye" to Blood Meridian. The kid is rarely given a voice, and we never occupy his thoughts, because his importance is as a witness to and actor in (in fact, more as a witness to than as an actor in) events that are greater than he is.

The kid's presence humanizes the presentation of history as violence and invites the reader to articulate a version of history through his fate. That the kid is the only survivor of the massacre of White's gang is in part a narrative necessity, but it is also an indication that he is the conduit for the book's narrative. He is the eye through which the cycles of violence are often seen. Ishmael-like, the kid "rose wondrously from among the new slain dead and stole away in the moonlight" (55). Having been conscripted to fight for Manifest Destiny, the kid escapes to await his next conscription by history, which comes for him in the form of the scalphunters who rescue him from a Mexican jail. This time he is conscripted to kill "Indians" for Mexicans (rather than to kill Mexicans for Americans), and his attitude toward his task is unrecorded. Some readers may want to see the scalphunters as mercenaries, less connected than the renegade Captain White to U.S. history. Actually, they are a version of White's last nightmare come to life. Although they are hired by a foreign government with which the United States was only recently at war, they are the shock troops for the coming American civilization. The fact that their employers are Mexicans rather than Americans shows that the war with Mexico was territorial rather than ideological. They were fighting over who would possess the Indians' remains.

Crucially, these shock troops are presented as if they were Indians. From their jail cell the kid and Toadvine see

> a pack of viciouslooking humans mounted on unshod indian ponies riding half drunk through the streets, bearded, barbarous, clad in the skins of animals stitched up with thews... and the trappings of their horses fashioned out of human skin and their bridles woven up from human hair and decorated with human teeth and the riders wearing scapulars of dried and blackened human ears and the horses rawlooking and will din the eye and their teeth bared like feral dogs and riding also in the company of a number of halfnaked savages reeling in the saddle, dangerous, filthy, brutal, the whole like a visitation from some heathenland where they and others like them fed on human flesh. (78)

The description echoes that of the Comanches who killed White's troop. Their actual encounter (the battle itself) with White's troop will continue through the acts of the scalphunters. As with the kid and White's men, the scalphunters will prove to be disposable—virtually every one of them will die before they arrive in California. Their acts live on, though, as ones that continue to define American history insofar as it can be known or described.

The key point about the scalphunters is that they kill regardless of their victims' national affiliation. Indians, Mexicans, and Americans compose their prey. Initially, they contract with Chihuahua City to kill Indians. Although their mission is less than successful, they are welcomed as great heroes when they return. Within a matter of days they kill the same people who hired them. Later, near San Diego, they conspire with the Yumas to capture a post held by an American doctor who is charging other Americans a toll to cross the river. At the same time they are negotiating with Americans who are camped out there to kill the "Indians." Without any true national identity, the scalphunters are disengaged from the usual paths of historical justification. Yet they are the actors who commit the deeds out of which histories are fabricated.

In *Blood Meridian* the scalphunters' actions are ordered by the narrative's most dominating figure, the judge. The judge first appears in the opening chapter, chasing a preacher out of a revival meeting as he accuses the preacher of sexually molesting an eleven-year-old girl while "clothed in the livery of his god" (7). The (presumably) falsely accused preacher calls the judge "the devil" (7). The ex-priest Tobin, a member of the band hired by the Mexican governor to kill the "Indians," enumerates for the kid the many "gifts of the Almighty" that have been reserved for the judge:

> You wouldnt think to look at him that he could outdance the devil himself would ye? God the man is a dancer, you'll not take that away from him. And fiddle. He's the greatest fiddler I ever heard and that's an end on it. The greatest. He can cut a trail, shoot a rifle, ride a horse, track a deer. He's been all over the world. Him and the governor sat up till breakfast and it was Paris this and London that in five languages, you'd have give something to of heard them. (123)

No task or accomplishment is too small or great for this Faustian figure. Were it not for the judge, Tobin tells the kid, the scalphunters would have already been massacred. They came upon the judge about "the meridian of day" sitting on a lone rock in the middle of the wilderness. Chased by Indians, without ammunition, they are near death. The judge "didnt even have a canteen," but he did have "a brace of pistols" and rifle emblazoned with the inscription "Et In Arcadia Ego." Sitting on the rock "like he had been expectin us," the judge leads them up into a mountain cave where he assures them "Our mother earth was round as an egg and contained all good things within her" (130). He takes them to a "rock of brimstone" from which they chip "pure flowers of sulphur," combine it with their urine, and make a kind of nitre-paste from which they can charge their rifle, patch balls together, and thereby make ammunition with which to slay "savages." Then he "called us all to fill our horns and flasks, and we did, one by one, circling past him like communicants" (134). Together these communicants, purified by an initiation into violence that they repeat out of material rather than spiritual necessity, kill fifty-eight Indians.

The judge's ability to make ammunition out of the elements of Mother Earth seems supernatural to Tobin, although it is really only the inspired stratagem of an educated man—rather like Twain's Connecticut Yankee, who suddenly landed in medieval England and "predicted" an eclipse. The judge's trick is a necessary gesture of civilization. Elsewhere, the judge enigmatically tells his companions that God speaks in stone, trees, the bones of things. Following Francis Bacon, whom no doubt he has read, the judge is trying to say that humanity's knowledge, constantly expanding, means nothing unless it is put to use. Thus, the judge is as interested in the wilderness as the subject of study as he is in the unparalleled opportunity to kill without great risk of legal consequences. A proto-Darwin, the judge collects and records natural specimens from the desert. According to Tobin, even while the judge was being chased by "Indians," he "would stop to botanize and then ride to catch up. My hand to God. Pressing leaves into his book" (127). The judge, we will learn, destroys what he finds, as if to make himself sole geologist-historian-naturalist of the landscape, but the process that he represents is the conversion of the landscape into something other than what it was prior to his arrival. The judge's answer to the question of why he collects specimens and records their attributes in his book defines how he conceives his relationship to nature and to the other scalphunters:

> He looked about the dark forest in which they were bivouacked. He nodded toward the specimens he'd collected. These anonymous creatures, he said, may be little or nothing in the world. Yet the smallest crumb can devour us. Any smallest thing beneath yon rock out of man's knowing. Only nature can enslave man and only when the existence of each last entity is routed out and made to stand naked before him will he be properly suzerain of the earth. (198)

Mountains, rivers, leaves, insects, people—the judge takes possession of them all equally, as everything that he encounters exists merely to be converted to his use. The will to violence that he inspires in the scalphunters he understands to be common to "the smallest crumb." As he says of his own relationship to birds, anything that exists without his consent is an insult to him (198). The judge will know the world and make the world subject to his knowledge.

The judge is no Captain White. White is presented as a dumb Christian, an extreme ideologue, who never doubts that he represents a nation destined by God's will to control the continent. White is history's fool—or tool—and his foolishness consists in believing that his or anyone else's history might be true. The judge usurps nature's authority (often attributed to something called

God) and claims it for himself. As he explains, "A suzerain rules even where there are other rulers," and his "authority countermands local judgements" (198). Like *Blood Meridian*, the book that the judge keeps means to contain the world—including even specimens from before human history existed. If he discovers specimens that he views to be unique, the only ones existing, the judge copies and then destroys them. His desire is "to expunge them from the memory of man" (140). To be suzerain over the dead and the living is to be a god. At one point, Webster, one of the men, says to the judge, "No man can put all the world in a book." To be polite, the judge agrees, but it is nevertheless clear that this is his intention. Elsewhere, he remarks that the "man who sets himself the task of singling out the thread of order from the tapestry will by the decision alone have taken charge of the world and it is only by such taking charge that he will dictate the terms of his own fate" (199). To Webster, though, the judge's response points to a premise that the judge shares with the book that contains his story: "whether in my book or not, every man is tabernacled in every other and he in exchange and so on in an endless complexity of being and witness to the uttermost edge of the world" (141). For the judge, to control fate is to control the fate of every thing and person, living and dead. At the end of the novel, the judge will be described as "dancing, dancing. He says that he will never die" (335). The judge's dance enacts this endless complex exchange just as he is, surely, its embodiment.

The judge is, arguably, human history incarnate. "Every man in the company claims to have encountered that sooty souled rascal in some other place," Tobin remarks (124). They too dance to the judge's tune but the tune exists independent of the judge's ability to dance to it. In this respect, the judge too is a narrative necessity—a way to make concrete what is actually to McCarthy a transhistorical process. We know hardly anything of the scalphunters prior to the judge's entrance. McCarthy gives no hint why they are in Mexico killing Indians. Presumably, they come for the same reason that the kid does: a taste for mindless violence. From the time of their first meeting, the judge is the scalphunters' leader, representative, priest. He gives them their life and their power to kill others. They are his "communicants" within a process that absorbs them, and neither they nor the judge, except as a symbol, can themselves absorb. Without the organizing agency of the judge, though, they more quickly become other killers' victims, blood for others' communion. Webster asks the judge to be excluded from the book, but the judge scoffs at this possibility: "my book or some other book" (141).

To the judge, history is the most powerful form of dominion because it seems to order the world. Actually, nothing orders the world, and this is why violence is the world's only sustained, permanent, form of expression. History, however, is the form by which humans displace this knowledge into something that we can claim to control. History is inevitably created as a consequence of destruction, just as the past enters the judge's book as it is destroyed. Moreover, if the judge can expunge from the memory of man what he puts in his book, then the judge's book becomes the only true record of the world. No rival versions can exist, because the judge's version will contain within it all possibilities. This point is important, because the judge lends order to what might otherwise be seen as chaos, random bloodshed, killing for its own sake. Yet the opposite to the judge does not exist—some readers may want to make the kid into the judge's opposite, but he can no more be opposed than the Hindu god Shiva can. The hermit warns the kid at the outset "that when god made man the devil was at his elbow" (19). In other words, concepts such as good and evil are human inventions that disguise the knowledge that the world and man are neither good nor evil. Whether the judge's book is also McCarthy's book I consider when I address the kid's refusal of the judge, but readers who think that merely by refusing the judge's logic they are safe from his history are as naive as Webster. The judge is the reigning spirit of the New World. Insofar as we Americans live on a landscape that is totally transformed from what it was when Europeans first arrived here, we exist as characters in the judge's book.

Even the skeptic Tobin is "of two minds" about whether or not the judge was "sent among us for a curse," because Tobin knows that his acts are sanctioned by the judge (131). The judge's example says that American civilization, like any other civilization, is violence *refined*, not eradicated. The Europeans' history on the continent is compressed. In this tableau of the judge making his away across the desert, McCarthy compresses the Europeans' history in the New World. The judge carries

> a parasol made from rotten scraps of hide stretched over a framework of rib bones bound with strips of tug. The handle had been the foreleg of some creature and the judge approaching was clothed in little more than confetti so rent was his costume to accommodate his figure.... He seemed some degenerate entertainer fleeing from a medicine show and the outrage of the citizens who'd sacked it. (297–98)

Here the judge represents the civilized European returned to a primitive state and the hearty pioneer making his way across a barren and dangerous landscape toward an idealized haven. He totes along rifles, but the parasol, fetid and rank, lends the judge a hint of decayed elegance. Carrying his parasol as if he were going to an afternoon tea, the judge promenades toward the future, where suburbanites who live in this same desert will serve sumptuous meals of beef and turkey in air-conditioned houses situated near rock gardens and flowing fountains bubbling over a desert landscape. The judge's parasol is of a piece with the scalphunters' dress—"tattered, stinking, ornamented with human parts like cannibals" (189). Each displays the layering of American civilization that *Blood Meridian* seeks to unearth—the bones that we have buried but still use to fasten and reinforce "exceptionalist" fantasies of American moral innocence.

The judge's inscription on his rifle, "*Et In Arcadia Ego*," warns of the impossibility of expunging the judge's macabre promenade through American history. Renaissance writers used this Virgilian expression ("Even in Arcadia, there I am, Death") as a grim exhortation. Erwin Panofsky notices that most post-Renaissance readers have mistranslated this line as "I, too, was in Arcadia," transforming a grim reminder into a nostalgic yearning for a world without death. After the Renaissance, this ideal realm is transplanted from northern Greece to the New World. William Shakespeare's *Tempest* and John Locke's remark that in the beginning the world was America both equate the New World with Arcadia. The revisionist would argue that the judge brings death into this New World Arcadia with his gun, forgetting (or never knowing) that death was already present in Arcadia. Bringing rifles (or smallpox-infested blankets) into the West did not cause Arcadia to be lost; rather, death was embedded in the European dream of America as certainly as the judge's book is created out of the life that he destroys. As Leo Daughtery explains, "The point of the gun's name is not that because of its appearance in the landscape, or by synechode the judge's appearance, death has been introduced into an idyllic Arcadia: the entire novel makes clear (primarily though the judge, who continuously emphasizes the point in his preachments) that the human world is, and always has been, a world of killing" (126–27).[13] To the judge, the challenge of the New World is to create something that will not become the material for someone else's creation but will endure as your own. This challenge is great because it involves more than possessing the fates of the scalphunters or creating the world of the future; it means, as his botanizing indicates, usurping the place of the dead. And in the New World the dead are present before the Europeans arrive. Those whom Americans call "Indians" enacted worlds that cannot be conquered by Europeans simply because they ended before the Europeans arrived. Thus, the judge destroys the relics he finds, because until all evidence of previous people's presence in the New World is abolished, its conquest will not be complete. Yet the judge suspects that the past cannot be conquered, and this knowledge enrages him: it makes him like human history—partial, incomplete.

Standing before the ruins of the Anasazi, the judge tells the scalphunters a parable about the European presence in the New World. He explains that, some years before, a harness maker lived in the "wilderness" of the Alleghenies. He "fell into the habit" of "dressing himself up as an Indian" and asking travelers for money. He met with success until one traveler, a young man, refused to give over money, "having recognized the harnessmaker for a white man" (142). The shamed harness maker then invited the traveler to his home. The traveler endeared himself to the harness maker and his family, and when he left, the family cried. The harness maker kept the departing traveler company until they were deep in the deep woods, whereupon the harness maker killed the traveler with a rock and took his money. The harness maker then tore his own clothes and bloodied himself in so that he can convince his wife that he and the traveler had been set upon by thieves. On his deathbed the harness maker told his son what he had done. His son forgave him but then went "away to the west and he himself [became] a killer of men" (145). At this point the judge's audience interrupts with variants to the tale that they have evidently all heard before. The judge quiets them, saying:

> There's a rider to the tale. There was a young bride waiting for that traveler with whose bones we are acquainted and she bore a child in her womb that was the traveler's son. Now this son whose father's existence in this world is historical and speculative even before the son has entered it is in a bad way. All his life he carries before him the idol of a perfection to which he can never attain. The father dead has euchred the kid out of his patrimony. For it is the death of the father to which the son is entitled and to which he is heir, even more so than his goods. [Consequently,] the world he inherits bears him false witness. He is broken before a frozen god and will never find his way. (145)

This "rider" explains how the judge's audience (his men and the readers too) came to be where they are at the time of the tale's telling. They are the sons gone west to become killers of men. Their fathers are strange versions of the primal New World scene depicted in the massacre of White's men by the "legion of horribles." Their father masquerades as an impoverished Indian to exploit the guilt that westering Americans feel about displacing Indians from their homeland. They are happy to hand over blood money rather than confront what they have done and are about to do. Likewise, the harness maker robs and kills other white men as an Indian, thereby ensuring that the cycle of violence against the Indian by the white man will be continued indefinitely. Yet the fact that white men must conduct their transactions through the figure of the Indian suggests that they have not altogether displaced the Indian from their self-understanding. The fact that the white man's image of the Indian is not real matters less than the fact that the Indian has become a frozen god whom he cannot displace.

Before telling the story, the judge is asked, "What kind of indians has these here been?" One of the men jokes they are "dead ones," but the judge insists they "are not so dead" (142). The tale explains how the vanished Anasazi still abide on this continent. Drawing an analogy between the coming American civilization and the ruins of the past Anasazi civilization that they uncover, the judge suggests that the spirit of the Anasazi will continue to dominate the landscape. Referred to by the judge as "the old ones" and "the dead fathers," these people can be remembered by future generations because they worked in stone—"passable masons" one of them says (142). The judge then makes a distinction between those who would create and those who exist as material for the creators to shape. Whereas he who makes "a shelter of reeds [and] has joined his spirit to the common destiny of creatures . . . [w]ill subside back into the primal mud," he "who builds in stone seeks to alter the structure of the universe and so it was with these masons [the Anasazi,] however primitive their works may seem to us" (146). Although countless tribes have passed over the ruins of the Anasazi, it is the Americans who have a spiritual kinship with these "dead fathers." What makes them kin, though, is the Americans' desire to transform those ruins into a new kind of stone that will be the American civilization. The Anasazi remains, however, "the tools, the art, the building—these stand in judgement of the later races" (146). The question is not whether the European Americans will conquer the continent but whether they will displace these dead fathers. To topple these frozen gods when their "spirit is entombed in the stone" is a mighty challenge, the judge suggests (146). Displacing the dead fathers is a form of seeking the sacred, which, as Girard says, "consists of all those forces, whose dominance over man increases or seems to increase in proportion to man's effort to master them" (31). "Violence is the heart and secret soul of the sacred," Girard also tells us (31). If so, then the murderous acts that the scalphunters perform in their attempt to replace the Anasazi ruins with the American civilization mark the heart and soul of what is sacred within American history.

Such speculations are of little interest to the judge's audience and possibly to many readers of *Blood Meridian* as well. Who wants to think of the American civilization as a continuation of the Anasazi ruins? Must the choice that history leaves Americans be between an understanding of ourselves as resurrected Indians or happy Indian killers? Yet, except for the judge and possibly the kid, these are the only historical roles available to the white men in *Blood Meridian*. The judge speaks to his men not to raise these questions but to assure them that they pursue an honorable quest in the sense that there is, finally, no other. He points to "these ruins wondered at by tribes of savages" and asks if they do "not think that this will be again? Aye. And again. With other people, with other sons" (147). When Tobin asks the judge how the fatherless child of the tale should be raised, the judge gives a list of choices that involve putting him in the wild and letting him fend for himself. He asks, "If God meant to interfere in the degeneracy of mankind would he have not done so by now?" In essence, the judge says that the son should do as the scalphunters do. What they do—playing these "games" for "stakes"—is worthwhile because it is an effort to surpass the deeds of the old ones. As the Anasazi are to the Americans so is the judge to his men. After he spoke, the judge rested, and "his eyes were empty slots" as if to suggest that the judge had become an ancient statue. "So like an icon was he" that the men "grew cautious and spoke with circumspection among themselves" for fear of waking him. The judge himself cannot replace the Anasazi except by binding himself to their spirit. Moreover, the judge himself becomes the frozen god whom the men will not be able to displace. God-like, he is their suzerain.[14]

The only one in *Blood Meridian*'s universe who seems to have the chance to usurp the judge's authority is the kid. In my view, to frame the kid in this way is more dramatic necessity than true possibility. Here the judge challenges the kid's apparent defiance:

You came forward, he said, to take part in a work. But you were a witness against yourself. You sat in judgement on your own deed. You put your own allowances before the judgements of history and you broke with the body of which you were pledged a part and poisoned it in all its enterprise. Hear me, man. I spoke in the desert for you and you only and you turned a deaf ear to me. . . . It was required of no man to give more than he possessed nor was any man's share compared to another's. Only each was called upon to empty his heart into the common and one did not. (307)

This accusation comes as the kid sits in jail for crimes that the judge has assured the authorities the kid has engineered. The kid denies authority: "It was you." The question is whether, even if he wants to, the kid can reject the judge's power to order him, to write his destiny. Again, in this novel, acts take precedent over intentions. As the judge points out, the kid passed up two opportunities to kill the judge. Ultimately, the judge will seal the kid's destiny by killing him.

The judge tells the kid that he has a "flawed" heart because "You alone reserved in your soul some clemency for the heathen" (299). This may or may not be true; there is no question that the kid often seems apart from the group. When given the task of executing a mercy killing, he refuses to do so. When David Brown, a member of the group, has an arrow in his leg, the kid pulls it out against the advice of others. (The judge, however, knows the kid will do this and in a sense assigned him the task.) A fortune-teller gives the kid the four of clubs, which indicates in Tarot terminology one who goes his own way. Still, the kid goes along until the group is no more. He is portrayed early on "lying on his belly holding the big Walker revolver and letting the shots off slowly and with care as if he'd done it all in a dream" (109). Shooting Indians, he appears not to be committed to the task in the same way that his fellows are, but nonetheless he still shoots at them.

The judge asks the kid, "For even if you should have stood your ground, yet what ground was it?" (307). That is, the kid has no perspective from which to challenge the judge that has not already been given to him by the judge. His confrontation with the judge changes the kid, because it obligates him to act on his heretofore unrepresented feelings. Phillips is right to suggest that the kid has no real self—he is either a projection of an inchoate will to violence or the tool of others. Like Achilles or Hector, he is a narrative device whose acts serve a larger narrative purpose than illuminating his character. His capacity to resist the judge is as beside the point as his capacity to acquiesce to the judge. The judge could kill the kid at any point but chooses to let the kid live far into middle age. Why? Once again, I think that the answer lies in the judge's Anasazi parable. There the judge proclaims, "it is the death of the father to which the son is entitled and to which he is heir" (145). The kid ran away from his father; the narrative does not tell us what became of him. In the scene where the judge confronts the kid in jail, the judge says to him, "Dont you know that I'd have loved you like a son?" (306). The judge is willing to acknowledge the kid as his heir if the kid will only acknowledge the judge as his father. Together they are a part of the same process in which the living and the dead are "in possession of the fruits of their election" (300). Each is possessed by the acts of violence that he has committed.

After this confrontation the narrative skips ahead thirty years to 1879. No longer are there "terrains so wild and barbarous to try whether the stuff of creation may be shaped to man's will" (4–5). Those who are moving across the western landscapes are now buffalo pickers scavenging the desert for bones they can turn into a meager profit. The kid, now a man, still moves amid the waste that he told the hermit he had headed straight for, but he no longer practices mindless violence. He joins an outfit that helps "pilgrims"—victims of the sort of violence he once committed—find their way. This stunning passage in which he confronts, as it were, a victim of one of his deeds shows that he wants to make amends for what he has done. In this moment he encounters a woman whom he takes to be the lone survivor of the sort of massacre in which he used to participate. He has to wade through the dead to speak to her:

He made his way among the corpses and stood before her. She was very old and her face was gray and leathery and sand had collected in the folds of her clothing. She did not look up. The shawl that covered her head was much faded of its color yet it bore like a patent woven into the fabric the figures of stars and quartermoons and other insignia of provenance unknown to him. He spoke to her in a low voice. He told her that he was an American and that he was a long way from the country of his birth and that he had no family and that he had traveled much and seen many things and had been at war and had endured hardships. He told her he would convey her to a safe place, some party of her countrypeople would welcome her and that she should join them for he could not leave her in this place or she would surely die.

He knelt on one knee, resting the rifle before him like a staff. Abuelita, he said. No puedes escucharme?

He reached into the little cove and touched her arm. She moved slightly, her whole body, light and rigid. She was just a dried shell and she had been dead in that place for years. (315)

The passage is beautiful and moving unlike any other in the book. This is the only moment when the kid is revealed as someone who hurts because of what he has done; it is the only moment in the book when a character is portrayed as psychologically vulnerable. To this woman's remains, the kid expresses guilt and, possibly, remorse. As a scalphunter, he had seen elderly Indian women scalped for their "receipts"—including one who was dead before the scalp-hunters found her. His desire to convey this woman to a safe place may or may not make restitution for past acts.

Her quartermoon blanket recalls the fortune-teller the kid met earlier. I doubt that this woman is the same fortune-teller, although she could be. Through this dead woman, the kid confronts what is, for him, the truth of his destiny. Recognizing his complicity in her death is what enables him to iden-tify himself as an American. (The narrative repeatedly names the scalphunters as "Americans" when they are murdering the defenseless.) The kid is identi-fied as such himself, because the narrative associates his prior actions with "Americaness." Not twenty pages earlier, he had left to die pilgrims he had promised to help. The kid's gesture to the "abuelita" invites the contemporary American reader to identify with his implied confession of "wrongdoing." Returning this corpse to her "countrypeople" acknowledges that Americans ventured upon land that did not "belong" to them in any morally sanctioned way, destroyed cultures they did not understand or care to understand, and returned to the scene of their transgressions crying repentance long after their original deeds had been done. But the body is dead—the act commit-ted cannot be taken back. McCarthy suggests that for "true" American his-tory, the one that has killed and killed and killed again to build the American empire, Americans substitute this other sentimentalized history to salve their conscience—to avoid seeing present acts embedded in prior acts. Like the kid, contemporary (white) Americans shy away from acknowledging dependence on the violent transformations undergone in the creation of a shared American history. If modern-day Americans are but a version of the kid pleading mercy from a dead woman, then can Americans approach this dead Indian woman as our "abuelita," or grandmother, as the kid calls her? If so, then are all of our contemporary debates about identity not just versions of old wars where one side longs to trade positions with the other? The kid finds the grandmother, as the judge finds the Anasazi, gone before he arrives. The kid cannot but see himself as an orphan who has killed his mother and grandmother. The kid's only atonement, then, is to acknowledge his life as one among the living dead. The desire to join his "abuelita" is also to admit that he would prefer not to have been born. Having been born, he destroyed the world that he entered, in order to make way for the world to come. He does not look to the future that his acts have created; he waits to join the dead he has sought through his life.

Having admitted his complicity in the judge's design and having tried to apologize for it, the question becomes what course of action would be appropriate for the kid to follow. He is doomed to repeat his eloquent gesture of apology. He can object to what the judge has done and even object to his role in it, but he cannot unwrite the history that they made except to claim that it is all false and that he died truly with White without, in fact, wondrously rising. His position is paradoxical because at the very moment when the kid discovers that he has a will and chooses to express it, he learns that he has no true will and his choices do not belong to him. Drifting west does not bring him unlimited freedom. With no mother alive to receive him, the kid can only return to his author-father, the judge, who will definitively end the kid's story. He is as chained to his history as Faulkner's Quentin was but he is without the means to make it beautiful and tragic.

We might think of the thirty-year interval between meeting the judge in jail and meeting him for the last time in the North Texas tavern as the time during which the kid tried to gain possession of a history separate from the one that has already made him. That the kid knows he cannot undo what he has done is suggested in his other significant encounter between the time that he was released from jail and his final meeting with the judge. This time he meets a version of himself, an "otherkid," a fifteen-year-old boy who is one of a group of five "sullen wretches dressed in [buffalo] skins" (318). This group is a pale reflection of the "viciouslooking humans" who were once the scalphunters. The older "kid" now wears a scapular of ears that had once belonged to his companion Brown. The kid's audience speculates that the scapular is a fake, refusing to believe that its wearer has a true relationship to the events it commemorates. It is as if the kid has been put in a museum to be gawked at and disbelieved by a tourist who predicts Jane Tompkins' experience in the Plains

Indian Museum in Cody, Wyoming. Later, however, the older kid kills the fifteen-year-old kid, when the young man appears in the night to challenge him. The kid kills his challenger. In so doing, he kills the boy's history before it can be lived or known. "You wouldnt have lived anyway," the kid remarks. This most likely is his brutal judgment on himself and his way of preparing himself for his final death at the hands of the judge (322). He may kill his double because his double has trivialized the kid's acts. He may kill to avenge the memory of those he killed. He may kill to destroy symbolically those future Americans who will pretend to distance themselves from the history that his acts have given to them. It is also possible that he has reverted to an earlier identity: he kills not for the fun of it but to commemorate the fact that he never passed beyond his taste for mindless violence.

Having symbolically killed himself, the kid can only wait for the judge to complete his living death. He finds the judge in a North Texas tavern, not far from the tent where they first met. Amid the swirl of the music and the dancing strangers, the judge and the kid come together as they did in another Texas tavern at the outset of the novel. "Do you believe it's all over?" the judge asks the kid (327). The scene revisits their previous conversation in the San Diego jail cell, except that now, as the judge points out, they are the only ones from their group left living. The tavern is filled with characters who cannot know that their presence has been dictated by the judge, and they surely represent the audience who is reading *Blood Meridian*. With this coincidence of audiences in mind, the judge explains to the kid why the future will deny the past that made it:

> As war becomes dishonored and its nobility called into question those honorable men who recognize the sanctity of blood will become excluded from the dance ... and thereby the dance will become a false dance and the dancers false dancers. ... [O]nly that man who has offered up himself entire to the blood of the war, who has been to the floor of the pit and seen horror in the round and learned at last that it speaks to his inmost heart, only that man can dance. (331)

The judge claims this legacy, and the kid denies it. When the kid says to the judge, "You aint nothin," the judge replies, "You speak truer than you know" (331). The judge's witticism acknowledges that they have fallen out of the timeless desert where they could express the murderous spirit of civilization in the open. The West is about settled; the New World is, for now, won. Its inhabitants are simulated Indians. As the American masons build their civilization, the warrior skills that the kid and the judge possess will no longer be so obviously needed—at least not on American soil. Toadvine's complaint—"You wouldnt think that a man would run plumb out of country out here, would ye?"—is the epitaph to their adventure (285). They will give way to the one depicted in the epilogue: striking fire out of the rock, trying to hem the judge in with fences and then with zoning laws for future construction sites. *Blood Meridian* reminds us that their ultimate meaning will be known only as ruins.

In this final encounter with the kid, the judge asserts, "There is room on the stage for one beast and one alone" (331). After lecturing the kid this final time, the judge kills him as he enters "the jakes" (333). In the seconds before dying, the kid "looked again at the silent tracks of the stars where they die over the darkened hills" (333). The moment recalls the stars that fell the night of his birth. It also recalls the incident in the first chapter when the kid ventured upon a "man coming up from the jakes" who would not give way and nearly murdered him. Then the kid had engaged in a fight that left him face down in a puddle of water. "He'd have died if someone hadn't turned him over" (9). The kid's hold on his life has always been tenuous; it seems a matter of luck that he has survived, and it is even questionable whether he has. This time when he steps into the jakes, he finds "the judge seated upon his closet." Here *closet* refers to the lavatory, but it can also mean a judge's chambers. The judge rises to kill the kid in an ambiguous gesture of love: he embraces him to death. The novel implies death by sodomy (333). An act violent and intimate, the judge seems to be claiming the kid for his own. The act (the judge) consumes the witness (the kid), yet the witness contains the act. History creates itself through acts of endless violation of others and the stories that humans write to affirm or counteract the memory of those acts.

III

Before the conclusion of this chapter, it is worth returning to the kid's encounter with the "abuelita," since there is another way to read it that does not obligate us to see it as only a futile gesture. On this view, the kid's conversation with the dead Indian woman lets him see himself as the one who is homeless, as the despoiler who cannot find a home except through his identification with those whom he has rendered homeless. Having no family of his own, he addresses her as if she were his family; this is why he calls her "Abuelita," literally "little grandmother," but more colloquially "old dear one." The judge's history is father-son driven and directed, seemingly, at the kid who has never known his mother. For the kid, to ask forgiveness of the grandmother is perhaps to seek to be united with his mother rather than his father. The kid has run away from his father, only to find the judge. Choosing to identify himself with the mothers, he renounces his birth and life to join himself with the raped and unknown, a gesture that he willfully repeats with the judge at his death. For his part, the kid may oppose the judge by choosing to become one with the tradition of the lost Indian tribes. He is the one figure who connects the previous world (the one of his "abuelita") to the New World that is America. If so, his annihilation takes the form of a communion with an ancient memory. The judge's empire—America—remains inhabited by the "antiwarriors pendant from their mounts," who are described as "souls broke through some misweave in the weft of things into the world below" (109). These antiwarriors haunt the judge's landscape and it may be that even the judge's rage for order cannot overcome their presence. Such would be the only context that I can think of in which the kid might plausibly be imagined the victor over the judge. To identify yourself with the memory of these lost ones, as the kid does, is to remove yourself from American history, if not yet history altogether.

In the end, *Blood Meridian* says that history is unknowable except as a contingent ordering because either acts of humans or nature will have destroyed the evidence of what was done and remembered. The account that McCarthy gives of the massacre of the Tiguas is as close as any human can come to telling what has happened to those histories for which we have no record. The act that frames this massacre is the judge's attempt to repress this telling. The judge finds some pictographs that he copies into his book. This history, he thinks, will be known only to him. He then "rose with a piece of broken chert and he scrappled away one of the designs, leaving no trace of it only a raw place on the stone where it had been" (173). In the next paragraph we learn that "in three days they would fall upon a band of peaceful Tiguas and kill every soul" (173). Killing the Tiguas' "every soul" is a version of scraping those pictures and leaving only stone. By describing the Tiguas' remains, McCarthy's "agentless" narrative strives to represent what might have been lost:

In the days to come the frail black rebuses of blood in those sands would crack and break and drift away so that in the circuit of a few suns all trace of the destruction of these people would be erased. The desert wind would salt their ruins and there would be nothing, no ghost nor scribe, to tell any pilgrim in his passing how it was that people lived in this place and in this place died. (174)

This is an account of a history lost to the historian. The battle that it depicts has no meaning except that a history has been lost, and it has no archive except what is *Blood Meridian*.

The passage does not strike me as a tribute to the judge's enterprise. Do these people and the memory of them deserve to die merely because they did not build in stone? Or is this battle just the likely last account, written before it is read, of what will once be the gone American empire? Is the suggestion here that we cannot know the Tiguas (or the Anasazi) and therefore cannot know ourselves? The text of *Blood Meridian* is tissued together out of such moments and questions. At such times it seems to speak, haltingly, for the lost ones. Perhaps McCarthy points to what cannot be told. Or perhaps Shaviro is right to say that McCarthy's voice "is not a perspective upon the world, and not a vision that intends its objects: but an immanent perspective that already is the world" (151).[15] Only such an "immanent perspective" can portray how histories have been embedded into the landscape that absorbs their remains. The force that animates the judge's acts one day will blow the dust over our American remains. That force, which we may call history, cannot ever be seen whole. Telling two histories at once—the one made in the name of America and the one that cannot be unmade because it contains all possible empires—*Blood Meridian* endures as the first and last book of American history.

Off Faulkner's Plantation
Toni Morrison's *Beloved* and
Song of Solomon

Too many books by Negro writers are addressed to a white audience. By doing this the authors run the risk of limiting themselves to the audience's presumption of what a Negro is or should be; the tendency is to become involved in polemics, to plead the Negro's humanity. You know, many white people question that humanity, but I don't think the Negroes can afford to indulge in such a false issue. For us the question should be, What are the specific forms of that humanity, and what in our background is worth preserving or abandoning?
—Ralph Ellison

I

William Faulkner's *Absalom, Absalom!* imagines a fictional universe in which African Americans have no say over their history and thus no future separate from white control. For unrepentant, post–Civil War white Southerners, Faulkner's novel implied a future in which the past would not have to be forsaken or forgotten but cherished as an abiding memory that becomes the context for the continuation of white Southern mastery over their environment. A hundred years passed after the Civil War before black Americans in the South could vote with impunity or attend the same universities that white Southerners attended. It took another forty years for the whites who killed those who tried to make Civil Rights in the South a reality to be brought to meaningful trial. Faulkner by himself did not create this future, but *Absalom* is not any more out of place within it than is Margaret Mitchell's still beloved *Gone with the Wind*. How does an African American writer, working in the long shadow of Faulkner, imagine a history that does not reduce one to being merely one of Faulkner's inventions, to some latter-day Clytemnestra or Jim Bond? When Ralph Ellison was introduced to Faulkner for the first time, he jokingly identified him as a kind of patriarch of African American literature: "You know, you have children all around now," he deadpanned to Faulkner. "You won't be proud of all of them, just the same they're all around" (Ellison and Murray 45).

Ellison does not record Faulkner's response, but one wonders what Faulkner would make of the fact that, other than Cormac McCarthy and the Latin American magical realists, the writers who have best engaged his work have been African Americans. Richard Wright, Ralph Ellison, James Baldwin, David Bradley, Ernest Gaines, Gloria Naylor, Charles Johnson, Edward P. Jones, and (most prominently) Toni Morrison have transformed Faulkner's legacy into a legacy for African American literature. Edouard Glissant argues that "Faulkner's oeuvre will be complete only when it is revisited and made vital by African-Americans" (55), and he credits Morrison with the initiation of the process. As Morrison's work perhaps best shows, these writers have responded to Faulkner not so much in terms of form (as James Joyce attacked the realist novel or Thomas Pynchon reconfigured Joyce) as in terms of content. That is, Morrison does not challenge Faulkner's modernist narrative strategies—she uses many of Faulkner's tricks in her own works—but she challenges the interpretive uses to which they are put.[1] As Harold Bloom observes, "Faulkner's mode of narration is exquisitely modulated by Morrison, but the accent of Faulkner can always be heard in Morrison's narrators" (*Toni* 3). As I argue, Morrison's work is most challenging not as a response to Faulkner the novelist but as a refutation of Faulkner the historian.

In addition to rewriting the stories of Faulkner's African American characters, Morrison's work shows how a powerful critique of history can become a type of history itself. Walter Benn Michaels's *The Shape of the Signifier* (2004) asserts that *Beloved* is a pivotal work for understanding how postmodernism engages with history. Michaels identifies *Beloved* as a key text of his "grid" for mapping what "a real history of recent American aesthetic and theoretical production might look like" (15). Michaels's argument is emblematic of those that insist that postmodern critiques of history are merely indulgent displays of postmodern identity politics. Grouping *Beloved* with Leslie Marmon Silko's *Almanac of the Dead*, Art Spiegelman's *Maus*, and Richard Rorty's *Achieving Our Country*, Michaels characterizes the novel as being "about those 'contingent historical circumstances' that have produced their authors (when causes replace reasons, historicism will naturally loom large), and they all understand themselves as technologies for the production of that paradigmatically identitarian notion, pride" (78). For Michaels, "Morrison's race," not her work, "provides the mechanism for as well as meaning of the conversion of history into meaning" (136). Thus, "it is racial identity that makes the experience of enslavement part of the history of African-Americans today" (136). Since Morrison's "deepest commitments are to categories of racial or cultural difference," her work privileges experience over interpretation (13). Morrison's ancestors experienced slavery, whereas the ancestors of others did not. According to Michaels, this gives her (and other African Americans) a unique claim to an identity that cannot be shared with or transmitted to Americans who are not black. On this logic, her authenticity as a writer is based not on what she writes but on what she is, or claims to be, which is black. This logic, says Michaels, is used to justify "the proliferation" of identity politics novels "that not only repeat the privileging of experience over belief but seek to extend it to the possibility of our experiencing (rather than learning about) things that never actually happened to us" (14). "The point here," says Michaels, "is not that our sense of whose histories need to be taken into account must be extended; it is instead that no one's history need be taken into account, that the recognition of inequality makes the history of that inequality irrelevant, and that the question of past injustice has no bearing on the question of present justice" (166).

Michaels examines *Beloved* to argue against two mistakes that he sees as endemic in "identitarian" politics. First, he argues, a book such as *Beloved* presents history as a form of self-knowledge, because it posits that "things that didn't happen to us can nonetheless be part of history" (*Shape* 167). Second, books such as *Beloved* may be right to suggest that "history makes us who we are, but [that suggestion is] also, for the purpose of making our society more just—at least if we identify justice with equal opportunity—irrelevant" (167). Michaels is not exactly objecting to how *Beloved*, in Michael Rothberg's words, "processes the legacy of the past by textualizing the process of slavery" (502). Rather, he seems to question the very idea of history, postmodern or pre-postmodern. In so doing, he endorses the very logic of identity that he would seem to critique. "Books like *Beloved*," Michaels argues, "imagine societies organized by identity" and thus cannot truly "serve as a source of identity because things that didn't happen to us can't count as part of our history" (150, 158). On this understanding, history is reduced to personal history, grounded in experience and limited to identity.

Actually, books such as *Beloved* and *Almanac of the Dead* are hardly "personal" since they imagine societies driven by and organized around shared communal visions that are understood to be versions of a living history. This sense of history is expressed through cultural conflicts that partly have to do with identity but mostly have to do with the sense of being a people with a shared story. These books are not about "culture" in the narrow and mostly symbolic sense that Michaels claims has been the basis of American literature since modernism. For Morrison or Silko, it is more than a contingent historical circumstance that black Americans and descendants of Indians continue to be disadvantaged socially and politically when compared with white Americans. For them, the question of social equality is not something that can be argued in the present without a historical perspective that accounts for why assertions of equality for everyone in American society are, in practice, usually disingenuous or naïve. In arguing that Morrison seeks to articulate not a living sense of African American history but merely an impregnable position in the culture wars, Michaels trivializes Morrison's work and justifies the pretense that history is something that does not exist except as someone else's talking point. David Harlan says, "Conservatives bewail the spread of identity politics, which they see as little more than tribal politics played out on a national stage. But this objection is pointless, for identity politics is as old as politics itself" (180). At one point Michaels acknowledges that the history of slavery is relevant to contemporary social problems and black poverty, but he nonetheless insists that reminding people that slavery existed is more likely to prevent rather than facilitate the fair distribution of wealth to all Americans (161, 168). To be sure, Michaels's larger worry is that the logic of identity politics makes it impossible for Morrison, Silko, and Michaels himself to live in the same country and share the same history. Yet why would any reader deny that these authors' histories are plausible from the point of view that they imagine and for the audience that they address, unless it is to deny these writers their point of view entirely? Until very recently, has it been possible to claim that African Americans live in the same country, share the same prospects, and understand themselves within the same past as white Americans? Does Michaels really think that the past can be sealed from the present—that the past is past and not only unknowable but also unrepresentable? Does he think that the future is now because the past no longer exists except as a trumped-up memory? Does he want to say that white people enslaved black Africans in the seventeenth century so that twentieth-century black Americans could use the fact of their ancestors' past enslavement to accuse twentieth-century white Americans of not living up to the professed ideals of their nation? If so, then Michaels's book does seem to stake positions that go well beyond anything Faulkner's work ever does.

Michaels's conclusion that "history, as of this writing, is still over" is tacitly an extension of the kind of modernist history that Faulkner canonizes (*Shape* 182). This complacent perspective Morrison's work explicitly rejects. One does not have to go to Faulkner to find a version of American history that is premised on racial inequality as a kind of given of American life, but one does have to go Faulkner to find such a history that contains as part of its story a powerfully sympathetic engagement with the plight of African Americans. Morrison, who wrote her master's thesis at Columbia University on William Faulkner and Virginia Woolf, has tried to warn critics away from reading her works as being entangled with Faulkner's. Eminent critics such as John Duvall, Philip Weinstein, and Patrick O'Donnell have written perceptively on what Duvall calls "the Faulknerian intertext" in the works of Morrison.[2] Following Morrison's lead, critics have sometimes been uneasy in connecting Morrison's work to Faulkner's, as if it is somehow disrespectful to Morrison's achievement to say that she might have been influenced by a powerful white male writer.[3] Weinstein's *What Else but Love?*—as fine a book as we are ever likely to have on Faulkner and Morrison—discusses the two authors primarily as "major novelists of racial turmoil" (xix). "I am not concerned with questions of influence," he adds (xix). Referring to Morrison's own critical "mapping of her intertextual relation to white writers," O'Donnell says that "the playing out of this relation" obligates "a casting of Morrison before Faulkner—in a sense, as if she were the precursor" (225). O'Donnell's point may seem incongruous until one recognizes that it betrays how closely tied Morrison's work is to Faulkner's. Such claims can only underscore that "influence" and not just "intertextuality" is crucial to understanding Morrison's response to Faulkner, since her aim is in its way explicitly Faulknerian: she would write Faulkner's influence out of her work as surely as Faulkner's work would deny African Americans a future in a transformed American society. Her works consistently expose Faulkner's "literary" achievement as one that created a version of African American history so powerful yet so limited that it denied African Americans both a past and a future alternative to the one that Faulkner named for them. At the same time, her formal narrative strategies are so implicated in Faulkner's that it is difficult to disentangle Morrison's writing from Faulkner's writing except through her very different view of Southern American and African American history.

To understand why *Beloved* is not merely an expression of "identity politics" in the sense that Michaels describes, one must recognize that Morrison's quarry is not only the kind of Southern history that Faulkner endorsed but the kind of American and African American history that Ellison celebrated. In ways that her critics have not sufficiently recognized, Morrison's writing responds both to the racist Southern history that Faulkner's work often implies and to the failed optimistic inclusiveness that Ellison's work advocates.[4] Prior to Morrison, Ellison had given the most powerful response to Faulkner in American literature. Unlike Morrison, Ellison was always willing to claim Faulkner as an influence. Ellison made it clear that he was not afraid of Faulkner's legacy and that he was ready to put it in its appropriate—that is to say Ellisonian—context. In the address that he gave at the presentation of his National Book Award for *Invisible Man*, Ellison brilliantly denied the history, if not the art, that Faulkner's great novels implied. Ellison has observed that "except for the work of William Faulkner, something vital had gone out of American prose after Mark Twain" (*Collected* 152). Ellison was identifying and praising writers—such as Herman Melville, Ralph Waldo Emerson, Henry David Thoreau, and Mark Twain—who had taken "responsibility for the condition of democracy"; "indeed, their works," he added, "were imaginative projections of conflicts within the human heart which arose when the sacred principles of the Constitution and the Bill of Rights clashed with practical exigencies of human greed and fear, hate and love" (153). Although Faulkner's commitment to democracy was tempered by his identification with the Old South, as Ellison well knew, the African American characters in Faulkner's work that most compelled Ellison's attention were created in response to the egalitarian concerns that *Absalom, Absalom!* suppressed and Ellison advocated. Ellison remarks, "I can accept Sam Fathers or Lucas Beauchamp in Faulkner," the characters who resisted white assumptions about what they could and could not do, "in ways that I couldn't accept Jim in *Huckleberry Finn*" (*Conversations* 154). He told interviewers, "If you would find the imaginative equivalents of certain Civil Rights figures in American writing, Rosa Parks and James Meredith, say, you don't go to most fiction by Negroes, but to Faulkner" (131). Such affirmative comments about Faulkner's work conveyed Ellison's sense that Faulkner's post-*Absalom* fictional portrayal of African Americans—his aesthetic rendering of what Ellison would call Negro identity—prompted the reader to see that African Americans were more complex, more defiant, and more human than their seemingly servile social place would indicate. For Ellison, Faulkner "has presented [Negroes] in terms of both the 'good nigger' and the 'bad nigger' stereotypes, and yet who has explored perhaps more successfully than anyone else, either white or black, certain forms of Negro humanity." As a result, Ellison acknowledges that in Faulkner's fiction "the dual function of this disassociation seems to be that of avoiding moral pain and thus to justify the South's racial code" (*Collected* 97).

As an artist who was also African American, Ellison recognized the power of Faulkner's fiction as history and the attendant need for African Americans to answer Faulkner's example. Ellison suggests that Faulkner is not just a repository of imagined figures (literary precursors to Rosa Parks), but indeed more fundamentally he recognizes Faulkner's work to be a source of historical knowledge and practice. "If you want to know something about the dynamic of the South from, roughly, 1874 until today," Ellison said in 1968, "you don't go to historians; not even to Negro historians. You go to William Faulkner" (*Conversations* 149).[5] Ellison's oeuvre—the novel *Invisible Man* (1952) and the unfinished novel published as *Juneteenth* (1999), along with shorter fictional works and numerous essays and speeches—could be seen as an attempt to refute the history, though not the literary artistry, that Faulkner's work implies. His friend and critic Albert Murray notes that Ellison "accepted the challenge of William Faulkner's complex literary image of the South" (Ellison and Murray xxii). Actually, though, Ellison would resist such a narrow interpretation of his works. He would say that if his work answers Faulkner's specifically, then it does so as part of the ongoing fight to determine what our nation's founding ideals truly mean. From Ellison's perspective, the goal of the American, no less than of the African American, was to escape the history that Faulkner's work implies. Ellison would make Faulkner over into an explicitly *American*, as opposed to Southern, writer whose primary value was his literary artistry. In this way, Ellison gave the canonical view of Faulkner as a high-modernist dandy.[6]

Morrison, writing after Ellison, cannot affirm the Ellisonian proposition that American and African American history share the same ideals and future. Ellison gives the kind of broad affirmation of American identity that Rorty advocates in *Achieving Our Country* and Michaels criticizes as another kind of identity politics. Like Michaels, Rorty identifies Silko's *Almanac of the Dead* as a key text for understanding how postmodern fiction now "assumes that democratic government has become a farce" (*Achieving* 6). Rorty argues that Silko's novel, which focuses "on the relation of European-Americans to Native-Americans and the descendants of the slaves brought from Africa," endorses a national politics "of national self-mockery and self-disgust" (6, 8). Rorty contrasts Silko's novel with muckraking novels of the early twentieth century, such as Upton Sinclair's *The Jungle* or John Steinbeck's *The Grapes of Wrath*, that "were written in the belief that the tone of the Gettysburg Address was absolutely right but that our country would have to transform itself to fulfill Lincoln's hopes" (8). Comparing Silko's vision of history to the vision of Martin Heidegger or Michel Foucault, Rorty argues that she "associate[s] American patriotism with an endorsement of atrocities: the importation of African slaves, the slaughter of Native-Americans, the rape of ancient forests, and the Vietnam War" (7). Against this "image" of American history, Rorty proposes a more affirmative one, modeled on the optimism of Walt Whitman and John Dewey, who insisted that "the point of society is to construct subjects capable of ever more novel, ever richer, forms of human happiness" (31). Rorty, like Ellison, understands American history as a long march of progress toward greater opportunity and equality for all of its citizens. One chooses to be an American and with that choice earns the benefits of American society through one's willingness to participate in it as an equal among equals. Aware of the kinds of ongoing historical conflicts that Michaels's argument represses, Rorty concludes, "The argument between Left and Right about which episodes in our history we Americans should pride ourselves on will never be a contest between a true and a false account of our country's history and its identity. It is better described as an argument about which hopes to allow ourselves and which to forgo" (14).

Perversely, it seems to me, Michaels equates Rorty's Ellisonian argument with Morrison's rejection of American innocence and optimism. Michaels asserts that "the relevant identity in *Achieving Our Country* is American," and thus Rorty's only achievement is the expression of "pride" rather than a meaningful historical vision (*Shape* 78). It is worth noting, though, that it is precisely the multiculturalist point of view that allows him to dismiss Rorty's argument as being merely identity (or ethnicity) driven. His dismissal of Rorty's quite traditional assertion of American identity as something Americans assent to rather than being born into as yet another ethnic identity position confirms how powerful so-called identity politics critiques have become. Michaels and Rorty agree on one point: that, in Rorty's words, "Leftists in the academy have permitted cultural politics to supplant real politics, and have collaborated with the Right in making cultural issues central to public debate" (*Achieving* 14). Yet neither Morrison nor Silko can be assimilated easily into the categories "Left" and "Right" that Rorty assumes identify the boundaries of political discourse in America, because their points of view are not part of the traditional conversation by which the "identity" of America is generally defined. Their work suggests that critiques of American history that these white male Americans would dismiss either as identity politics or bad faith actually reflect long-standing, never confronted, intractable conflicts within American history that are not going away.

As a matter of politics, it may seem naïve to think that Silko's scenario of indigenous Americans driving European Americans off their ancestral homeland is going to happen anytime soon. However, as a form of collective desire and a will to believe in a history other than the one that has seemed to replace yours or that of your ancestors, its expression is likely to be with us until "America" is a word one finds only in scattered manuscripts or scratched on the rocks of the Grand Canyon. In other words, you cannot argue away or kill the collective desire that Morrison and Silko portray. Neither Morrison nor Silko can be as optimistic as Rorty and Ellison, and it is not because Heidegger or Foucault has corrupted their belief in American history. Rather, Morrison and Silko portray how their peoples' history has been corrupted by invaders' histories and how now they are fighting back. Morrison, like Silko, writes history that accepts as a given that the type of tribal racism that Faulkner portrayed cannot now be eradicated, and therefore, each wants to figure a way out of the bad history that has been inflicted on the people that she identifies as her audience. From this perspective, Rorty is misguided when he invidiously compares Silko with Sinclair or Steinbeck, because neither of these earlier authors represents a point of view or a criticism of American history at all consistent with Silko's. The point here is not just that Morrison and Silko are not white (and that Rorty's heroes are) but that by the end of the twentieth century the kind of optimism about America that Rorty associates with Whitman, Dewey, and Sinclair is, for many, no longer possible.

Morrison's work would suggest that Michaels is wrong to say that "history, as of this writing, is still over" but perhaps right to say that the America that Rorty hopes to achieve is no longer achievable (*Shape* 182). In other words, Michaels's rejection of Rorty's argument is right only to the extent that it affirms the logic that Morrison or Silko enacts. In the wake of the ongoing postmodern critique of history in general and the multicultural critique of American history in particular, the question to be confronted now is not which history you are going to choose or even which history are you going to reject as invalid, but which history has already chosen you. If one can say that the kind of history that Rorty or Ellison advocates now seems less possible as a viable American present or future, then one should also say that neither Faulkner nor Morrison, nor anyone else discussed in this book, would say otherwise.

II

In a brilliant essay that assesses *Beloved*'s somewhat ambiguous status as a postmodern novel that also aspires to be a type of history, Kimberly Chabot Davis notes that "while the novel exhibits a postmodern skepticism of sweeping historical metanarratives, of 'Truth,' and of Marxist teleological notions of time as diachronic, it also retains an African-American and modernist political commitment to the crucial importance of deep cultural memory, of keeping the past alive in order to construct a better future" (75). Thus, as Davis's argument suggests, Morrison rejects the kind of Rorty–Ellison American history metanarrative in favor of one that emerges from a specifically African American tradition. Yet simply calling *Beloved* a postmodern text alarms many readers—especially African American readers. As Davis notes, Barbara Christian insists that "the power of this novel as a specifically African-American text is being blunted" by attempts to explain its postmodern qualities (qtd. in K. Davis 76).[7] To be sure, Morrison understands as well as Hayden White does that history is always a type of fiction told according to the desires and beliefs of a particular audience. Morrison has characterized *Beloved* as a type of "literary archaeology" because she aims to write a kind of history (African American) that other historians (American) have missed (qtd. in K. Davis 112). Morrison is well aware of the large body of scholarship that has had a similar aim—whether it is Eugene Genovese's *Roll, Jordan, Roll* (1975) or recovered slave narratives such as Harriet Jacobs's. For Morrison, though, the novelist, rather than the historian, can better portray a "true" history precisely because the form of the novel allows the search for an abiding, underlying Truth (as opposed to merely a contingent ordering of facts) that the conventional practice of history can never claim. As Davis notes, "Moments of self-reflexivity" in *Beloved* suggest "that a fictional account of the interior life of a former slave might be more historically 'real' than actual documents" (81). On this view, *Beloved*'s Sethe—Morrison's fictional version of Margaret Garner, the slave whose "real" life inspired the novel—is truer than the real Garner, whose remains are to be found moldering in historical archives.

Morrison's commitment to an authentic and abiding African American history conflicts with her general postmodern skepticism toward metanarrative. To the extent that *Beloved* is an example of Linda Hutcheon's historiographic metafiction, as Davis argues that it is, the novel must be read primarily as a mere critique of the metanarrative of American liberty that Rorty advocates.

Davis is right to say that *Beloved* "makes us question the more extremist voices [such as that of Michaels] asserting that postmodern culture is bereft of history," but I would add that this claim is meaningful only to the extent that Morrison can identify a historical narrative alternative to those that she questions, one that is useful for orienting her audience within their present (75).[8] That is, her novel works as history, and not just historiographic metafiction, only as it transcends (or radically alters) the context of its own critique. Linda Anderson has noted Morrison's interest in "missing history." Anderson says that Morrison tries "to write from a position of a female subject whose connection with the maternal places her outside the socio-symbolic contract in the way [Julia] Kristeva describes" so that one could write from a "timeless place" in a language that emerges from "within an almost impossible void" (137). Yet I would suggest further that if Morrison's work betrays a modernist commitment to a poetics of memory, it is also emblematic of how powerfully Faulkner's influence, both as a novelist and as a historian, imbues her work. Thus, while Morrison's latent modernism is the mechanism by which she searches for an authentic past, it also threatens to compromise her postmodern project of inventing a history that she and her closest readers (whom I take to be readers who can orient themselves within an African American history that is not necessarily American) can use to move toward a future better than their memory would suggest is possible.

Davis observes that Morrison has always demanded that readers view her work as a type of history. Morrison defined her ambition to interviewer Elissa Schappel as follows: "to write novels that were unmistakably mine, but nevertheless first fit onto African-American traditions and second of all, this whole thing called literature" (118). To the question of whether she defines her work as being first African American rather than a part of the whole of literature broadly conceived, Morrison responded, "Yes" and then "Oh yes" (118).[9] Moreover, Morrison has said that her work is written to stand in the place of lost folk traditions:

For a long time the art form that was healing for Black people was music. That music is no longer exclusively ours; we don't have exclusive rights to it. Other people sing it and play it; it is the mode of contemporary music everywhere. So another form has to take that place, and it seems to me that the novel is needed by African-Americans now in a way it was not needed

before—and it is following along the lines of the function of novels everywhere. We don't live in places where we can hear those stories anymore;
parents don't sit around and tell their children those classical, mythological archetypal stories that we heard years ago. ("Rootedness" 340)

In other words, Morrison understands her work to be a form of cultural
memory—history—that she preserves and passes on to an audience who
also affirms it as theirs. Anderson rightly observes that for Morrison "what
becomes 'known' as history is not all there is to know," yet this unknown is
precisely what Morrison seeks and wants to make known as the basis of her
critique of others' metanarratives (141). This view even implies that her work
is less interpretation than it is a return to a kind of authentic history where
the community is so in tune with itself that conflicting interpretations about
community identity would be impossible because they are unthinkable. This
is why Michael Awkward is right to say that a novel such as Song of Solomon
presents a monomyth (in the Joseph Campbell sense) that performs the "dual
functions" of preserving "traditional Afro-American folktales, folk wisdom,
and general cultural beliefs" that can be adapted "to contemporary times and
needs" (69).[10]

Yet when Morrison searches for this community that preserves these beliefs, or the ancestor that authorizes it, she finds some version of her past
already imagined by Faulkner. Ironically, although Faulkner and Morrison are
at odds in obvious ways, they both share a deep suspicion about the efficacy of
the liberal American tradition. They both write about Civil War–era America
without devoting much attention to war itself or its political aftermath. Each
understands the individual to be a function of a particular narrative history that
is community driven. To be outside the community is to be outside or beyond
history. Morrison, though, indulges in a kind of utopianism (inconsistent to
be sure) that hopes that by returning to the ground of the past, her history can
create a different, more livable, present as well as a more hopeful future. In an
oft-cited remark, Morrison identifies the premise that animates her practice
of history: "There must have been a time when an artist could be genuinely
representative of the tribe and in it; when an artist could have a tribal or racial
sensibility and an individual expression of it" (Rootedness 339). In Playing in the
Dark, she argues that the course of American self-definition, by whatever form
we define it, has resulted in "a master narrative that spoke for Africans and
their descendants" (50).[11] Refusing to make a distinction between literature

and history, Morrison says "Whatever popularity the slave narrative had … the slave's own narrative, while freeing the narrator in many ways, did not destroy the master narrative" (51). If Morrison writes in the hope of creating a narrative that is authorized by the continuing power of her ancestors, her work also raises questions about how she can ever confirm that her history is true to her ancestors' vision—that is, independent of her own creation of her ancestors' vision as her history's authorizing spirit. As such, its history would be unique and perhaps incommunicable to anyone outside the group (again, not unlike Faulkner's aim.)[12]

In the map that he drew to accompany the text to *Absalom*, Faulkner referred to himself as sole owner and proprietor of Yoknapatawpha County. Faulkner's fiction also drew a map of ownership over Southern history and took possession of Southern history and everything contained by it. Faulkner's property includes the imaginary slaves, their descendants, and their stories. Early in *Beloved* Morrison introduces a concept that is crucial to the novel, "rememory," which seems recognizably Faulknerian. "If a house burns down," Sethe explains, "it's gone, but the place—the picture of it—stays, and not just in my rememory, but out there, in the world" (36). The peculiar quality of "rememory," as Michaels points out, is that it has a reality independent of one's memory of it and thus poses as a danger for those who were witnesses to or victims of the event that is being "rememoried." Michaels finds this conception dubious because "slavery needn't be part of your memory in order to be remembered by you" (*Shape* 136). For Michaels, this becomes the logic by which Morrison can portray slavery as a living memory that is still part of her living history. He calls this a "racial memory" because, presumably, only blacks were slaves in America (actually, some Indians were made slaves too) and thus the racial memory is available only to contemporary African Americans to recall today as rememory. However, what *Absalom* suggests is that the rememory of slavery was not the experience merely of slaves but also of whites such as Quentin. *Absalom* may be a reactionary Southern history but this should not obscure the fact that the narrator-historians of *Absalom* are traumatized by their "rememory" of slavery within their community. They are so traumatized by slavery, or its communal rememory, that they blame its practice on the outsider, Sutpen, rather than on themselves. One could even argue that Quentin's suicide was his admission that his "rememory" of slavery was too much for him to bear. In any case, Morrison's concept of rememory is a deft reformulation of Faulkner's premise that the past is never really past and, as a consequence, the serenity of one's present is always at the risk of being destroyed by a living danger of one's past. "Rememory" is also Morrison's apt reformulation of Faulkner's narrative strategy of using endless plot repetitions with slight variations within a single story. Just as *Beloved* is a "rememory" of *Absalom*, so is Morrison's redeployment of Faulkner's narrative techniques a bid to reject his story.

It is no coincidence that Morrison's narrative appropriation of Faulkner focuses on a house. Symbolically, the house referred to in *Beloved* restores the one that burns down in *Absalom*. Morrison also reworks the symbolism of Judith Sutpen's famous "loom passage" in *Absalom* as the starting point for *Beloved*. I quoted the first part of the passage in Chapter 1 but left off before Judith addresses the question of how she will be remembered:

> And so maybe if you could go to someone, the stranger the better, and give them something—a scrap of paper—something, anything, it not to mean anything in itself and them not even to read it or keep it, not even bother to throw it away or destroy it, at least it would be something just because it would have happened, be remembered if only passing from one hand to another, one mind to another, and it would at least be a scratch, something that might make a mark on something that *was* once for the reason that it can die someday, while the block of stone cant be *is* because it can never become *was* because it cant ever die or perish. (101)

Judith's stunning speech offers a dream of history that is at odds with the understanding of memory and time that the novel elsewhere presents. In the first place, she imagines that her history can be known by strangers. If her identity is no longer a tangled string on a loom but "a scratch"—a mark on paper and therefore knowable to others who come after her—then she can be known by someone outside the family. Her identity may take on a new form; instead of being known only in terms of how she relates to someone else, she can come undone from her implication in others' lives and histories. Scratches on paper may last longer than scratches on stone because they are not as subject to the elements of wind, sun, and rain. To Judith, paper can tell a history that is separate from the past and therefore "was," whereas inscriptions on marble absorb the present into the past and your history remains an unending "is." Yet in *Absalom* Judith's history must yield to that of Quentin, Rosa, and Sutpen: no stranger will tell her story, unless it is Shreve, who can know it only through Quentin. Morrison will not tell Judith's story either. However, Judith's wish to be rescued by someone outside her story's frame is precisely what

Morrison hopes to do for Clytemnestra and the other black female characters in Faulkner.

The "block of stone" to which Judith refers dominates *Absalom* and is the point of departure for *Beloved*. In *Absalom* the image of the graveside marble headstone is in its way as important as Sutpen's mansion. Sutpen has shipped from Europe the tombstones that will mark his and Ellen's graves. He then drags them around on his own from battle to battle during the War. Later, Quentin and his father stand in the Sutpen family cemetery contemplating their graven images for pages and pages; and then there is the recounting of the stories of how those headstones came to be there through the unstinting labors of Judith and Clytemnestra. *Beloved*, too, revolves around the image of a headstone on which is marked the title of the novel and the name of Sethe's slain daughter. Its history is not so grand. In exchange for ten minutes of sex with Sethe, a mason carves "Beloved" on the stone. Sethe wonders whether if she had given the mason "a half hour, say," she "could have had the whole thing, every word she heard the preacher say at the funeral" (5). Instead, her daughter's name on the stone is incomplete ("Dearly" is the unspoken part of her name), and thus so is her symbolic remembrance. The novel will complete this unfulfilled gesture of remembrance. The ideal audience the novel addresses is gathered to put to rest (or to pass on) Beloved's legacy. In this sense, *Beloved* seeks the past to create a context for understanding the present and then moving on.

Ostensibly, the novel depicts the story of Beloved's unrepressed return to Sethe and the mother's reluctance to surrender even the ghost of the child she murdered. On a deeper level, the novel is an act of memory and love for the child who could not live for her story to be told but whose "rememory" continues to animate those who would recall Beloved's presence in the world. From this perspective, *Beloved* is a defiant, not altogether postmodern, expression of the belief that history cannot be destroyed—cannot be told or written away. As a history that responds specifically to *Absalom*, though, the work seeks to answer Judith's plea by putting the past in the way that a funeral address should. To be put to rest, "Beloved" must be called; to say the word *Beloved* is to recall the past for an audience who wishes to make it dear (to themselves). But when her full, unspoken name, "Dearly Beloved," is spoken, the summons for one to return becomes a call for many to gather. The writing on the tombstone, the eternal "is" that names the dead child who haunts Sethe, calls out to passing strangers who have been unable to hear its cry because her name cannot truly speak for itself. Eventually, the scratches on the tombstone will become the letters that name Morrison's history, *Beloved*.

Judith's tombstone has no life in *Beloved* except as metaphor. In *Absalom* it is Clytemnestra who must make sure that Judith's grave has a headstone and that the grave is among the others whose lives defined her: the "scratch" that is her name will be obliterated by the elements. Morrison's characters, though, bury not their owners but their own. Clytemnestra, in fact, pays (with the help of Quentin's grandfather) her own money to make sure that Judith is properly buried—an act that is rewritten by Morrison into Sethe's more tortured burial of her own child. Clytemnestra's extraordinary efforts to bury her half sister carry the suggestion that Clytemnestra should be seen as the Sutpen who remains to preserve the family story. Like Sethe, though, she will kill a member of her own family—her white half brother, Henry. Arguably, Clytemnestra would end the Sutpen story herself by burning down the Sutpen mansion. Ultimately, Quentin, not Clytemnestra, will be the one who gets to shape the communal memory of the Sutpen story. This story includes the story of Clytemnestra's suicide, which, in an eerie sense, is a mirror version of Quentin's own suicide. The image of Clytemnestra looking out the window frames the beginning and end of *Absalom*. In the first chapter, Clytemnestra stares with Judith at Henry/Sutpen fighting the slaves. In the last chapter, Clytemnestra is looking out the window as the house burns—as if she were casting judgment on the story Quentin tells, thinking that it is about him and not her. The possibility that Clytemnestra might have a story to tell, or could offer some reflection on the history that brought her to this act, is one that Faulkner raises but represses. Instead, he sends Jim Bond howling like an idiot into a present that Shreve names as the future. "So in a few thousand years," he tells Quentin, "I who regard you will also have sprung from the loins of African kings" (302). This is precisely the future history that Quentin refuses to join and the history that Shreve and Quentin conclude that Sutpen has rejected.

Morrison, however, will answer Bond's howl and Shreve's mocking challenge through a reimagined Clytemnestra. In Sethe's account of "rememory," the burning house is an image of the past as past in an old-fashioned historical sense; it is something that exists independent of one's perception of it and cannot be destroyed. It "stays, and not just in my rememory, but out there, in the world" (36). Quentin's suicide resulted from his inability to escape the past; as history, it was a desire for the present to remain forever as it is. Quentin did not want Sutpen's "burning house" to remain in the world; he wanted to take its image with him. Therefore, to undo *Absalom*'s history, Morrison's "rememory" of Faulkner's burning house must reclaim that house as the possession of those who gather to bury "Beloved." This includes Morrison's readers as surely as it does the characters that are led by Ella—she who "didn't like the idea of past errors taking possession of the present" (256). Morrison's "rememory" of *Absalom* addresses Faulkner's idea that the present can be known only as a repetition of the past with a quasi-postmodern orientation toward history. On one hand, she imagines that the ancestor can be recovered. On the other hand, the search for the ancestor transforms the seeker's understanding of the present. Thus, the past renews and transforms—even if its truth is unchanging and, in a sense, impossible to hold as one would an object. Morrison revises Faulkner by suggesting that the present can remake the past as *something other than what it was* (or what Faulkner claimed it was in *Absalom*). Such a view is impossible in Faulkner's world but absolutely necessary if Morrison is to deliver to the present an African American history that is estranged from the one Faulkner imagined.

Unquestionably, *Beloved* is about possession and repossession, about being held in bondage to the past, and about mastering one's own bondage until it is transformed into freedom. "Freeing yourself was one thing," observes Morrison's narrator, "claiming ownership of that freed self was another" (95). Every major character in the novel—Sethe, Baby Suggs, Paul D Garner, Stamp Paid, Ella—confronts the difficulty of extricating one's self from another's past. To be possessed by the past is to be owned by those who own the past. Well after he has become a free man, Paul D will recall that his idea of being an independent man derives from the man who once owned him. Can Paul D ever truly be a man if he learned to be a man as a slave?[13] When Sethe is raped by Schoolteacher's proxies—"students" conducting a science experiment—there is the sense that a rememory of an inescapable past will become this event's persistent legacy. Its rememory is certainly behind Sethe's murder of Beloved and thus behind the novel's notion of the past as insatiable ghost devouring the present. Schoolteacher's proxies' rape of Sethe is the searing and perfect image of how slavery remains with us even today, a rememory that cannot be lost as long as the effects of its violation remain evident. Faulkner did not tell the reader how and with whom Sutpen engendered Clytemnestra. Instead of portraying the rape of Clytemnestra's mother or the image of Clytemnestra burning down slavery's mansion, Morrison portrays Sethe as the great fecund black female body being ravaged by insatiable white boys at the behest of another patriarchal figure, Schoolteacher. Their violation will engender no child; instead, it deprives Sethe of her mother's milk and thus her children of their nourishment. As awful as Schoolteacher is, he evokes Faulkner as the artist of Sethe's debasement who is writing her history as an animal.

That Sethe's rape can become a paralyzing, inescapable rememory can be seen in that Sethe's husband, Halle Suggs, is presumably destroyed simply by witnessing it. His view is never known because he, like Quentin contemplating the Old South, never leaves this moment. "Last time I saw him," Paul D tells Sethe, "he was sitting by the churn. Had butter all over his face" (69). Morrison suspends Halle's story at the point where he saw his wife being raped to suggest how psychologically paralyzing the experience of slavery could be as well the remarkable strength required to overcome its constant degradation. Stamp Paid suffers an experience similar to Halle's, when he must confront the fact that the slave master is sleeping with his wife. Neither he nor his wife can talk about it without jeopardizing their love for each other. Stamp, though, will endure, guide others to freedom, and eventually help rescue Denver and Sethe from the ghost of Beloved. Halle will not. Halle is an ironic critique of Ellison's *Invisible Man* and the upward-bound optimism of Frederick Douglass's first autobiography. Neither of these archetypal narrators of African American literature suffers from rememory. For them, the past is the place you left on your way to the happier future.

In *Beloved*, Sethe, not her husband, escapes Sweet Home. Briefly, she seems to possess the self that slavery denied her in exactly the way Douglass might have implied. Because she is a figure for a communal history, her success cannot include only herself. Understanding the slaves' journey into freedom as an essentially individual journey distorts the experience of the slaves—the majority—whose journey could not have mirrored that of Douglass. This "individual" story of Douglass or Ellison also distorts the future, since it fairly obliterates the fact that the slaves' flight to freedom was a *collective* experience and that their history would have to be shared even after each was individually free. The freed slaves never fit into the free-market American paradigm in which entrepreneurs could work their way up the ladder of American success. The future for the freed slaves would continue the logic of slavery insofar as African Americans would be grouped as a type of American subclass dependent on the rise of other groups (first, post–Civil War European immigrants and, more recently, Asian immigrants) for what meager share of American wealth trickled down to them. Sethe's journey contrasts with that of Douglass or with that of Ellison's invisible man and better represents African American life in postmodern America, because she is neither allowed to shed her past nor able to be true to her people by succeeding alone (even if that were a possibility for her).14

As an escaped slave, Sethe carries with her literally her past and her future (in her womb). Here Sethe explains to Paul D how her journey was inconceivable without the knowledge that she was bringing others with her:

> I did it. I got us all out. Without Halle too. Up till then it was the only thing I ever did on my own. Decided. And it came off right, like it was supposed to. We was here. Each and every one of my babies and me too. I birthed them and I got them out and it wasn't no accident. I did that. (162)

For Douglass or for Ellison's invisible man, self-reliance comes by virtue of his escape; for Sethe, escape comes by virtue of her self-reliance. Above and beyond running away to some hoped-for sanctuary, Sethe must *herself* be a place of sanctuary. "I was big, Paul D, and deep and wide and when I stretched out my arms all my children could get in between" (162). In a way she never could before, she claims her children *as hers*. She brings her future with her, and her escape recalls Douglass only insofar as the future can be assumed to replace the past. However, the past returns to her in the form of Schoolteacher's deputies. Rather than see her future—her children—absorbed again as the repetition of her past (as a typical Faulkner character would), she tries to kill it. She surrenders to what she thought she escaped.

This twenty-eight-day period of safety is crucial to Morrison's history. It represents a dream-idyll during which Sethe seems to be able to transcend her history. For Morrison, however, no such transcendence is possible without time and the communal work of rememory. To reinforce this point, Morrison underscores the fact that the slave catchers capture Sethe because of a lapse on the part of the community of former slaves. Instead of looking out for her inevitable pursuer, whom they all know to be coming, they are attending a feast given by Sethe and her mother-in-law, Baby Suggs. The purpose of this feast mirrors the purpose of Morrison's history: to re-member—in the sense of putting back together—one's history as a collective experience that belongs to all. A successful re-memory will transform the shared experience of slavery into a shared history of communal affirmation. Of all the freed slaves in the book, Baby Suggs seems most able to re-create—or rememory—the formative communal experience shared while in slavery. This experience, or history, is the foundation of the African-American future. "We scattered," Baby Suggs tells Janey Wagon, "but maybe not for long" (143). Symbolic as the space where the bad part of their past can be cleared away, the Clearing marks the location where Baby Suggs tries to extricate from the past a perspective that might make a future. The mixture of joy and sorrow that Douglass heard in the slave songs receives pure expression in the dancing, crying, and laughing women, children, and men who gather to hear Baby Suggs offer "up to them her great big heart." In the Clearing, Baby Suggs gives the sermon of what we might call the Church of the Freed Slave:

> We flesh; flesh that weeps, laughs; flesh that dances on bare feet in the grass. Love it. Love it hard. Yonder they do not love your flesh. They despise it. . . . And O my people they do not love your hands. They only use, tie, bind, chop off and leave empty. Love your hands! Love them. (88)

Baby Suggs urges the members of her community to take possession of themselves, and this possession begins with the body that once belonged to a slave owner. Morrison suggests that for the slaves it was most likely easier to imagine themselves free in spirit than in flesh, since the slave owners were more interested in the slaves' bodies than they were in their minds, which could not yield crops and could only be a source of potential resistance. If the name "the Clearing" suggests that old torments are being swept away, then what Baby Suggs clears away is not the past but the forces that have blocked the way to that part of the past, which the community needs to sustain itself as a community.[15]

Baby Suggs could easily have been the focus of this novel. She too goes from slavery to freedom, but her freedom is purchased for her by her son. Instead, Morrison suggests that her community was not ready for Baby Suggs's message. The community is less moved by Baby Suggs's eloquence than by the suspicion that the feast that she and Beloved offer is too bountiful: "Too much, they thought. Where does she get it all, Baby Suggs, holy? Why is she and hers always the center of things?" (137). The problem is not that Sethe and Baby Suggs have too much but that they have claimed too much for themselves too soon. The slave catcher sneaks up on them because the community has not yet repossessed its past, and the people's jealously of the "holy" Baby Suggs indicates this failure. Baby Suggs and Sethe understand the power of what they have carried with them—what they will keep as theirs. A past with so much unacknowledged pain cannot be jettisoned so easily—even when confronted with courage and beautiful words. Rather than give her history to Schoolteacher, Sethe will symbolically kill it and her future too. This act is also too much for the community, but symbolically her act will clear (remember she is situated in the Clearing) the fog that prevents them from connecting their present to their past. Sethe does not mean to kill a future that excludes slavery; she means only to kill slavery itself. Insofar as she goes to jail and her living children are not returned to slavery, her act is successful. To the community, though, Sethe is a pariah because she has acted out their own most cherished, most repressed desire. Provisionally, they will accept as valid the white newspaper accounts of Sethe's murder of Beloved (as if accepting *Absalom*'s word as true) instead of seeing her act as a reflection on their common experience. Stamp will even show these clippings to Paul D to dissuade him from loving Sethe. Replicating Schoolteacher's history and thus showing how hard it is to escape, Paul D will do as the whites would and label Sethe a four-footed creature (165).

To survive as part of a healthy community, Sethe and the other slaves who make the crossing into freedom must bring with them the resilience that they used to survive the Sweet Home slavery.[16] In a sense, they are their own ancestors. In the scene last quoted, Sethe tries to explain this idea to Paul D in justifying why she killed her child. Signifying upon Douglass's famous image of the circle, Morrison describes Sethe as "circling, circling" her subject. In so doing, Sethe tries to describe how she imagined her free self could be part of her slave self. "Sethe knew that the circle she was making around the room, him, the subject, would remain one. That she never could close it in, pin it down for anyone who had to ask" (162–63). Sethe has no conception of what it means to abandon the self that she made while she was a slave. Without the resilience that she found as a slave, Sethe could not have experienced the joy of bringing her children over into freedom. Yet without experiencing the twenty-eight-day joy of being her own sanctuary, Sethe would have had neither the strength nor the vision to murder her children when the slave catchers came. These overlapping circles of identity, slave and free, prompt her to the terrible moment where, borrowing Morrison's words again, "the best thing that is in us is also the thing that makes us sabotage ourselves." How can she separate the past that is hers from the past that includes the evil Schoolteacher, since she cannot kill one past without killing the other?

When Beloved returns to Sethe, she does so as the material incarnation of Sethe's rememory. At first Beloved's return seems joyful—the happy reunion of mother and child that returns the mother to her true self. Speaking in an eerie sing-song voice that seems to be beyond language, Beloved prompts Sethe to remember aspects of herself that she had forgotten. She helps Sethe forget what had become each day's primary chore: "the day's serious work of beating back the past" (73). Beloved's fingers are "cool and knowing" and through them Sethe feels "the anguish rolled down" (97). She remembers that her mother did not have enough milk to feed her, and this reminds her of when her breast milk was stolen. "I know what it is to be without the milk that belongs to you; to have to fight and holler for it, and to have so little left. I'll tell Beloved that; she understand. She my daughter" (200). Gradually, though, the past comes back as a desire for death. "When I put that headstone up," Sethe apostrophizes Beloved, "I wanted to lay in there with you, put your head on my shoulder and keep you warm" (204). Beloved's return not only makes this wish come true but also threatens to become the moment that Sethe can never escape.

Instead of possessing herself, Sethe and her "freedom" are possessed by the past. Sethe's murder of her child is to *Beloved* what Henry Sutpen's murder of Charles Bon is to *Absalom*. Sethe can no more escape that fatal moment than Quentin can escape Henry's fatal act. Thus, both Sethe and Quentin fall in love with the past and fall into it as Narcissus fell into his own reflection. Sethe is misguided, though, to think that Beloved is her child. Her child is dead, unnamed while living, and presumably unresurrected in death. To be sure, Sethe "knew death as anything but forgetfulness," but this is a function of her rememory not of the ghost of her daughter. Instead, Beloved is the ghost of a collective memory. As Sethe's daughter, Beloved represents Sethe's specific experience of slavery, but Sethe's experience and haunting are singular to her. Theoretically, Morrison could have invented different episodes specific to another character's experience of slavery. Sethe's history rather than that of others is chosen as emblematic because her act of repudiating the experience of slavery is the strongest imaginable. The "dismemberment" from each other and from themselves that the other former slaves feel Sethe makes explicit by dismembering her family.

In this way, Sethe, like Oedipus, is a tragic figure who is burdened with the knowledge that the community cannot confront. This communal knowledge is rooted in "the mark" that she inherits from her mother that has been passed, through Beloved, to her (and perhaps through her to Beloved as well). Sethe's fate is to carry with her the history of this mark's meaning. Indeed, she must act out its history in the horrible murder of her daughter. Not coincidentally,

Beloved's return prompts Sethe's rememory of her first encounter with the mark. In this crucial passage, Sethe tells Denver and Beloved the buried story of her inheritance:

> One thing she did do. She picked me up and carried me behind the smoke-house. Back there she opened up her dress front and lifted her breast and pointed under it. Right on her rib was a circle and a cross burnt right in the skin. She said, "This is your ma'am. This," and she pointed. "I am the only one who got this mark now. The rest dead. If something happens to me and you can't tell me by my face, you can know me by my mark." (61)

This mark has several different meanings, all of them interrelated. First, it is the sign by which Sethe's mother's captor tried to fix her identity as a slave. As such, it represents the suppression, or at least the distortion, of her African identity. Yet this fixed meaning is unfixed by the marked person herself, because she takes possession of the meaning of the mark. She has earned the right to be known by this mark, since she is the only one of her group to have survived its imprint on her person. Her lesson to her daughter, Sethe, is that you are more than a piece of property; you are a self, capable of owning your own desires.[17] But that self is known only through the mark, which is at once a version of her own self-individuation and the means through which she knows herself to be connected with her ancestors. For *Beloved*'s African American readers, the story of the mark may become a way for the community to know and affirm its story. This reading best contradicts the historical mark of *Absalom*, where slaves, in effect, remain slaves even after Lincoln. [18]

What Sethe learns of her mother's children creates a less complicated genealogy than any in Faulkner's books. Where Faulkner makes the issue of miscegenation central to *Absalom, Absalom!*, Morrison dramatically dismissed it in *Beloved*. Nan tells Sethe that her mother threw away children who were the product of rape by the white man. "She threw them all away but you. The one from the crew she threw away on the island. The others from more whites she also threw away. Without names, she threw them. You she gave the name of the black man. She put her arms around him" (62). Still, even if her mother did not have to be raped by a white man for her to be born, Sethe cannot escape her enslavement by white people. In *Absalom*, Clytemnestra's black mother is not given a name—she is introduced as a necessary afterthought. (Telling Quentin that Clytie was Sutpen's daughter too, Quentin's father offhandedly remarks, "Miss Rosa didn't tell you that two of the niggers in the wagon that day were women?" [48].) Presumably, she too is the product of a rape. Like Morrison, Faulkner was aware that the history of whites in the South is inextricable from the history of blacks, which is why the last surviving Sutpen is black. Indeed, Sutpen is portrayed as an ominous outsider to the community in part because the community cannot disassociate him from his wild slaves. He fights with them, and he speaks their strange tongue. He owes his "design" and thus his history to the "nigger" who showed him his place through the mansion's backdoor. *Absalom* attributes tremendous power to blacks to shape and create white identity. However, that very power is a product of the whites' fear of them. Their blackness does not have to be an essential, determining fact, even if for *Absalom* Bon's blackness is the determining fact of the narrative, the only fact that the narrators cannot or will not explain away.

Thus, one could argue that *Beloved* strives for a "pure" African American history, except that Morrison knows that a pure black identity is as unlikely to be fulfilled as Quentin's wish that history cease with him. However, Morrison does not think that Quentin's history can be overcome without the recognition that African American history persists (as Michaels acknowledges) through the re-creation of the experience of slavery. Morrison, I suspect, rejects not the obvious historical reality of miscegenation but Faulkner's portrayal of it. For Faulkner, the representation of miscegenation revealed the white man's folly—his helpless desire for those he had enslaved. Whites procreating with blacks remained somehow a story about white people—about white power, white guilt, white despair, and so forth. By rejecting Faulkner's miscegenation frame, Morrison takes authorship of the history of African Americans since slavery and writes for a community of readers untroubled by how "black" their story may be. Her most powerful and subtlest presentation of this narrative aim occurs in the story of Paul D's escape from the chain gang in Georgia. Technically, Paul D is no longer a slave, but the chains of slavery have become the shackles of the chain gang. For all practical purposes, his status has not changed at all. Paul D reflects that even as a prisoner (or a slave) the pleasure of listening to the doves was denied him, since he had "neither the right nor the permission to enjoy it because in that place mist, doves, sunlight, copper, dirt, moon—everything belonged to the men who had the guns" (162). Yet one thing does belong to Paul D, and that is the experience that he shares with the other prisoners, the feeling that they know from being chained to one another, hand by hand, link by link. Together they "sang it out and beat it up, garbling the words so they could not be understood; tricking the words so their syllables yielded up other meanings. They sang…of pork in the woods, meal in the pan; fish on the line; cane, rain, and rocking chairs" (108). Like Sethe's mother with her mark, Morrison's singing prisoners create an identity separate from their imprisonment, one that enables them to survive their imprisonment.

Although each prisoner is locked within his own box, collectively they are still chained to one another, a group. When rain pours down, filling up each cubicle with water, there is the possibility that each man will drown—alone. Suddenly, "somebody yank[s] the chain," the prisoners move as one, burrowing under the mud, and arrive safe outside their imprisoning box. "For one lost, all lost. The chain that held them would save all or none" (110). Locked in his makeshift cell, Paul D can feel only the terrible burden of his own ego. Within that cell there is no relief, except what he can draw from those to whom he is attached. Yet the terrible irony is that Paul D and the other prisoners free themselves by breaking the bond that has sustained them: they cut their chains in order to escape. Ironically, freedom only returns each one to the prison of his cell. Isolated, Paul D's postslavery self is symbolized by the rusty tobacco tin that he carries with him, a memento of the prison that he now carries within. One can imagine him a version of the grieving Lucas Beauchamp in Faulkner's "Pantaloon in Black."

Ultimately, in *Beloved*, the future must do the work of absorbing the past. This work is hopefully attributed to Denver, who initiates the community action that results in Beloved's expulsion. Denver will be a teacher and, presumably, work to overturn the vicious lessons of the Sweet Home Schoolteacher—although it is unlikely that she will be doing it in classrooms where Faulkner's white literary descendants will attend. Denver is also receptive to the affirmation of self that Baby Suggs precipitously offered. Her courage would be impossible without Baby Suggs, who reminds Denver of her heritage and tells her, "Know it, and go out in the yard. Go on" (244). The novel, however, seems to offer Denver's promise more as a defensive hope than a hard-earned reality. Certainly, the book's ambiguous epilogue undermines any sense of genuine hope that the past has been reclaimed and the present has been made safe. When we last see Beloved, she is pregnant. Morrison has said that the dedication, "Sixty Million and more," refers to slavery's dead, who go on re-creating even in death. Beloved is pregnant with the memories that Morrison would have her audience know and dismiss. Beloved represents the idea that history, or a past, exists, even if you do not know it. This past cannot be made up to suit the needs of the present. We are told in the epilogue that down at 124 Bluestone

Road Beloved's "footprints come and go, come and go." Although "they forgot her like an unpleasant dream during a troubling sleep," Beloved lives still even if she cannot be seen or registered cognitively. Thus, she "is not the breath of the disremembered and unaccounted for, but wind in the eaves, or spring ice thawing too quickly. Just weather. Certainly no clamor for a kiss" (275). The weather is the atmosphere of rememory—the air through which rememories move and gather. The narrator says twice, "This was not a story to pass on," and once, "It was not a story to pass on." The story must be told so that it can be told as something else. On this reading, the community's forgetfulness is a triumph of postmodern history—a sign that its members may be able to accomplish what the Judith or Quentin in *Absalom* could not: to make themselves other from their past.[19] By a different reading, however, the past cannot be left behind; it travels with you and its rememory may trap you, as it seems to trap Sethe, in the chair where you sit.

III

In presenting Beloved's legacy, Morrison gives a more ambivalent interpretive turn to the dilemma that defines her other major Faulknerian novel, *Song of Solomon*. The protagonist of *Song*, Milkman Dead, like Sethe, suffers from an abiding emptiness that is a consequence of having been cut off from a meaningful relationship with his past, or ancestors. The family name, Dead, is bluntly symbolic. Milkman is Morrison's version of one of Faulkner's Northern blacks lost from the "Sweet Home" of the South. The past holds more for him that the present, but can its lessons be captured and then used? His father, Macon, has given himself over to the pursuit of conventional bourgeois American success; his financial success as a landlord comes at the expense of poor blacks. Macon Dead fulfills Morrison's version of the American Dream as the dubious promise of individual fulfillment that comes at the African American community's expense.[20] Like *Beloved*, *Song* imagines the past as something that can be recovered. It is there, whether or not you know it. To be severed from the past, or knowledge of it, is to be dead. To discover the past is not only to find an identity that you may not have known you had; it is also to be born as if for the first time. *Song* is what Robert Stepto calls a "descent" narrative, in that Milkman's quest for identity moves directionally opposite to the classic slave narrative: He journeys from North (Detroit) to South (Virginia), where his past remains to be found. Once there, Milkman decides that "All that business about southern hospitality was for real." In fact, "he wondered why black people ever left the South" (260). Ostensibly on the vulgar quest for lost gold, Milkman finds, instead, the animating spirit of what has made him who he is (and is not): the secret of the bones that his aunt Pilate Dead carries with her (actually the remains of Macon's paternal grandfather); the mythological Circe who, like Clytemnestra, guards the *Absalom*-like mansion that might have been his; and, most profoundly, Solomon, or Shalimar, the ancestor who magically leaps from the South to fly home to Africa.

As he is traveling South toward Circe, Milkman wonders about the word *people* and the contexts in which he has heard the word spoken. He knows that the word has a special, coded meaning. "All his life he'd heard the tremor in the word: "I live here, but my *people* . . ." or "She acts like she ain't got no *people*" or "Do any of your *people* live there? But he hadn't known what it meant: links" (229). As the character that links Milkman to his history and to his family, Circe is another version of Pilate and a key link to discovering his true relationship with his "people." As Wahneema Lubiano notes, "Pilate 'teaches' Milkman to read history" and thus "represents not only embodied history but the praxis that comes with recognizing history's effects" (113). Finding Circe allows Milkman to understand the role that Pilate has been performing in keeping the ancestors alive. Whereas his father exploits poor blacks for social position, Pilate carries in her jewelry the slip of paper on which her name was first written. She also carries her father's bones wherever she goes, but she does not know whose bones they are. More than Pilate, though, Circe is a semidivine figure living on past death, who is the keeper of the authenticity of the past. Circe is the one who will help Milkman determine that the bones that Pilate preserves are his grandfather's. Her memory of the past will enable him to learn that his grandmother is named "Sing" and that thus the injunction to "sing" that Pilate has heard from ghosts [her father] has been a call for Pilate and later Milkman to reconnect themselves with the ancestral past from which they have been separated. The identity of Sing is a key to finding Solomon, whose song Milkman follows and which also names the novel: "Jay the only son of Solomon / Come booba yalle, come boobe tambee," one version goes (264). Throughout his journey through the South, Milkman hears versions of this song sung by children who may or may not know something of its origin; the implication is, however, that the song connects all of them to a shared ancestor. As Milkman puts together the clues to his past, he is described as never having been so happy.

Circe does not know all of these details, but without her Milkman's quest would be incomplete. When confronting the rage-filled Guitar Bains at the end of the novel, he would not have known what his ancestor Shalimar, or Solomon, knew: "If you surrendered to the air, you could ride it" (337). With this knowledge Milkman can, like Solomon running in reverse historical time, jump out of his slave-inherited identity and ride all the way back to Africa. Circe, like the Circe that Homer's Odysseus encounters, is unable to use her magical powers to achieve her own desires. She remains trapped on her island, in this case the mansion where she served the white family who killed Milkman's grandfather and converted the Deads' land into their own. The truer literary precursor for Circe is not Homer's unhappy goddess, though, but Faulkner's Clytemnestra. Like Clytie, Circe seems doomed to live in and look after her white master's house until the end of her days. Faulkner's Clytie, though, is Sutpen's daughter and thus has a family connection to the house. Morrison does not reveal her Circe's family history—she seems to have been autochthonous. Circe's family connection, if she can be said to have one, is to look after the land that was to be "Lincoln's Heaven. "Why did black people ever leave the South?" is the book's recurring question. Through Circe, Milkman learns the answer: because they were driven off. Circe, however, holds her post and this makes her an ambiguous character. She saves Macon and Pilate from their would-be murderers while she serves the white usurpers, but her true role is as proprietress of their history. She is a version of Morrison the historian.

In *Absalom, Absalom!* Faulkner refused to confront the narrative implications of having Clytie be the one who burns down the family mansion. The fact that her story was embedded in Sutpen's story—indeed, the fact that her story went back not only through Sutpen but through the "wild niggers" he brought with him from Haiti—did not concern Faulkner (although he was too good a historian to leave it out). Her destruction of the mansion was a final gesture of protection to those whom she served, even a gesture of protection to her, in effect, murdered Henry, the murderer of Charles Bon. In *Song*, Morrison's Clytie serves the Butler family but she does not love them. She is their servant, not their kin. Although her account of the furnishings of the house recalls how Sutpen furnished his home for Ellen (the family goes to Europe, where they buy "pink veined marble from across the sea for it," just as Sutpen acquired marble across the sea for his and his wife's tombstones), her intention is to distance herself from any history that is shared with the Butlers. Thus, she pointedly tells Milkman that the last living Butler, her mistress, commited suicide rather than live on in a kind of shared equality with her servant:

> She saw the work I did all her days and *died*, you hear me, *died* rather than live like me. Now, what do you suppose she thought I was! If the way I lived and the work I did was so hateful to her she killed herself to keep from having to do it, and you think I stay on here because I loved her, then you have about as much sense as a fart! (247)

Morrison's Clytie is no suicide victim. Her account has a satisfying moral clarity absent in Faulkner. Sutpen's mansion decays as a result of the Civil War, a decay that becomes irreversible during Reconstruction. The Butlers, by contrast, rob Lincoln's Heaven from the Dead family but die out anyway. In *Absalom*, Clytie and Judith live on almost as sisters (although Clytie is really Judith's half sister) and together share the burden of raising Bon's son and grandson. Clytie and Judith share an intimacy implied by no other characters in the book (with the possible exception of Henry and Bon).

Racial difference in *Absalom* does not forbid love between white people and black people; rather, the narrative forbids acknowledging such love. Morrison, however, refuses to portray this intimacy between the races. She seeks, instead, the expression of love between black people. For Morrison, the legacy of slavery is not only that white people must acknowledge their complicity in robbing African Americans of their history and their identity but that African Americans must confront and address the division, or wound, suffered by the African American body, or community, as a consequence of having been robbed of their story. Her works confront how knowledge of this ancestor is lost, but not permanently, and how learning about the connection to a specific ancestor creates a wholeness of self denied to those who live in ignorance of the past. Guitar's shooting of Milkman is an ambiguous image of this quest. Tellingly, the Butlers' story is only implied. The point that Circe makes is that her mistress is neither Judith Sutpen nor Scarlett O'Hara. Whereas Faulkner's Judith cares for her lover's black offspring, Morrison's Judith is helpless, not strong, and doomed to die at her own hand for her family's failure to realize its ambition.

Morrison replaces Faulkner's ambiguity with moral anger. The Butler woman thus suffers Quentin's fate but without his atmosphere of poetry or noble suffering. Milkman will be liberated by his discovery of his past, but he will not live beyond his rediscovery of his heritage. Explaining his mission to Circe, Milkman says that he has returned to the South to see whether anything remains from his father's and his aunt's experience in the cave. Circe praises him for his seeming veneration of the ancestors. She tells him that this is "a thought worth having," since "the dead don't like it if they're not buried" (245). Although Milkman was lying to Circe, in the end her words will more truly characterize his journey. Ironically, the reason for his journey is not that different from the motivation that he believes to explain his father's coldness. He wants gold. Morrison constructs the story so that the gold he seeks is a version of his grandfather's bones—the reader understands that what he seeks is self-sufficiency, something that Morrison imagines can be achieved by claiming your history rather than by achieving wealth. However, when Milkman confronts Guitar and is presumably murdered at the end of the book, questions remain. Is veneration of the ancestors really a version of a person's own death? Can the discovery of the ancestors salvage the present? When Milkman flies like Solomon away from death, what is his destination? Africa? To whom does the present belong? Is the Reverend Mr.Cooper right to tell Milkman that the Butlers are "dead now" because "things work out, son" (232)?

We might argue that Milkman's meeting with Guitar at the end of the novel is a confrontation between the living dead, Guitar, and the formerly dead now resurrected. Guitar, so much more attuned than Milkman to the historical context of being black, has tried to get revenge by matching hate with hate. His organization, the Seven Days, is dedicated to answering as fully as possible each white person's murder of a black person with its own murder of a white person by a black person. Morrison sympathizes with Guitar's rage but does not countenance it, since Guitar ultimately turns against Milkman (a version of Ellison's Battle Royal) and makes him a victim of Guitar's self-fulfilling prophecy that everyone wants a black man dead, even other black men. Yet another character suggests that Guitar's vengeance is merely a form of God's work. The Reverend Cooper assures Milkman that the death of the Butler family was holy retribution for what they did to his family. "The ways of God are mysterious," says the Reverend, "but if you live it out, just live it out, you see that it always works out." I am not sure that we can say that Milkman's story works out. Although he gains a new appreciation of his father as a man who inspired respect and who, in his way, wanted Milkman to share his own story, he is also confronted with a lost legacy still unrealized. This lost future is articulated movingly in the now unsalvageable vision that his grandfather (Jake Dead) had for what was to be Lincoln's Heaven:

> We live here. On this planet, in this nation, in this country right here. No-where else! We got a home in this rock, don't you see! Nobody starving in my home, and if I got a home you got one too! Grab it! Grab this land! Take it, hold it, my brothers, make it, my brothers, shake it, squeeze it, turn it, beat it, kick it, whip it, stomp it, dig it, plow it, seed it, reap it, rent it, sell it, own it, build it, multiply it, and pass it on—can you hear me? Pass it on!!! (235)

Pass it on: What is there for Milkman to pass on in the moment of his death but the knowledge of a lost communal identity? Grandfather Jake knew everything that Milkman has lost, but still his story ended when "they shot the top of his head off and ate his fine Georgia peaches" (235). Does Milkman's knowledge of his inheritance protect him from Guitar's bullet?

At the end of *Song of Solomon*, Morrison places Milkman's name among other actual historical figures of African American expression: "Muddy Waters, Pinetop, Jelly Roll, Fats, Leadbelly, Bo Diddley, Cat-Iron, Peg-Leg, Son, Short-stuff, Smoky Babe, Funny Papa, Bukka, Pink, Bull Moose, B. B., T-Bone, Black Ace, Lemon," leading all the way up to "*Dat Nigger*" (330).[21] The book begins with the problem of naming. "Not Doctor Street" is not only the black commu-nity's ironic commentary on the white community's concerted efforts to deny them a place of their own, but also a symbolic way of protecting themselves. This list of names at the novel's end is a celebration of African Americans who named themselves and claimed the world according to their own version of it. Certainly, they also stand as expressions of Morrison's commitment to the endurance of the African American folk tradition. *Beloved*, she says, aspires "to be both print and oral literature" ("Rootedness" 341). "It should deliberately make you stand up and make you feel something profoundly in the same way that a Black preacher requires his congregation to speak, to join him in the sermon, to believe in a certain way, to stand up and to weep and to cry" (341).

Sethe cannot hear such a roaring at the end of *Beloved*. *Song of Solomon* re-names Faulkner and in the process hopes to initiate a history that is alternative to the one that he inscribed. Whether Morrison's *Song* incites in her audience the same reaction that she attributes to the folk figures and mythical black preachers is open to question. Like Faulkner, hers is a poetics of memory and thus only partially postmodern. *Song of Solomon* denies *Absalom*, but is the future of her black characters really that different from the one that Faulkner implies? What alternative to the life of Macon Dead is there for contemporary African Americans? These works can be characterized as "postmodern" in that they suggest that history for Morrison is not final. Morrison leaves it to her readers to transform her characters' stories into something better for themselves. Certainly, Morrison seeks and celebrates the viability of a living African American culture, best expressed in *Song* through the game songs that the children sing that go all the way back to Africa. Yet the book's conclusion can also be taken to suggest that the postslavery African American is, as it were, born dead. Circe cannot leave the mansion and virtually everyone in the book seems to be dead or dying. From this perspective, *Song* seems more like a novel than a postmodern history.

Song ends with Milkman's flight to the ancestor; *Beloved* does not erase the suspicion that the descendants have killed their own ancestor. This is why Morrison's history is never quite as triumphant—even when singing an African American song—as Ellison's *Invisible Man*. In *Beloved* the community casts Sethe out and then takes her in again. Sethe is a figure of awe and dread because she both kills and gives birth to the ancestor that is the enabling figure for Morrison's fiction and her imaginary community. In *Song* the ancestor may be unreachable. As we have seen, Morrison says, "When you kill the ancestor, you kill yourself" (344). Sethe has both killed and birthed their ancestor—which may make her a sacred figure. As Morrison told Naylor, she writes of a "woman who killed her children [because she] loved her children so much; they were the best part of her and she would not see them sullied" ("Interview" 584). Morrison's response to *Absalom* portrays Africans who became Americans as required to leave and thus kill their ancestors. They are then reconstituted as a community by the Middle Passage, but that community is broken when they are sold as slaves. The slave ship takes them from their homes; as slaves they are divided again, and then as "free" African Americans they are asked to abandon and forget their past.

This act is precisely what Sethe cannot accomplish and Milkman may fail to achieve. Like Faulkner, Morrison wonders whether the dead's claims on the present can be overcome. At best, Sethe and Milkman find that rediscovering the experience of slavery (and its aftermath) is the precondition for a meaningful engagement with the present—a chance to find an identity that cannot be defined as mere politics. However, both novels suggest that having been enslaved may not be as hard to endure as losing the communal bond created by slavery, since it seems to lead to either the alienation that defines the Dead family or the anger that drives Milkman's friend Guitar. In this respect, the tragic dilemma that Sethe suffers when she kills her children rather than have them returned to slavery, or Guitar's wish to avenge the deaths of innocent black children that leads him to murder Milkman as well, is the recurring threat to a healthy communal history that Morrison's work identifies and seeks to exorcise. It may be that Morrison is suggesting that as long as African American history remains tied to American history, the rememories of the past are too much to overcome. On this view, Morrison is not a postmodern historian at all but a tragic one who, as bleakly as Faulkner's Quentin, sees no way out of the present that the past has made. On another view, presumably the one that Morrison wants her African American readers to share, the continued search for the lost ancestor will culminate in a future that will be better than either the present or the past. With this future will come an understanding of history through which the group knows itself not as the abandoned property of another but as the continuation of and belief in the ancestor's authorizing presence.

The conclusion to *Beloved* finds Sethe in the same room that she had earlier declared, in the company of Beloved, to be the world. To Paul D's assurance, "You your best thing," Sethe responds with questions: "Me? Me?" (273). Morrison strands Sethe in order to embolden her audience. Sethe's question incites the reader to answer, "Yes," an affirmation that is self-directed rather than Sethe-directed. As such, *Beloved* rewrites the famous endings to *Invisible Man* and *Absalom, Absalom!* Ellison's novel ends with a question: "Who knows, but that on the lower frequencies, I speak for you?" (*Invisible* 572). There Ellison invites the audience to see themselves in his protagonist. Morrison, by contrast, challenges her readers to estrange themselves from the figure with whom they identify: to create a history different from the one that has entranced them. In this way the ending of *Beloved* answers Faulkner's conclusion to *Absalom* as well. Sethe, like Quentin, will probably remain trapped within her rememory. However, *Beloved*'s readers are asked to do as Paul D did with Sethe or as Denver did with Beloved: to invent histories that will allow them to move past the present (and the past) into the future. Sethe succumbs, but the reader should not. To Faulkner, Morrison seems to want to say, history is malleable, changeable like the weather. History is for the living, not for the dead.

4

Thomas Pynchon's *Mason & Dixon* Drawing a Line in the Sands of History

I should perhaps have thought the rest not worth preserving, but for their testimony against the only history of that period which pretends to have been compiled from authentic and unpublished documents. Could these documents, all, be laid open to the public eye, they might be compared, contrasted, weighed and the truth fairly lifted out of them, for we are not to suppose everything found among Genl. Washington's papers is to be taken as gospel truth. . . . With him were deposited suspicions & uncertainties, rumors and realities, facts and falsehoods. . . . From such a Congeries history may be made to wear any hue, with which the passions of the compiler, royalist or republican, may choose to tinge it.
—Thomas Jefferson

What is at issue, therefore, is how historians use documents not to establish discrete facts, but as evidence for establishing the larger patterns that connect them. Are these patterns, these connections already there waiting to be discovered by a neutral process of cognition, or do historians put them there themselves?
—Richard Evans, *In Defense of History*

History is a line we ourselves must rig up, to a past we ourselves must populate.
—David Harlan, *The Degradation of American History*

I

Thomas Pynchon's *Mason & Dixon* imagines an America other than the one we have inherited. Set in 1786 Philadelphia, on the eve of the writing of the U.S. Constitution, the 776-page text is an implausible one-night bedtime story told by an avowedly biased narrator, the Reverend Wicks Cherrycoke. In form and content, the book clearly parodies popular histories such as those written by Walter Isaacson, David McCullough, and Joseph Ellis in that it rejects the assumption that American history can be reduced to the tale of its founding by a handful of great and divinely inspired men. Replete with thousands of obscure facts and numerous impossible happenings in a kind of reductio ad absurdum of the logic of conventional historiographic practice, *Mason & Dixon* suggests that by 1786 U.S. history was already doomed to fail to fulfill its utopian dreams. The grid was mapped and the future already drawn.

The novel's apparent focus is the tale of the exploits of Charles Mason and Jeremiah Dixon, whose surveying work for William Penn and Lord Baltimore (Charles Calvert) resulted in the creation of the famous Mason-Dixon Line. Through these unlikely heroes, small cogs in an enormous historical wheel, Pynchon documents a shift in Euro-American thinking from belief in God to a belief in Science as the rationale for explaining and understanding the world and humans' place in it. In *Mason & Dixon* America is seen as the dream of seventeenth-century science wedded to post-Renaissance capitalist mercantilism. Pynchon illustrates how learning to plot and predict the turnings of the cosmos became a method for conquering the world as a rationalist endeavor. Within this context, the discovery and mapping of America becomes almost a secondary plot; thus, fewer than half the pages address the actual drawing of the Mason-Dixon Line.[1]

Pynchon also implicates history (and with it fiction) within a variety of other disciplines. In a sense, his book enacts the history of historiography that historians such as Robert Berkhofer, Richard Evans, and Keith Jenkins have described.[2] David Harlan worries that "there is no sense of urgency in American historical writing, no sense that we must use the books and ideas we have inherited from the past to put our own lives to the test" (*Degradation* xxxii). *Mason & Dixon*, by contrast, has this sense of urgency, perhaps because Pynchon already writes from a perspective that, according to Harlan, historians have yet to find: "the point where we no longer feel that if we cannot refute contemporary skepticism" and "all is lost, [as] history will slide into fiction" (xxxi). Pynchon's novel is history and historiography both, and it is perhaps the best answer available to the question of what a truly postmodernist history might be.[3] No work discussed in this study contains more historical "facts" or makes as comprehensive a use of historical research. Its methodology, though, is the decidedly postmodern one of "textualism" that Berkhofer defines as "fusing past and present" in a way that "unites history and historiography, in contrast to usual disciplinary practice" (22). I would venture to say that no other post-Faulkner writer so well exemplifies (and puts to scrutiny) Hayden White's point that history must be plotted to be known or so successfully points to how any given history might lead its readers to a vastly different conclusion if only it were plotted differently or subjected to a different methodology. As a historian, Pynchon sometimes takes on the role of scientist in that he wants to explain in a factual way, indifferent to narratives that might be constructed about its discoveries, how the world works. Often, although not always, he suggests not the historian as scientist but the scientist as historian, since technological innovation is always transforming the way that we know and manipulate the world. Yet Pynchon does present history as a text, and he seems to agree with medievalist historian Nancy F. Partner's assertion that historical "facts" inevitably become "constructed artifacts no different in cognitive origin than any made thing or 'fiction'" (qtd. in Evans 70). Pynchon's work also addresses the implications of Dominick LaCapra's claim that "all history . . . must more or less blindly encounter the problem of a transferential relation to the past whereby the processes at work in the object of study acquire their displaced analogues in the historian's account" (qtd. in Evans 70). One can spend much time tracking down Pynchon's historical sources—which include the journal that was kept by Mason—looking for instances where Pynchon adapts or rewrites his source for a purpose that is presumably alternative to that of the source's intention.[4] What one will find, though, is that Pynchon cannot give the facts straight. The historian's return to the facts—to the archive—requires him to perform an elaborate mediation between the past he verifies and the present that he must invent. Moreover, as an exercise that tests the limits of historical commentary, *Mason & Dixon* asks this: when the facts seem to require it, why not invent the past since the past has obviously invented us?

Insofar as the novel concerns itself with American history proper, it recalls the *Blood Meridian* premise that American history, so intent on forgetting the past in order to create the future, *has never transcended the historical moment of its origins* and thus can only replay this beginning in ever-expanding contexts.

Mason & Dixon preserves the initial distinction between European and non-European that we saw with *Blood Meridian* and, in fact, makes that distinction the necessary condition of its narrative performance. For Pynchon, American history cannot be known except through the repression of other histories—the most obvious example being those of the Indian tribes. Where McCarthy indicates that Europeans, the unhorsed Saxons, could not truly conquer the New World except by becoming a conjoined being with their Other, Pynchon will not quite imagine a New World history separate from a European point of view. The story of America that Pynchon tells through Cherrycoke is inevitably the story of exponentially increasing exploitation undertaken in the name of progress. What begins in the eighteenth century as a story of Europeans exploiting the North American continent becomes by the end of the twentieth century the story of Americans exploiting the global "world markets."

Describing Pynchon's earlier masterpiece, *Gravity's Rainbow* (1973), Richard Poirier aptly addresses the blurring between history and fiction that has characterized all of Pynchon's work since *V*, his first novel (1963): it is not enough "to say that Pynchon's fictions have historical analogues or that he allegorizes history. Rather, his fictions are often seamlessly woven into the stuff, the very factuality of history" ("Importance" 53). Yet, never merely historical fiction, Pynchon's work is so rich with the absurd that readers suspect that what they know to be true is as unlikely as what they suspect is invented. Tony Tanner is right to say of *Mason & Dixon* that "what Pynchon realizes, beyond any other contemporary writer, is that the best way to be deadly serious is to be whimsically unserious" (234). Its pattern comes specifically out of the history of the novel as a formal innovation. Its structure often recalls Laurence Sterne's *Tristram Shandy* (1759–67) and Miguel de Cervantes's *Don Quixote*. Interpolated stories, multiple narrative frames, and intentionally forged historical documents make it hard for the reader to know where he or she stands in relationship to "truth." As Pynchon knows, this sense of epistemological and even ontological uncertainty is not only the invention of postmodernist theory; it is coincident with the birth of the novel.[5] In direct contradiction to the methodology of most conventional histories, Pynchon's "history" alerts the reader to the unreliability of all narrative histories except as the expression of a contingent, and interested, point of view. Despite its obvious fictions and anachronisms, however, *Mason & Dixon* should be read as a work of history that reconstructs and explains how America came to be and implies its past, present, and future, all at once, in its every sentence.[6]

The novel's central conceit is that mapmaking is a method of both ordering and reducing the world so that a few specific, narrow political interests may fashion it to their will. Once Europe discovered America, the forces of empire and mapmaking went hand in hand. David Seed argues that the novel "demonstrates how surveying and mapmaking are implicated in vested commercial and political interests as well as in the processes of civilization" (85). Conversely, most critics understand Pynchon's reliance on an unreliable narrator as a protest against the oppressive imperialism that is America's historical legacy. Thomas Schaub suggests that "*Mason & Dixon* is surely a novel for the people, as antigovernment as any Idaho militiaman" (195). Arthur Saltzman says the novel "continually impeaches the dream of precision, reviving the wilderness against our most elevated, exacting presumptions" (65), whereas Jeff Baker observes that the "novel sets about to explore the very 'fork in the road' America never took" ("Plucking" 168). Where this fork in the road might lead is difficult to say. I certainly agree with Stacey Olster, who says that the novel is "a critique of American exceptionalism" (283), and with Victor Strandberg, who says that the novel confirms "the temperament of a hippie rebel against tradition, convention, and all forms of social hierarchy" (103). Some readers may hope that the novel, with its many-layered and competing stories, will create an American history alternative to the oppressive story of conquest and dominion that *Mason & Dixon* portrays as the canonical version of America. At times Pynchon's novel offers a refuge from history, since Cherrycoke's marvelous story-making abilities allow his audience a chance to spend a cold, wintry night dreaming of a world better than the one they know. Yet the novel's amusements inevitably become a path back into the history that has made the United States what it is today. Cherrycoke's long night's tale is, finally, a funeral commemoration of Mason and Dixon, and Pynchon's novel rests with the knowledge that the only possible escape from history is through death.[7]

Mason & Dixon implies a modernist reader, one tutored by James Joyce and T. S. Eliot and willing to work through the maze of the text to find the pattern its many facts conceal even as they reveal. More than any of the other works discussed in this study, *Mason & Dixon* plays on the reader's desire to distinguish between history and fiction. Pynchon's argument with history is also an attempt to re-create a discredited form. In a sense, he wants to claim history as fiction's province. Like Toni Morrison, Pynchon rewrites history to create a future better than the one implied by the present he knows. Hence, as Tanner suggests, Pynchon writes history in the subjunctive tense: "The great subjunctive premise underlying Pynchon's work is—*had* America taken a different path" (224). At times Pynchon verges on suggesting that U.S. history is so corrupt that all that remains for readers of conscience is to counter-fabricate a history that at least amuses. Replacing realist history with fictional history is, for Pynchon, a moral imperative, since it is the only way to recover senses of wonder and alternative modes of perception that the colonizing of America destroyed.

Pynchon thus presents conventional history as a tool of the powerful. His characters seek, without quite finding, fictional ways to confront the stories that powerful interests persuade others to believe as true. As one character notes:

> To rule forever, it is necessary only to create, among the people one would rule, what we call…Bad History. Nothing will produce Bad History more directly nor more brutally, than drawing a Line, in particular a Right Line, the very Shape of Contempt, through the midst of a People,—to create thus a Distinction betwixt 'em,—'tis the first stroke,—All else will follow as if predestin'd, unto War and Devastation. (615)

Whereas William Faulkner, Toni Morrison, and Cormac McCarthy master history through their narrative art, Pynchon shows in *Mason & Dixon* how narratives of science and technology become all-powerful narratives virtually invulnerable to the types of counterhistories that authors such as Pynchon or Cherrycoke would write. Writing in his *Spiritual Day-Book*, Cherrycoke observes that Mason and Dixon are "united, they pursue a ride through the air, they are link'd to the stars, to that inhuman Precision" (440). Although Cherrycoke's "inhuman Precision" refers to an idea of God, his words also recognize that the time period of the novel portrays the consequences of humanity's mastery of the heavens as a means for knowing the world. Pynchon's Cherrycoke resists this logic that weds scientific with imperial narrative, conjuring up alternative possibilities as if they might have been real—might have become history.

In Pynchon's "Is It O.K. to Be a Luddite?" in the October 28, 1984, *New York Times Book Review*, Cherrycoke's creator observes:

> In ways more and less literal, folks in the 18th century believed that once upon a time all kinds of things had been possible that were no longer so. Giants, dragons, spells. The laws of nature had not been so strictly for-mulated back then. What had once been true working magic had, by the

Age of Reason, degenerated into mere machinery. [William] Blake's dark Satanic mills represented old magic that, like Satan, had fallen from grace. As religion was becoming more and more secularized into Deism and nonbelief, the abiding human hunger for evidence of God and afterlife, for salvation—bodily resurrection, if possible—remained. (1)

In *Mason & Dixon*, America is the space where scientific rationalism collided with and destroyed realms of magic and wonder. "America," says one character "for centuries had been *kept hidden*, as are certain Bodies of Knowledge. Only now and then were selected persons allow'd Glimpses of the New World" (487). Pynchon will frequently invoke America as an unspoiled garden full of mystery and wonder, and generally the Indians are the keepers of that Garden. Mason and Dixon, the astronomer and surveyor hired to mark its landscape and render it symbolically as maps, are allowed glimpses of the "Magick" of the New World: giant vegetables, golems, burial mounds that refuse to be known by European instruments of measurement. They are also allowed to see the destruction taking place in the Garden. As Mason and Dixon are warned at one point, "This Age sees a corruption and disabling of the ancient Magick. Projectors, Brokers of Capital, Insurancers, Peddlers upon the global Scale, Enterprisers and Quacks,—these are the last poor fallen and feckless inheritors of a Knowledge they can never use, but in the service of Greed. The coming Rebellion is theirs,—[Benjamin] Franklin and that Lot,—and Heaven help the rest of us, if they prevail" (487–88).

Cherrycoke's story makes clear that the "Brokers of Capital" will prevail yet invites the reader to believe that some forms of discredited magic are still possible. Cherrycoke's family members will listen to their daft relative's stories, not to be preached at but to be entranced by the magic of storytelling and the diversion it affords. "Snakes! Bears! Indians!" Mason's boys scream when they learn their father is headed to America, and thus to a land of wonder (201). In its stubborn insistence that a world of wonders exists despite mostly successful attempts to erase alternative modes of perception from the map of the known world, *Mason & Dixon* is, arguably, a post-postmodern novel. Postmodern works have generally denied the possibility of a transcendent, omniscient point of view, arguing instead for a world that can be known only through contingent perspectives. Despite its critique of "history" as congeries of lies and truth constructed to promote the profitable interests of a select few at the expense of the many, *Mason & Dixon* often seeks to reoccupy a perspective from which transcendence still seems possible.[8] Its search for transcendence—a time beyond time, so to speak—-is at odds with the historical progression it portrays.

As a narrator, Cherrycoke is part primary witness, part archival historian, and part fabulist.[9] Yet his perspective is framed by a late-twentieth-century narrator, giving the novel a kind of doubled temporal frame of reference. Throughout, Pynchon brilliantly conflates the eighteenth century with the twentieth century in a way that defines his postmodernist historical method. In a typical episode, his heroes visit a tavern framed as an eighteenth-century (when coffeehouses first flourished) version of a contemporary Starbucks-like coffee shop.[10] They enter a "Bar [that] seems to vanish in the Distance," where "invigorating Liquid" of coffee is served all day, providing a great "*stimulus*" to political discussion. When a Quaker dryly notes that they customarily imbibe "a sweetness of immorality and corruption," since their coffee is "bought as it is with the lives of African slaves," the past and future Starbucks dwellers respond that they "wish no one ill" but "it helps to have a lick of molasses to look forward to" each day (328–29). As a matter of defining what the past was and has done, *Mason & Dixon* says there is no story to tell about America other than its transformation of the world and its resources into pleasure for a limited number of Americans. The "Distance" into which the "Bar seems to vanish" becomes, in a sense, the contemporary Starbucks, where Pynchon's reader is possibly consuming his book (along with some designer coffee). American history is too brief and too transparent to see any pattern other than a series of alternatively ingenious and brutal methods for destroying God's bounty (and those who inhabit it) while renaming what one finds as one's own. Pynchon sees no coincidence in the fact that the first American president was, by trade, a land surveyor. One of the novel's funniest moments occurs when George Washington first meets Mason and Dixon and hears of their mission to plot the westward line. He responds by giving free advice: there is "no reason you fellows shouldn't turn a Shilling or two whilst you're over here . . . and have ye considered how much free surveying ye'll be giving away,— as the West Line must contribute North and South Boundaries to Pieces innumerable?" (276). Washington's observation hints at the conflict that will be the Civil War, but Pynchon's point is that America was always organized as a murderous land-development scheme.

A few pages later, outside the coffee tavern, Mason and Dixon will confront the stories of those who are being displaced. They will hear of Indians being "massacr'd ev'ry one," by "that brave Paxton vermin," as one Pennsylvanian describes them, so that "now the entire Tribe is gone, the lot" (304). These proto-Americans' disgusted account of how soldiers allowed the Paxton group to kill the Indians will be no proof against the ultimate destruction of thousands of like tribes in the course of America's development. Americans identified themselves as such through the displacement of Indians and the importation and use of slaves, all in the service of expanding "democracy" or promoting "freedom." Pynchon underscores this reading by having his narrator, Cherrycoke, interrupt his account of his hero's first meeting with Washington to draw a moral for his audience, only a few years removed from the events described. "Unfortunately, young people," he says, "the word Liberty, so unreflectively sacred to us today, was taken in those Times to encompass even the darkest of Men's rights,—to injure whomever we might wish,—unto extermination, were it possible,—Free of Royal advice or Proclamation Lines and such. This being, indeed and alas, one of the Liberties our late War was fought to secure" (307). Cherrycoke's commentary frames the American Revolution as something that defends this sinister conception of liberty. Cherrycoke's listeners want to object to his interpretation, although one protestor "does not remain to press the Point" (307). Another observes the annihilation of Indians by Colonel Henry Bouquet and General Thomas Gage during the French and Indian Wars by giving "gifts" of smallpox-infected blankets established a policy of genocide that the Paxton Boys are merely carrying out.

John Wade LeSpark, the aptly named weapons dealer and Cherrycoke's de facto host, assures the Reverend that he "may ever speak freely here,—killing Indians having long ago ceas'd to figure as a sensitive Topick in this house" (307). "Killing Indians" is already, in 1786, an old subject. The discussion is typical since it neatly overlaps the present with the past. Cherrycoke's allusion to the passage of time, "in those Times," is deeply ironic since the Reverend refers to a period only thirty years gone (as if to say George W. Bush's war with Iraq is of a different epoch from the hardly passed Vietnam War). Cherrycoke knows, and his audience understands *and accepts*, that the Revolutionary War, this merely "late War," is one of many to come, from the Civil War to the myriad wars of the twentieth century and beyond, a succession (to use Gore Vidal's phrase) of perpetual wars for perpetual peace endlessly fought in the name of Liberty.

11

Brian McHale suggests that Mason & Dixon dramatizes the dominance of space over time but actually Mason & Dixon portrays how the human maintenance of time allows for the creation and then the calculated distribution of space as a form of imperial power ("Mason" 43–63). Nowhere is this more evident than the curious relationship between Mason and Dixon and the Indians they encounter. The novel's most important line is not, as it turns out, the Mason-Dixon Line but the Warrior Path that divides the realm of the Indians from "civilization." Working at the behest of "civilization," Mason and Dixon have been "order'd" to "continue the West Line 'as far as the Country is inhabited' " (470). Their line drawing will cease when they reach a well-traveled Indian line known as the Warrior Path. Although Mason and Dixon will have marked the transit of Venus for the Royal Academy and the Mason-Dixon Line for future generations of Americans, they can neither mark nor cross the line that is the Warrior Path. In a sense, the Warrior Path is the shadow line to Mason and Dixon's. Once one line is crossed, the other disappears; the question is whether the Warrior Path can ever truly be crossed since it defines the boundary of not only the surveryors' journey in America but also Mason & Dixon's history of America's origins. In the wilderness, Mason and Dixon learn that along the Warrior Path European conceptions of distance and time do not always apply. Moreover, as Hugh Crawfford, a white man "accompanying the Indians" explains to the King's cartographers, "the Great Warrior Path" marks "one the major High-ways of all inland America." Mason and Dixon's job, however, is precisely to regulate time and distance. That "major High-way" of the Indians will be overrun by new concpetions of distance and time. At one point, Benjamin Franklin, "speaking as Postmaster-General," will tell Mason and Dixon that he sees "our greatest problem as Time" (287). How can messages be relayed across the continent and remain, as it were, timely unless those sending and receiving them can calculate the importance of their messages against the time that it takes to receive them?

Before coming to America, Mason and Dixon were sent by the Royal Academy to chart the transit of Venus so that more precise maps of the earth can be made. As a practical matter, it makes sense for them to stop their colonial venture at the Warrior Path since the purpose of their work is to settle the dispute of "civilized" men, and, by definition, "civilized" men do not (yet) live beyond that line. Besides, they might be killed for trespassing. By implication, though, Mason and Dixon's line will obliterate the line of the Indians' Warrior Path.

Although Mason and Dixon may chart their line for the purpose of establishing the Ohio–Pennsylvania border, they are actually charting the inevitable course of westward expansion by the descendants of Europeans. "Going West was all futurity," the narrator remarks at one point (499). Jorge Luis Borges famously described maps that would include within them the maps that are being made of the world that was being mapped. To say that "Time and Distance mean something else out here" is to say that European instruments cannot map the Warrior Path and where it leads the white man cannot know. The Warrior Path challenges their basic hypothesis that time and distance are complementary concepts through each of which the other may be defined. Mason is "made dizzy" the first time he witnesses an "Indian" entering into and emerging out of the forest. Watching his movement "is like seeing a bird take wing,—each moves vertiginously into an Element Mason, all dead weight, cannot enter," just as "contrariwise, watching an Indian emerge, is to see a meaningless Darkness eddy at length into a Face, and a Face, moreover, that Mason *remembers*" (647). At one with the landscape that Mason can know only mathematically, the Indian's face, haunting and strange, is a symbol of what Mason cannot penetrate. Mason is made "anxious before the advent of these Visitors how Strange, who belong so *without separation* to this country crypticK and perilous," because he suspects that even when he cannot see them, they are there. His "remembering" is Pynchon's reflection on how future Americans will understand the Indians' history—as ghosts of a dimension of time and space unrecorded and hence unknown.

When the "Indian" disappears into the bush and renders Mason "dizzy," he disappears not just from white man's encroaching empire but also, more specifically, from the realm of empiricism that began during the Renaissance when Europeans came to believe that what cannot be known empirically and through experience does not count as knowledge or even "humanity." Arguably, the key historical event of the novel, one that the novel portrays indirectly, is the solution to the longitude problem that so baffled seventeenth- and eighteenth-century scientists. As Dava Sobel explains in *Longitude* (1995), understanding the importance of the longitude problem takes one back to Galileo, Johannes Kepler, and Isaac Newton and leads forward to the creation of the British, Spanish, and American empires.[11] In order to plot and successfully execute voyages across the sea, sailors had to know how to determine the longitude. Otherwise, neither wars nor mercantile excursions could be confidently waged. The riches of the New World could hardly be capitalized upon without adequate means of transportation. To determine longitude required knowledge of the time in two different places at once, and this required a means of keeping time that could withstand the dislocations of sea travel.[12] Empires literally depended on solving the longitude problem. So pressing was the issue that in 1714 the British Parliament passed the Longitude Act, offering a prize "equal to a king's ransom," or what would be in the millions of dollars today, for its solution (Sobel 8). Famous astronomers such as Giovanni Cassini, Galileo, Edmond Halley, Christian Huygens, Johannes Kepler, and Isaac Newton all attempted to solve the problem by plotting the relationship between the moon and the stars. This technique (known as the lunar method) proved unwieldy, however, because it required a vast number of specific charts with precise plotting of the position of the moon in relationship to the stars. Ultimately, though, it was the clockmaker John Harrison whose invention of a clock that would keep time over the oceans solved the problem. As Sobel suggests, "Some modern horologists claim that Harrison's work facilitated England's mastery over the oceans, and thereby led to the creation of the British Empire—for it was by dint of the chronometer that Britannia ruled the waves" (153). Thus, she adds, "in the course of their struggle to find longitude, scientists struck upon other discoveries that changed their view of the universe," including "the first accurate determinations of the weight of the Earth, the distance to the stars, and the speed of light" (8).

Pynchon portrays fanciful versions of both approaches to the longitude problem in order to show the wide (indeed world-encompassing) historical consequences that its solution would have. The first example occurs when Mason and Dixon are sent to South Africa to chart the transit of Venus. Briefly, a Dutch clock will replace Mason as Dixon's traveling partner, and then later a second clock replaces Dixon. The two Dutch clocks, doubles for Mason and Dixon, literally speak to each other, a comic representation of the idea of man as machine. Similarly, "as part of a small but global scientific armada," Mason and Dixon are supervised by Nevil Maskelyne, the chief proponent of the lunar method of determining longitude and a nemesis not only to Mason and Dixon but also to Harrison. Although Mason and Dixon are not directly involved in Harrison's quest for a clock, their activities are a consequence of the search for longitude. Their supervisor from the Royal Academy employs them to find a lunar method for solving the longitude issue. Although they seem to work as part of a global science experiment, their "obs," or observations, are really done in the service of empire building. Thus, years later, when they are hired to settle the Maryland–Pennsylvania boundary dispute, their ability to plot a map by using the stars is what makes possible not only the creation of the boundary between the two states but also future dislocations of Indians from their ancestral landscapes.

At that point Pynchon's Mason will be distressed to have his skills reduced from those of an astronomer to those of a surveyor. He became an astronomer to survey the skies and to marvel at God's works, not to plot dubious property lines for kings and lords. Yet part of Pynchon's message is that the eighteenth century marks the point where humanity's ability to mark time and its relationship to space became a means for controlling what humans could and could not do. Dividing the space of the world into minutes on a map parallels the drive to divide days into minutes that will measure a person's productivity. The clock, the knowing of time irrespective of location, made the longitude possible; the clock also mechanized humans, making human beings versions of the clock. The tension between humanism and technology is a problem that was given philosophical form in Julien Offray de La Mettrie's *Man a Machine* and fictional form in Laurence Sterne's *Tristram Shandy* and Denis Diderot's *Jacques the Fatalist*. Pynchon registers these historical recognitions of the duality inherent in technologies of human control by including a second clock in the premise of his narrative. This clock, which becomes a character in the novel, is invented by Dixon as a perpetually running clock. Subsequently swallowed by another character, it ticks on and on inside the man's stomach. The clock that cannot stop is emblematic of a new understanding of time that contains within its processes all human activity. You sleep; the clock ticks. The sun sets and rises; the clock just measures and ticks. Humans cannot void the clock so they become instead a version of Newton's perfect mechanism. The ticking of the clock replaces the beating of the human heart, which, after all, must stop one day (or second), whereas the clock ticks on.

Mason & Dixon shows how this technological innovation reveals not only human mortality but also time's immortality. From this point (although Cherrycoke will significantly disagree), Europeans exist in *time* rather than in God. This moment will lead to Ernest Becker's observation that "in the missile age man finally crowned Newton's beginning, and completely secularized the stars; now we yearn toward the moon to plant a national banner" (17). Becker adds, "Man having lost the capacity to marvel, it was inevitable that good and evil should have become merely an affair of technical calculation. As we know, the great prophet of this outcome, of the bureaucratization of good and evil, was Max Weber; he saw that man's own organized efficiency would threaten to degrade him completely" (17). *Mason & Dixon* portrays the degradation that Weber describes as the inheritance of American history.

For Pynchon, the question of how distance relates to time is not only a historical matter but also a narrative problem. Mason and Dixon look to the stars to plot the contours of the earth. Rather than have the future make the past over according into its own logic, Pynchon looks to insert what he knows of the present into the past so that the past predicts the future. Pynchon's Cherrycoke will refuse conventional chronology. To many, this gesture might seem to be a refusal of history altogether (although it is more likely a refusal of the scientific premises that seem to drive this story)—for what is history if it is not the ordering of events? Pynchon's answer is that (a) time is an invention, not a discovery, by humans and (b) the invention of time is the means by which Europeans have justified and accomplished taking over the New World and, once taken, the New World has merely made it possible for humans to become willing slaves to time. In this way Pynchon's novel enacts its own version of time. The novel invents a narrative dimension within which its history can plausibly violate conventional rules of time and space.

The novel's complex doubled-narrative perspective can be seen in the portrayal of Cherrycoke's immediate audience as protosuburbanized Americans. Their home is their world, and the world seems to have become their home. Inside their houses they amuse themselves with an orrery, a makeshift home solar system built by "the renown'd German engineer" Dr. Nessel during one of his many visits to America (95). The LeSpark Orrery includes the most up-to-date astronomical finds: "the outermost Planets, Saturn and the new 'Georgian' " (95). The central "lanthorn" of the contraption is the sun, and its light reveals the other heavenly bodies. Evoking modern-day Americans who imagine they have access to the world though their television sets, Pynchon portrays these early Americans as having already contained the universe within their own domestic space. When questions of astronomy arise—as they often do in the narrative—the family has recourse to its orrery to settle them. The children speculate about the topography of the newly discovered planet and enjoy, in their fashion, the presumption that by discovering a world, they have made it. "The children have since pass'd many an hour, Lenses in hand, gazing upon this new World, and becoming easy with it. They have imagin'd and partly compos'd a Book, *History of the New Planet*, the Twins providing the Wars, and Brae the scientific Inventions and Useful Crafts" (95). This is world making domesticated—their games make literal the connection between science and imperialism. The sky's seemingly infinite expanse has been contained under a single rooftop and so a family now has the power to claim the universe as their own. The family's game of science fiction suggests too the relationship that they enjoy, as Americans, with the New World. Their orrery provides them with the means to "discover" the world, which, in turn, gives them the right to name it and quantify its properties—an extension of Mason and Dixon's more painstakingly undertaken efforts in America and South Africa. "I get to light the Sun," one child cries, as they all dash for the orrery. And one day, future Americans will again light the sun, in the form of atomic bombs.

The book reminds us that the discovery and use of the atomic bomb became possible only because humans had learned to manipulate spaces so microscopically small that the spaces had to be imagined before they could be discovered. The contemporary reader can make such historical connections and may even see that although Pynchon's astonishing re-creation of eighteenth-century America is itself a kind of world making, it is not finally as significant as the fact that Mason and Dixon could plot the transit of Venus to determine the solar parallax. The extraordinary power that this knowledge brought underpins the phenomenon of complacent late-twentieth-century U.S. consumers' exploitation of a significant portion of the world's natural resources for their own amusement. Pynchon chooses a random point from the eighteenth century and reconfigures our postmodern world from that point. Thus history is presented as a problem in geometry. The implication is that other points might have been chosen, but since any single point eventually connects with other points that lead to the same end, one beginning point is as good as any other. In this regard, *Mason & Dixon* displays pretense to totality that surpasses the epic inventions of Faulkner and McCarthy because it makes the epic beside the point—a naïve belief that poetry will not only have the final say but will also turn whatever "history" has happened into mere fodder for the poet's poem.

To understand this claim, we need to consider the true extent of the obscurity of Mason, Dixon, and the meaning of their line. Why base an epic-length work on a pair whose claim to fame was having completed the basically boring work of clearing a vista 8 miles across and 334 miles long through Maryland and Pennsylvania? The West could have been settled without them—not that settling the West was their purpose. Their actual job was to resolve a boundary dispute that in a decade would be rendered pointless by the Revolution that would eliminate the both parties' claims to ownership. Nor can we quite say that Mason and Dixon were significant because they were the ones who mapped the line. Neither was a genius; they merely applied a set of rules that they had been taught. Nor are they significant because their names outlived their act, so that virtually every American knows the term *Mason-Dixon line*. Americans are familiar with them only by a quirk of history: the line that they drew happened to become a symbolic marker that divided slave states from free states. That Mason and Dixon had relatively interesting lives of their own, were distinguished in their day, were known to many "important" historical figures is certainly true, but it is hardly sufficient reason for a novel as large in scope as Pynchon's. Yet Pynchon chooses to focus on these two figures about whom "only a few dated articles have been written" not only to render them surprisingly heroic (which he does) but also to show that the terrifying logic of history intersects with all lives, no matter how seemingly forgotten (Clerc 1).

Wherever Mason and Dixon go, they are made aware that their actions are part of a plot that they can only dimly surmise. Avatars of the future U.S. Empire, they mark the moment when a belief in the wonder of God's world gave way to a rational world that could be known and exploited. Mason sums up this crucial tension in his own story: "As if there were no single Destiny but rather a choice among a great many possible ones, their number steadily diminishing each time a Choice be made, till at last 'reduc'd,' to the events that do happen to us, as we pass among 'em, thro' Time unredeemable,—much as a Lens, indeed, may receive all the Light from a vast celestial Field of View, and reduce it to a single Point" (45). In this passage the telescope is a metaphor for the control of history. The telescope identifies the desired end of its viewer and frames that view as desirable. Likewise, as the novel progresses, we see that the telescope is a device that controls, rather than being controlled by, Mason. Mason uses it to chart the skies, but it does not take Mason outside of himself or suggest a broader fate than his own. Mason may think the "single point" to which he refers implies the omniscient Christian God, but the telescope does not, in fact, reveal the majesty of God's universal plan. Rather, with the aid of the telescope, the stars have become mere guideposts for mapping the earth.

Mason's reflections are an occasion for Pynchon to look back at revolution in the understanding of the world that is now complete. A world that was once made by God so that humans could achieve the divinity within them has become material to be shaped according to human will. With the telescope, the earth became no longer a place to be escaped or joined through a journey to God's paradise; it became the material for creating the paradise that humans would make for themselves merely by plotting maps out of heaven's twinkling lights. As Becker has observed, "The great meaning of the medieval world view was the Creator, in His design, had a stake in the Earth: the Earth was a staging ground for salvation." This meant "that the world was a place of decadence and was doomed, sooner than later." Thus, "the great significance of the Newtonian world picture was that it put an end to this whole period of anxiety—at least on a conceptual level.... [B]y mechanizing nature Newton actually reversed the gloomy vision of a chaotic universe cold to man's fate; instead he offered man the comfort of a new harmony and security" (4). At this point, science, not God, rules the universe. Once it is determined that the world is mechanistic and subject to natural laws that need only be identified and interpreted by humans, then the world is either a mechanism that humans learn to control or, less grandly, a mechanism within which humans learn to accept their place.

Many of course tried to suggest that the Newtonian order was not so harrowing and could be transferred to the surviving older order. The universe has laws; it runs like a clock, but God remains the clockmaker. As John Locke observed, "The works of Nature everywhere sufficiently evidence a Deity" (qtd. in Becker 5). Certainly, Mason and Cherrycoke understand scientific discovery to be a way of serving the Creator. When questioned about his politics, Mason gravely asserts that he and Dixon serve an authority higher than a political one intent on only secular observation: "'Surely, at the end of the day, we serve no master but Him that regulates the movements of the Heav'ns, which taken together form a cryptick Message,'—Dixon now giving him Looks that fail, only in a Mechanickal way, to be Kicks,—'[that] we are intended one day to solve, and read'" (59). Mason's belief that he is doing God's will in the name of science is undercut when he and Dixon observe the transit of Venus in South Africa. They are part of a legion of scientists, positioned by the Royal Academy all over the world, who are collecting data so that an accurate rendering of the earth's longitude may be registered. This feat will make maps more accurate and travel easier. The management of trade and armies will become more economical; it will be possible to live closer to the minute, so to speak, and the management of time will be commensurate with the management of the world's affairs. Pynchon underscores what is at stake for this enterprise when he has Cherrycoke observe that "somebody somewhere in the World, watching the Planet go dark against the Sun,—dark, mad, mortal, the Goddess in quite another Aspect indeed," recites a line from Sappho's Fragment 95 that addresses Hesperus, saying, "You bring back the bright day scatter'd,—you bring in the sheep, and the goat,—you bring the Child back to her Mother" (96). The speaker's interlocutor points out that the reference is wrong—that Sappho refers to a sunrise and not the sunset. The real point, though, is that the speaker recalls Sappho, an ancient, to memorialize the passing of an old cosmology no longer adequate to explain what is happening. Sappho's poem is of a time when the stars inspired myths and stories and wonder—not points on a map. At that moment, "a sort of long black Filament yet connects her to the Limb of the Sun, tho' she be moved well onto its Face, much like an Ink-Drop about to fall from the Quill of a forgetful Scribbler," and then someone shouts, "Quick! someone, secure the Time!" (96). They have become the Scribbler, or a legion of Scribblers, serving the interest of the telescope. Mason and Dixon witness in order to record—the material of poetry has become data to study and to exploit. What they experience is not an isolated moment of wonder but the moment when the world becomes smaller and the sky the earth's servant.

The astronomical magic that Mason and Dixon might experience when they observe the transit of Venus is not a singular experience but the creation of science. Mason and Dixon watch the three astral bodies line up in a row according to a specific set of instructions with a specific end: the skies bureaucratized. "Observers lie, they sit, they kneel,—and witness something in the Sky. Among these attending Snouts Earth-wide, the moment of first contact produces a collective brain-pang, as if for something lost and already unclaimable,—after the Years of preparation, the long and at best queasy voyaging, the Station arriv'd at, the Latitude and Longitude well secur'd" (97). What is lost is the wonder that such a moment might produce. "Eh? where am I?" Cherrycoke imagines such an astronomer thinking (97). Humans define the shape of earth and their physical place on it, but the responsibility of such a God-like act causes doubt and anxiety. Eclipses are no longer mysterious portents from God—not a prophecy or something to be divined by Apollo's priest—but events in this newly conceived history of humans. Dixon recognizes the transition that they record when he speaks of Galileo before the cardinal recanting his famous recantation. "Nonetheless, it moves," Galileo muttered beneath his breath, and Dixon knows that what was at stake " 'twas not only seeing the Creator about his Work but Newton and Kepler, too, confirm'd in theirs. The Arrival, perfectly as calculated, the three bodies sliding into a Single Line.... Eeh, it put me in a Daze for fair" (98, emphasis mine). Perfectly calculated: Dixon is not amazed by what he sees but that what he sees can be calculated in advance by a human-devised formula. As Cherrycoke explains to his audience, Mason and Dixon's method of observation allows them to determine the earth's size as it would be seen by an observer from the surface of the sun. What an extraordinary claim that must have seemed—to write down an equation that encompasses the entire space that encompasses humanity! What is at stake is the ability of science, not God, to command a third-person, omniscient point of view from which to view the doings of earth. Science presumes an objectivity based on the observable data. The earth is merely a matter of minutes and seconds, properly recorded, easily calculable. Once the earth becomes divided into minutes, it becomes smaller, more manageable. Humans do as well.

Reverend Cherrycoke resists the progressive compressing of the world into scientific formulas, maps, and diminishing markets that *Mason & Dixon* documents. In his *Spiritual Day-Book* Cherrycoke observes that "Pennsylvania is a place of spiritual Wonders amazing as any chasm or cataract" (481). Like Mason and Dixon, Cherrycoke is obsessed by boundaries; he chases after territories unmapped and unexplored. Where Mason and Dixon trace boundaries to measure the world and make it known once and for all, Cherrycoke values those boundaries as points that should not be crossed or even named. Against knowledge, transparent and evident, Cherrycoke values mystery, doubt—the realm where his "true Christ" lies. Mason and Dixon seek the certainty of precision; Cherrycoke's doubt is his faith. Cherrycoke remarks, "How might I speak of my true 'Church,' of the planet-wide Syncretism, among the Deistick, the Oriental, Kabbalist, and the Savage, that is to be,—the Promise of Man, the redemptive Point, ever at our God-Horizon, toward which all Faiths, true and delusional, must alike converge!" (356). The surprise of the narrative is not Pynchon's presentation of American history as the empire created by Europeans who had mastered certain scientific equations but his willingness to return us to a historical moment where what we now know was not already self-evident—to pretend for the duration of the evening that Cherrycoke's tale takes place in an America that could have been other than what we now know. "These times are unfriendly toward Worlds alternative to this one," Cherrycoke says as if addressing us rather than his immediate audience (359).

Cherrycoke lets the reader occupy a perspective where magic, fantasy, and alternative worlds still seem desirable. His history not only opposes the process by which sky and earth are reduced to a set of equations but also works to create a space other than the space that Mason and Dixon were assigned to mark—to make it possible for us to work our way back through history's tangled lines to construct a history more pleasing than the official history that we have inherited. One such alternative history that Pynchon recovers through Cherrycoke is the controversy of the missing Eleven Days. In 1752, eleven days were removed from the British calendar by act of Parliament. September 2 slid into September 14, and this "Theft of the People's Time," as Cherrycoke has it, infuriates, among many others, the people of Mason's hometown: "Not only did [the members of Parliament] insult the God-given structure of the Year, they also put us on Catholic Time. *French* time" (192). "Would that I might restore to them their Days, and be done!" Lord Macclesfield, president of the Royal Society, tells James Bradley, expressing the anxiety many felt about seeming to usurp "God's-time." (193). As a friend of Bradley's, Mason feels implicated in the theft too. He invents a story for his disgruntled townsfolk concerning a people imported from the land of the Eleven Days who do not fear the passing of time. His story seems to allude to the ongoing European discovery of "new peoples" who, free of civilization, are free of the sense of time as a burden—something to be prolonged or escaped.

Later Cherrycoke imagines Mason telling Dixon that he discovered the realm where the missing Eleven Days continue to exist. While everyone else awoke the morning of September 14, Mason awoke the morning of the September 3 in "*Tempus Incognitus*" (556). There he encounters ownerless horses and cows, "Apples nearly ripe," and "Waggons half-laded" (557). "'Twas as if the Metropolis of British Reason had been abandon'd to the occupancy of all that Reason would deny" (559). Mason stands before "a Barrier invisible, which," he says, "I understood I might cross if I will'd." There, he says, he receives "a distinct Message that the Keys and Seals of Gnosis within were too dangerous for me. That I must hold out for the Promises of Holy Scripture, and forget about the Text I imagin'd I'd seen" (560). Mason determines, "The dark Presences that had caus'd me such Apprehension, prov'd to be the Wraiths of those who had mov'd ahead instantly to the Fourteenth, haunting me not from the past but from the Future," until finally he is drawn back into the town and the world of the Fourteenth and his wife, Rebekah (still living then) (560). It is an extraordinary passage. Mason chooses to interpret the dream as a foreshadowing of what awaits him in death: his long dead wife and heaven. Ordinary waking life is like the dreamed Eleven Days—a transitory region on the road to Life Everlasting. Actually, though, the dream reveals what the Age of Reason and its servants (including Mason and Dixon) work to suppress. On one level, the dream betrays the nascent romantic fear that warns humans against aspiring to the secrets of heaven—Mason compares himself with Johann Goethe's Faust. Yet for Cherrycoke, as well as for Mason, the dream seems to be about a realm that science cannot know and about finding again a time that, according to the New Science, cannot exist. Mason characterizes his journey within the Eleven Days as "a lapse of consciousness," because it is an awakening into sensation that the Age of Reason discounts or denies.

The "wraiths of the future" are likely the future readers whom Mason's work serves: readers who can only laugh at those who believe that the calendar could be anything other than what it reads or that there might be a realm where the missing Eleven Days continue as part of a universe parallel to the one that erased them. Comfortable in the twilight between superstition and enlightenment, Mason serves the Age of Reason but would revolt against its claims. The Learned English Dog (L.E.D.), another of Pynchon's antirationalist inventions, intuits this quality of Mason's when he takes time to address Mason using the king's English. " 'Tis the Age of Reason, rffff," the Dog barks, mocking the claims of the enlightenment with a comic, articulate growl. Like Cherrycoke, Mason is attentive to forms of expression beyond the measure of sense: the ear he visits in the museum; the recurring apparitions of his wife; the dog Fang, whom he perceives to have the ability to speak (although the dog chooses not to). It is no coincidence, then, that Cherrycoke, Mason, and Dixon share more than apprehension regarding the casual manner in which the English government is displacing people in its name. Cherrycoke tacitly compares Mason's consciousness and historical situation with that of the displaced African slaves or the Indians of the New World. Cherrycoke's Mason is keenly aware of the powerful and frightening union that science and government form. His family was on the losing side of the Weaver Rebellion: "I was expell'd from Paradise by General Wolfe and his Regiment. One penetration, and no Withdrawal could ever have Meaning. My home's no more" (313). Ironically, Mason himself will become symbolic of similar imperial acts of population displacement.[13]

That technology changed what it meant to be human was certainly not evident to Mason when he was a boy viewing the amplified sky. Then Mason stargazed because he liked it and because, in a related way, it brought him closer to the heavens. Cherrycoke reports that Mason's father mocks him bitterly for giving his life over to stargazing—a word he associates with the practice of masturbation—and for breaking with his region and its way of life. But to young Mason his humanity was enriched by what he did and saw. Through his telescope, Mason experiences his own identity to its fullest dimension. Mason is content to be a creature under the stars, and to the American reader it is hard not to associate Mason's pleasure with the pleasure that Ralph Waldo Emerson described in *Nature* as his transformation into a "transparent eyeball" (*Essays* 10). If Mason is humbler than Emerson, less inclined to confuse God's authority with his own, in such moments Mason nonetheless seems to approach Emerson's admonition that each individual is unique, a universe unto him- or herself, and that to be alive is to experience the sacred. This intimation of one's own connection to the divine is rendered incongruous by Mason's actions as an astronomer, since his job is to colonize space in the name of time. One wag's remarks regarding the missing Eleven Days points to the fact that Mason's longing for God is exchanged for merely secular ends: "Time, ye see, is the money of Science, isn't it. The Philosophers need a Time, common to all, as Traders do a common coinage" (192). Or, as the ale cup that addresses Mason notes, "The business of the world is trade and death" (247).

Mason's story of the missing Eleven Days suggests that *time, civilization,* and *death* are interchangeable terms. The Europeans, controllers of time and space, bring death to the black men and women of Africa as surely as they bring death to the Indians of America. Throughout the novel Mason and Dixon are collaborators in and witnesses to a process of national-cultural transformations that are truly global in scale. Rarely do they see themselves as being implicated in this process of displacement. As employed by Cherrycoke, though, Mason and Dixon are positioned in the narrative as Henry Jamesian *ficelles*: the link that allows Pynchon's phenomenal capacity to imagine the universe from the most abstract conceptions of it down to its minutest material consequences. In one of the most remarkable scenes in the novel, Pynchon, incredibly, inflects Mason's arrival and the ultimate meaning of his and Dixon's story through the experience of a "Darkling Beetle." Having recently arrived in South Africa, Mason brushes from his face a "Darkling Beetle" that, in its way, has traveled as far to find Mason as Mason has traveled to find it. Like the arrival of the beetle, Mason's arrival in Capetown is a consequence of the European mania to map the world. Although Mason is one medium through which Europeans are mastering the globe, he is no more secure about his sense of control over his own personal situation than is the beetle. In this paragraph Pynchon prepares us for the conjoining of the perspectives of Mason and the beetle:

> In a corner, the Darkling Beetle rustles in its Cage, its Elytra the same unforgiving white as the great sand-waste call'd 'Kalahari' lying north of here, where the creature was taken up, brought Leagues overland to the Cape with hundreds of its kind, arriving hungry and disoriented, to be set out with the others, like a great sugar-iced Confection, at some Harborside Market frequented by Sailors and the Strange. So far in its Life, it has never seen Rain, tho' now it can feel something undeniably on the way, something it cannot conceive of, perhaps as Humans apprehend God,—as a Force they are ever just about to become acquainted with. (88)

The storm arrives and Pynchon's narrator suspends the conclusion of the beetle's journey to tell us how Mason and Dixon explore Capetown. The beetle's plight is all but forgotten when suddenly Mason yells "Ahrrh!" and "plucks from his Face a Beetle, about half an inch long and emitting green light as if bearing a Candle within" (89). Such beetles, he realizes, are all around him, a storm like rain. The reader sees that the beetle and Mason are part of the same process. As Europeans colonize Africa and the Americas, humans are transforming the globe as never before. Whole populations, animal and human, will have to accommodate to the transformation.[14]

What other novelist would include in his account of the colonization of Africa the transformation wrought by the existence of a type of insect and then use the transformation of that insect to suggest a commensurate transformation of what it means to be human? Moreover, the white/black beetle displaced from one part of Africa to another becomes emblematic of the slave trade that made colonization possible. Mason will forget the beetle but neither he nor Dixon will forget their Capetown initiation to the practice of slavery, which they will see on a much broader scale in America. The flight of the "Darkling Beetle" might be said to symbolize the European appropriation of the slave trade in Africa were it not for the fact that Pynchon is as sympathetic to what he imagines to be the beetle's perspective as he is to any human. The beetle is not exactly a symbol for something else. Thus, in the same incident, Pynchon manages not only to deflate the practice of history by making it something other than the justification of human presence on this earth but also to suggest that the ultimate end of history as a practice is to tell stories that justify human achievements regardless of what we (or they) accomplish.

If creation's design can be mapped and explained by humans, then anyone or anything that gets in the way, be it "ignorant Indian savage," "Darkling Beetle," or superstitious Englishman, is just an obstacle that needs to be removed. I will say more about how Pynchon depicts slavery and the virtual extermination of the Indians, but for now it is worth noting that one of the most disturbing elements of the book is the insignificance of Mason's desires in the context of the history that he serves. Even Mason's dream of an alternative time-dimension ends with his subjection to the time occuring outside his dream. America, says Cherrycoke, is a dream of "pure space," but if so, it is one that the line must violate, just as the line is an affront to Zhang's belief that the earth is "a living creature" (586, 602). Dividing the days and topographical spaces into minutes is a precondition for creating contracts that assign certain "territories" to certain peoples. This precondition determines the perception that all subsequent "Americans" will have of their history. Mason's refusal to cross the barrier he imagines in his dream of the Eleven Days anticipates his later unwillingness to cross the Warrior Path that separates the encroaching Europeans from the Indians. But what can this unwillingness really mean? The wonder, for instance, that Mason experiences gazing at the stars will eventually become part of a mechanism for displacing others from their view of the skies that they have known and seen.

Mason & Dixon raises a question present in all Pynchon's work: to what extent can one's own self be separated from the controlling will of the state? On one hand, Cherrycoke's tale cannot be a form of such narrative ordering: Cherrycoke, who has come to Philadelphia to bury his friend Mason, offers his story to the LeSparks in exchange for board. Cherrycoke's narrative sympathies are with his vision of the "true" Mason—the soul separate from the Royal Academy, the Crown, or even futurity. Cherrycoke's account—affectionate, humorous, frankly ridiculous—would resist the incorporation of Mason into larger histories and return to the dead Mason his proper, sacred, individual life: the joy he found in looking at the sky through a telescope or the love he shared with his now dead wife. Cherrycoke, that is, would make Mason (and Dixon) something other than a helpless coefficient of history. However, Cherrycoke's narrative cannot protect Mason or his work from the history that writes him. The outside frame narrative—the one we may attribute to Pynchon—contains Cherrycoke's tale within this more somber knowledge. The reader who would identify with Mason's resistance to the end that he serves and endorse Cherrycoke's tale over Pynchon's novel (the author of Cherrycoke is one such reader) must choose to remain within Cherrycoke's alternative time and space. This whimsical reader may align his or her point of view with that of history's dispossessed and the pursuit of alternative stories that likely will be defined by most others as fantasy.

The novel implies that fantasy may be one's only recourse against the state's awesome powers to define an individual citizen's identity in terms of the state's own interest. At its bleakest, Pynchon's fable suggests that without the state's sanction, the individual does not exist. As the novel progresses and as Mason and Dixon confront evidence of the Indians' displacement and the slaves' unhappy bondage, the reader understands that their sense of dispossession makes them kin to Cherrycoke himself, whose path to the land named "America" was also the result of forced displacement. If the Reverend Cherrycoke sometimes betrays a fascination with America as an exceptional entity, humanity's last best hope, then this is because he wants to imagine America as a refuge from those forces that drove him from England. The Reverend is the ideal American: a European immigrant who flees his homeland to create a history different from the one he has experienced. Yet even though the United States' history as a country separate from Europe has hardly begun, Cherrycoke already sees that this seemingly newborn history cannot escape the circumstances that made its birth. He is as homeless in America as he was in England since the history he fled there awaits him here. Although a dream of America as pure possibility unfettered by the past will prompt him to flights of poetry, neither his poetic and often playful language nor his tale can conceal the darker prospects of his—our—American dreaming. Cherrycoke asks:

Does Britannia, when she sleeps, dream? Is America her dream?—in which all that cannot pass in the metropolitan Wakefulness is allow'd Expression away in the restless Slumber of these Provinces, and on West-ward, wherever 'tis not yet mapped, nor written down, nor ever, by the majority of Mankind, seen,—serving as a very Rubbish-Tip for subjunctive Hopes, for all that may yet be true,—Earthly Paradise, Fountain of Youth, Realms of Prester John, Christ's Kingdom, ever behind the sunset, safe till the next Territory to the West be seen and recorded, measur'd and tied in, back into the Net-Work of Points already known, that slowly triangulates its Way into the Continent, changing all from subjunctive to declarative, reducing Possibilities to Simplicities that serve the ends of Governments,—winning away from the realm of the Sacred, its Borderlands one by one, and assuming them unto the bare mortal World that is our home, and our Despair. (345)

This gorgeous passage summons the appeal of America as an unrealized possibility—F. Scott Fitzgerald's "fresh Green breast" passage from *The Great Gatsby* is endlessly displaced westward unto the next horizon. In 1786 Cherrycoke should not yet be able to sense that the country is exhausting its possibilities, surrendering already the realm of the sacred. The tinge of regret that often peeks through the tale is Pynchon's narrative frame overlapping with Cherrycoke's. The passage cited above moves from "dream" to "Despair"; it peeks out beyond its frame to include the future, present-day America—the one that has been mapped by Rand McNally and can be bought, over and over, for about twenty dollars at Wal-Marts and gas stations across America. The romance that the passage evokes, though, is all the more poignant because its author knows what its narrator cannot: that America has been converted from the subjunctive to the declarative and every day brings with it a new assertion of U.S. power at home and abroad.

Telling his story from an eighteenth century perspective, Cherrycoke hopes to redeem his heroes from the ominous historical forces that shape them; he seeks what might be called a pure history, one that redeems the relentlessly materialist world that absorbs Mason and Dixon. To counter the claims of science, Cherrycoke holds to the claims of Jesus Christ. "As Savages commemorate their great Hunts with Dancing," Cherrycoke asserts, "so History is the Dance of our Hunt for Christ, and how we have far'd. If it is undeniably so that he rose from the Dead, then the Event is taken into History, and History is redeem'd from the service of Darkness,—with all the secular Consequences, flowing from that one Event, design'd and will'd to occur" (75–76). For Cherrycoke, any true theory of history cannot be separated from a faith in Christ's eventual resurrection. Having such faith is the only strategy available to Cherrycoke for denying the otherwise all-consuming power that the state exacts over individuals. On this view, Mason and Dixon belong to Christ, not to the Royal Society, the British Empire, or the future America. Cherrycoke's Christ offers refuge for history's passed over, its preterite as they are called in *Gravity's Rainbow*, and it offers hope that the America that his heroes mark will become the "very Rubbish-Tip for subjunctive Hopes" (345). Ethelmer, Cherrycoke's nephew and a possible version of the younger (*Gravity's Rainbow*)

Pynchon, ridicules Cherrycoke's Christological perspective. The college student scoffs, "Including ev'ry Crusade, Inquisition, Sectarian War, the millions of lives, the seas of blood. What happen'd? He liked it so much being dead that He couldn't wait to come back and share it with evr'body else?" (76).

Although Ethelmer's withering skepticism does not answer Cherrycoke's optimistic faith any more than Cherrycoke's idealism answers Ethelmer's materialism, their exchange reveals that *Mason & Dixon* contains two, possibly contradictory, novels in one binding. One might remark that *Mason & Dixon* is Cherrycoke's novel and Pynchon's history, but only to underline that Pynchon's history of America can be known only through Cherrycoke's fiction. At one point a character observes that elders such as Uncle Ives consider novels to be dangerous. They are dangerous because they can reveal prevailing history—in this case the one that makes Uncle Ives, a weapons manufacturer, rich—to be, from a different perspective, fiction. Cherrycoke, who longs for a just society predicated on Christ's teachings, tells his tale to a skeptical audience looking for easy entertainment, for home theatricals. For his part, Pynchon writes his novel for readers who dare to believe in the alternative America Cherrycoke summons forth despite the overwhelming "historical" logic of Mason and Dixon's line. Possibly, Cherrycoke's novel is Pynchon's as well, and the author of *Gravity's Rainbow* affirms the Christological perspective. There is no way to know, and, besides, the competing time frames of the two versions of *Mason & Dixon* seem impossible to reconcile into one. History is a matter of belief and those who would be redeemed must make their stories known.

Too humble to pretend that he is writing Christ's history, or what might be styled the truth that leads to resurrection, Cherrycoke will settle for not telling the kind of history that justifies a particular social order. He is not on the side of property, and therefore his only point of view in this world is as an outsider—a beetle, an Indian, or a member of the clergy preaching divinity in the age after science removed the Christian God as the ruler of the cosmos. Yet Cherrycoke's narrative stance is, for a Pynchon hero, remarkably *unparanoid*. Along with identifying Cherrycoke's unapologetic sympathy for the oppressed, Pynchon flaunts Cherrycoke's unprecedented ability—for a Pynchon character—to remove himself from the sinister material implications of his story. Once exiled from England, Cherrycoke accepts his position as cultural outsider: a man of God in the atheistic age of enlightenment, a man without property in a nation consecrated for the sole purpose of acquiring property. As a narrator, he need not seek secret histories, conspiracies of *The Crying of*

Lot 49's Trystero, or, as in *Gravity's Rainbow*, the doomed resistance of a shaky "We" against an all-powerful "They." His characters sometimes fear that they are the unwitting victims of others' plots—specifically, members of the Royal Academy and the Jesuits—but this is mainly Cherrycoke's joke, since they have become characters in his tale. Cherrycoke makes the story but does not make himself quite its subject. He refuses the position of Byron the Bulb, the true hero of *Gravity's Rainbow*: a postmodern Manfred doomed to suffer both the despairing knowledge of the world's depravity and the awareness that he is powerless to communicate this knowledge to others who might act to stop it. Having made his protest against the powerful as a young man, he is free to become the rarest possible Pynchon character: the unparanoid, happy exile.

The importance of Cherrycoke's religious belief cannot be exaggerated, because it is what allows him to be a part of the story and to lift it above a perspective of either gloomy melancholy or whimsical bitterness. If you believe in the mediating power of Jesus Christ as the one who will save you and the fallen world in which you live, Cherrycoke says, you have no reason to be paranoid. Cherrycoke's most revealing expression of his Christianity is not technically part of his tale at all; it is inserted as an epigraph to Chapter 52 and comes, apparently, from one of his own written works, playfully titled *Undeliver'd Sermons*: "The Ascent to Christ is struggle thro' one heresy after another, Riverwise up-country into a proliferation of Sects and Sects branching from Sects, unto Deism, faithless pretending to be holy, and beyond, ... the America of the Soul. . . . Doubt is the essence of Christ," Cherrycoke reasons. This means that "the final pure Christ is pure uncertainty. He has become the central subjunctive fact of a Faith, that risks ev'rything upon one bodily Resurrection" (511). No doubt this sermon remains undelivered because Cherrycoke is perfectly aware of how controversial most parishioners would find its message. Whereas for most traditional Christians accepting Christ as the son of God and humankind's savior means discovering the one true faith that obliterates all others, for Cherrycoke accepting Christ means opening one's mind to William James's view that faith can never be final and will always be subject to change. As "the central subjunctive fact of a Faith," the meaning of Christ cannot be understood except as a conditional possibility contingent upon the final resurrection on Judgment Day making it true. Cherrycoke's concern is that the final resurrection renders everything before it irrelevant: "Wouldn't something less doubtable have done? A prophetic dream? A communication with a dead person?" (511). Cherrycoke is skeptical of any perspective that encourages meek assent to the divine right of kings and the infallibility of popes. Cherrycoke is a peculiar (although not unique) Christian, because he seeks Christ but resists authority. Remember, his "crime" against the state consisted of his rejection of the state's claim to assert its right over the property of others—what *Gravity's Rainbow* named "the preterit." Although Pynchon's works from V to *Mason & Dixon* portray Christianity as the cloak with which Western Europeans drape themselves in order justify taking dominion of everything they see in the many "New Worlds" they discover, *Mason & Dixon* revises Pynchon's established stance because Cherrycoke's hopeful democracy cannot be separated from his commitment to Christ.

Choosing to believe in the contingency of social order and refusing a final order not ushered in by a resurrection that he himself cannot bring forth, Cherrycoke's brand of Christianity is closer to Søren Kierkegaard's than it is to that of his eighteenth-century contemporary George Whitefield (who is mentioned in the novel). Through Cherrycoke's eschatology of uncertainty, Pynchon is subtly subverting the traditional exceptionalist American myth in which Christ's resurrection becomes a metaphor for the fulfillment of America. Cherrycoke imagines the resurrection as an event that will efface the moral contradictions of Euro-American society. Where the exceptionalist myth of America invokes a truly sacred hope (the dream of Christ's order) in order to justify a base secular order (the American empire), Cherrycoke dreams of Christ's resurrection to redeem an otherwise debased secular history. Cherrycoke is no meliorist, since he does not meekly await the second coming. Cherrycoke's theory of history implies that Christ's resurrection cannot occur until American history is made right with Cherrycoke's utopian dream of a world without dispossession.

To those who would dismiss *Mason & Dixon* as a long-winded parlor trick, an exercise in whimsical despair (a possibility Pynchon probably allows), Cherrycoke offers a hopeful definition of history as something always being made; thus he celebrates histories that are defiantly idiosyncratic, deeply biased, and very personal. Pynchon begins Chapter 35 with this quotation from Cherrycoke's otherwise unknown *Christ and History*:

History is not Chronology, for that is left to lawyers,—nor is it Remembrance, for Remembrance belongs to the People. History can as little pretend to the Veracity of the one, as claim the Power of the other,—her Practitioners, to survive, must soon learn the arts of the quidnunc, spy, and

Taproom Wit,—that there may ever continue more than one life-line back into a Past we risk, each day, losing our forebears in forever,—not a Chain of single Links, for one broken Link could lose us All,—rather, a great disorderly Tangle of Lines, long and short, weak and strong, vanishing into the Mnemonick Deep, with only their Destination in common. (349)

Through Cherrycoke, Pynchon resists the conventional understanding of history, one persistently reinforced by the American public school system, that would insist that history is a knowable, basically permanent collection of facts and shared principles. This is the view of Leopold von Ranke, which says that the past is easily distinguished from the present and is therefore easily known—something that may be compressed into a pamphlet or a textbook and regurgitated by all. Yet, says Cherrycoke, how easily this idea that the past cannot be changed translates into the belief that the present cannot be changed either. Learn the Pledge of Allegiance; learn the significance of the dates 1607, 1620, 1776, 1789, 1861–1865, 1918, and December 7, 1941; become Good Americans. By injecting personality—whimsy—into his history, Cherrycoke acknowledges that history's purpose is to allow people to justify their lives and, with any luck, improve them. History is something that belongs to people; it is not given to them. Cherrycoke proves that history is, at bottom, a form of religion. Cherrycoke's history would discover the divinity he understands to be carried within all people of all races.

The good Reverend Cherrycoke's aspiration as a historian is, ironically, to desacralize American history—to portray it as something other than the empirical proof of an imperialist science equation that demonstrates that white people are morally destined to rule the world through their ingenious gadgets and hypocritical Christianity. Cherrycoke mocks the sort of favored history that requires larger than life "Founding Brothers or Fathers" whose outsized scale must be equal to the epic sagas that they are supposed to enact. Cherrycoke declines to depict these Founding Fathers as colossi bestriding history; instead, he portrays them as comical figures somewhat ineptly equating their self-interest with that of the new nation. Benjamin Franklin is portrayed as a genius of the occult who is also a hardheaded sneak and a spy. There is a marvelous scene in which Franklin takes a group of people who have been listening to his harmonium in an inn and leads them out into the night to chase lightning and worship electricity.[15] Thomas Jefferson is a well-read country gentleman looking for a phrase that he will later use in the Declaration of Independence, whereas George Washington is a giggling, marijuana-smoking landowner whose sidekick is a black slave who doubles as a Jewish stand-up comic.[16] By rendering these "heroic giants" comically marginal without compromising Pynchon's massive historical overview of the period, *Mason & Dixon* identifies what our infatuation with these figures represses.

The received version of the Revolutionary War for most Americans is that the British were "oppressors" of and "tyrants" over the Americans. Yet American history does not begin with the Revolutionary War; it is itself a consequence of European history. In tracing the combined interests of European scientific invention and vast national mercantile greed, Pynchon radically suggests that the failure to recognize that American history was never truly a new beginning has blinded us to the true meaning of our history. A consequence of this national blindness is nicely expressed in Cherrycoke's portrayal of the Sons of Liberty—a revolutionary group committed to securing prompt freedom for the colonies—when they explain to Mason that he is, in reality, a slave to the British Crown (404–7). The historical irony of course is that the Americans and the English were both slave owners, and it would be the Americans' legacy to continue what was actually a European practice. However, because the foundling nation could not sort out its slavery problem, the ideals of the republic were doomed to fail. Dixon makes this point to the Sons of Liberty on a subsequent visit. He argues, " 'Tis not how British treat Americans [but] 'tis how both of You treat the African Slaves, and the Indians Native here, that engages the Friends more closely,—an old and melancholy History" (568). Dixon speaks as a Quaker but also represents a view that has been available in American history virtually since its inception, although Americans continue the pretense of asserting that it did not appear until the Civil War, the Civil Rights era, or yesterday. The Sons of Liberty allow Dixon his verbal liberty because he adds that, as a Geordie, he could never support an English king. His audience toasts the second statement and ignores the first. Cherrycoke's Dixon, though, knows not only that it is absurd for revolutionaries to claim that they are slaves to the Crown when real slaves exist beneath their very noses but also, as his answer suggests, that his revolt against the king would be inseparable from a revolt against the practice of slavery.

What is the proper historical method for addressing a nation famously dedicated to the proposition that all people were created equal yet whose material wealth depended on (and in a way depends still) on the exploitation of slaves? One can make the familiar argument that the understanding of equality written into the Declaration of Independence has become more inclusive with the passage of time, but not from Cherrycoke's "Christological" perspective. Pynchon suggests that the conflict between American myth and American reality is so entrenched that we cannot approach it honestly except through parodic humor. In this context, consider Cherrycoke's account of Mason and Dixon's visit with George Washington. Cherrycoke portrays a protovaudeville act between master and slave, where the slave invents the master at the price of the master's humanity and the slave's freedom. A comic note is struck immediately when the general, in response to Dixon's inquiry about his manner of speech, observes, "Up in Pennsylvania they tell me I talk like an African" (276). After sketching out in a disarmingly casual manner the Americans' eventual occupation of the continent—Americans "will fight Indians whenever they please" and will fight "Baits wherever they must"—Washington calls for his servant. Gershom enters in his best slave-lackey manner: "Yes Massuh Washington Suh" (278). Washington's assumption that Americans will control the continent and its history is of a piece with his assured mastery over Gershom.

The visitors, however, are impressed by neither Washington's imperial manner nor his slave's servile manner. The Quaker Dixon is enraged when Washington, citing John 1:49, identifies Gershom as "an Israelite in whom there is no guile." Dixon insists that only one savior can make such a judgment, and a duel seems imminent, when Gershom enters again and explains that the quotation is the general's way of making a joke. The joke is that Gershom actually is an Israelite, or at least is of the Hebrew faith, and he shows them his yarmulke to prove it. This sets off a chain of gags between master and servant appropriate to Gershom's other career as a stand-up comic. (His specialty is King George III jokes.) Washington then requests some Kasha Varnishkies, and, upon being told that there are none, requests hog jowls instead. At this point, Gershom, playing Stepin Fetchit, shouts, "One bi-i-i-I-g mess o' Hog Jowls, comin' raaight up, Suh!" (279). Together they playfully send up the institution of slavery and their implied relationship to each other as if to suggest to their visitors that the perniciousness of slavery has been greatly exaggerated. The peculiar institution, when observed up close, is actually a barrel of laughs.

With Gershom singing "Hava Naghilah," Pynchon freely piles anachronism upon anachronism. The joke is not on Mason and Dixon, but on Washington and the white male nation he is said to have fathered. If Gershom and George send up any notion that they are, in Cherrycoke's terms, knight and serf of the castle, then their comedy cannot conceal and indeed can only point to

182 Thomas Pynchon's *Mason & Dixon*

the fact that slave and master are mutual creations, dependent on each other. Much has been made of Jefferson's likely intimate relationship with his slave Sally Hemings and the children they probably made together, but the comedy imagined here involves a greater intimacy between master and slave than even concubinage affords. Gershom's primary role to is to entertain George. Yet, like the Fool in King Lear, Gershom's care for his master also involves his having authority over him. Thus, Gershom becomes the de facto adviser to his master's guests as Washington surrenders control of the scene to Gershom. He is free to joke about their impending deaths at the hands of Indians and the backwoods Presbyterians who will mistake them for atheists. The latter joke is one already made by Washington, leading the reader to suspect that so close is the relationship between master and slave that they say the same things regardless of whether they are together. The real joke—one that Americans approach painfully when they approach it all—is that Washington is somehow black and his slave is somehow white. Gershom speaks like Henny Youngman, and Washington, by his own admission, speaks like an African.

This so-called secret that George and Gershom joke about comes out in the open briefly, three hundred pages later, in a Virginia tavern where Mason and Dixon once again encounter Gershom. Complaining of the imperious way that the British are perceived as treating the colonies, someone observes that the British are "not only presuming us their Subjects, which is bad enough,—but merely that we're another kind of Nigger,—well that's what I can't forgive" (572). A bystander quickly objects to the use of the n-word as a "Very shark" in "this quiet Pool of Reason" but remains untroubled by the analogy (which previously troubled Dixon) that the white colonists and the black slaves have the same relationship to the British Crown (572). Then, as if on cue, Gershom materializes, spouting more jokes about King George—a slave earning laughs by mocking his white audience's "oppressor." He creates a sensation not just because of his antiroyalist stance but also because "half the Company believe this is a white Customer, impersonating an African." As those who recognize Gershom call out for favorite routines, such as "the Crocodile that can walk" or "the Rabbit in the Moon," the revelry is interrupted by a voice asking whether there might be "a real Negro in here." Someone responds with an observation funnier than even Gershom's best King George jokes: "Hell, maybe even more'n that one." Suddenly, the evening dissolves into chaos as "ev'ryone suspects ev'ryone else of being Gershom" (573).

In American history, the irony of the joke is nearly endless since white Americans have generally justified their power in terms of racial purity. African American intellectual history from Frederick Douglass to Toni Morrison has emphasized that white Americans have relied on the logic of racism to justify the repression of African Americans. Arguably, Gershom's joke allows Pynchon to acknowledge W. E. B. DuBois's contentions in *Souls of Black Folk* (1903) or Ralph Ellison's assertions in various essays that American history and identity are irreducibly African American. Gershom's joke, however, does not defiantly proclaim the essential blackness of American identity, as DuBois and Ellison did, but ironically surrenders the hope that the majority of contemporary white Americans would accept a version of themselves consistent with an African American point of view. *Mason & Dixon* does not address an explicitly African American audience as *Beloved* does. I believe that Pynchon, as perhaps is true of Morrison as well, would prefer a history that could be accepted by all Americans, but this history no longer seems possible. Pynchon underscores this pessimistic view through his ingenious use of anachronistic humor. Only an audience that had been sensitized by the attorney Johnnie Cochran's use of the term n-*word* instead of *nigger* during the 1994 O. J. Simpson trial could appreciate Pynchon's satirical jabs at political correctness in this scene. Pynchon's knowing postmodern anachronistic point of view, though, also satirizes best-selling popular histories about the Founding Fathers. Such works enact a collective will to situate American history forever in the time before the question of slavery and its consequences need be permanently addressed. From this perspective, Gershom's jokes suggest that any historian who fails to acknowledge how deeply embedded racist points of view continue to be in mainstream American history is a historian who writes fantastic, or unbelievable, history. The pluralist dream of an America in which all ethnicities can prosper was never, we now know, possible. The reader of *Mason & Dixon* despairs to affirm this point of view but also knows that any history that celebrates itself through anachronism can exist only on the margins, as irony. Yet this sort of postmodern skepticism, as Cherrycoke's knowing winks to the latter-day reader attest, is to be preferred over the type of exceptionalist American history that perpetuates itself as a form of unknowing anachronism committed by writers and consumed by audiences who choose to believe that the Revolutionary War is the endpoint of American history or that the Civil War truly ended at Appomattox in 1865.

III

Despite the persistent postmodernist skepticism of the outer narrative frame, Cherrycoke's heroes emerge from the narrative as heroes in what is nearly a premodernist way. Cherrycoke tells Mason and Dixon's story not simply to amuse his immediate audience, his various nieces and nephews, or to earn his night's lodging, but also to pay tribute to his friends' humanity as something that transcended the immediate circumstances of its expression. Cherrycoke portrays Mason and Dixon as devout men with honorable instincts that are worth preserving. Their Pynchonian humanity consists in their understanding that they cannot keep from violating their own sense of what makes a proper human community. This recognition is, to Cherrycoke, what makes redemption—for individuals and for history—possible.

Toward the end of their story, Dixon asks Mason, "Didn't we take the King's money, as here we're taking it again? whilst Slaves waited upon us, and we neither one objected. . . . Where does it end? No matter where in it we go, shall we find all the World Tyrants and Slaves? America was the one place we should *not* have found them" (693). Cherrycoke would have his audience remember Dixon's question while believing in the possibility of a Christ-redeemed history, one in which transcendence is possible. As Dixon tells Mason when they are on the verge of crossing the Warrior Path, "They [the Indians] want to know how to stop this great invisible Thing that comes crawling over the Land devouring all in its Path." It is a "tree-slaughtering Animal, with no purpose but to continue creating forever a perfect Corridor over the Land" (678). Dixon's ability to make this observation is what makes him fit to be one of Cherrycoke's heroes.

Moreover, Mason's and Dixon's acts that question the emerging status quo are prompted by a religious faith that cannot be accommodated to the exploitation or murder of human beings for profit. At one point Mason asks Dixon whether it is true that the Quakers sit still and quiet waiting for Christ to come. Dixon explains, "We spoke of it as the Working of the Spirit, within. 'Tis a distinct Change from ev'ryday. . . . Tha wouldn't be able to miss it, should it happen" (101). When Dixon protests the colonials' treatment of the Indians and the slaves, he speaks as a Quaker. As he tells the Sons of Liberty, "My allegiance, as a Quaker born, would lie, above all Tribes, with Christ" (568). Pynchon, the taproom historian looking for a link to the past that might justify a history other than the one the Founding Fathers left us, sees this allegiance when Dixon heroically confronts the slave trader in Baltimore near the end of the book. Unquestionably, it is one of the most important confrontations in the novel. At this point Mason and Dixon have completed their work in America and are on the verge of heading back to their native lands. Likewise, Cherrycoke's tale is near its end, and perhaps for this reason he allows his protagonists to seek a moral to their work: "Here in Maryland, they had a choice at last, and Dixon chose to act, and Mason not to,—unless he had to,—what each of us wishes he might have the unthinking Grace to do, yet fails to do. To act for all those of us who have so fail'd. For the Sheep" (698). The "Sheep," a version of the preterit in *Gravity's Rainbow*, include not the LeSparks but Pynchon's immediate audience, his readers. Cherrycoke's comment and Dixon's encounter with the slave trader identify American history in terms of our persistent failure to live by Dixon's "Spirit"—whatever notion of justice that might have authorized Americans as a group to act as Dixon does when he challenges the slave trader. For Pynchon, as for Morrison, the point is not that some Americans did not on occasion have the right impulses but that our ordinary histories continue to require works such as *Beloved* and *Mason & Dixon* to make our failures known and one day, perhaps, right.

Dixon's desire, a hopeless one, is to drive the slave trader off the street and outside of history. As the slave trader announces his auction, with the promise that each of the Africans is "a flower of the Tribe they had been taken from," Dixon initially tries to repress the desire, "strong as thirst, to get up, walk over to the fellow and strike him" (696). Pynchon's portrayal of the slave trader denies that slavery was ever about anything more than the gratification of having complete control over another human being for one's own private pleasure; this desire to own—whether economic, sexual, or even moral—matters more than its justification. "And so I hope ev'ryone will come down and have a look, dusky children of the Forest, useful in any number o' ways, cook and eat 'em, fuck 'em or throw 'em to the Dogs, as we say in the Trade, imagine Gents, your very own Darky, to order about as you please." He then addresses Dixon directly: "You, Sir, in the interesting Hat. A fine young Mulatto gal'd be just your pint of Ale I'd wager, well tonight you're in luck, damme 'f you're not" (696). When the slave trader adds that "everyone wants a slave, at least one, to call his own," Dixon responds "far too brightly," "Sooner or later a Slave must kill his Master" (697). As the reader knows, the trader's jest is on target, since Dixon continues to desire Austra, a slave girl he first met in Capetown and then would see again in Pennsylvania. The next day Dixon again encounters the trader, driving his slaves through town, disconsolate because he has not sold them all. Having secured Mason's promise to back him up, Dixon declares, "That's enough" and "stands between the Whip and the Slaves" (698). The trader warns Dixon not to interfere with his property, but Dixon counters by taking away the slaver's whip. Dixon then, apparently, whips the humiliated trader with his own instrument. The trader cries out for mercy while his own slaves watch briefly before unchaining themselves and escaping. Dixon tells his victim, "Now be a man, face me, and make it easier, or must I rather work upon *you* from the Back, like a Beast, which will take longer, and certainly mean more discomfort for *you*" (699). Dixon wants to kill him, but his conscience prevents him. Instead, he keeps the trader's whip and warns him, "Dead *you'll* be, ere *you* see again this Instrument of Shame. For it will lie in a Quaker Home, and never more be us'd" (699).

How different Dixon's "Spirit"-infused stance against slavery is from that of the greedy and niggardly Dutch Vrooms, whom Mason and Dixon encounter in South Africa. The Vrooms's pious Protestantism adorns their greed for acquisition. Their desire for wealth is insatiable and inseparable from their status as slave owners—a point that Pynchon makes humorously by portraying them as clever hawkers of sex. The Vroom women (mother as well as daughters) excite the desire of Mason and Dixon so that the gentlemen will satisfy their sexual desires elsewhere—on the bodies of the slaves. The Vroom women sit on Mason's lap or appear before him alone, with their breasts exposed. Then in the night, slave girls appear as if they were succubae sent from the men's dreams to ease their priapic pain. In the dark, slavery seems a dream, a romance of the night. Actually, it is a carefully orchestrated, quite rational manipulation of sexual desire. The children engendered—or perhaps we should say engineered—will augment the property of the Vrooms. The Vrooms justify their transaction to themselves through their belief (which they understand to be fact) that they are redeeming Africa for the fulfillment of Christianity. In so doing, the Vrooms perpetuate a cycle of white ascendancy and black dependency in the eighteenth century that persists to this day.[17] Thus, it is crucial to note that Dixon's revolt against the slave trader is also a revolt against his continuing desire for Austra, the slave girl he met in Africa. Dixon's heroism consists of his ability to acknowledge his own desire for sexual possession of another but still reject it. Of course, given that Austra is not present during Dixon's revolt, his desire for her may be repressed rather than abolished.

Moreover, Pynchon's strategy of having Cherrycoke tell his tales of slavery to the LeSparks as a form of entertainment implies that slavery is but one long-running production, in which each of us has a role, in a theater that we have never escaped.

Still, as a tableau for how Americans might have confronted the evil of slavery, Dixon's attack on the slave trader and his confiscation of the whip are irresistible. Instead of retiring the whip of slavery as soon as conscience rose up against it, Americans have too often invented a history that conceals how we have craved the whip—as the slave trader knew—and that repeats the rationalizations of the past in order to excuse what was done and to ignore that descendants of slaves are now more likely to be poor than any other people in American society.[18] Cherrycoke suffers from no moral ambiguity regarding either the practice of slavery or its role in the creation of the republic. How would American history be different if the perspective that informs Cherrycoke's tale—given before Washington became president—had become the canonical version of the birth of America? What if American history had not been a narrative of ongoing repression of "others" and dissenters in the name of liberty? What if it had instead been one that confronted the *repression* of "others," and not the "others" themselves, as the central threatening impulse to an enlightened communal ideal?[19] Then the moral outrage of slavery and the dispossession of the Indians' territory would always be in the open for those to deny if they dare. Would subsequent Americans have been compelled to square the justifications given by their country for its acts with the acts themselves? Or, like the LeSpark family, would Americans have learned to pretend that the imperious, self serving-justification that has passed as "American history" is, in fact, "true," and thus, in the end, is all for the best? Again, Pynchon suggests that all along only the latter scenario could have been the American fate. Most white Americans live more or less happily in an endless present severed from any knowledge about those conflicts of the past that have, in fact, never been resolved, while the "others" who protest are dismissed as "identity politics" troublemakers (people who that so-called American history often labels as those targeted by the Alien and Sedition Acts or, perhaps one day soon, the Patriot Act).

Pynchon, as despairing as his history may be, remains in part a resolute post-modern idealist. This Pynchon represents the futile, if still longed for, dream of escaping the premises of American history through Cherrycoke's "Indian" vision, a version of the Sioux holy man Black Elk and others have described when in touch with their dead ancestors or their gods. In this dream—"I pray 'twas Dream," Cherrycoke says—he is flying "some fifty to an hundred feet above the Surface, down the Visto, straight West" (649). Here Cherrycoke is either transcending the course of the Mason-Dixon Line and thus escaping its implied history or merely continuing its progress. He decides what he experiences, " 'Tis no Dream, but a form of Transport," but where he is transported or for what precise purpose he cannot say. Like the "unearthly blue flame" that he sees that he associates with a "waggoners' Forge or Mr. McClean's Oven," the Mason-Dixon "Line makes itself felt,—thro' some Energy unknown" (650). Perhaps in opposition to his image of an engine burning in the wilderness, the Reverend fashions himself "an heroick Scout" who is "seeking the Warrior Path." Cherrycoke whispers to a future from an unrecoverable past:

> We all feel it Looming, even when we're awake, out there ahead someplace, the way you come to feel a River or Creek ahead, before anything else,— sound, sky, vegetation,—may have announced it. Perhaps 'tis the very deep sub-audible Hum of its Traffic that we feel with an equally undiscover'd part of the Sensorium,—does it lie but over the next Ridge? The one after that? We have Mileage Estimates from Rangers and Runners, yet for as long as its Distance from the Post Mark'd West remains unmeasur'd, nor is yet recorded as Fact, may it remain, a-shimmer, among the few final Pages of its Life as Fiction. (650)

Again, Cherrycoke speaks to the past and the future simultaneously. Both implied audiences have shared the same fantasy that the Indians are unapproachable beings, children lost to (our) history, figures from other cultures' fables. By reading the book we become de facto members of Mason and Dixon's party. In speaking the dream of his "transport," the Reverend seeks the way (or a road to a road) back to the Warrior Path. To find this path, one would have to be "transported" beyond the enlightenment and Christianity as well: one would have to abandon time and distance as one knows it. Cherrycoke implies that although the West may be settled and the burning engine of technology may have overwhelmed the wilderness all the way to the Pacific Ocean and into futurity, somewhere within a still unmapped space the "Traffic" of the Warrior Path continues unabated and undisturbed. We—his audiences—have written over the Warrior Path's line but we have not erased it, because we have not crossed it, for the simple reason that *we have not yet invented the equipment to mark the path or what it means.* How can you cross what you cannot see or know? Borrowing the words from Wallace Stevens's poem, "The Idea of Order in Key West," Americans have yet to find demarcations ghostly enough to register the Path. That part of our "sensorium" still lies undiscovered, and it is to that still unknown country that Cherrycoke's "transport" pays tribute.

Through Cherrycoke's transport, Pynchon's encyclopedic awareness of early America in all of its European dimensions will surrender any claims to narrative authority over the story of the Indians. As one Indian tells Mason, we are also your dreams. Although the Europeans have faith in their technology—that "the finer the Scale we work at, the more Power we dispose"—the Indian's remark suggests that his people cannot be vanquished or vanished at all. Cherrycoke leaves for the Indians the prospect of escaping Mason and Dixon's "looming" line. "On November 5th," he remarks, "two things happen at once,—the Visto is completed, and the Indians depart" (681). One seems to be a necessary consequence of the other. In turn, Cherrycoke surrenders his ability to imagine himself as an Indian, since that flight of fancy also stops at the boundary of the Warrior Path. He cannot find the path: no exact mileage estimates exist. Cherrycoke can only remember it, as Mason does that Indian face, as something he cannot know.

In *Days of Obligation*, Richard Rodriguez writes bitterly of contemporary Americans' tendency to romanticize what used to be called the "American Indian": to equate them with an idealized version of nature. This version of the "American Indian" can only cry, as he does in a famous commercial from the 1970s at the polluted disaster that white people have made of the landscape. This version of the Indian must remain static, a figure who represents his or her people's despoilment and the white people's triumph, however ambiguous. In his refusal to represent the Indian as a part of Western culture, Pynchon may partake of the kind of romanticism that Rodriguez derides. On my view, what makes Pynchon's treatment of the Indians striking, and not merely romantic, is that it refuses to represent the Indians at all. (Even *Mason & Dixon's* parodic version of the Puritan captivity narrative involves not Indians but Jesuits as captors.) They are not understood to be hosts to the Europeans or exactly stewards of nature. Rather, the existence of the Indians forms a line, a boundary against which Europeans have defined and continued to know themselves. Portraying America as the invention of the enlightenment and empiricism, Pynchon represents the Indians *as never having been there/here at all.* To be sure, people known as "Indians," or the Six Nations, existed and were allied with the French against the British in the French and Indian War. They endured as mercenaries (bodies, creatures), who could wield weapons and be employed by another European nation to further the European ends. As a threat, they needed to be expunged—with smallpox-infested blankets if necessary (another fruit of science). However, to understand the Indians as a people with a set of historical premises that govern their actions and that may be adapted by Europeans is unthinkable within the historical frame Pynchon establishes.

Cherrycoke gives Mason something of this paradoxical way of perceiving. If Dixon fought the slave trader (and with him his own desire to possess slaves), Mason is the one who seeks to commune with the Indians. Working from Mason's actual preserved logs, Cherrycoke re-creates Mason's visit to the site where the Paxton boys massacred a group of Native American men, women, and children—an event that haunts Cherrycoke's narrative and Mason in particular. Mason writes in his "Field-Record" of his visit to Lancaster Town, thirty-five miles off his course, "What brought me here was my curiosity to see the place where was perpetrated the Horrid and inhuman murder of 26 Indians, Men, Women, Children, leaving none alive to tell" (341). Typically, the winners, the American settlers, are there to justify what happened. Their logic is based on blood reasoning. They kill ours, and we kill theirs. Dixon objects that the slain were said to be members of a peaceable tribe—certainly the mothers and children were peaceable. The colonists say that this slaughter hurts them more. Mason remarks that they must hate the Indians very much. "We're out here as a Picket for Philadelphia," one says (344). Neither Mason nor Dixon, agents of civilization themselves, are moved by a logic that says, in effect, being "civilized" justifies any act, no matter how barbarous. The next day Mason returns alone to the site of the massacre and is moved to ask of himself and perhaps God, "What in the Holy Names are these People about? Not even the Dutchmen at the Cape behav'd this way. Is it something in the wilderness, something ancient, that waited for them, and infected their Souls when they came?" (347). Mason knows that such arguments are also specious, since they would deny civilization's complicity with the force that destroys in its name—as if once the wilderness is cleared, a truly refined civilization begins. Standing there as a witness to a barely remembered massacre, voluntarily confronting "blood in Corners never cleans'd" and places "where blows with Rifle-Butts miss'd their Marks, and chipp'd the Walls," Mason thinks that these acts were committed in a place "roofless to His Surveillance,—and to His Judgment."

How can the colonists commit these acts before God, who should seem so much closer to them in a place as yet untransformed by humans? The answer he comes up with is as good a definition of how Americans understand their relationship to the past as any. He tells Dixon, "Acts have consequences," and "these Louts" have "no Glimmer of all the debt they have taken on." He then adds that what he smelled there was not so much death but "Lethe-Water." "In Time, these People are able to forget ev'rything" (346–47). That is, Mason and Dixon encounter Americans indifferent to the horror of their acts *as they are being committed*. But what consequences have these acts for most Americans except that they have been forgotten as have the people who were eradicated? Mason aptly states, "In America, as I apprehend, Time is the true River that runs 'round Hell" (346). The Americans Mason and Dixon meet do not really die; they replicate themselves into the twentieth century and beyond.

Against this perpetual forgetting stand the examples of Cherrycoke and Pynchon, who desire a history that seeks its own transcendence. "To insist on the miraculous," Pynchon writes in "Is It O.K. to Be a Luddite?" "is to deny the machine at least some of its claims on us, to assert the limited wish that living things, earthly and otherwise, may on occasion become Bad and Big enough to take part in transcendent doings" (5). In *Mason & Dixon*, the instinct to preserve history must, for Cherrycoke, include the dream of transcendence as a condition for remembering anything at all. Cherrycoke speaks to children too young to have forgotten anything or accommodated themselves to the contradictions of history. He would instruct the uncorrupted even while adults protest. His history remains true to the young man who was removed from England for protesting notices of assize. There he was convicted, in his words, of "a Crime they styl'd 'Anonymity' "; he had posted around London "Accounts of certain Crimes I had observed, committed by the Stronger against the Weaker,—enclosures, evictions, Assize verdicts, Activities of the Military,—giving the Names of as many of the Perpetrators as I was sure of" (9). For such acts, he was confined to the Tower of London, "to understand that my name had never been my own,—rather belonging, all this time, to the Authorities, who forbade me to change it, or withhold it, as 'twere a Ring upon the Collar of a Beast, ever waiting for the Lead to be fasten'd on" (10). His memory of this "Ring" foreshadows his sympathy for the slaves and the Indians; it is what he brings with him to America when he is cast out of England. "Anonymity" is not so much his crime as his condition, one that he shares with his creator, Thomas Pynchon, who fashions himself as one whose books are the anonymous postings of an oppositional force in hiding. *Mason & Dixon* is a powerful protest against the claims of the powerful told by an anonymous man otherwise lost to history and its endless parade of crimes committed by the stronger against the weaker. For some readers, Pynchon's fantastic novel may be the truest version of American history yet written.

5

History after Henry Adams and Ronald Reagan Joan Didion's *Democracy* and Don DeLillo's *Underworld*

Historians undertake to arrange sequences—called stories,
or histories,—assuming in silence a relation of cause and
effect. . . . Where he saw sequence, other men saw something
quite different, and no one saw the same unit of measure. He
cared little about experiments and less about his statesmen,
who seemed to him quite as ignorant as himself and, as a rule,
no more honest; but he insisted on a relation of sequence, and
if he could not reach it by one method, he would try as many
methods as science knew. Satisfied that the sequence of men
led to nothing and that the sequence of their society led no
further, while the mere sequence of time was artificial, and
the sequence of thought was chaos, he turned at last to the
sequence of force.
—Henry Adams, *The Education of Henry Adams*

I

At the turn of the twentieth century, Henry Adams describes the historian's plight in terms that predict how Don DeLillo portrays the plight of historian Nicholas Branch in *Libra*. Branch, like Adams, is so overwhelmed by the inundation of "facts" about the subject of his inquiry and by the multiplying theoretical explanations that these facts suggest that he is helpless to construct a narrative that can adequately account for what has occurred. Adams's modernist plight predicts DeLillo's postmodern predicament: the inability to construct a linear narrative that connects the present to the past. Along with Don DeLillo, Thomas Pynchon and Joan Didion are the major postmodern American novelists whose work most clearly addresses Adams's concern that historians could no longer claim objective mastery over their subject. Pynchon's first novel, *V* (1963), was constructed as a kind of Adamsian inquiry into the nature of history and identity.[1] Works such as *Gravity's Rainbow* and

Mason & Dixon comment on the postmodern author's inability to overcome and outframe the great narrative strategists who represent the combined forces of Science, Government, and Business. Didion's debt to Adams, which is largely the subject of this chapter, is evident in her darkly ironic stance toward the practice of American democracy and the corrosive beauty of her prose. Where Adams, assuming corruption to be the prime mover of political action, is sanguine about the artist's irrelevance to political power, Didion extends Adams's arguments to reveal American democracy as a type of postmodernist novel in progress orchestrated by ingenious modernist-schooled narrators whose political power is a consequence of their narrative mastery. As we shall see, Didion and DeLillo both suggest that the line between art and society, between aesthetics and politics, has—since modernism—become irretrievably blurred and that when it comes to narrative structures and the art of deploying them, the work of the solitary historian or novelist is a feeble match for the overwhelming aesthetic presentation and narrative power of a Ronald Reagan or an I. G. Farben.

This dire situation would surely have amused Adams, who mordantly announced in his *Education* the end to history. Writing in 1906, Adams decrees, "In 1900, the continuity [that holds history together] snapped" (*Henry* 1137). As Adams drew closer to death, he repeatedly fantasized about a historical method, predicated on physics, that could predict the end of history. With varying degrees of irony, Adams's late works refined his earlier prediction of the precise date of the end of history (other end dates were either 1921 or 2025) but were consistent in asserting that history could be known only as a form of entropic decline. In his 1909 work, "The Rule of Phase Applied to History," Adams suggested that "if man should continue to set free the infinite forces of nature, and attain the control of cosmic forces on a cosmic scale, the consequences may be as surprising as the change of water to vapor, of the worm to butterfly, or radium to electrons" (*Degradation* 309). What Adams really meant was that in the physics-driven machine age, traditional historical narrative was losing its force—except perhaps in its conventional role to describe "the decline and fall" of any given age. In light of the discovery of entropy, "nothing remains for the historian to describe or develop except the history of a more or less mechanical dissolution" (206). Thus, Adams decreed that history as a form "must submit to the final and fundamental necessity of Degradation" (208). Adams's key claim is that human history itself has become a version of the scientific equations that allowed humans to redirect nature's seemingly immeasurable (and immeasurably inefficient) forces into technologies of control. Rather than comprise stories about how differing peoples invented themselves in light of the historical circumstances in which they found themselves, history would now become a function of new scientific equations whose chief effect would be to obligate humans to subsume their identities within physical forces that they only seemed to comprehend. "If values can be given to these attractions," Adams said, "a physical theory of history is a mere matter of physical formula, no more complicated that the formulas of Willard Gibbs or James Clerk Maxwell; *but the task of framing the formula and assigning the value belongs to the physicist*" (310). Significantly, Adams suggests not so much that the physicist has usurped the role of the historian as that the physicist's discoveries inevitably must alter what it means to be human and thus what it means to construct stories about being human as well.

For Adams, history was neither an object nor an idea about the past; it was a narrative problem to be solved. If history is no longer teleological, then such ordering that it can have is a matter of narrative art. Commenting on Adams's affinity with later theorists of postmodernism, David Harlan sees him as a kind of proto–Michel Foucault. According to Harlan, "the older Adams" and the "younger Foucault" both "looked into the past and saw nothing but a discontinuous series of sudden, unexpected, inexplicable and inexplicably violent ruptures" (*Degradation* xxvii). In his autobiography, Adams is uncertain how to define either history or himself as a subject. "One sought no absolute truth," he admits. "One sought only a spool on which to wind the thread of history without breaking it. Among indefinite possible orbits, one sought the orbit which would satisfy the observed moment of the runaway star Groombridge, 1838, commonly called Henry Adams" (qtd. in Harlan, *Degradation* xxvii). *The Education of Henry Adams* offers a narrative frame that insists on the inevitable contingency of all points of view. No chapter offers a definitive view of Adams, and each chapter challenges the claims to historical knowledge of previous chapters. In *Libra*, Branch can find no spool to wind his history of the John F. Kennedy assassination into coherent narrative. Where Adams imagines history as something that can communicate only a proliferating sense of dislocation and alienation, DeLillo imagines that in the postmodern era, history must turn to fiction as its last chance for inventing narratives that people will accept as true.

As powerfully as the works of Pynchon and DeLillo, Didion's work has addressed how writing history has changed since Adams predicted its death more than one hundred years ago. Her novel *Democracy*, named after Adams's *Democracy*, is her most concentrated and sustained response to Adams, but virtually every one of her sentences implies Adams in some way. All of Didion's works, fiction and nonfiction, toy with the stance of a narrator who is at odds with his or her own narrative, which Adams enacted in *The Education of Henry Adams*. What Didion takes from Adams, beyond a similarity in narrative style, is a certain skepticism regarding the historian's ability to represent the subject so that the audience will believe what the historian says is, in fact, true. Where Didion differs crucially from DeLillo is in her skepticism that fiction has any greater claim to narrative authority than history does. DeLillo's work when read through Didion's (and DeLillo has acknowledged Didion as an influence) reveals a kind of modernist nostalgia for the godlike narrative power of the master artist. Both *Libra* and *Underworld* imply that whereas the historian cannot stand outside the process that he or she describes, the novelist can. *Democracy*, by contrast, questions whether any narrative, regardless of whether it is called history or fiction, can be seen as true, except as the successful expression of a will to power on a massive scale. Like Pynchon and DeLillo, Didion attempts to offer an oppositional stance to the union of corporate power with governmental control, yet she worries whether a context exists in the postmodern age for this stance to be expressed. Critics of postmodern approaches to history have often worried that such approaches create a "political paralysis resulting from the reduction of lived experience to linguistic texts" (Berkhofer 16). Bryan Palmer argues that "the descent into discourse" has resulted in "a plurality of discourses that decenter the world in a chaotic denial of any acknowledgement of tangible structures of power and comprehensions of meaning" (qtd. in Berkhofer 15). The concern here is not that history becomes merely the whim of the historian but that forces labeled as racial, economic, or political no longer seem relevant to describe how a society works. From the other side of the postmodern divide, Keith Jenkins says that now that history "has ended as a groundable (epistemological/ontological) discourse," history can become whatever we want it to be, as we look forward "to possible future imaginaries exfoliating forever" (*Why* 2–3). Didion suggests that Jenkins's view is naïve and worries that a "groundless" postmodernist history becomes a tool to support the interests of the ruling classes. For Didion, history belongs to those who control the means of its representation and distribution—an ongoing movie, television, or radio show—and it is owned and operated by the program's sponsor. You, the viewer, watch the program and buy its products; otherwise, you are out of the picture.

Didion does not imagine, however, that a properly vetted postmodernist (or anti-postmodernist) approach to practicing history in the academy will rescue history from its current dilemma. More despairingly than perhaps even Pynchon, Didion suggests that the rise of postmodernism, combined with a global media culture that is, in fact, an expression of allied corporate and government interests, means that history as a source of memory and cultural continuity no longer exists except as the occasional expression of outraged marginalized groups. The works of writers such as Didion, DeLillo, and Pynchon occupy a critical perspective analogous to less well-known or read academic studies published by university presses. Academic arguments about the practice of history, or academic histories that challenge persuasively some received view of the past, can be made and exchanged between interested parties, but they will have virtually no effect on the national conversation about American history that takes place daily on television, in newspapers, or every two or four years at the ballot box. A work such as *Democracy* does not portray history as dead; it portrays it as an idea, or a memory, that no longer interests most Americans except as the confirmation of something that they already believe. Further, Didion suggests, what they believe is likely going to be some government-manufactured "lie" that is told as a pleasing story and distributed to reach the maximum possible number of viewers, readers, or listeners. *Democracy* shows that in the postmodern era one cannot say, as Faulkner did, that the past is not even past, because, in fact, the past never was at all.

Adams suggested that historians' inability to know the present compromised their ability to know the past. Jean Baudrillard says that in the postmodern era "perhaps history itself has to be regarded as a chaotic formation in which acceleration puts an end to linearity and the turbulence created . . . deflects [it] definitively from its end" (qtd. in Jenkins 65). Once you lose control of the present, you lose control of the past as an informing idea as well. The past becomes something that is invented, packaged, and adapted as needed. During the run-up to the 2004 election, there was much talk about "a senior adviser to [President George W.] Bush" who, according to a report by the journalist Ron Suskind in the October 17, 2002, *New York Times Magazine*, had offered this view:

Guys like me [Suskind] were "in what we call the reality-based community," which he defined as people who "believe that solutions emerge from your judicious study of discernible reality." I nodded and murmured something about enlightenment principles and empiricism. He cut me off. "That's not the way the world really works anymore," he continued. "We're an empire now, and when we act, *we create our own reality.* And while you're studying that reality—judiciously, as you will—we'll act again, creating other new realities, which you can study too, and that's how things will sort out. We're history's actors . . . and you, all of you, will be left to just study what we do." (http://www.nytimes.com/2004/10/17/magazine/17BUSH.html, emphasis mine)

The adviser blithely announces that "history" is not the past unless the government says that it is. His blunt declaration of power depends on an ability to use the media to name and therefore create reality. By seizing control of how the present is known and represented, a government administration need only maintain the appearance of consistency with the ideals of democracy, in order for most Americans to accept as true the reality that the government knows to be its own invention. For instance, if Congress passes something known as the "Clean Air Act," the name of the act alone is enough to ensure public approval. Whether the law fulfills its name's promise is irrelevant, since the name will characterize whatever most citizens hear about the government's actions regarding "clean air." That such a law may actually protect the industries that are responsible for a significant amount of world pollution is an irony for connoisseurs of postmodern discourse to savor. Any complaints about the law will be presented on television as mere entertainment, and every time environmentalists support the protestors' position, the media that covers them will further marginalize their view: How can any reasonable group protest a "clean air act"?

Baudrillard's "The Precession of Simulacra" describes a process whereby the mass media has effected what he refers to as a simulacrum of the real. As Linda Hutcheon explains, "Baudrillard argued that today the mass media have neutralized reality by stages: first they reflected it; then they masked and perverted it; next they had to mask its absence; and finally they produced instead the simulacrum of the real, the destruction of meaning and of all relation to reality" (*Politics* 31). One can question whether reality has been neutralized or a different way of perceiving has replaced another way of perceiving, but from either perspective the point is the same: whoever controls the means of media representation also controls history as most Americans receive it.[2] To DeLillo, as we shall see, Baudrillard's simulacrum is the space in which "senior advisers" such as the one that Suskind describes (and the interests that they represent) have become quasi-modernist narrative gods absorbing the world with all of its contradictions into one powerful, totalizing narrative frame. Michael Rogin's book *Ronald Reagan, the Movie, and Other Episodes in Political Demonology* (1987) gives a compelling account of the stunning representation of such narrative power in the political realm during the 1984 Republican Convention. The scene is the staged representation of the nomination of Reagan for a second term of office. The stars are Ronald Reagan, Nancy Reagan, and the awe-struck viewer. After showing a film that "cut from shots of her among children and drug abusers to a scene from *Hellcats of the Navy*," Nancy Reagan "repeats her faith in the commander as he leaves on his climactic voyage" (42). The commander in the 1957 film is, of course, Ronald Reagan. First in the film and then in televised real life, Nancy Reagan dramatizes for an audience larger than any who ever watched one of her films a process whereby a nearly thirty-year-old movie about a fictional war hero can come to life as contemporary historical reality. As Rogin's analysis makes clear, the audience's perception of the older President Reagan collapses into their perception of the younger, fictional Commander Reagan. Nancy on the podium forms the bridge between the real Reagan, whatever that is, and his image. Her live presence in the viewer's television set assures the audience that one Reagan is the same as the other and that to believe in him they need only call him President.

Even more extraordinary, though, is how the staged event will collapse Nancy Reagan, the twice-represented Ronald Reagan, and the television-viewing audience into one perceiving mass by placing actor (Ronald Reagan), fan (Nancy Reagan), and the audience (you or me) within a single frame of vision. As Rogin explains:

> In cutting from life to the movie, the republican National Committee may seem to have exposed the manufactured nature of its real-life image of the president's wife. But another film event suggests the media men deliberately dissolved the boundary between life and image [art] to offer us the reassurance of film. The president reelected in 1984 does not promote the telescreen as an instrument of surveillance and personal invasion on which big brother is watching you. Instead he offers freedom from public and

private anxieties by allowing you to watch big brother. When Nancy Reagan spoke at the convention following the film of her life, Ronald Reagan watched her on television from their hotel suite. "Make it one more for the Gipper," she urged, and the mass television audience (including him) saw her tiny figure turn with arms raised in support of an enormous image on the screen beside her, larger than her and larger than life. On camera in the hotel room, the image watched itself wave back, forming the truncated head and shoulders of her husband, the president of the United States. (42)

Rogin's account points to the diminished authentic presence of the president, who has become a cropped image that, as it happens, recalls the paralyzed hero that he played in an earlier movie, *King's Row* (1942). Rogin's descriptive phrase, "truncated head and shoulders," suggests a spectacle of humanity diminished and replaced by a mere image—a head shot. What is truly remarkable about this spectacle, though, is how the members of the audience become one with the president not by expressing their collective political wishes through Congress but by joining him as a spectator to his own staged regime. He stands out as the First Viewer, the man who controls the television channel that we all watch, and he himself is the representation that the screen projects. The scene implies both omnipresence and omnipotence. References to Reagan's films in which he retrospectively seems to have been a martyred hero (the Gipper from *Knute Rockne*) or a brave commander (*Hellcats of the Navy*) stand in for the political situation that he is presumably being elected to shape for the improvement of all. No one need question what Reagan does as president, because he is always with us, since the audience is situated within the television set with our friend and leader, Ronnie. As the actor, or self, who is being divided into millions of identical television images for an audience of people who are consuming history not as a subject or even as the past but as the immediate representation of themselves and their collective desire, Reagan watching himself wave to Nancy and to the rest of us performs a version of the spectacle that DeLillo portrays in *Libra*, with Lee Harvey Oswald dying while he watches his own death on a television placed nearby.[3] If watching the endlessly reflected images of Ronnie and Nancy waving to each other and to us—being part of their story on television as if it were also our story—is represented as if it were the same as making a political choice or choosing to believe in a kind of history, it is because in the postmodern era it is the same.

Who is the author of this image? Not Ronald Reagan, and not DeLillo or

Didion either. The author is a version of the president's senior adviser who described to Suskind how any government regime invents reality in the postmodern era. The works of Didion and DeLillo intersect at the point where one tries to make historical sense of narratives that seem to have no author and political processes whose power accrues from their ability to present history as the invention of a never-ending moment in time. As we shall see, in *Underworld* DeLillo portrays the aesthetic possibilities of the postmodern era as no longer being the province of only artists (novelists, sculptors, filmmakers) but also of masters of political surveillance such as J. Edgar Hoover. In *Democracy* Didion draws on the lessons of Adams to suggest that there is no way for her or anyone else to compete with narratives that can be compressed and conveyed instantaneously and continuously with such force as the narrative of Reagan waving to himself (and thus to everyone watching) at the 1984 Republican Convention. It is not that history does not exist but that its function has been usurped by political forces that claim to act in its name.

I I

During a long, eloquent speech concerning the corruption that is endemic to American political and social life, a character in Adams's *Democracy* (1880) laments that he will not live long enough to see just how corrupt American society will become in the future: "I do much regret that I have not yet one hundred years to live. If I could then come back to this city, I should find myself content—very much more so than now. I am always content where there is more corruption, and *ma parole d'honeur*" (*Henry Adams: Novels* 38). Published just over one hundred years after Adams's novel of the same title and in the same year as Reagan's televised apotheosis as the living end of American history that Rogin describes, Didion's *Democracy* confirms that Adams's view of history as a narrative problem predicts how history would come to be understood in the postmodern era. It also confirms Adams's prescient fears regarding the depressing fate of the American republic. In Adams's *Democracy* the presumption is that the central character, a wealthy widow named Madeleine Lee, moves from New York to Washington to observe the true operation of social and political power in America. "She wanted to see with her own eyes the action of primary forces; to touch with her own hand the massive machinery of society; to measure with her own mind the capacity of the motive of power" in order to discover for herself "the great American mystery of democracy and government" (7). What she discovers is "a government of the people, by the people, for the benefit of Senators" (17). At the center of Didion's novel, by contrast, are two heroines. One is Inez Christian-Victor, modeled after the widowed heroine of Adams's Democracy. Where Madeleine Lee moves to Washington to find the locus of power in America and is courted by a congressman and a senator, Inez Christian-Victor marries a congressman who becomes a senator only to find that the power that she seeks circulates not through her husband's office but elsewhere. The other heroine is Didion. Her narrative stance is borrowed not from Adams's Democracy but from The Education of Henry Adams, as she pursues a plot line that is held together by her inability to master the narrative that she presumes to tell. Where Adams's Democracy assumes a center of power that might be penetrated and known, Didion's Democracy assumes that any such center of power is a fiction that is designed to conceal how disconnected the claims of democracy and even history are from day-to-day political reality.[4] Beyond acting as a scathing attack on American imperialism, Didion's Democracy raises the question of whether attacks on imperialism or improper concentrations of power are even possible—not because people do not want to stage the attacks but because historians lack the narrative power to communicate their critiques to audiences increasingly devoid of that quality without which no history can exist: memory.

Didion's engagement with Adams is itself slyly Adams-like. Adams presents The Education of Henry Adams as if it were an autobiography, but in many ways it is more successful as a fiction than is his novel Democracy. Didion presents her work as a novel but in many ways it is more effective as a kind of history. Didion's characters are invented (although plausible real-life models could be adduced), but the author who enters the narrative is to be taken as the author of the book. In this sense, Didion's Democracy can be read as a veiled autobiography. Similarly, The Education of Henry Adams begins with an "Editor's Preface" that is attributed to Henry Cabot Lodge although, in fact, it is written by Adams. Adams deployed a fictional device as the frame through which the reader would apprehend what he presented as his life's story. Adams thus omitted crucial biographical facts of his life, most notably the story of his marriage to Marian Hooper and her eventual suicide, while he made the real historical figures of his novel—Abraham Lincoln, Henry Palmerston, William Gladstone—seem like fictional characters. Adams wrote Lodge that his goal was to adhere to "the rule of making the reader think only of the text" (Henry Adams: Novels 1220). Assuming the voice of Lodge in the preface, he identifies the work's central achievement in terms of a problem that he could not solve, remarking that "the point on which the author failed to please himself and could get no light from readers or friends, was the usual one of literary form" (719). Didion's problem in Democracy is also one of form, but her solution, following Adams's example, is to employ a narrative strategy that makes the history that she describes both personal and national and then to suggest that neither she as author nor America as history makes coherent sense in any way that she can authorize.

Didion borrows the plot for her novel from Adams's Democracy and then inserts the autobiographical narrative perspective from The Education of Henry Adams into that plot. In effect, she combines Adams's novel and his autobiography and then translates both into a late-twentieth-century, postmodern context.[5] Hutcheon, arguably the ablest taxonomist of postmodernity, could be speaking of either Adams or Didion when she says, "The postmodern's initial concern" is "to de-naturalize some of the dominant features of our way of life; to point out that those entities which we unthinkingly experience as 'natural' are in fact 'cultural'" (Politics 2). In Democracy Didion playfully acknowledges this stance as hers by including an excerpt of an assignment from a college textbook for freshman writers. The textbook assignment refers to an essay written by Didion. After noting that "Didion begins with a rather ironic reference to her immediate reason to write this piece," the textbook asks the student to "consider Didion's own involvement in the setting" (17). In a novel that asks the reader to "call" the narrator "Joan Didion," the move underscores Didion's ironic self-authorizing narrative given: to refuse to accept any narrative stance as definitive or authoritative. The book thus presents its characters and the events that it describes in the same light as it does its own mediating narrative persona: with ironic skepticism. The implied logic of Didion's rhetorical move leads us to Hutcheon's other central claim about postmodernism: that it exists in a space where "documentary historical actuality meets formalist self-reflexivity and parody" in that postmodernism admits its "own complicity with power and domination" (Poetics 7, 4). Certainly, Democracy seems to follow this form, as it gives a documentary account of the rise and fall of a powerful American political family, its point of view rendered as "real," since it is told by the well-known reporter and cultural critic "Joan Didion."

Moreover, as Alan Nadel notes, Democracy is "about the erosion of [Americans'] ability to believe in our personal and nation allegories" (96). To characterize Didion solely as a postmodernist writer, however, distorts both her achievement and her aims. Actually, Didion's work challenges Hutcheon's widely accepted claim that "postmodernism has called into question the messianic faith of modernism, the faith that technical innovation and purity of form can assure social order, even if that faith disregards the social and aesthetic value of those who must inhabit modernist buildings" (*Poetics* 12). To read Didion's *Democracy*, by contrast, is to see how widely pervasive the techniques of modernism have become in American society. Where obviously postmodern writers such Thomas Pynchon or John Hawkes foreground and render problematic their self-reflexive narrative strategies, the producers of "Ronald Reagan, the Movie" use postmodern narratives in order to conceal the unreality of the narrative that they put forward. Pynchon may question the faith that technical innovation and purity of form can ensure social order, but the aesthetic genius that presented Ronald Reagan at the 1984 Republican Conventions suggests that most Americans do not. In this sense, the association of Didion with postmodernism has obscured her position as a critic of the politics of postmodernism as a national aesthetic style that defines the post–Vietnam War political environment.

If postmodern critics see works of art and criticism as being complicit with the power structures that they represent and often challenge, then Didion shows us how agents of power often understand their acts to be complicit with the narrative structures (media) that disseminate them. In other words, postmodern political style, even when it seems to be enacted by people who know little of the history of modernism, makes use of typically modernist narrative strategies in order to conceal the complexity of contemporary history. Instead, they (remarkably adroitly) stage simplistic scenarios that assure the members of the audience that they need know only that "Ronald Reagan will fight the Evil Communist Empire" or that "George Bush will smoke out Osama bin Laden." In this respect, Didion's work does not look back to Adams's work as much as it portrays how Adams is being projected onto Didion.[6] Adams thought that the complexity of the universe made history unknowable, whereas Didion asserts that the postmodern narrative technologies allow powerful interests to make history unknowable except as a trite patriotic gesture. In the postmodern era, history is a matter of transmission and consumption that occurs instantly. This means that history is impossible to know because it is impossible to register and therefore impossible to construct except as an evanescent, though ever-present, distraction.

In *Democracy*, Didion's two rival artists are Billy Dillon and Jack Lovett. Dillon is a Karl Rove character who is adept at making the news media print the story about his boss, Senator Harry Victor, that he wants the audience to know. Lovett is someone who Oliver North or the Central Intelligence Agency (CIA) might hire to accomplish an unpublicized armed mission. Dillon crafts the mass multimedia presentation of an artificial image that voters will believe as true; Lovett enacts the secret policies (overthrowing governments, committing assassinations) that legally elected politicians approve without the voters' consent or knowledge. Each creates history in his own way, but the history that Dillon represents bears no "real" relationship to the history that Lovett enacts. Similarly, although the film version of Ronald Reagan bears no relationship to the real president, the image nonetheless stands in for the president's actions and the viewer (or voter) need not confront the contradiction that has been concealed through the mastery of the aesthetic presentation.

The modernist author-god paring his or her fingernails while contemplating the perfect world that he or she has made is no longer James Joyce but Ronald Reagan or George Bush. Whereas Joyce actually made the world that is *Ulysses*, Reagan and Bush only pretend to author the world in which the voters choose to believe. The fact that Reagan and Bush are, in fact, the creations of others is perhaps less significant than the recognition that political figures and corporate powers have themselves become private artists who are intent on making their audiences accept their work as "true" and "valid." Once history is understood to be nonteleological in the sense that Adams described, the past is replaced with a never-ending *justification of the present*. Works such as *Ulysses* or *The Waste Land*, which seemingly have little do with either scientific innovations or government formation, imply a world that is knowable only through radical and incessant reconfigurations of traditional narrative strategies. Didion's work asks the reader to see what happens when history becomes aestheticized and produced by the government. As Didion's *Democracy* shows, what drives history's machinery in the postmodern age is not just power, privilege, and the need to maintain the status quo but also the collective loss of memory that makes something that you see happen on television—whether live or replayed six hours later—come to have the narrative weight that is traditionally associated with the word or form *history*.

The loss of memory receives its fullest expression when Inez meets a reporter, "a stringer," from the Associated Press. The stringer's angle is to portray "the-woman-who-might-be-America's-next-first-lady." The exchange that occurs probably best captures the key theme of the novel. The stringer asks Inez "what she believed to be 'the major cost' of public life" (50). Didion's narrative makes it clear that this question is not intended to elicit a startling or truly informative response as much as it is intended to produce magazine copy and establish Inez as an "ordinary" person who is merely making the best of an unusual circumstance. Her spin-doctor, Dillon, has prepped her for this question: "The major cost of privacy, Inez, that's an easy shot. The hardest part about Washington life is finding a sitter at the Gridiron Dinner. The fun part about Washington life is taking friends from home to the Senate cafeteria for navy-bean soup. You've tried it at home but it never tastes the same" (520).

Such a scripted revelation, conducted repeatedly in different hotel rooms with different reporters and then recopied repeatedly in *Vanity Fair*, *Ladies' Home Journal*, *Family Circle*, *McCall's*, or the *New York Times Sunday Magazine*, underscores the fact that running for national office is a staged event in which only the status quo is at stake. In Baudrillard's terms, it is a simulacrum of the actual event that it is supposed to represent. The magazine profile is a mechanism through which candidates project personalities for the consumption (as opposed to the education) of the voting (re)public. This time, however, Inez declines to recite Billy's rehearsed speech—declines to stay on message—and instead speaks the unspeakable. With Didion in the room watching her, Inez replies that the major cost of public life is "memory, mainly" (52). Running for office is "something like shock treatment," she adds, because "you lose track" of what you said and where you are until you are like an airplane that must "drop fuel," "jettison cargo," "eject the crew" (51–52). The reply is shocking not only because it is truthful and invites real reflection but also because it violates the established protocol for an exchange between news reporter and news subject, a protocol that demands that nothing be said now that has not been said before. Indeed, "new" observations require special announcements and press conferences so that what is "new" can be contained and marketed in advance by those who are getting the "news" out to the reporters. Inez, momentarily, has escaped her handler, Dillon, and has said something that, as it turns out, only Didion is interested in hearing and is capable of decoding.

Loss of, or indifference to, memory characterizes Didion's novel. Issuing "a narrative alert," Didion warns, "I no longer have time for the playing out" of narrative suspense (164). Saying precisely what *Democracy* is about, what constitutes its plot, is difficult. "Call me the author," Didion may say, but she is the first to admit that the novel you are reading is not necessarily the one that she thought she was writing. The first three chapters begin three different novels and, throughout, Didion mentions other failed novels that she has abandoned in favor of the one we are reading. Ultimately, the novel would seem to focus on Inez. Details accumulate quickly to define Inez's character, almost as if we were reading an article for *Vogue* (the magazine where Didion worked in the early 1960s and where she implies that she met Inez): Didion suggests that Inez loves Jack Lovett but cannot marry him because she is too young and already married. Her father married outside his social standing and left his daughters with a broken home, and her mother abandoned her as a child. After marrying an ambitious politician, Inez thus only comes to be known only as "Harry Victor's wife," and her life of simulated pleasure and privilege estranges her children, who have been involved with illegal drugs and drunk-driving incidents. Each of the novels, including the one that we are reading, converges on Oahu, which Didion describes as "an emergent land mass along the Hawaiian ridge" or "a temporary feature [for which] every rainfall or tremor along the Pacific plates alters its shape and shortens its tenure as Crossroads of the Pacific" (18). That this location has become an extension of the U.S. Empire is, in the context of the novel, almost beside the point. Nor does Didion ultimately seem interested in what many readers might consider to be the novel's climax: the murder of Inez's sister, Janet, by her father, over a land deal that would displace an ancient burial ground with a housing development. Those readers who are looking for conventional "historical" morals can read every plot point in the novel through Didion's description of the Christian family "as a family in which the colonial impulse had marked every member" (26).

The symbolism of what Didion depicts is almost numbingly predictable. Corrupted U.S. "interests" in the Pacific, whether on Oahu or Vietnam, are the end point of the U.S. Empire: the Christians have converted the natives so successfully that the natives conspire to sell out their own dead, and so it will go, until the island is washed back into the sea. What is most interesting about the family murder is how inconsequential to the novel it seems. Whereas for Adams such a plot twist would constitute a moral climax, for Didion it is merely one more story, as usual, that is more important for the ease with which it is obscured or ignored than for the moral revelations that it might uncover. Without this story, Didion would have no novel; yet her novel can be about only her inability to make this story into a satisfying moral climax. Instead, Didion's family history presents us "clips," isolated pieces of information that are interesting in their own right but constitutive of a story that no one really wants to piece together. Her manner of presenting Harry Victor's political career follows this pattern. In machine-gun style, moving with the quickness of a fifteen-minute political infomercial, she tells us of his "two years in the Justice Department" and his entry into fame as the coauthor (with Billy Dillon) of the *New York Times Magazine* piece "Justice for Whom? A Young Lawyer Wants Out"; his involvement in the East Harlem "Neighborhood Legal Coalition"; his successful campaigns for Congress in 1964, 1966, and 1968; his appointment to fill a vacant Senate seat in 1969; his "fact-finding missions" to U.S. foreign policy hot spots, such as Jakarta, Santiago, and Managua; in short, his entire political resume leading to his unceremonious failure to become the Democratic nominee for president in 1972. These "clips" suggest not a heroic advocate of noble political causes but someone who is scripting a future role for himself, who is making himself ready to occupy an already defined campaign niche. When Harry's career founders, it is not because he lacks "ideas" but because someone else is more marketable. Inez's commentary on Harry's lost career stands in for Didion's: "You didn't start speaking for this generation until after the second caucus. You were only the voice of a generation that had taken fire on the fields of Vietnam and Chicago after you knew you didn't have the numbers" (180). In other words, Harry's positions are either retrospective or prospective. They have no relevance except as copy: potential clips or sound bites to be looked up for other campaigns.

Didion is more interested in Inez's story than in her husband's (just as Adams preferred his "innocent" heroine to the corrupt senators). Didion implies but does not write a history of the Christians, or a history of the Harry Victors, because they have become so familiar that they lack narrative traction. *Democracy* is not a jeremiad. Instead, Didion focuses on and identifies with Inez, because her disappearance down the postmodern memory hole seems to suggest something poignant that has been lost. If great modernists such as Marcel Proust and James Joyce understood memory to be the wellspring of their artistry, then Joan Didion understands that the loss of memory has become the social and aesthetic given of postmodern America, to the extent that it would seem to deny the relevance of history altogether. The stringer who asks Inez about the major cost of public life will not grasp Inez's point, in part because it does not conform to the script that she expects. Moreover, Didion, the other journalist on the scene, will not write about it except as fiction. Thus, when Inez says that the cost of being in the political process is memory—that you drop fuel, jettison cargo, eject the crew—her comment obliquely refers to the stance that is necessary for the ongoing charade that is her life to be successfully marketed, or advanced, as a representative instance of how democracy works. Billy wants Inez to present not a point of view but a lifestyle that the "voters" can identify with and fantasize about joining. To follow Dillon's advice, as she is supposed to do, represents the daily eradication of memory. Just as Billy makes Inez's image, he also helps create the postmodern context in which Didion—or any maker of narratives— tries to write her history.

In Adams's *Democracy* the disparity between those who are elected to office and those they are presumed to represent was, in a sense, a happy one. None of Adams's contemporaries who read his novel understood his heroine to be representative of democracy because, as a woman, she lacked the right to vote. Her rejection of Senator Silas Ratcliffe's proposal of marriage at the end of the novel could be seen as her choice to operate on a higher ground. In this respect, "power" was localized in senators and congressmen and those who did business with them. Of his heroine's first trip to Congress, Adams writes, "To her mind the Senate was a place where people went to recite speeches, and she naively assumed that the speeches were useful and had a purpose, but as they did not interest her she never went again. This is a very common conception of Congress; many Congressmen share it" (12). (One wonders what Adams would make of the C-Span channel where Madeleine's experience in *Democracy* is now available daily to anyone with access to cable television.) In Didion's *Democracy* those meaningless speeches are what Billy writes for Inez and Harry and they fill virtually every particle of the nation's public space. That is, Billy's words are no more empty or meaningless than the words of Adams's congressmen but through the ubiquity of the media, their emptiness has become the space, or the simulacrum, in which all discussions of democracy are transacted.

III

Didion's *Democracy* portrays how newspapers such as the *New York Times* and television networks such as CNN present history for consumption by mass audiences whose commitment to "democracy" is only symbolic. Hutcheon famously asserts that the postmodern artist's success as a force of political opposition may be in "jamming the system," but Didion suggests that any frequencies for insurgent activity have either been blocked or converted for the purposes of the state. *Democracy* anticipates the current cultural moment where seemingly important national "heroes" such as Ronald Reagan or George Bush, and seemingly crucial plot twists such as "9/11" or "the hunt for Saddam Hussein" are scripted into an ongoing drama that is designed to compel its television audience to accept as true whatever the presented heroes say and whatever the state say is true. For instance, when the World Trade Center towers were destroyed on September 11, 2001, what one saw on live television was not just a horrific image of three thousand people perishing at virtually the same moment. What one saw, according to contemporaneous reports, was "history in the making." There was no space to protest that what one was seeing may not have been what was, in fact, happening. The subsequent accusations on various Internet sites and blogs that the Bush administration had used 9/11 to further its own interests (which, on this understanding, cannot be seen as being coincident with the interests of the American people) were surely attempts to jam the system. However, these protestors were operating on an outdated model of history, one that assumes that claims of "reality" or "truth" can be disputed rather than created by fiat by whoever is controlling the television screens.[7] Questions about how the U.S. government may have co-opted 9/11 for its own subversive aims matter little in the face of its appropriation of the televised image of the twin towers' destruction as a certified instance of the "history" that the government is, as it were, licensed to market and control. On this logic, 9/11 fulfills a specific narrative function: to compel unity among Americans where otherwise none might exist. To transform an isolated event, an incident involving four hijacked airplanes and their consequent destruction, into a narrative that audiences will recognize as "history" requires an aesthetic sensibility and the means for reproducing it.

Before the smoke from the devastation had cleared, national media analysts and quasi-government-sponsored sources were talking about the "generation of September 11," and "the day when America lost its innocence," and "the day a president came of age." Such commentary suggested a general euphoria—a feeling comparable to what is experienced in successful Baptist revivals or Alcoholics Anonymous meetings—that inheres in the shared knowledge that from this date forward "nothing again would ever be the same." Before the smoke from the towers had cleared, 9/11 was not simply being memorialized but also *marketed* as an event not to be forgotten. Hats commemorating the bravery of the New York Police and Fire Departments were being sold and worn all across the country; telethons transmitting the earnest performances of celebrities—celebrities who might not be so visible until the next set of presidential conventions—were being replayed on thirty or forty television channels simultaneously; shots of politicians quickly communing at "ground zero" to express their dismay, anger, and concern about an event that "was beyond their comprehension" (but not their sense of political opportunism) were interspersed between the other commercials for history in the making. The patriotism of many and the bravery of a courageous few were all on display; what was not on display was any sense that the event had a context other than its own sudden shocking appearance. What was not discussed was the irony or the significance of conferring the weighty word "history" on an event that was understood to have made all events prior to it meaningless, occasions not to be remembered. Thus, the irony of defining and justifying future national political decisions—the notorious Patriot Act that curtailed long-standing civil liberties of American citizens, the wars in Afghanistan and Iraq—with the simple statement "9/11 changed everything" cannot, in the public discourse, be meaningfully confronted.

Thus, 9/11 became a copyrighted historical event that was staged and endlessly performed by the U.S. government and the national news media in the name of the Bush administration or the American people, which are supposed to be one and the same. In the face of such an unprecedented ability to create a fictional reality and then compel potentially billions of people to suspend disbelief, politically oriented postmodern authors cannot help but feel complicit with the forces that they portray. To understand how Didion exposes and criticizes the relentless reproduction of events such as 9/11 as history, we might contrast *Democracy* with DeLillo's exploration of similar issues in his history of the United States during the Cold War, *Underworld*.[8] DeLillo sees the same forces at work that Didion sees but refuses the explicit role of historian. "Fiction rescues history from its confusions," DeLillo has flatly stated. Fiction "provides the balance and rhythm we don't experience in our daily lives, in our real lives," he continues. "So the novel which is within history can also operate outside it—correcting, clearing up and, perhaps most important of all, finding rhythms and symmetries that we simply don't encounter elsewhere" (DeCurtis 56). In my view such sentiments are reassuring precisely to the extent that they deny the consequences of what his fiction actually portrays.

When DeLillo portrays his ideal postmodern artist, he looks to figures such as J. Edgar Hoover, Ronald Reagan, or the renegade CIA operatives who inadvertently drive the plot of *Libra*. Although DeLillo pays homage to the great modernist masters such as James Joyce and Franz Kafka (even saying that the JFK assassination marks the moment when the modernist difficulty of Kafka landed in America), the narrative forms that excite his aesthetic imagination are television, film, and photography—the media of advertising. DeLillo's work responds to the aesthetic and political power that are communicated by such mass media demonstrations of virtuosity as Reagan's image at the 1984 Republican Convention. DeLillo often portrays the Zapruder film as a starting point for exploring the way in which representation seems to replace reality in the postmodern age. In the Reagan example, though, representation creates reality by referring to a movie image that is presented as if it were a true event from the past rather than, as it in fact is, a fantasy from the past. DeLillo's success as a novelist is a consequence of the same talent for multimedia mimicry that turns a Reagan or a Bush into a television hero: an uncanny ability to transmit seriatim through his narratives a range of media forms. The question that Adams asked and that Didion and DeLillo reframe is not how to separate the artist from his art but how to separate the oppositional artist's narrative from the technologies by which it is reproduced. The very success of DeLillo's narrative mimicry may lead to concern that he is an impersonator co-opted by the narrative forms that he replays. In fact, DeLillo's narrative strategies have already been co-opted by the same political forces that his fiction exposes to critical inquiry. What DeLillo lacks, as does Didion, is access to the means of representation on a mass scale. Even a best-selling author cannot compete against 24/7 news.

In DeLillo's fiction film becomes a visible manifestation of human thoughts: we create the film and then the film creates us.[9] Thus, in *Underworld*, Klara Sax wondered whether "this home movie was some crude living likeness of the mind's technology" (495–96). Correspondingly, DeLillo's fiction has replaced the solitary and singular artist-observer familiar from Henry James and James Joyce with a multiplicity of competing aesthetic technologies. The presence of the film in the narrative—its celluloid shadow—disrupts the reader's confidence in the transparency of the word, which may suggest to many that DeLillo has surrendered to film the power that was once attributed to the novel. "The film was printed on her mind in jits and weaves," DeLillo writes of one viewer (445). *Underworld* takes its title from an imaginary word/film, *Unterwelt*, that is presented as if it were a lost work of the great Russian director Sergei Eisenstein.[10] Tellingly, the most important prior, nonliterary narrative precursor in DeLillo's fiction is a work that is not really a work at all and a narrative that is, arguably, not really a narrative. The Zapruder film of the JFK assassination appears in most of DeLillo's novels and is implied in all of them. In *Underworld*, Klara, watching the Zapruder film, wonders at how "it carried a kind of inner life, something unconnected to the things we call phenomena" and at how its "footage seemed to advance some argument about the nature of film itself." From Klara's perspective, the film is not about how Kennedy died or about who might have killed him and why. What matters is the medium, the shooting of the shooting, the fact that something happened and the camera was running, so it could be recorded. Moreover, the same characters who witness the rare showing of the almost secret *Unterwelt* are also present at an exclusive screening of the Zapruder film of the JFK assassination. Watching this film, the characters are less confronted with the death of the president than with "the famous headshot [that obliges them to] to contend with the impact" (488); that is, they have to confront the existence of the event as film.

Why does DeLillo take the title of his book from a film that he himself has invented, as if it were a real film created by the real Sergei Eisenstein? In part, this move speaks to the ubiquity of technological representation in the postmodern era. Arguably, film blurs the line between fiction and truth more effectively than the novel does. More important, DeLillo, a novelist who pretends that his novel is a film, points to a conception of himself as a narrative maker that is consistent with the reality makers that Suskind describes or the anonymous directors who (as they did at the 1984 Republican Convention) brought to television the movie version of Reagan as president. In *Underworld* the two films, one real and one not, provide a kind of textual subconscience to the novel. With the Zapruder film, what begins as a commemorative home movie becomes a document that is classified as a threat to national security because it might undermine the "official truth" of the assassination. Both texts dramatize a disjunction between author and text that works to make the text seem more real than any force, human or otherwise, that is said to authorize its meaning. *Unterwelt* has an author, Eisenstein, but no existence; the Zapruder film actually exists but, in effect, has no author. In this respect, DeLillo's novelistic ambition is to absorb the unauthorized cultural power of the Zapruder film and fuse it with the artistic authority that he attributes to the Eisenstein film. Presenting his novel *Underworld* as the double to the film *Unterwelt*, DeLillo invokes the possibility of mimicking something that does not exist in order to assert through the form of the novel his status as creator. Walter Benjamin imagined a degrading of the aesthetic product because of the separation between artist and art enforced by the technology of mechanical reproduction.[11] DeLillo, by contrast, understands the aesthetic product created by the technological forces of reproduction to have achieved an augmented power that he aims to capture as an artist.[12] Yet what happens when DeLillo's point of view is shared and enacted by Rove or Reagan?

In *Libra* DeLillo suggests that *Hearings before the President's Commission on the Assassination of President Kennedy* is "the megaton novel James Joyce would have written if he'd moved to Iowa City and lived to be a hundred" (181). As I noted in my Introduction, DeLillo implies that *The Warren Report* is the logical successor to *Finnegans Wake*—a mythical novel posing as a history or documentary compiled with knowledge of the same narrative techniques that were mastered by Joyce. Insofar as *Libra* is a rival narrative to *The Warren Commission Report* that uses the same information to tell a different story, DeLillo may think that he is identifying himself and his work as the successor to Joyce, but he also acknowledges that his work forms a link between modernist aesthetic technologies and postmodern government systems of disinformation and control. In this respect, DeLillo's artistry is not so different from that of a brilliant CIA agent or National Security Adviser: the artist's job requires the mastery over massive accumulation of detail and the ability to control multiple contradictory narratives existing simultaneously as valid explanations of a historical event and to reduce them to a message for which the audience, or the polity, will suspend disbelief. Works such as *Gravity's Rainbow*, *Libra*, and *Underworld* all posit a "reality" that may or may not be America as a historical "text" made up of facts ready for narrative organization. Whereas, for instance, Julio Cortázar's classic postmodern novel *Hopscotch* (1966) imagines the possibility of rearranging narrative sections into endless possible other versions of the novel, DeLillo's emblematic *Warren Commission Report* becomes a tool kit for constructing rival and even contradictory histories. Either Don DeLillo or J. Edgar Hoover (or Lyndon Baines Johnson) can piece together stories from *The Warren Commission Report*, and the result is either one novelist's fiction or one nation's historical record. The confusion, or melding, of seemingly distinct genres, history and fiction, is precisely the narrative's goal.

Underworld extends *Libra*'s portrayal of how high modernist narrative strategies are now the methods that renegade government agencies and the people who direct them employ to control Americans' perception of "truth" and its relationship to history. The prologue to *Underworld*, which *Harper's* magazine originally published under the title "Pafko at the Wall," re-creates the legendary October 3, 1951, baseball game between the New York Giants and the Brooklyn Dodgers, which was won by Bobby Thomson's ninth-inning home run. On that same day an event perhaps more momentous also occurred: the Russians successfully exploded their first atom bomb. Andy Pafko was the left fielder for the Dodgers when Thomson hit his home run over Pafko's head and into

American cultural memory. Many living midcentury Americans still recall that day fondly as "the miracle at Coogan's Bluff." The phrase "Pafko at the wall" marks the boundary between the nostalgia of the game itself and the covert, even secret, history of the atom bomb that Americans have repressed. Yet the secret history of the bomb, or the Cold War, is infinitely more important than Thomson's more celebrated home run to understanding how American lives would be shaped for the next forty years.

Brilliantly, DeLillo chooses to retell the histories that intersect on that day partly from the perspective of Russ Hodges, the baseball announcer for the Giants whose radio call of the game was recorded (like the JFK assassination) by an amateur recording enthusiast. If, for many readers, baseball is an emblem of American identity, DeLillo lovingly recontextualizes Hodges's famous call as a kind of imaginary radio transmitting again and again (because the call has been replayed on radio and television thousands of times) over an empty, decontextualized American history. DeLillo's Hodges transmits a simulacrum of American history: a memory that is itself only a memory of a pleasant memory repeating into an endless present that also includes the present in which DeLillo is writing.[13] To DeLillo, what is compelling about this moment is not merely the game but also how the game seems to be played in isolation from the cultural context that surrounds it. Ironically, the cataclysmic event of the Soviets' successful dropping of the bomb, which would ensure that the Cold War would run for another forty years, seems relatively insignificant in the context of an epic baseball game that ended with Thomson's "shot heard around the world."

Throughout *Underworld* these two events—the game and the nuclear bomb—become intertwined. Memory of the game replaces memory of the bomb. The game becomes a metaphor for how easily the "real" history that makes the present possible can be subsumed beneath a cover narrative telling an appealing story whose relevance is only its ability to divert. In *Underworld* the impulse to history as a form of communal memory and renewal becomes instead a type of nostalgia. The game stands as a cultural marker for an abiding American will to innocence. Such innocence makes it possible for Americans to believe that we are bringing democracy to the deprived peoples of Vietnam or Iraq or to conceal from ourselves the increasingly frightening and dangerous world that U.S. policies have nourished since World War II. Such innocence makes it possible to believe that Thomson's home run really was the "shot heard around the world."

In discussing DeLillo's masterful re-creation of recent U.S. history as the implications of a particular baseball game, we should bear in mind John Duvall's observation that Ronald Reagan began his public career as a baseball announcer who specialized in re-creating for his audience games that he had not seen.[14] Through Hodges, the Reagan presidency hovers over the narrative as an unnamed but permeating presence. DeLillo re-creates the Thomson game as a commentary on how the U.S. government itself authorizes its own story through endless media re-creations of fictional news events made to placate an audience eager to be deceived. Just as Hodges and Reagan once re-created already completed games over the air as if they were being played that moment, DeLillo re-creates this day from October 1951 as if it were the endless present of the second half of the U.S. twentieth century. Waiting for the game to begin, DeLillo's Hodges recalls how he "spent years in a studio doing re-creations of big league games. The telegraph bug clacking in the background and blabbermouth Hodges inventing ninety-nine percent of the action. And I'll tell you something scout's honor. I know this sounds farfetched but I used to sit there and dream of doing real baseball from a booth in the Polo Grounds in New York" (25). Relying solely on the facts that the telegraph provided, an announcer would simulate a game as if witnessing it live. The announcer—with the help of an engineer—worked into his description of the game prerecorded details of authenticity: crowd noise, the sound of the ball striking the bat, the umpire's voice. Before Baudrillard explained to intellectuals the cultural perils of simulacra, Hodges and Reagan were already past masters of the art of simulation for mass audiences. In a simulated game what is important are not the actual facts that make up the experience but the experience that is being re-created. Thus, along with telling who made which out when, the announcer might describe, as Hodges says that he did, "a carrot-topped boy with a cowlick (shameless, ain't I) who retrieves the ball and holds it aloft" (26). That such details were as canned as the recorded sounds of ball striking bat matters less than the fact that the moment described was part of an established ritual meant to comfort the members of the audience, who already knew that what was being heard had "actually" happened.

The sense that the baseball game one hears through the radio is happening live and is therefore authentic depends on the audience's willing suspension of disbelief. The red-haired boy is only one of hundreds of details that the announcer would have to fabricate in order to make the game seem real. Knowing that most of the details of the game that is being broadcast are, in fact, invented does not threaten the pleasure that the audience gets from listening to a game whose outcome, at least, they know to have been real. It is the experience of the game that they want—something that they already know from listening to other games and thus can experience from an invented game as well as from a genuine live one. Even if you had never heard a game before, the first live one you hear would follow the same form as this made-up game. Analogously, when American audiences watch a president's inaugural address or are told in print and on television and on the radio that the United States is intervening militarily in the affairs of sovereign nations such as Nicaragua, Colombia, El Salvador, Venezuela, Lebanon, or Iraq to further the "interests" of "democracy," they need not be concerned when it turns out that the details of the interventions conflict with the cover story. Virtually every American "knows" that Americans promote democracy wherever "we" go, even if "we" in fact do not. A narrative that is simple, transparent, and satisfying to its audience is all that matters. Although the story that conveys this happy illusion is simple, the techniques for conveying it are perhaps more complicated and multilayered than those that Joyce used to fabricate *Ulysses* or *Finnegans Wake*. Certainly, to DeLillo, Didion, or Pynchon, one's artistry had better be assured, and the expectations of one's audience well scripted, to compel Americans to believe that Reagan's policies in Latin and Central America were promoting democracy and a safer world.[15] In the baseball game, Hodges, like the Reagan–Bush administrations, works to collapse the distance between what actually happened and the narrative that is told in place of what happened. DeLillo or Didion, by contrast, attempt to complicate such an exercise in willed innocence by historicizing it through their "fiction." This ambition is difficult to accomplish, however, when you do not control the media that tell the story.

In *Underworld* Thomson's home run ball, which falls in and out of the hands of many characters during the fifty-year time period that the novel encapsulates, symbolizes the postmodern desire of America to re-create perpetually the conditions of its own cultural innocence despite the obvious conflicts of its history. Once again, Rogin's analysis of Reagan's movie presidency should help elucidate what is at issue here. With Reagan playing the president,

the oppositions that traditionally organized both social life and social critique—oppositions between surface and depth, the authentic and the inauthentic, the imaginary and the real, signifier and signified—seem to have broken down. The dispersal of the subject into space, as Fredric Jameson has put it, replaces the alienation of the subject in time, and nostalgia for imitating historical surfaces replaces concern with the actual character of public and private history. From this point of view, Reagan's easy slippage between movies and reality is synechdochic for a political culture increasingly impervious to distinctions between fiction and history. (9)

Similarly, DeLillo's presentation of the recording of Hodges's radio transmission dramatizes not the easy slippage between nostalgia and history but the absolute effacement of history in exchange for the pleasure of nostalgia. As the recording of the game comes to replace the experience of the game, the memory of the game—its sound bite—acquires a near transcendent meaning. Similarly, as Rogin explains, the remembered movie image of Reagan, and all of its pleasant connotations, replaces and stands in for the real President Reagan. By virtue of the game's ending having been recorded, the game becomes detached from the moment that it records, and thus that moment can be continually reexperienced outside the history in which it happened. The memory of the home run replaces the history that surrounds it. In the same way, words such as *freedom* or *democracy*, whether or not the ideals that they represent are being pursued, can be detached from their presumed context of association and used to justify any act of war or change of legislation, regardless of whether the cause of "freedom" is being advanced. "Courageous" heroes, such as the one who made movies rather than join the "greatest generation" in fighting World War II or the one who not only bypassed service in Vietnam but also left his domestic National Guard unit without finishing his tour of duty in order to help run a political campaign, can always be found to fulfill the role that is required of them.

DeLillo's *Underworld* portrays the drama of the game and the drama of the Cold War as inverted versions of the same event. For DeLillo, if not for Hodges, the communal camaraderie of the ball game exists only in the context of "the secret of the bomb" (51). Shrewdly, DeLillo highlights the fact that it was a technological accident that Hodges's call and hence the game ever became ingrained in our cultural memory. The game was filmed, but it was not officially recorded for audio. The recording exists only because an amateur with a tape recorder (a prematurely jubilant Dodgers fan who wanted to tease his Giants-fan friends about the game) happened to preserve Hodges's call. The point is not that without Hodges or without Thomson's home run the Cold War would not have existed but that the need for the Cold War would have required a plausible—a patsy—narrative to justify that it could be justified as an event worth replaying. The forces that we associate with the Cold War—the Federal Bureau of Investigation (FBI), the CIA, Hoover, and presidents from Harry Truman to George Bush—act in the vacuum created by feel-good emotions that communal narratives such as this faked baseball game generate. Of all the administrations since World War II, the Reagan administration best exemplifies a regime whose power is based on its ability to re-create any event as a satisfying aesthetic spectacle. That Reagan's great gift was to act a role in a satisfying simple moral drama makes him a compelling figure not only for artists such as DeLillo but also for those people who would use Reagan's symbolic power to further their own geopolitical ends. Once the Reagan image or brand is able to make all political decisions a referendum on whether the nostalgic America that Reagan enacted is real and therefore worth preserving (in the same way that the second Bush administration appeals to the memory of 9/11 to justify its political acts), then debating the merits of funding Nicaraguan rebels or investigating whether Republican operatives were clandestinely conducting secret negotiations with the Iranians who were holding the American hostages in 1979 in order to deliver the 1980 election to Reagan need not be part of the condensed history that Americans know as real.[16]

Present at the game is *Underworld*'s other key artist figure, J. Edgar Hoover. If DeLillo uses Hodges to advance the art of historical re-creation, then he portrays Hoover as his master conspiracy-theorist-as-artist. In this respect, Hoover marks the culmination of a series of characters (Globke in *Great Jones Street* [1973], Murray Siskind in *White Noise* [1985], and David Ferrie in *Libra*, among others) who are adept analysts of media forces and are themselves conspiracy theorists. Hoover is the only character present at the game who is capable of making and deploying in real life the sorts of cultural and historical connections that DeLillo demands of his readers. In ways that are as disturbing as they are compelling, DeLillo makes reader and author complicit with Hoover. One might say that Hoover is included in the novel almost as an homage from one narrative artist to another. Watching the baseball game, Hoover "can almost hear the wind blowing across the Central Asian steppes, out where the enemy lives in long coats and fur caps, speaking that old weighted language of theirs, liturgical and grave. What secret history are they writing?" (50). Although the ultimate answer to this question is the history that DeLillo presents in *Underworld*, this passage also points to Hoover's own skill at writing secret histories. A messenger informs Hoover that the Soviets "have exploded a bomb in plain unpretending language." The "news is hard, it works into him, makes him think of the spies who passed the secrets, the prospect of warheads being sent to communist forces in Korea" (23). Ostensibly, Hoover is enjoying the ball game, but his thoughts predict the next forty years of U.S. foreign and domestic policy: "The genius of the bomb is printed not only in the physics of its particles but in the occasion it creates for new secrets" (51). As a reader of the game whose thoughts shift from intuiting the writing of a "secret history" to interpreting that history immediately in "plain unpretending language," Hoover is more than just a particularly skilled postmodern reader. His skills lie in deciphering the text of history before it is even written and then rewriting it as his own in the name of the FBI.

None of DeLillo's prior conspiracy theorists has Hoover's astonishing imaginative power. Moreover, DeLillo portrays Hoover as a dominating figure (as he often does Joyce), both real and mythical. As an artist he wants to usurp Hoover's power.[17] As DeLillo and DeLillo's Hoover both recognize, aestheticized cultural representations and refigurations often work to anaesthetize their audiences. Like DeLillo, Hoover stands apart from the ball game even as he predicts how the game might be re-created by the future. The ball game is open: the home run is for everyone to enjoy and remember. The bomb is also for everyone, but it releases layers of information unavailable to all. Hoover reflects on the importance of announcing the news before the Soviets do. "By announcing first, we prevent the Soviets from putting their sweet spin on the event. People will understand we've maintained control of the news if not of the bomb" (28). If spies cannot control the Soviets' ability to develop nuclear technology, then the U.S. government can produce agencies that can create information for the purpose of concealing it. Hoover's power derives from his recognition that secrets must be invented or found yet must remain secret in order for him to augment his own aura of cultural and narrative power. Sitting with the celebrities Frank Sinatra, Jackie Gleason, and Toots Shor, Hoover "admires the rough assurance of these men.... [T]hey have a size to them, a natural stamina that mocks his own bible-school indoctrination even as it draws them to the noise" (29). Hoover cannot blend into the scene without knowing that "their hidden lives are in his private files, all the rumors collected and indexed, the shadow fact made real" (17). What the secrets are matters less than the fact that people believe in and fear their existence. Their belief in stories with so many levels that they inspire fear of of making known their ultimate meaning is what allows Hoover to control those whose lives he, in effect, writes. Hoover's mastery of what his audience and victims understand to be multiple intersecting narratives is what makes him powerful. As the author of *Underworld*, DeLillo would co-opt Hoover's narrative mastery by re-creating the baseball game as if it were the bomb and the many secrets that its detonation at once creates and conceals. If unpacking the layers of history that are embedded into this seemingly innocent baseball game allows DeLillo to explode the mythology of the Cold War, it will not allow him to displace Hoover as, arguably, the Cold War's most dominating author and artist.

In other words, co-opting Hoover's narrative power does not eliminate Hoover or safely expose him as some sort of terrible cultural presence. It is important to understand that DeLillo is undermining Hoover's political intentions, not his aesthetic mastery. DeLillo is not so naïve as to think that by exposing Hoover's aesthetic practice he can eradicate Hoover's pernicious cultural legacy. Demonizing Hoover or the technology that Hoover employs does not alter the fact that Hoover was capitalizing on possibilities inherent in the culture that were available to anyone with an all-consuming will to power and access to the nation's "secrets." Years after the baseball game, caught in the midst of the 1960s, DeLillo's Hoover reflects on his "enemies-for-life," observing that

> the way to deal with such people was to compile massive dossiers. Photographs, surveillance reports, detailed allegations, linked names, transcribed tapes—wiretaps, bugs, break-ins. The dossier was a deeper form of truth, transcending facts and actuality. The second you placed an item in the file, a fuzzy photograph, an unfounded rumor, it became promiscuously true. It was a truth without authority and therefore incontestable. Factoids seeped out of the file and crept across the horizon, consuming bodies and minds. The file was everything, the life nothing. (559)

As DeLillo recognizes, Hoover's dossier becomes a kind of novel in progress— a counterpart to *The Warren Commission Report*. As a new form of media, Hoover's dossier is more powerful than *The Warren Commission Report* not simply because it is never released and is thus never readable. Rather, it acquires power because it does not attempt to formulate a cohesive narrative or reveal an organizing authorial agency. The mere fact of its existence—its unlimited capacity for rumor and innuendo—implies omnipotence. DeLillo describes Hoover's dossier in terms that are traditionally associated with the novel—a deeper form of truth, transcending facts and actuality. By showing how Hoover co-opts novelistic strategies, DeLillo imagines Hoover inventing the kind of postmodern novel that DeLillo writes. Implicit in DeLillo's presentation of Hoover is the uncomfortable recognition that Hoover's ability to combine politics, aesthetics, and capitalism makes him an exemplary postmodern theorist, reader, and even artist. By DeLillo's reasoning, Hoover is to postmodernism as Joyce is to modernism. Although DeLillo writes *Underworld* not to supplant Hoover but, in a sense, to out-Hoover Hoover, the reader cannot help but wonder whose "file" is more powerful—the fictional file that DeLillo imagines in *Underworld* or the undoubtedly real file marked "DeLillo, Don" on record at the offices of the FBI and the CIA.

IV

DeLillo insists that the novel can be separated from history—indeed that the novel can contain and co-opt the other narrative forms that it portrays without having them become lesser versions of that form. DeLillo also implies that the author can be distinguished from his or her text, a text that is separate from the world that he or she "creates." Didion, however, does not deny her own authorial complicity with the narratives that she would undermine, which is why it is hard for her to write her story. Her recognition is that their means of reproduction and dissemination are more powerful than hers, in part because she has little confidence in the number of sympathetic readers that her work can attract.[18] There is no Hoover in Didion's *Democracy*, perhaps because Didion cannot imagine that a single genius exists who runs the whole show. The senator, Harry Victor, is a "radio actor" (as Jack Lovett calls him) for various corporate interests, and neither Dillon nor Lovett is portrayed as having the power that DeLillo's Hoover has (103). Rather, it often seems that the machinery of representation is the most powerful force in the novel. Didion thus situates her perspective within an already existing network, or process, of endlessly recycled disinformation.

Didion the narrator is ineffectual, hapless, impotent. In the scene in *Democracy* where Inez describes her loss of memory, Didion flaunts her own narrative irrelevance to the larger narrative point made by Inez. When Inez challenges the Associated Press reporter to articulate a view about Inez that does not come from previous prefabricated sources—from "the clips"—the reporter looks to Didion for help. "I looked out the window," Didion writes. Didion looks out the window because she has seen it all before; she also looks out the window because there is nothing that she can say that will change the reporter's understanding of the situation. Moreover, the reporter's version, not Didion's, will be the historical record accepted by most. Thus, again, Inez speaks for Didion when she tells the reporter, "You might as well write it from the clips," since "I've lost track. Which is what I said in the first place" (53). The reporter obliges, Didion tells us, in the story that appears the next day under the headline "Inez Victor Claims She Is Often Misquoted," a headline that can only further undermine Inez's ability to say anything that she has not been represented as saying before. The scene involving Inez and the Associated Press reporter predicts Didion's "true" account of the 1988 Democratic Convention in her essay "Insider Baseball" (first published in *After Henry* [1992] and then later reprinted as the signature piece of *Political Fictions* [2001]). In "Insider Baseball," Didion focuses on the "communicants in what we have come to call, when we want to indicate the traditional ways in which power is exchanged and status quo maintained, 'the process'" (*After* 48). "The process" is not "'the democratic process,' or the general mechanism affording the citizens of a state a voice in its affairs, but the reverse: a mechanism so specialized that access to it is limited to its own professionals, to those who make policy and those who report on it, to those who run the polls and quote them, to those who ask and answer [on] the Sunday shows, to the media consultants, to the columnists, to the issues advisers, to those who give the off-the-record breakfasts and to those who attend them; to that handful of insiders who invent, year in and year out, the narrative of political life" (49–50). Didion identifies "the last true conflict of cultures in America, that between empirical and theoretical America. On the empirical evidence this country was about two-toned Impalas and people with camouflage hats and a little glitter in their eyes, but this had not been, among people inclined to be theoretical, the general assessment" (52). When Didion stands in the rain among journalists watching candidates address scraggly crowds of unenthusiastic people who are unlikely ever to find themselves in suites at luxury hotels, she quotes Joe Klein, another political reporter but one who is well insulated within the process, describing the same event in terms of eager crowds and gathering electoral excitement (52). This report is entertainment for "theoretical America," those whose "demography is good," "upscale" targets for the advertisers, "the kind of audience you want if you are Merrill Lynch and you have decided to buy commercial time for the 1988 Republican convention" (51).

When "empirical" America has been sacrificed for "theoretical" America, or what twenty years later people would call the sacrifice of "reality"-based

America for "faith"-based America, "news" stories are covered only in terms of how effectively the candidates advance their campaigns. That is, media and politician combine to present the appearance of what is happening rather than what may, in fact, be actually happening. "It was taken for granted," Didion observes in "Insider Baseball," "that these 'events' they were covering, and on which they were in fact filing, were not merely meaningless but deliberately so: occasions on which film could be shot and no mistakes made" (54). In this context, reporters can say that a candidate's main challenge is "not to make any major mistakes"—to tell the story about the navy bean soup at the commissary and not the story about the loss of memory that makes it possible for (to choose just one easy example) President George Bush to appoint to high office someone (Elliott Abrams) who was indicted and convicted of lying to Congress during Bush's father's administration. Well before the celebrated Valerie Plame Affair exposed the cozy link between high-level government officials and high-level media types of the Sunday morning talk show variety (and resulted in a perjury conviction for Vice President Dick Cheney's Chief of Staff, I. Lewis "Scooter" Libby), Didion details how eagerly reporters from major weeklies such as *Time* and *Newsweek*, not to mention all the "experts" employed by the television networks, trade a critical point of view on what they observe in exchange for that more prized commodity, "access."[19] Thus, in the Plame Affair, Lewis "Scooter" Libby, who was found by a jury to have lied about his possible role in the outing of an undercover CIA agent, Valerie Plame, claims as exculpatory evidence that he heard high-level secrets from Tim Russert, the media host of the NBC Sunday morning talk show *Meet the Press*.

The public exposure of the national media in the Plame Affair as a de facto branch of the government so powerful that its interests transcend even those of the CIA is a revelation unsurprising to readers of Didion. In contrast to that of Russert, Didion's premise as a reporter is to recognize, as she told Sara Davidson, that "in the life of the body politic the actual movement is going on underneath," and, she continued, "I am interested in what's going on underneath" (15). Didion looks for truths seemingly unknowable and unrepresentable: information that cannot be traded or revealed in exchange for "access," since "access" ultimately means just reporting what one is told. One does stenography. In "Insider Baseball," when Didion says that those "covering" the campaign conduct their own poll to see who will win, she suggests that this mock election perfectly represents the process that they presume to witness. During the 2000 presidential election, none of the major media outlets questioned the propriety of the candidate George Bush when he interrupted television coverage to announce that the state of Florida had been called inaccurately in favor of his opponent, Al Gore. Bush assured either the viewers or the media (it was hard to tell which) that this mistake would soon be corrected, and as authority for this claim he pointed to his brother, Jeb Bush, who was sitting in the same room with the candidate and, more important, was also the sitting governor of Florida. This astonishing moment, where a candidate conducts a hypothetical vote count with no ballots on live television and then announces his projected account to be true, was not part of the story that night. Instead, the media surrendered their role to the candidate and then quickly retracted their exit polls in favor of the future president's preferred version of what had happened. In that moment, the media proved that it would follow not the person who won the most electoral votes but the person who most effectively seized the media to authorize the process of his own election.

Two weeks later, when the nation was treated to the spectacle of truckloads of ballots being driven across Florida as news outlets covered lawsuits about whether it was actually legal to count the actual ballots to determine the "real" winner of the election, the simulacrum-like nature of the event was either impossible to register or taken completely for granted. Then, when the Supreme Court decided the election by a 5–4 vote in lieu of counting accurately the millions of votes cast by Floridians, their election process did not seem that different from the straw vote among reporters portrayed by Didion as being the logic of the 1988 presidential election. In Didion's account in *Political Fictions*, the reporters are not voting for who they think would be the better candidate but for the one they guess will be chosen, by whatever process, as the winner. In the 2000 election, the reporters got to vote by presenting as "true" a process that millions of Americans may have seen as a presidential election stolen live on television. As Didion remarks of the process generally, "The only outsider was the increasingly hypothetical voter, who was seen as responsive not to actual issues but to their adroit presentation" (60). Even as a novelist— perhaps especially as a novelist—Didion knows that she risks being perceived by those within the process as a hopeless outsider, "someone too 'naïve' to know the rules of the game" and therefore someone unfit to participate in the game (65). One can object that even if Didion is right to say that in the United States democratic elections have degenerated into staged events that are meant to celebrate a "process" that can only signify its own emptiness, that does not mean that Didion cannot write a counterhistory, as Adams did, to the one that is sanctioned and sells every week at the newsstand and every night on television. Didion shows, however, that even dissenting views become included within "the process" that they would oppose. The process is a perfect perpetual motion machine: it does not need Inez or Harry or even Billy in order to continue running smoothly. In the end, to try to oppose the process is only to expose how easily the process renders irrelevant any oppositional view.

As a real political reporter, Didion can portray only how beside the point her view is when it is placed next to official history. "Call me the author," she writes as her opening statement in Chapter 2 of *Democracy*, invoking Herman Melville's opening to *Moby-Dick* but also suggesting that her authorship is merely a matter of accidental naming. Like Adams in the The *Education of Henry Adams*, she remains an uncertain narrator, ever skittish about what role she is to play and what narrative line she should pursue. Reflecting on the multiple and conflicting details of her story, she observes, "Consider any of these things long enough and you will see that they tend to deny the relevance not only of personality but of narrative, which makes them less than ideal images with which to begin a novel, but we go with what we have" (17). Elsewhere she says, "I am resisting narrative here" (113). At one point she characterizes the novel as being written "at a point in [her] life when [she] lacked certainty, lacked even that minimum level of ego which all writers recognize as essential to the writing of novels, lacked conviction, lacked patience with the past and an interest in memory" (17). Her journalistic prose is noticeably absent of such reticence. However, if her journalism defines the process that seems to make memory and therefore history irrelevant, her fiction provides her with an opportunity to explore whether it is possible in this age even to write history except as a type of fiction.

She alludes to this challenge in *Democracy* when she discusses her role in a class that she "happened" to be teaching at Berkeley in the spring of 1975. The course's aim is "to discuss the idea of democracy in the work of certain post-industrial writers" (71). The four writers she mentions are George Orwell, Ernest Hemingway, Norman Mailer, and—predictably—Henry Adams. Excepting Adams, each was an expressly political writer who wrote and even acted to oppose specific political regimes. Excepting Adams, each believed that he articulated a historical perspective that might contradict or even change the course of history that he wrote against. Pointing to her own role as author of *Democracy*, Didion asks her students "to consider the role of the writer in a post-industrial society" (72). In the context of these other writers, Didion comes across as a political writer stranded without an audience or a usable history. "Consider the social organization implicit in the use of the autobiographical third person," she adds, again invoking *The Education of Henry Adams* (not to mention Pynchon's 1963 *V* and Mailer's 1968 *Armies of the Night*) (72). Just as Inez says to look it up in the clips, Didion points to other writers who have described the loss of democracy in the twentieth century. Her heroine, though, is no Nick Adams, Norman Mailer, or even Madeleine Lee. Inez Christian-Victor is not the logic of heroic individualist resisting the claims of society. She is, rather, the culmination of U.S. imperialism in the postmodern era and, as such, is just another character implicated within a system that uses her for its own self-perpetuating ends.

Some readers might want to find appeal in Inez's decision to renounce her family and its implied privilege in favor of lending aid to victims of U.S. imperialism. Inez's flight from her life and family suggests that a disastrous U.S. history can be confronted and recuperated. This interpretation would indicate that Inez's personal history cannot be reduced to the recurring clip of her dancing on the roof of the St. Regis, one that Didion admits "temporarily obliterated [her] actual memory of Inez" (219). Didion even gives to Inez a sort of epiphany that explicitly points to this reading. Her moment of revelation occurs after Jack Lovett has rescued Jesse Victor from Vietnam. In a plot twist consonant with the symbolic overkill of naming her heroine "Inez Christian-Victor," Didion has Jesse, "the crazy eight in this narrative," skip Janet Christian's funeral and fly into Vietnam at the precise moment when the United States is abandoning the war (164). Jesse's hope that going to Vietnam will help her to get her life in order parallels the U.S. effort to get its house in order by stopping the war. Setting into motion a series of events that eventually lands her in Kuala Lumpur, Inez travels to Vietnam to rescue Jesse. Once she learns that Jesse is safe, Inez decides that "she could no longer grasp her or their own uniqueness, her own or their difference, genius, special claim" (208). Seeing that "the world that night was full of people flying from place to place and fading in and out," she no longer saw any reason that she or her family "should be exempted from the general movement." They have been exempted, she realizes, "just because they believed they had a home to call. *Just because they were Americans*" (208, emphasis mine). If this were only a novel about the U.S. colonial-imperial imperative, this might be a shattering moment of self- and national recognition. It might, like the judge's actions in *Blood Meridian*, stand as a twentieth-century replication of the nineteenth-century cycle of Manifest Destiny. Inez Victor, though, recognizes here that her "passport did not excuse her from 'the long view,' " by which she means, according to Didion, "history" (210). Inez's recovery of her private life might be said to initiate a newly awakened sense of her identity as an American. By rejecting her role in her husband's public fantasies of power, she could renounce her "exemption" from moral consequences that her place in U.S. history has seemed to grant her. In other words, Inez would be the United States evacuating Vietnam, appropriately chastened by the experience and ready to redress the wounds of those she has injured.

Didion, however, does not commit herself or her reader to this morally redeeming ending. Instead, she points to the "history" that is being made while we are not watching or, more pointedly, while we are being entertained by what is supposed to pass for official history, some of which may include staged events of moral affirmation. "Most often these days," Didion admits, "I find my notes are about Jack Lovett" (30). Some critics call Jack the novel's hero.[20] Yet he is an arms dealer, a sometime CIA contract player, the kind of person who sells weapons to the Iranians and gives a piece of the cash to the Contras in Nicaragua to help fund their revolution.[21] He, like Dillon, is Didion's narrative double. He speaks the novel's first words: "The light at dawn during those Pacific Tests was something to see" (11). Because his words are given without identifying quotation marks, they seem to come from a controlling narrator. Moreover, his words establish one of the political contexts of the novel: U.S. nuclear dominance after World War II. Didion writes, "According to Jack Lovett himself he was someone who had 'various irons in the fire.' Someone who kept 'the usual balls in the air.' Someone who did 'a little business here and there.' Someone who did what he could" (39). Jack is the "something going on underneath" that Didion identified as what interested her about U.S. politics. Jack is a source for Didion's narrative, but he also marks a critical destination point for her narrative. Didion knows that Jack is the key to her story, and she cannot quite ever truly locate him.

Unlike the Victors, Jack's name will not be found in Who's Who. Didion suggests that even if names like Jack's were to be found, "even the most casual reader" might be able discern "the traces of what intelligence people call 'interest.' " Of course, Didion's statement is purposely ironic since part of her point is that the most casual reader is not interested in such correspondences and that, for most, if you are not in Who's Who then you have no identity. As Inez knows, Jack is Harry's opposite. After experiencing one of Jack's quick arrivals and departures, Inez remarks, "He's running a little coup somewhere, I just bet" (34). As Didion's narrative double, Jack tracks Inez as surely as Didion does; usually, he beats her to Inez. While Harry runs for office and visits places such as Jakarta during the civil unrest of 1969, ostensibly to promote democracy, Jack is there as well, visiting Inez and likely at the same time having a hand in the civil unrest. Jack says of Harry what Didion and Inez both know, even if neither voting populace nor the media that cover politics seem to know it: that "he's a congressman," which means that "he's a radio actor" (103).

Jack lives, in fact, what Didion longs to expose in fiction. Didion's interest in Inez cannot be separated from her interest in Jack—a character that Henry Adams could never have imagined. Describing Jack's relationship to "democracy" is as difficult as describing Inez's. Ironically, but inevitably, Didion searches "the clips" for clues to Jack's whereabouts. After she taught class, she would go to the newsstand to buy the day's papers and then return again in the evening to see "the same dispatches, under new headlines and with updated leads," from different papers, and she would try to piece together which details were new and which had disappeared altogether (73). Didion attempts to decode from the scraps of "official" history what the headlines seek to conceal. Here the character Joan Didion models the reading strategy that the author Joan Didion would have her readers employ when they confront "official" government-media-sanctioned news accounts. Analogously, Lovett is also obsessed with the crucial misleading detail that conceals an identity, usually his. His addresses are forged, and his business cards do not describe his business. "It was possible," Didion says, "to see this tendency to obscure even the most inconsequential information as a professional reflex" (41). Jack "lived in a world where the collection of information was indistinguishable from the use of information and where national and private interests (the interests of state and non-state actors, Jack would have said) did not collide but merged into a single pool of exchanged favors" (218). This is the world that obsesses Didion, the one about which she hunts for news in official dispatches, because it contains the history that "the process" conceals.

As an emblem of the "the process" that cannot be "officially" acknowledged, Jack—however unsavory his actions—is an ambiguously heroic presence in *Democracy*. Jack is the rugged individualist who gets things done. Jack, not Harry, makes U.S. foreign policy happen. Jack is the one who saves the heroine. Didion admits that she sees the image of Jack watching Inez fly to Honolulu to confront her father's murder of her sister as her "lone figure on the crest of the immutable hill" (78). What plot the book has is structured around this meeting, and Didion plays it over and over as if it were the central scene in Akira Kurosawa's *Rashomon*. In Jakarta, Jack says to Inez, "We've still got it" (105). In Honolulu, Jack rescues Inez from her family, and they catch a flight to Hong Kong that Inez describes as being "exactly the way she hoped dying would be. Dawn all the way" (188). For Jack, the perfect dawn is seeing the light off the Pacific after the "Wonder Woman Two" nuclear test bombings (11). If Jack represents the secret history that the official history conceals, then his relationship with Inez is also the narrative force that keeps Didion's history from being only snarled skeins of narrative discontinuity.

Ironically, what survives in this novel of abandoned novels is the romance between Jack and Inez. Jack saves Inez and her daughter, Jesse, while Inez and Joan look after Jack's memory. When Jack suddenly dies in Indonesia, Inez is forced to do for Jack what he has always done for her. Using great ingenuity and courage, she rescues Jack's identity from a precarious situation by getting his body out of Indonesia and back to Honolulu. She runs the kind of mission that Jack used to run, and she carries it off with a flair for romance that Jack would have appreciated. In Hawaii, no doubt near where they once watched the test nuclear bombings together, Inez buries Jack, secretly, in a place of honor away from "the hedge that concealed the grave of the executed soldiers" near a Jacaranda tree that will drop petals on his headstone (226). Inez then calls Didion to tell her this story, a story that Didion cannot tell in any personality profile on Inez that she might think of writing and a story that she could not know without access to Inez. What Didion writes instead is this novel, a novel in which Jack appears, in my view, as Inez would see him.

It is significant that in conclusion Didion refers to the time when Jack's "name was just beginning to leak out of the various investigations into arms and currency and technology dealings" but only to emphasize that it would be naïve to view him as merely a traitor (217). "That there is money to be made in time of war is something we all understand abstractly. Fewer of us understand war itself is a specifically commercial enterprise" (159). Jack understands this aspect of war; the U.S. Empire has been good business for him. Inez, like Didion, knows even better than her "radio actor" husband that Jack worked for "overt and covert agents of the United States government" and that "he regarded the country on whose passport he traveled as an abstraction, a state actor, one of several to be factored into any given play" (219). Besides wanting to protect Inez in her portrait as well, Didion admires Jack's mastery of his form. As Inez's protector and as the executor of secret U.S. plots, Jack makes

Democracy happen even if few will recognize him as the author—any more than few will read and reread successive editions of the major papers and identify how characters such as Jack are the real authors of events beneath or behind the newspapers' bylines. Didion wishes that she had such narrative control over the "history" that she attempts to engineer.

The ultimate lesson for Didion, inevitably, is that all acts are narrative ones. Her own narrative is merely one among many, afforded no special privilege because it is "art" and unlikely to prevail over the no less aesthetically powerful narratives that the Billy Dillon/Karl Rove types distribute as "news." In Lovett's "system," "all information is seen as useful. . . . All behavior was purposeful, and the purpose could be divined by whoever attracted the best information and read it most correctly" (36). To Didion, the narratives that Jack or Billy create are both mutually sustaining and untenable except as a form of aesthetic mastery. Neither Jack nor Billy is concerned that his narratives are mutually constitutive, although they are made to intersect through the agency of Didion and Inez. Jack may rescue Inez (and Inez may rescue Jack), but he cannot rescue Didion, who—concluding the logic that was first advanced by Henry Adams—writes history as fiction in deference to her recognition that in the postmodern era history can be known only as a type of successful fiction. The conclusion of *Democracy*, with its image of Didion trailing Inez into the Pacific distances, allows the reader to pretend that Inez and the author can escape the logic of *Democracy* only as refugees from history. In this age of postmodern history, the possibility of escape is at best a harmless fiction with which to distract ourselves.

Denis Johnson's *Fiskadoro*
Postcolonial America

A space of time is fixed for every nation and when their hour is come, not for one moment shall they hold it back.
—The Koran

I

The texts discussed thus far have been either postmodernist histories or postmodernist-oriented critiques of history as a practice. Denis Johnson's *Fiskadoro* (1985) is a prophecy about how American history will end. The novel implies that the U.S. Empire ended with the fall of Saigon and that everything after that date pointed to the inevitable nuclear holocaust. The concluding episode of U.S. involvement in the Vietnam War is portrayed through the eyes of a young girl, Marie, who will later survive the nuclear holocaust that destroys the United States and will become the oldest living person in the world of *Fiskadoro*. The novel ends with her death and with her death also ends any memory of the world that the present-day reader can know. As such, the novel is a myth about where history comes from, what history does, and why history as a practice can never end. The novel may also be read as a critique of postmodernist assumptions in that it insists that there are no differences between humans of any time or place that cannot be resolved through a shared understanding—or surrender—to the divine. Johnson's "Acknowledgments" thank such "teachers of humankind" as Joseph Campbell, Victor Turner, Oliver Sachs, Bruno Bettelheim, and Marcel Grialie for their inspiration. Arguably, the pivotal episode of the book, in which the protagonist, Fiskadoro, undergoes a rite of penile subincision that initiates him into a higher form of consciousness, bears the influence of all these thinkers.[1] Thus, the novel situates its understanding of "history" within a variety of other intellectual disciplines—anthropology, religion, science, and the study of myths. Like McCarthy's *Blood Meridian*, *Fiskadoro* is history as omnitext—a book that creates the world that it tells as it compresses the reader's world into the book that is being read. The process of world conversion requires an analogous conversion of the reader, who must believe that the world one knows has become the book that he or she reads. Where *Blood Meridian* presents the will to violence as the ground of history, Johnson sees history as the search for God.

Despite receiving positive reviews, prestigious grants, and earning the imprimatur of Harold Bloom—who includes three of Johnson's works (*Fiskadoro* among them) in his *Western Canon* (1994)—Johnson's writings are underrepresented within the academy. Because the plot of *Fiskadoro* hinges on a nuclear holocaust, critics have approached the book either as a science fiction novel or a holocaust novel.[2] Connecting the island setting of *Fiskadoro* to the "early modern utopias," Jacqueline Foertsch, for example, argues that despite its clear intention "to condemn the disastrous nuclear war that is visited on their settings," the novel "fails to frighten and thus convince in a way that we expect from this kind of narrative" (82). It is certainly arguable that its genre is the utopian novel, as it implies a future society more desirable than any the reader knows. Moreover, Johnson uses his imagined nuclear holocaust as a way to reconstruct a mythical pattern that results in the regeneration of human society. In this sense, the holocaust matters to Johnson less as a potentially real event (although it is) than as a narrative device necessary for exploring human meaning that goes deeper than any one isolated event, no matter how cataclysmic. Multiculturalist, if not postmodernist, in orientation, the book's reference points and vernacular rhythms are of post-1960s America: it implies that the end of America nation dominated by white men has already begun. Many readers may find *Fiskadoro* quite frightening since its premise is that you, the reader, are dead and now you have only the narrative of *Fiskadoro* to orient you in a world that you no longer know. The book's opening paragraph states, "A little ways north of them the bodies just go on and on," and eventually the reader realizes that he or she is understood to be among those bodies (3). The lesson of *Fiskadoro*, which it gives more forcefully than any postmodern theorist, is that narrative orders the world you know or claim to know. Its appeal inheres in its total commitment to the power of narrative to compel belief. History can be only the story that you believe to be true.

Although published in 1985, *Fiskadoro* can be read as a post-9/11 novel. In the wake of 9/11, Americans became aware that their empire is fragile and subject to destruction. The plot premise of *Fiskadoro*—that the United States has been destroyed by nuclear bombs—may be more plausible after 9/11 than it was at the height of the Cold War. To add to its uncanny aura is the fact that *Fiskadoro* is patterned after the key text of Islam, and it addresses its reader from a future in which readers of the Koran rule the world, or at least America. In light of the destruction of the World Trade Center towers (apparently by Islamic warriors), *Fiskadoro's aura of prophecy takes on an even eerier dimension.* Like the Koran, it commands the uncertain and the faithless to ready themselves for the next world. The present of the novel occurs in an unknown future, addressed to an unknown audience, and concerns itself mostly (though not entirely) with events that happen around 2065. The events concern stories about the past that have mythical importance for the unknown future audience. They are recalled to have taken place in a region known as "the Quarantine, in a time between civilizations and a place ignored by authority" (12). Questions concerning the scope and power of the U.S. Empire, its relationship to colonized people from the pre-Columbian era to the fall of Saigon, and the attendant traumas suffered by millions of people throughout American history are raised and dismissed as no longer important. To the extent that *Fiskadoro* reflects contemporary America, it reveals an America that has truly become a polyglot of cultures separate from the white Anglo-Saxon culture that has dominated the country since its inception. Yet the reader recognizes signs of the lost American civilization in the world of the Quarantine. The music of Jimi Hendrix, Bob Dylan, and various reggae bands plays through amplifiers running on dying batteries. One character, Mr. Cheung, walks through "a pocket of industry, passing the bottle factory and the candle factory" and thinks of the "other buildings in the neighborhood that had never hosted any such resurrections and inside of which machines hulked inscrutably, scaring away the people who might have lived in them." He "walked past these places with a dread of something that lurked here hoping to churn people into grease" (158). Mr. Cheung intuits the connection between the creation of these machines and the destruction of the world that made them. Instead of suggesting how much "better" Mr. Cheung's world would be if these machines were made to run again, *Fiskadoro* assumes that it is fruitless to wish that Mr. Cheung's world were ever otherwise.

Mr. Cheung is the novel's representative historian and representative American. He wants to preserve in memory the world that was lost. As with Don DeLillo's Nicholas Branch, Denis Johnson's historian cannot find a historical method that is adequate to account for what he wants to know. *Fiskadoro* does not question the practice of history as a worthwhile goal; rather, it shows that absent a structuring narrative that compels belief, historical facts mean virtually nothing. Mr. Cheung thinks that through his study of history he can address his present situation merely by recovering and preserving a past that is actually irretrievably lost. However, the past is truly past—unknowable. Moreover, Mr. Cheung lacks the skill and the desire to reinvent the past in light of his present. Unfortunately for Mr. Cheung, any ordering narrative that might allow him to rig a lifeline from his present to the past that he seeks has been destroyed; lacking this lifeline, Mr. Cheung and the American history that he seeks will be stranded not only from the past but from the future as well. *Fiskadoro* imagines American history from a perspective that does not assume the realization of a U.S. Empire to be history's desired end point. *Fiskadoro* shatters the belief in an endless present continuous from the American Revolution to today that underpins the most prevalent versions of American history.

Mr. Cheung is introduced to the reader with this telling sentence: he "believed in the importance of remembering" (10). All Mr. Cheung really knows is that his fragment of America survived because "they'd been too far away from the holocaust to witness it" (11). The compulsion to preserve artifacts of the past consumes Mr. Cheung. He has memorized the fifty states of the Union, the Declaration of Independence, and the U.S. Constitution. In the world of the novel, these fifty states no longer exist except in the mind of Mr. Cheung and there only as the completion of a mnemonic device centered on the first girl he ever loved. When Mr. Cheung recalls his lost love, now known as "The Fifty States in Alphabetical Order," he thinks of himself on his knees before her. This memory calls to mind the phrase "*I'll ask her*," which becomes "Alaska." The recollection of the other forty-nine states follows (11). that Mr. Cheung "could recite but couldn't quite explain the texts of several famous speeches and documents" indicates that he understands history to be a static rather than a living thing (10). It also suggests how irrelevant these documents are except as propaganda. For Mr. Cheung, memory cannot be, as it was for modernists such as William Faulkner and Marcel Proust, an act of cultural or personal renewal. Johnson seems to be parodying not only the hagiographers of the Founding Fathers but also any historian who thinks history can be found only in the archives or by the preservation of precious information or facts. Mr. Cheung's ability to recite the facts of the fifty states, the Declaration of Independence, and the Constitution does not help him to understand what America was or what its destruction meant. The history that connected these words is gone and so is the logic that made them come into being and make sense as more than words on a map. He is the historian who possesses facts but no sustaining narrative to connect them.

This historian, seeking to know the past's objective truth, is a charter member of the Society for Science. They believe that they are the last surviving humans and thus responsible for the rebirth of a new world. To achieve this future, the group is dedicated to studying—one might say worshipping—the past. In fact, they are the last surviving remnants of a past that the future will know only through fragments of the Society's limited perspective. The future, *Fiskadoro* implies, will not mourn the past that the Society cannot reconstruct, but will marvel instead at how the Society foolishly concerned itself with what it could not recover. The Society has access to the few books that survived the blasts. Among them are *The Sun Also Rises* (1926) by Ernest Hemingway, *All about Dinosaurs* (1956) by Roy Chapman Andrews, and *Nagasaki: The Forgotten Bomb* (1969) by Frank Chinnock. At one meeting a conflict occurs. One member of the group, Maxwell, wants to continue to read *The Sun Also Rises*, but the others want to go forward with *All about Dinosaurs*. The group's presumption is that these books will explain who they are. Maxwell thinks that Hemingway's book has the most immediate relevance because young hoodlums on the island are calling themselves Jake Barnes. Maxwell insists that reading this book will explain why these boys cannot commit themselves to rebuilding the lost civilization the Society wishes to reconstruct. What is curious about the survival of Jake Barnes is that it is doubtful that any of these new Jake Barneses can read. Hemingway's creation has survived the nuclear holocaust but escaped the context of its invention. The point that the Society cannot grasp, because it would deny their reason for existing, is that history as a practice is meaningless without a plausible narrative framework that gives meaning to its knowledge, or facts. *Fiskadoro*'s Jake Barnes has achieved a degree of alienation (and immortality) unimagined by Hemingway, but the Society cannot appreciate this irony, and it would not matter if it did. The Society can understand neither Hemingway's Jake Barnes nor their own Jake Barneses. The cultural connection has been lost.

Stranded from a narrative that would order what they know (or would know), the Society can do no more than read the books literally—as a fundamentalist reader reads the Bible. Their laborious study of the dinosaurs is a case in point. The Society rightly intuits that the dinosaurs are their precursors: "These animals lived in tropical regions like ours. But today they are extinguished and are no more," William Park-Smith says. They are "extinct," another character observes "with relish" (43). Patiently, painstakingly, the readers work their way through the Text that they hope will explain their presence.

They learn of humans' discovery of the dinosaurs (1818) and the fact that the dinosaurs were already extinct when they were discovered. Mr. Cheung is the one who perceives the important connection—that he and his friends will one day, like the dinosaurs, be extinct. Upon hearing the words "One hundred and forty million years is a long time, and many changes took place," Mr. Cheung "saw the truth of his own extinction and it made him dizzy. They were ghosts in a rotten room" (45). Later, Mr. Cheung, "thinking of the personal ghostliness of his friends, how they would all someday be gone ... was surprised to hear [someone] say, 'Probably the rocks containing their skeletons lie out to sea'" (46). This passage echoes another passage in which Fiskadoro looks to the sea, where skeletons from the holocaust also lie, and thinks of the ghosts rushing out to meet him. Mr. Cheung, by contrast, imagines himself becoming one of those ghosts, and we are to understand Mr. Cheung as a ghost that *Fiskadoro* preserves as a parable. As a historian, Mr. Cheung sees himself as the last tenuous link to a past that would not exist were it not for his memory of it. Actually, his connection to the past is more intimate: *he is the past and, as such, must be destroyed.* The future society, in the form of Fiskadoro, will require that his knowledge be sacrificed and destroyed.

To a reader who is accustomed to modernist-oriented literature, what is disturbing about the Society's pursuit of history is that its members are doomed to experience their death *as a form of memory*, instead of experiencing memory as type of personal or cultural renewal. Mr. Cheung best represents this tendency. In one passage, Mr. Cheung walks out of the meeting, dizzy, only to find "himself transported through a tunnel of dust that narrowed toward the Tiny White Dot.... The profound familiarity of all this was nauseating. The White Dot rushed in utter silence up against this sight and exploded with unbelievable brilliance, the All White, Ever White, the Ultimate White of the Nucleus, the Atomic Bomb" (47). Later, when he hears about the American nuclear bombing of Japan, Mr. Cheung will suffer a similar sensation. As he listens to the account of Lieutenant Nobukazu Komatsu's reaction to witnessing the destruction of Nagasaki, Mr. Cheung believes that he is undergoing the same experience: "I was there. My eyes burned up. It was the only thing I felt. I remember." Others who are listening endure the same reaction and together they try to withstand the sensation that "by reading about the bomb they might wipe themselves off the earth tonight" (151). They do not disappear at this instant, but the point is that they cannot escape this originary moment and thus their continuing existence is a form of communal destruction. Their interest in the past, in history, only returns them to an instant that they can neither understand nor move beyond. Just as their discussion of *The Sun Also Rises* (1926) undermines the value of secular literature for anything except entertainment, their reading of *Nagasaki* questions the discipline of history for anything except the preservation of relics. Their commitment to "history" as an end point rather than as a way to make the future traps them in a living death. They have indeed become the dinosaurs: living fossils unfit for preservation except as narrative remains for a future that will demand stories that keep the past distinct from the present. Others—the future readers of *Fiskadoro*—will talk about them, but the future will have no mechanism to remember them as they were, which is to say, as they wanted to be known. Incapable of understanding history as anything other than an accumulation of facts, Mr. Cheung's destiny is to become someone else's fact in someone else's narrative. Mr. Cheung and his Society must persist as faintly ridiculous figures put to the holy purposes of others. They wanted to invent themselves by shaping the past but instead have become the past that is shaped.

II

Insofar as the novel assumes that America and the memory of America must be destroyed before the regeneration of its descendants can occur, *Fiskadoro* is deeply American and, despite its use of the Koran, recognizably Christian fundamentalist in its orientation.[3] Not unlike the novels in the Tim LaHaye/ Jerry Jenkins *Left Behind* series, which preach that the End Times are here and Jesus Christ will return soon to initiate a worldwide reign cast in the image of an American theocracy, *Fiskadoro* imagines that the goal of history is to reveal the truth that orders the world and one's place within it. Johnson's narrative aspires to the same power claimed by Allah in the Koran and it is for this reason that Allah is portrayed as the governing authority of the world of this novel. Using the Koran to help structure his novel enables Johnson to portray a creation myth and and tie it to a specific national history, as the Koran is tied to sixth-century Arab nationalism. Like the Koran, *Fiskadoro* promises a particular community of believers not only rebirth—a promise that Joseph Campbell's writings also emphasize—but also endless judgment given in the voice of God.[4] "This Book is not to be doubted," the Koran begins (Dawood 11). Neither is *Fiskadoro*. Insofar as its audience is contemporary America, Johnson's voice frames us as "unbelievers" or, as the Koran states, those who "believe in God and the Last day, yet they are no true believers." For these people "there is a sickness in their hearts which God has aggravated: they shall be punished for the lies they tell" (111). "They are like one who kindled a fire, but as soon as it lit up all around them God put it out and left him in darkness. Deaf, dumb, and blind, they will never return to the right path" (11–12). The fire in the Koran becomes the nuclear bomb in Fiskadoro, and the "desechados" live in a darkness the book seeks to bring to light.

The book portrays the aptly named Cassius Clay Sugar Ray as a prophet whose authority comes from the Koran. Attesting always to his faith in Allah, Ray is known as the Flying Man. He demonstrates that the Koran, not the Bible, is the key religious text that has survived the holocaust. In the same way that Ray prepares the way for the boy, Fiskadoro—the magical figure who preserves for the world to come whatever the destroyed world has that is worth keeping—the Koran prepares the future world that Fiskadoro contains and authorizes. "Thanked be the compassion and mercy of Allah," the narrative asserts on the first page, and periodically thereafter, before observing that "the bodies just go on and on, and the Lord, as foretold, has crushed the mountains" (3). The reference likely is to the surah in the Koran, often translated as "The Mountain," which describes the day of apocalypse and final judgment. "On that day the Koran states, the heavens will shake and reel, and the mountains move and pass away. On that day woe betide the unbelievers, who now divert themselves with vain disputes" (369). The dead bodies are the bodies of people who "on that day," as foretold, "shall be sternly thrown into the fire of Hell" (361). Although it is not quite accurate to say Johnson is writing another version of the Koran, or even writing to confirm the ultimate truth of the Koran, he is both transforming history into religion and reflecting on the inevitable religious dimension to history. Whereas most traditional historians are concerned with establishing the disputed and often lost facts so that a coherent narrative may be constructed from them, Johnson is concerned with writing a narrative so powerful that all facts, even those unknown, will become subject to it.

The Koran warns that "poets are followed by erring men" (264). Yet what Johnson does is more blasphemous since he writes history as received Truth. Fiskadoro's narrative strategy is implied by this astonishing declaration on the book's opening page:

It's true that starting a little ways north of them the bodies just go on and on, and the Lord, as foretold, has crushed the mountains; but it's hard to imagine that such things ever went on in the same universe that holds up the Keys of Florida. It strains all belief to think that these are the places the god Quetzalcoatl, the god Bob Marley, the god Jesus, promised to come to and build their kingdoms. On island after island, except for the fields of cane popping in the wind, everything seems to be asleep. (3)

Out of this serene eeriness the name "Bob Marley" stands out as either incongruous or prophetic, depending on your sense of the divine. Many readers will know of Bob Marley's status as a prophet among Rastafarians; others will not know that Marley, a hero of truly godlike status to impoverished black Jamaicans, was a legendary reggae musician who, in the eyes of his followers, died a martyr's death from cancer that was abetted by his habitual and defiant use of marijuana, an herb that he considered conducive to religious visions. Johnson's narrator does not imply a hierarchy that would elevate one of the three named gods above another; rather, they are all equal as gods who have presided over civilizations that are now gone or passed over. At best, they are avatars who prepared the way for the narrator's present, a time and a world that Johnson never makes known because it is assumed that the audience has the same knowledge (or ignorance) as the narrator.

In his book about the postmodern critique of the practice of history, Robert Berkhofer observes, "One of the popular lessons of history according to professional and lay persons alike is summarized in the aphorism that there is nothing new under the sun except the history you don't know. Such a slogan implies either that past episodes recur or that their organization duplicates standard plots" (136). Although Berkhofer subsequently suggests that these plots inevitably serve "ideological needs and cultural practices," his statement implies that contingent cultural practices may be only the dressing, or the costumes, that the shape of history takes. *Fiskadoro* powerfully suggests that the search for cultural order drives all attempts to understand history or its possibilities and even invites the reader to judge all previous empires of all epochs as equivalent. Although Johnson presents history as a search for transcendence in the sense that Berkhofer (or, more appositely, Joseph Campbell) describes, *Fiskadoro* also points to the "ideological needs and cultural practices" that have shaped American history since the Europeans first began to transform North and South America into their own self-image. From this perspective, *Fiskadoro* is both an imaginary history and a specific critique of the failures of American history.[5]

Contained within *Fiskadoro*'s eerie invocation of the gods that have authorized the dominions of different American empires is a critique of contemporary Americans' arrogance about their nation's so-called world supremacy. The triumphant secular accomplishments of the American civilization—the Declaration of Independence, the U.S. Constitution, the freeing of the slaves, all the wars won between 1776 and 1945, the technological mastery of nature, and the freedom from toil and disease as the world had previously known it—are all lost, converted to fallout. What remains are vestiges of various histories that collided in the name of America: Spanish, Jamaican, Protestant, European—a mélange of African, European, Native American peoples who, it seems, serve as material for the creation narrative of the unnamed, apparently Muslim, future. In its evocation of "a time between civilizations and a place ignored by authority," *Fiskadoro* recalls the Europeans' discovery of the New World and the inevitable mingling of European and indigenous cultures: the god Quetzalcoatl confronting the god Jesus. Those who live in the Quarantine are "desechados," the Spanish word for "the rejected," and are the inheritors of the vanished empires associated with the Americas. The "lost ones" are those whose people lived under but never benefited from American rule. They are also we who read the novel who are like the unbelievers in the Koran upon whom "God has set a seal upon their hearts and ears; their sight is dimmed and grievous punishment awaits them" (11). *Fiskadoro* portrays that grievous punishment as having already happened and suggests a future heavenly world to which we would be denied entrance. In this sense "desechado" marks an ongoing historical condition since the inception of America as a historical reality.

The Koran proposes to integrate the Jewish and Christian religions with the Islamic religion of Mohammed; similarly, *Fiskadoro* proposes the displacement of the U.S. Empire by dispersing its history among these three equal gods. Repeatedly, the Koran portrays the Israelites and Christians as "people of the Book" who have received the true word of God only to fall away from God's truth. Mohammed is instructed to tell the skeptics:

We believe in God and what is revealed to us; in that which was revealed to Abraham and Ishmael, to Isaac and Jacob and the tribes; and in that which their Lord gave Moses and Jesus and the prophets. We discriminate against none of them. To Him we have surrendered ourselves.

He that chooses a religion other than Islam, it will not be accepted from him and in the world to come he will surely be among the losers. (50)

The point of this passage is that there are no true gods other than the Lord God, or Allah, and that Allah has authorized certain figures to speak in his name. The Koran identifies, among others, Moses, Abraham, Lot, Noah, and Jesus. Similarly, although the Israelites and the Christians may have once been favored by Allah, their transgressions against the Lord have caused them to lose favor with Him. Their prophets are to be honored, but Islam is now the one true religion of the Lord.

In the Koran the narrative voice comes from God, although the speaker is usually designated as "we." *Fiskadoro* blasphemes against the Koran by identifying Quetzalcoatl and Bob Marley as "gods," with a lower-case "g," but the sense of the text is to portray them, particularly Marley, as prophets rather than as usurpers of "the real and current blessing being showered down on us in every heartbeat out of the compassion and mercy and bounty of Allah" (12). To those who are skeptical of Mohammed's preaching, a consistent and powerful response is given:

> Who is more wicked than the man who invents a falsehood about God or denies His revelations. Such men shall have their destined share, and when Our angels come to claim back their souls they shall say: "Where are your idols now, those whom you invoked besides God?" "They have forsaken us," they will answer, and will confess that they were unbelievers. (111)

Like a chant, variations of this response recur as the Koran tranquilly numbers the many civilizations that have been destroyed whose peoples did not acknowledge the Lord as the one true Lord. "Do you not see that God has created the heavens and the earth with truth? He can remove you if He wills and bring into being a new creation" (181). Thus, "as for Noah's people, We drowned them when they denied their apostles"; "the tribes of Ad and Thamud were also destroyed and so were those who dwelt at Rass, and many generations in between" (255). Many more nations might be cited but Johnson's point is that American civilization, too, is on the list. Americans are the nonbelievers for whom there is only "the Fire." "But when the supreme disaster strikes—the day when man will call to mind his labors—when the Fire is brought into sight of all—he that transgressed and chose the present life shall have his home in Hell; but he that feared to stand before his lord and curbed his soul's desire shall have his home in Paradise" (418).

The disorientation that the reader of *Fiskadoro* experiences upon encountering "the god Bob Marley" is intensified through the recognition that the novel assumes the reader to be—again, like the reader of *Blood Meridian*—subject to its narrative authority. We know only that the world that the novel describes is from a period of "Quarantine" in "a time between civilizations and a place ignored by authority" (12). The Koran states, "When the sky is rent asunder; when the stars scatter and the oceans merge together; when the graves are hurled about: each shall know what it has done and what it has failed to do" (420). The time of the narrative, as opposed to the events the narrative describes, seems to be after the Disaster and the Resurrection. *Fiskadoro* can be seen as the answer to the skeptic, as proof that the Lord's words were true and the mountains have been crushed to dust. The reader who tries to assert his or her authority by piecing together into a recognizable whole the novel's hints about chronology and action faces an impossible task. The novel invites the appeal of this typically modernist gesture but gives the reader no way to effect it. By making the god Jesus equal with the god Quetzalcoatl, *Fiskadoro* in effect effaces the whole epoch of history since the European conquest of America. Quetzalcoatl was forced to abandon his reign and the ancient city of Tollah when he was chased off by Texcatlipoca, the warrior-hero of the Aztecs. Likewise, so have Christ and then the god Bob Marley now followed Quetzalcoatl, to give way to Allah. First, Christ replaced the Aztecs through the agency of Hernán Cortés and then Bob Marley became a god during the Quarantine period that the novel relates. Jesus is an "old" New World god because the New World was conquered in his name. Conquistadors and Catholic missionaries, emissaries of Jesus, mixed their blood with the blood of the indigenous peoples. Northern Europeans, often fighting the Catholics in the name of Jesus, came bearing African slaves, who also added to the polyglot of American history. As the son of a white English soldier and a black Jamaican woman and as a prophet of a New World religion that combined Christianity, Islam, and pan-African identity, Bob Marley is the embodiment of a cultural transformation by which the New World eventually absorbed the Old World.[6]

In *Fiskadoro*, a group known as the Israelites carries on in Marley's name: reggae-playing, marijuana-smoking Jamaicans. Cultural syncretism abounds. The priest of the Marley cult is a white woman named Mother, identified by one character as an "old Baptist sorceress" (124). She represents the transformation of Protestant Christianity into a force that can accept Marley and then Allah as a god. Mother preaches the return not of Christ but of Marley: "*Our father Bob Marley a-coming to take us home!*" (123–24). Those who worship Bob Marley congregate at "the Key West Baptist Church of Fire," located next to Mr. Cheung's place. As the unwitting prophet for the world that will replace hers, Mother understands Marley to be a messiah who will return to this world to rescue the faithful and bring them to a better place. "And if we *believe, only believe*, that we are the *people*, and that Bob Marley a-coming to take us *home*—," she prophesies (124). Mother's "faith" in Marley is an honest attempt to confront her world's fallen state. Living amid nuclear devastation, she knows that the word of the old Christian God has become literally radioactive. If the American Puritans of the seventeenth century believed that the visible world must be interpreted for signs that reveal God's proper order, then the good Marleyite Mother instructs her followers how daily happenings in the Quarantine are signs from the god Bob Marley. One recognizes in her new religion vestiges from earlier fundamentalist Christian sects. Debates about the merit of teaching evolution have survived the holocaust and it is clear that the scientists lost the battle. "Wait a minute! Wait a minute!" Mother shouts at the damned. "I got something to tell you-all—we're turning into monkeys! Monkeys is the point of it, backsliding out to the deep down primitive state where Bob Marley can't never find us" (120). Mother's faith in the healing power of Bob Marley is all that prevents humanists such as Mr. Cheung from turning into the very monkeys that the lost tribe of "evolutionists" (evil-lutionists) said were humans' precursors.

Thus what is startling about the god Bob Marley's role in the world of *Fiskadoro* is how easily and perfectly he has replaced Christ. Except for the sentence in the book's opening paragraph that links Christ to Marley, Christ is never mentioned in the novel. Mother's fear of being turned into a monkey may seem at first a sly dig at modern-day Creationists—those who deny the truth of Darwin and want the Bible taught in schools as "science." Mother may at first seem to be a parody of the familiar televangelist or traveling sidewalk show preacher: the would-be prophet who makes a profit by preparing her audience for the approaching End Times. The world of *Fiskadoro*, however, makes her figure sympathetic because history has given credence to her fundamentalism: the world that invented itself in the name of Christ has been destroyed. Probably, the New World Christ has not been forgotten so much as discredited by history since Christ's teachings were corrupted by his followers who endorsed global imperialism and, with it, the atomic bomb. Likewise, since the Darwinists were aligned with "science," "rationality," and "technology," they helped create the tools that made possible the destruction of creation by Christ's betrayers. In *Fiskadoro*, destruction is the work of humans and redemption the work of God, or Allah. Hence Allah makes more sense as the originator of the universe than does an explosion that took place billions of years ago. *Fiskadoro* portrays a world that has already begun anew so what use is a science that says that the earth's history goes back in time billions of years? Ironically, for Mother, the Darwinist position has become a type of eschatology: if monkeys can become humans, then why not humans monkeys? More than just transform this modern-day anti-Darwinist into a kind of backwards-Darwinist (for whom evolution runs in reverse), *Fiskadoro* transforms Darwinism into a kind of discredited Bible story. It also portrays how since the 1960s a born-again Christian mentality has been recapturing the America that the Puritans ceded to the secularists three hundred years ago.

Of the three gods mentioned on the book's opening page, Bob Marley is the one who is most powerful to the future world, because he provides a bridge between the world of the Quarantine and the world to come. Marley is an intermediary figure, as Christ is in the Koran. In the Koran the Israelites are praised for being the first people to whom God revealed his Word and with whom He made his covenant. *Fiskadoro*'s "Israelites" are "ceremoniously building" a mysterious white boat in anticipation of those who will come at the conclusion of the novel to end the Quarantine and usher in the next world (115). Although the Israelites of the Koran are a tribe lost from God, the Israelites of *Fiskadoro*—descendants of the colonial conquest of the New World—are bringing Allah nearer. From the perspective provided by the Koran, one surmises that Johnson's "Israelites," although they possess divine authority, will be superseded, as Mohammed superseded Abraham and Christ. The Koran's "people of the Book" have become "the people of the beat." *Fiskadoro* appropriates into the logic of its narrative two central themes of Jamaican reggae: the reunification of the scattered African tribes and the critique of European imperialism that this reunification would realize. Their reggae music and its Rastafarian ethos are a type of folk history embedded in the holy text. Such figures as Desmond Dekker (who performed the great reggae anthem "Israelites"), Peter Tosh, and the great Jamaican reggae band the Melodians become prophets of Allah whose warnings were ignored by the white people (the Americans and the English) who bought their music. At the end of the novel the Israelites' reggae rhythms signal the ceremonial end to the Quarantine.

In preaching the gospel of Bob Marley, Mother's congregation is allied with the Israelites. They appear as if from nowhere at the outset of the novel chanting "an old hymn" that seems to explain their purpose and to confirm Mother's prophecies. By the end of the novel we understand that they are mediating agents for the beginning of the New World that will usher in the reign of Allah. They sing:

> Let's seize the time now
> Let's seize the time
> Let's make the sys-tem
> Pay for its crime (14)

The Israelites' name derives from another "old Israelite hymn" that the narrative mentions: "By the Rivers of Babylon," which was first recorded by the Melodians (36). In that song the Melodians liken themselves to the biblical Israelites who were enslaved by the Egyptians. They sing of being taken from their homeland—Africa—to a strange land where they are enslaved by white men. Their ability to sing is the only possession they can keep. Although the white man demands to hear this gift for his pleasure, the African descendants retain it as a kind of secret tongue. As with the American slaves, their "song" becomes their history—a form of memory and expression that is their means for situating themselves in the strange land to which they have been brought. Their song becomes their home, and they make their new land their home through their song. Survivors of the European Conquest and the nuclear holocaust, *Fiskadoro*'s Israelites are fulfilling such prophetic Marley anthems as "Four Hundred Years," written by Tosh (which protests the history of the enslavement of blacks by whites in the New World), and "I Shot the Sheriff" (which calls for the revolution that would overthrow white imperialism in the New World). Neither of these songs apparently survived *Fiskadoro*'s holocaust, but their spirit has. To the Israelites of Marley's own time, Columbus discovered America and Cortés conquered Montezuma so that one day Bob Marley could promise the beginning of a new world. In *Fiskadoro*, the nuclear holocaust, brought on by the U.S.'s relentless drive for world domination, has made Marley's prophecy true.

Like the chanting Israelites, who every day prepare the boat with which they will greet the ships of the next civilization, Mother's role is to prepare her parishioners for the end of the Quarantine. Her presence in the novel takes up only a scattered handful of pages, but the present-day reader clings to Mother—with her reconstituted Southern Baptist fundamentalist fire—precisely because we recognize her in ways that we will not be able to recognize Fiskadoro. Along with Mr. Cheung, Mother is the character who most resembles the reader—although most readers are likely to be made uncomfortable by this connection.

Has some vestige of the Southern Baptists absorbed the religion of Bob Marley, or have Rastafarians absorbed the Southern Baptists? This strange question is for the fallen present-day audience to contemplate but it points to the syncretic understanding of religion and humanity that *Fiskadoro* champions. Presumably, the future world sees Mother as an honorable prophet of divine apprehension, one who served a lost and now dead god. Indeed, the destruction of race-based Christian America is more compelling—truly total—if the god that replaces Christ is replaced as well. "Someday," the otherworldly narrative voice reminds us, "the sand would rise up and cover the old high school, and then slowly collaps[e] the church next to it, the Key West Baptist Church of Fire" (7). Until then, Mother survives as a tribute to humanity's need to believe in a force stronger than its own to shape the creations of the human world and as evidence that how one perceives history need not be based on race.

III

Fiskadoro's central wisdom reveals that "to concern ourselves too greatly with the past is a sin, because it distracts our mind from the real and current blessing being showered down on us in every heartbeat out of the compassion and mercy and beauty of Allah" (12). These words accommodate the reader to the annihilation of their world, since the destruction of the present must be embraced as the transformation necessary to fulfill our destiny. The narrative, not the reader, is the book's ultimate authority and in this sense the book is neither modernist nor postmodernist. It is, in fact, *fundamentalist*, and it positions you as a fundamentalist reader in two distinct ways: you are either trying to imagine yourself as one with the future, or you are trying to deny the version of history the book presents. Johnson's aim, which is similar to Milton's in *Paradise Lost* but arguably more radical since the context of his writing is more truly secular, is to make you, the reader, believe that the text you read authorizes the world in which you live. To understand the god Bob Marley or, more crucially, the character Fiskadoro, the book requires you to accept that the end of the U.S. empire is inevitable and to be welcomed. Part of the narrative's brilliance, thus, is that it makes you take Bob Marley seriously as a religious figure and it does so by converting your secular impulses into religious ones. In converting its secular reader into a fundamentalist one, *Fiskadoro* asks its reader to accept that no notion of history can be separated from a religious desire to become one with God, or Allah. Johnson thus uses the present-day reader's fear of nuclear holocaust to prepare the reader for a potential conversion—to what, it cannot quite say. Preparation is enough; how hard after all to throw over everything you have been taught about your country's history and your place in it.

Consequently, *Fiskadoro* works to bind the reader to the world of the Quarantine. This means not only that you are an aspirant waiting to be rescued by the true Word but also that you cannot fully understand the past that created you or the present in which you live. And even that formulation is imprecise since by the novel's uncanny logic it is the future—not the past—that gives you your identity. This is a difficult position to accept, especially since the remains of "America" are everywhere in the novel and the question of being American seems to be at issue. When Fiskadoro makes his first appearance in the novel, he is asked two questions: "Do you speak English?" and "Are you an American?" (6). Neither question, however, can be answered with a simple yes or no. "Sugar es por la candy" is Fiskadoro's answer. As his answer suggests, "English" has become a language in flux. As the English tongue crumbles into a mixture of other tongues—Caribbean, African, and European—so has America disappeared into the scattering of multiple ethnic, cultural, and historical possibilities.

Besides its junked technology, what remains of America and its culture is preserved and transmitted through the medium of rock and roll. Mr. Cheung reflects, "History the force of time . . . are washing over us like this rocknroll" (122). In the world of *Fiskadoro*'s future, America has been recolonized by its own multicultural Otherness. Rocknroll is the form of displaced memory, or history, through which that message is communicated. It is difficult to convey how powerfully the voices of Marley, Dylan, and Hendrix pervade the novel, floating through the narrative like cries from ghosts. Listening to the voice of Dylan as Mother preaches Marleyism and the Israelites gather to prepare for the time when they will make the system pay for its crime, Mr. Cheung thinks, "I don't wish to be caught up inside these forces. They aren't my forces" (117). Mr. Cheung cannot recognize that these forces represent the authentic (only living) history of the time he mourns. Rocknroll survives because in its time it imagined the truest vision of the future. What remains of American culture after the nuclear holocaust is not its Constitution or its Gettysburg Address but the music made by and for its "desechados," or lost ones.

Identified in the novel as "the great poet of the times of hard rain," Dylan's voice surfaces when a loudspeaker plays one of his more obscure songs, "Man of Peace," which was released two years before the publication of *Fiskadoro* (122). Johnson clearly invokes the then recently born-again-Christian Dylan as a Jeremiah-like prophet whose warnings went unheeded. Instead of truly listening to the prophets on the radio, most Americans were lost in a present they could not escape. Indeed, we are to understand that Fiskadoro has transformed the historical frequencies, the coded messages, that rocknroll has preserved into the sacred text we are reading. Through these rocknroll voices, Johnson points to a U.S. Empire that was rotten to the core, destroyed by the very cultural forces that it was unable to incorporate into its own body. Now rocknrolll is washing over Mr. Cheung and carrying him away; it is completing the devastation of the holocaust and making it irrevocable.[7] He wonders whether such premonitions might not become the medium for a "memory belonging to a ghost, which the ghost shoots into [his] head for viewing, the way a recording plays over *Cubaradio*" (49). The connection that Mr. Cheung intuits between spirits from the lost world and the rocknroll that plays on the mysterious "Cubaradio," which also comes to them from an origin unknown, captures precisely the relationship that rocknroll bears to history in this novel.

Fiskadoro, for his part, not only hears the music but also seems attuned to its hidden message. One of the most memorable passages in the novel occurs when he hears Hendrix's 1967 "Purple Haze" playing on his battery-operated radio. Fiskadoro has heard Hendrix "a dozen times at sound-shows," but this is the first time he hears Hendrix being broadcast from one of the outlaw radio stations that transmit mysteriously from outside the Quarantine (19). In this context, "Purple Haze" seems to name this world's condition. Fiskadoro hears Hendrix stutter, "Scuse me-scuse me-scuse me," and the suspended phrase "while I kiss the sky" alludes to the apocalypse that has truly fallen. "Purple Haze" repeats over and over until another voice intrudes, riffing on Hendrix's voice. "Scuse me," the radio announcer's voice interrupts:

Guess what, this ain't the program as usual like you thought it was, this is Junior Staff Sergeant Bud Harmon from Nawtha Nawlins Texas and me and Danny and Rick Ames and the Pork-jumper himself Junior Corporal George Wills caught the typhoon and busted up at I guess approximately thirteen hundred hours on them rocks right down there, I can see 'em from the window, and I can see *you too*, motherfuckers, and *I got rounds left*. (20)

After some discussion among his radio audience, Harmon continues:

And we killed six a them and they killed three a us, and I got this radio station and *I love Hendrix!* So phone in your requests, only the phone here don't

have a number on it, so fuck you. I'm thirty-six years old and I just believe
I'll *rock all night*. My dad was a Staff Sergeant and he made me one, and he
loved Hendrix, and *his* dad loved Hendrix, and *I* love Hendrix—nobody never
told me I was own die in Cuba, but I really don't give a shit, if that's how it
is, that's how it is. Because it feels like once the other boys eat it, you know,
and you're just the last one left, who cares. All I own do is gepback home.
But ain't no way I'm own gepback home. I got this radio station and I got
rounds left. Goddamn I have rounds in possession—got two real shiny
stainless-steel thirty-round clips and I love Hendrix and *I am going to rock till
I die!* Fuck Cuba! (20–21)

To the reader, if not to Fiskadoro, this extraordinary passage not only con-
jures up the recognizable voice of a Vietnam-era soldier (for whom the music
of Hendrix was not an anomaly but often a battlefield necessity) but also
suggests the cultural fluidity that has occurred in the aftermath of the U.S.
Empire's destruction. No government exists to authorize the speaker's voice;
he speaks his mind only and is heard via the medium of a dying technology.
A system of authority that determines and legitimates a specific hierarchy
of rank no longer exists. Apparently, military classification can be achieved
either through hereditary privilege or simply by virtue of naming yourself to
your rank. It is possible that this gunner is himself a guerrilla fighter and is no
proof that all authority has broken down everywhere. To the speaker and most
likely to Fiskadoro, however, what matters is that Harmon's license to express
himself comes through the agency of Hendrix. Hendrix provides continuity
and a sense of history to three generations of Harmons, and Hendrix also can
be invoked as a figure who sanctions the usurpation of authority. The sergeant
understands his authority to be invested in him *by the power of Hendrix*.[8]

In *Fiskadoro* Hendrix's postcivilization legacy is claimed by the "completely
white-blooded Soundman," nicknamed "Hendrix Is," who "owned the generator and batteries that lit up their surroundings and shot the power of life"
into the equipment that amplifies the recorded and live music that booms
through the community (34). Hendrix Is shoots the "juice" to the amplifiers so
that the Israelite singer "Little Sudan" can perform. Hendrix Is presumably is
the one responsible for playing "Purple Haze" so often that Fiskadoro knows
it when he hears it on "Cubaradio." Like a rap MC, Hendrix's authority derives
from his ability to manipulate and project sound. Fiskadoro holds him in awe,
because he is the "proud possessor of light and dark" (35). Described as a

god, Hendrix Is actually occupies an intermediary position, because the source of his power, the battery-operated generator, will one day burn out.

"Hendrix Is" is, so to speak, but he will not be. He recalls the destroyed society, the one that Mr. Cheung longs for, which also fancied itself the proud possessor of light and darkness—and time and distance too. The narrative often describes the detritus of the previous century—"emergency signal-lights flashing constantly, the radio emitting a low steady wash of static, these things hooked by cables to an auto battery that rested on a sill and served to hold open a window" (28). It sometimes appears that cars are as prevalent in the twenty-first century of *Fiskadoro* as they were in the twentieth (though many current estimates in fact predict that the world will be virtually out of oil by the 2050s, the time when most of *Fiskadoro* takes place). Furniture, clothes, even household decorations are made out of junked cars. In Fiskadoro's house there is a "red bucket seat—one from amighty Thunderbird autocar—" that has been converted into a rocker (29); Mr. Cheung wears straw shoes with soles "cut from the treads of car tires" (41); auto lights and reflectors adorn walls. If this new world continually invents itself out of the remains of the old one, then the characters also know that they cannot remake what they use. Speaking of the boats they use to fish and the fuel required to run them, one fisherman states, "The oleo gone dry up outa these Keys tomorrow but when we can't run the engines no more, we can forget about boats. Don't talk to me about no boats" (16). The engine-powered boat runs still, but only to run down. Jimi Hendrix, a voice salvaged from the wreckage, continues to rule this battery-operated world, but his refrain to "Purple Haze" now predicts the world's decay into oblivion. "In Hendrix's Purple Haze, the singer asked if the haze that surrounded him was tomorrow or the end of time. Yes, and yes, says *Fiskadoro*.

Staff Sergeant Harmon plays "Purple Haze" over the radio both as his own death song and as the perfect envoi to a world that is being reborn in the nuclear haze that engulfs it. Johnson's other rocknroll reference here is likely Prince's 1984 song "Purple Rain," which was widely popular the year before the novel was published. "Purple Rain" explicitly transformed the conceit of Hendrix's "Purple Haze" into a version of the world being destroyed by a nuclear apocalypse. In "Purple Rain," Prince converts personal "wastedness" into the wasting of an entire society. In *Fiskadoro* the "purple rain" has long since fallen, and the "purple haze" remains—in the barrels of contaminated kerosene that people burn for light and heat and oil, in the radiation-sensitive badges that have long since lost their ability to register anything but their own corruption, and in the cancerous tumors that afflict so many at such young ages.

Fiskadoro hears "Purple Haze" on the radio the night before his father dies, which sets in motion the chain of events that lead to his sacrifice and finally to his readiness to meet the new civilization when it comes to rescue the world that is already, symbolically, gone. Indeed, one should understand that moment as the beginning of the ritual that prepares Fiskadoro to meet his fate and that signals the final end of the world that Hendrix and Hendrix Is represent. Not coincidentally, Fiskadoro tries to learn to play Hendrix on his clarinet but fails (19). Hendrix will not survive Fiskadoro's ascension. Harmon, in contrast, represents the death of the human that precedes human rebirth in Fiskadoro. Harmon calls on Hendrix to memorialize his life, which he has lost, even if he does not know it, in the name of technology. In Harmon's final moment, his life, whatever it might have been, has been reduced to a voice only. Hence the narrative uses "the radio said" to introduce Harmon's monologue. Harmon has become a function of the technology that transmits him; his essence (and perhaps afterlife) is (as) a ghostly radiowave. His fate is to be a signal that will soon be lost. The last song he plays is Hendrix's version of the American national anthem, Francis Scott Key's "The Star Spangled Banner." In other words, Harmon's death song is America's as well.

To the modern reader ignorant of *Fiskadoro*'s implied future, the death of America is the only historical message that can be understood. Thus, Mr. Cheung, the reader's proxy in the novel, seems to be forever remembering the end of America, but it is his mother, Grandmother Wright, who better symbolizes America's end as ongoing, dying memory. Grandmother Wright, also known as Marie, was born in Vietnam in about 1959 and dies (probably) in 2065, in the novel's concluding sentence, as the boats arrive to usher in the New Age. She retains her memories of the world before the fall but is unable to speak or communicate her memories to those around her. The world of the future makes Grandmother Wright's silence the saving moral to her story but the contemporary reader sees her story as the missing link to understanding how America was destroyed. Other than the fact that Marie was in a Key West motel room when the nuclear bombs began to fall, the reader knows only how she escaped the fall of Saigon after the Vietnam War to arrive in America. Because her story is so closely tied to Fiskadoro's story, though, she commands the reader's attention as the second most important character in the book. She is described as having "the power to see through walls," because "it was a usual thing for her to bore with the smoldering chill of her vision through the center of the earth and the layered decades" to see through the past until her father's face materialized (71). Grandmother Wright preserves in her person what Mr. Cheung seeks: the past, a living version of the history that is seemingly lost. Hence Cheung remarks, "Just by surviving, she's turned into the most important person in the world" (51). However, since she cannot speak except in random sentences that bubble out of her own sealed-off, interior consciousness, she cannot share her memories. Mr. Cheung often tortures himself with the thought that had he only asked more questions years ago, he would know more of what happened than he does now. The lesson of Grandmother Wright, though, is that the past is actually past and therefore cannot be known. If she has a history to communicate, the words she speaks do quite well: "Bremerton, Seattle, Tacoma... are blown to shit" and then "Is Denver gone?" (69). Again, the only history that exists is the fact of the characters' virtual extinction—their history is the destruction of history as it was known before the holocaust.

The end of the world and the end of America are the same event in Marie's mind. Each ending begins with "that small war, between the Americans and the Vietnamese Communists [which] was turning toward its end on the day of her father's death" (72):

> Whenever she imagined, against her will, that triumph of death over the world, the hordes of skeletons dragging the sacks of their skin through the flaming streets, the buildings made out of skulls, the empty uniforms coming inexorably through the fields, the bodies of children stuck full of blast-blown knives and forks—the bottom of everything, the end of the world, a gray blank with nobody to remember it, the vision described, passed on, preserved by *no one*—it was in that city she saw it, in the city of her father's death. (71–72)

That city is Saigon, and her father, Arnold Wright, is a British importer—a descendant of the seventeenth-century East Asian Trading Company. He identifies "authentic" items of Asian culture and arranges for them to be sold to English customers avid for a piece of the Orient in their own small domains. With an English father and a Vietnamese mother, Marie, like the god Bob Marley, is the child of imperialism. She will become her father's last shipment overseas. As she comes of age, her family is coming apart under the pressure of the U.S. withdrawal from Vietnam. That war was begun by the French, continued by the United States, and won by the North Vietnamese. Her father's suicide is presented as if he were a casualty of the U.S. withdrawal. To the reader of the future, these events are just scenery, part of an incommunicable past. To the present-day reader, the father's act seems ceremonial, a European hara-kiri. Symbolically, his act sets the sun on the British Empire and on the age of world conquest by the Europeans and their inheritors, the Americans, the beginning of which *Mason & Dixon* portrayed. Marie's disinclination to distinguish "that small war" between the United States and Vietnam from the more substantial conflagration that consumed the world as she had known it obligates the reader to see the former as preparing the way for the latter. Historically, from this moment on, as *Fiskadoro* itself suggests, stories of historical fusion and cultural uplift will no longer be subject to the British-American-Christian point of view.

Mr. Cheung surmises that the nuclear holocaust was precipitated by a war between communist Cuba and democratic America, and, following the frustrated historian's assumptions, the reader can choose to regard *Fiskadoro* as a Cold War novel. However, by emphasizing the religious nature of the future civilization, Johnson ultimately makes this interpretation untenable. What seems to have occurred is an unimaginable fusion of cultures present within American culture at the time that the bombs dropped, but the fusion favors peoples whose identity lay outside America's traditional WASP–dominated structure. Marie is a prophetic instance of this fusion. Without mother or father, this child of China and Britain via Vietnam escapes Saigon and comes to America, an imperial orphan ready to receive all that American culture has to offer. Following the trajectory of American Empire, but in reverse, she stops in the Philippines, where apparently she has a child. America receives her in the form of her uncle, Kin-lau Kaung, who takes her to "a quick-stop store," where he buys her "a tube of toothpaste, two bars of bath soap, and some roll-on underarm deodorant" (94). It is a perfect initiation into American culture: a convenience store where one can obtain at any time of day or night the ceremonial but so practical items necessary to rub away the accumulated grime of history. In this moment it seems she is Huck Finn in the territory of his dreams or Ishmael home at last after a terrible ordeal, ready to begin anew. She, too, believes herself to be destiny's child: "as if she'd lost her father and abandoned her mother, been raked across life after life, in order to stand here in the enameling brilliance and receive these things" (95).

Her final destiny, however, does not lead exactly to America, and her story is not the traditional American story of an individual who triumphs over history and society to become "truly" herself. An unwanted by-product of the U.S. Empire, she is a cultural bomb landing on American shores. Her presence in the United States suggests that the country is being transformed by the very peoples it once tried to subjugate. The fusion of previous irreconcilable identities that she represents predicts the future as the nuclear holocaust seems to have melted down traditional ethnic allegiances. Polyglot persons such as Marie survive; the WASPs do not. Mr. Cheung's ceaseless invocations of the United States throughout the narrative only highlight the absence of the kinds of "real Americans" that both the America of popular culture (John Wayne) and of politics (the Adams, Bush, Clinton, and Kennedy families) have made into the story of itself. While it may seem overly teleological to suggest that America was destroyed by the non-Europeans it included within its borders, the fact is that in Fiskadoro the ghost of America survives in the bodies of people who normally fall outside the mainstream of American stories. In this context one thinks of the conversation that Mr. Cheung has with Flying Man. A comic routine is begun when Flying Man says, "The oxrago playing depachu, Man-jah." Mr. Cheung, whose own English includes Spanish words, cannot understand what Flying Man says to him. Mr. Cheung eventually determines that oxrago means "orchestra." The reader is left to translate the sentence: "The orchestra is playing at the departure, Manager" (54–55). Flying Man is telling Mr. Cheung that his orchestra (the Israelites) will be playing the day the ships come to end the Quarantine. Cheung's inability to understand Flying Man's polyglot language is connected to his ignorance of his imminent "depachu" into the next world. Nor can he perceive the association of man with God, or Allah, that occurs when Flying Man joins "jah" to "man." Marie, however, will be prepared for the "depachu," since she is the symbolic mother of such conversations and the world in which they occur.

Marie prefigures a fusion of identity unimaginable within the America she joins, but this is not her primary narrative purpose. Her value to the future is that she is the only survivor of the destroyed world. Sealed in her mind are the last images of the world before the holocaust. These memories must fail to survive Marie. By the novel's logic, Marie's story must be completed by Fiskadoro's story: the past gives way to the unimaginable future. Thus, the narrative carefully binds the two so that whenever Marie is thinking about her past the reader is thinking about Fiskadoro (and vice versa). To understand Fiskadoro's meaning, we must surrender our belief in American history, which is why I have saved my discussion of him for the end. We cannot know him except as a species of myth, which is apparently how the future civilization knows him as well. His name links him both to Christ (fisher of men) and to fisher king myths well worked since T. S. Eliot's "The Waste Land." These myths do not explain either the character or the novel, but they help us to understand how Fiskadoro becomes the mysterious narrative principle by which the future present of the novel identifies itself, albeit tenuously, with the past.

I V

A fisherman's son, illiterate, Fiskadoro lives in a world bounded by the daily setting and rising of the sun. Although he owns a clarinet and his family has a radio that still works, he, unlike Mr. Cheung, exists outside of the bounds of civilization as the reader understands it. Unlike Huckleberry Finn, *Blood Meridian*'s kid, Alcott's Jo, or virtually any adolescent that one may remember from classic American literature, Fiskadoro is impossible to identify as a representative American.[9] The closest approximation to Fiskadoro in American literature would probably be the Pacific Islanders among whom Tommo lost himself in Melville's *Typee*. In that novel, the white American joins the Pacific Islander community and participates in their rites, but he stops short of having his face tattooed or becoming a cannibal (acts that to the nineteenth-century American were roughly equivalent). Refusing to be tattooed marks Tommo as an American, prompting him to return to the civilization that he had nearly—and happily—abandoned. Fiskadoro, by contrast, is no white American. When he descends among the swamp people in the novel's climactic symbolic passage, his surrender to the rite separates him from everyone he knows (Mr. Cheung most obviously) and prepares the way for the arrival of the future world.

Among the swamp people, Fiskadoro at first will be made "like all other men" but then later he will be made "different from all other men" (193). Described elsewhere by Mircea Eliade, Victor Turner, and Bruno Bettelheim, Fiskadoro undergoes the rite of subincision, a ceremony that initiates young men into their community. Like the other boys his age, Fiskadoro suffers having his urethra sliced so that his penis has two heads. This ceremony initiates the young men into their community. Fiskadoro, however, is not meant to receive this rite because he is an outsider to the community. He is included because he has been mistaken for a lost boy who drowned a few days earlier. The mistake makes sense, though, because Fiskadoro will become someone through whom other lost souls live. The Islamic text that justifies and explains the ceremony makes it clear that Fiskadoro's astonishing role is to save the world. Before he is cut, Fiskadoro is told that "a long time ago" there lived a man named Mohammed to whom "the Sovereign Lord" gave half His power to "save" others when "Hell was brought near" (180). Mohammed's followers doubted his power from the Lord, even after Mohammed moved a mountain to prove it. In the Koran the disbelievers were warned that when the day came that "Hell was brought near," they would not have the power to continue living. One man followed Mohammed's warning, though even he had doubts. When "Hell was brought near," this man alone survived. Mohammed challenged the survivor to follow him into a cave, whereupon the survivor encountered a two-headed snake that claimed to be Mohammed. The survivor denies that the snake was either Mohammed or a man, but the snake contended that he could be part of a man and commanded, "Where I go between your legs, make yourself like me" (181). When, after some time, the survivor escaped from the cave, he "went to relieve himself, and he found the two-headed snake there" (181). Fiskadoro is then told, "This is the man we, the Quraysh, all come from" (181).

The ceremony of the subincision connects the men of the community to the only survivor of the time when "Hell was brought near," to the one man who heeded Mohammed's warning. For the community of the swamp people, the ceremony is a way to keep the faith in God that the lost ones lacked. They also become a version of the Quraysh, or (as one character notes) "the original first tribe of Mohammed," and through them Fiskadoro is connected to this tribe (166). Cutting the urethra of every male in order to express submission to God's power suggests an extraordinary literal mindedness, but the act has a regenerative power that is not only symbolic. The lost ones who did not heed Mohammed's warning had the arrogance to claim that they themselves possessed "the power to make babies and keep generations living on the earth" (180). For the swamp-people, this power belongs neither to them nor to Mohammed but only to God. Fiskadoro, however, does not understand the story or its relationship to the ceremony. Fiskadoro is not compelled by tradition; he undergoes the ceremony by his own choice. He can see that the other men on the island carry a snake with two heads between their legs, and he determines that he must "go through the ceremony" to "make himself like other men" (179). However, because he will return to his home, where the ceremony does not exist, Fiskadoro actually will be marked as different from other men. If anything, his extraordinary decision makes his act closer to the original initiate's act than anyone who has undergone the ceremony since the original rite occurred.

Fiskadoro takes the place of the man from the swamp people's story. He is the survivor whose faith makes possible the continuation of the world. In this way his initiation serves to join him not to the swamp people but to those of the future. During the ceremony Fiskadoro is made to repeat the part of the Koran story that says, "*When the earth is crushed to fine dust, and your Lord comes down with the angels, in their ranks, and Hell is brought near—on that day man will remember his deeds. But what will memory avail him*" (183). To the swamp people, the story is about creating a community by recounting what others have either denied or forgotten. It is a story about memory. These words are addressed to the arrogant ones who would claim the power of creation—memory will not avail them because they can remember only having denied the Lord in the form of His representative, Mohammed. Fiskadoro, by contrast, is chosen by Allah to be the survivor who takes the place of those whose arrogance caused them to be destroyed. One easily summons here a vision of an all-encompassing American empire obliterating all limits and borders, all nations and cultures, in an ever-expanding war, to create a secular heaven that makes each and every soul a servant to Exxon or McDonald's or Microsoft in an unending dream of infinite consumption and gratification. The American world is destroyed not through reckless expenditure of creation's resources (the green reading) but through the presumption that the world exists for America to create in its own name (the fundamentalist reading).

In *Fiskadoro* there is no Mohammed figure to warn the doomed ones (unless it is Bob Dylan or Bob Marley) and thus there can be no survivors of the time when "Hell was brought near." Instead, there is Fiskadoro, who enacts for the liminal world of the novel the rebirth of humanity into a new cycle of being. As Johnson acknowledges at the book's outset, the work of Turner influenced his conception of the novel. According to Turner, "liminality may be partly described as a stage of reflection" (105). Fiskadoro is not so much one who reflects as he is the occasion for reflection. He represents the historical process that the sacred narrative of the novel portrays. He is no more a hero in the conventional novelistic narrative sense than Jesus Christ, Buddha, or Bacchus were. Rather, he literally embodies the process of renewal from death to birth that makes for the continual creation of humanity and with it the endurance of memory and eventually history.[10] That such renewal effaces previous stories of origin is not contradictory but proof of how contingent and time-bound any particular history must be. Thus, through the process of subincision, Johnson portrays how, in Turner's words,

> those ideas, sentiments and facts that had been hitherto for the neophytes bound up in configurations and accepted unthinkingly are, as it were, resolved into their constituents. These constituents are isolated and made into objects of reflection for the neophytes by such processes as componential exaggeration and dissociation by varying concomitants. The communication of *sacra* and other forms of esoteric instruction really involves these processes, though these should not be regarded as in series but as in parallel. The first is the reduction of culture into recognized components of factors; the second is their recombination in fantastic or monstrous patterns and shapes; and the third is their recombination in ways that make sense with regard to the new state and status that the neophytes will enter. (105–6)

The liminal process Turner describes from his time among the Ndembu tribe clearly defines the pattern Johnson employs to structure Fiskadoro's role in the novel. One could say that the subincision is a version of the bombs that blew up the world, but it may be truer to the novel to say that the bombs that blew up the world are a part of Fiskadoro's ritual. By contrast, Mr. Cheung and the Society for Science know the most about the past and they are the ones in the novel most like the destroyed ones They are a version of the process that led to the destruction, not the re-creation, of the world. Fiskadoro comes not to rescue them but to rescue the future from them. This role explains the otherwise enigmatic statement that "in the dream, his first purpose had been to go through the ceremony and make himself like all other men," but that "now he was awake, [and he] was different from all other men who were awake" (193). The ritual of the subincision marks Fiskadoro, as Turner says of the members of the Ndembu tribe who also employ this ritual, as "symbolically sexless or bisexual...as a kind of human *prima materia*—as undifferentiated raw material" (98). As "human *prima materia*," Fiskadoro is born after the time of hell among people who cannot know of their fallen state, in order to prepare them for their impending resurrection into a new civilization. He lives in what Turner calls "the peculiar unity of the liminal: that which is neither this nor that, and yet is both" (99).

Fiskadoro's allure to the future ones who tell his story comes in part from their recognition that his ignorance of his exalted position is what makes him holy. He has both known hell and forgotten it. Here I stress that Johnson's novel pointedly rejects a narrative assumption prevalent since modernism: that the hero of a novel is the carefully mediated perspective—one's so-called consciousness—of a particular character or number of characters in combination. Johnson gives no credence to the sanctity of the individual's consciousness except as the expression of a group belief. A peculiar component of the subincision ceremony that Johnson portrays is the pill made of "memory juice," apparently some chemical concoction, perhaps LSD, that the initiate ingests. You take the pill, says one character, and "first you remember every single thing in the world, then you don't remember a-tall. Zip. Nothing. Nada" (162).[11] The pill initially allows the initiate to realize that which Mr. Cheung most devoutly seeks: to remember everything and thus to know everything. However, memory—history—is less important than faith and this is why the initiates take the pill, not to enhance memory but to lose it. After the ceremony Fiskadoro will forget why he is not like other men. He will even forget who his own mother is and will repeatedly try to sleep with her. "They never do get back the memories that happened before all that craziness, and the cutting," a character remarks (163).

Before Fiskadoro's process of forgetting truly begins, though, he must experience and then forget the event that so devastated the world that another savior was required. Upon returning home from the subincision ritual, Fiskadoro's first act is to relive the nuclear holocaust as if he were present at the moment it began. Floating along the coast of what used to be "Miami ef el ay," he sees that the words he spoke during the ceremony had come true: "The earth had been crushed to fine dust." He then "put his arms around himself as the tears fell down his face. Today he would remember his deeds." He sees an endless line of cars full of people who die trying to escape the city the day the missiles fell, persons "made of brown bones who didn't shift or flicker or turn" their heads. Sobbing violently, Fiskadoro is certain that the dead are aware of him and that "his purpose in this dream is to die." He waits to be received by his keeper, hopes for "the vigilant guardian to note down each word," listens for "the trumpet-sound." Bawling "out loud for his lost life," he is saved from his trauma only when "his memory [leaves] him" (188–89).[12]

In this scene Fiskadoro, a fisherman's son and hunter of men, assumes for himself responsibility for the world's destruction. He relives each death as if it were his own. In a matter of moments, he goes from experiencing the holocaust, to remembering the holocaust, to remembering the experience of remembering, to remembering nothing at all. The properties that the swamp people attribute to a "soul" illuminate Fiskadoro's state and its relationship to Johnson's attitude toward history and the reader's part in it. To them a soul is "like a baby who hasn't been born," so that "a soul with a new body has a new face and a new name and remembers new things" (176). Fiskadoro will wear the mark of his difference between his legs but will not recall how it came to be there. He has accepted the burden of the past, but the past will not burden him. If Fiskadoro's willingness to go through the ceremony made him dear to Allah, then Allah returns the gift by allowing Fiskadoro to forget the past that he has assumed unto himself. Fiskadoro, the narrative asserts, "is the only one who was ready when we came," because he is the only one who has lived through the experience without creating, denying, or preserving it. He allows himself to live by Allah's will alone and therefore is truly chosen to survive.

The present-day reader, however, is denied Fiskadoro's gift. We know that we are the ones dead in the cars and we are placed in the position of wanting to rise up out of our destroyed cars to speak to the one who the narrative tells us was ready for the next world when it arrived. Fiskadoro will meet versions of the reader in the form of "ghosts who had appeared out of the sea—from the shipwrecks, from the End of the World, from the plagues, from the cold time, from the kill-me—drowned sailors and frozen children, young maidens bleeding down their legs, sick old men and women and cancer-wasted fish-wives who seemed to wander hopelessly near the place of their burning; but all of them were smiling and no longer touched with pain" (196). This biblical passage, with echoes of Bob Dylan's "A Hard Rain's A-Gonna Fall," summons the reader's American future in the form of the likely stages of decay that are projected to occur after a nuclear holocaust. The meeting of worlds described here suggests that Mr. Cheung is not delusional to think that he has memories of the nuclear explosion ("new things now remembered") even though he was not yet born when the bombs fell. Fiskadoro takes possession of the memory that tries to possess Mr. Cheung, just as these ghosts of sailors trying to escape the sea find rest with Fiskadoro. More important, Johnson imagines a present-day America that will be destroyed but that also might one day be saved by the narrative's protagonist. In this one moment the reader of the future and the reader of the present may meet in a shared belief in the power given to Fiskadoro.

Fiskadoro does not, in the end, damn the American reader to everlasting perdition. If the reader cannot quite understand the meaning of the character Fiskadoro except as a symbolic principle, then Johnson seems to allow the historical American reader the same chance at salvation that Marie is given when she falls into the ocean and nearly drowns after escaping from Saigon. Again, Fiskadoro's story completes Marie's story, just as her story underlines the moral to his. The pages that depict her survival in the sea may be the most beautiful in the book. Floating on the water, waiting to be rescued, Marie's extraordinary effort to save herself seems tiny when compared with the ocean's power to absorb her. Unlike Crane's "The Open Boat" or Melville's *Moby-Dick*—obvious models for Johnson—the sea that surrounds Marie does not become a merely literary symbol for nature's indifference or rage. The qualities that might be ascribed to it—cold or warmth, calmness or rage—are not directed at Marie. The sea is only a living place that provides the form in which organisms live and die. Marie thinks how different the sea seems once one is in it rather than flying above it in a helicopter, as she had been a short while earlier. "The surface that seemed so black and heavy from above, whose motions had seemed so blubbery and incidental, now proved active, populous and resourceful, throwing up generations of fingers that clawed her face, worms that raced across her nose and mouth and choked her, small whirling mouths that swallowed and abandoned her hair" (211). The sea is anthropomorphized here, but only because Marie is flailing among others from her helicopter, who are also trying to survive. They brush up against her as they struggle for their lives as willfully as she struggles for hers. In this environment life is swiftly stripped to its most elemental quality. One man dies because he refuses to part with his shoes, for fear that his feet will be eaten by sharks. The weight of the shoes exhausts his strength, and he goes under. Soon the living, Marie among them, maintain their place by standing on the bodies of the dead who float next to them. The obvious moral—that the living must always walk on the bones of the dead—speaks to the future civilization and the dead present reading the book of their (our) death.

Eventually Marie thinks that she has "reached the bottom of everything." But, the narrative tersely notes, "she was wrong" (215). Her experience will exhaust her every reserve of life, yet she will go on living. At one point she wakes from a dream only to find herself drowning. The "shock of finding herself here where she'd always been was like a birth" (215). Paradoxically, since Marie is remembering this memory as she dies, she must wake into a death that she does not actually live—not yet. When she does reach bottom, she does not know it, and—like Fiskadoro reexperiencing the holocaust as if for the first time—she might as well be dead. In the end, only three from the helicopter are saved, Marie among them. Despite their almost inconceivable efforts to stay alive, they are not portrayed as the authors of their survival. The extraordinary passage that recounts Marie's survival enacts what is the key message of the book:

> Marie was the last of the three to be taken out of the water—Captain Minh and one other woman had been saved, and now the young girl Marie. Saved not because she lasted, not because of anything she did, or determined in herself to do, because there was nothing left of her to determine anything; saved not because she hadn't given up, because she had, and in fact she possessed no memory of the second night, and couldn't believe, to this day, that she'd spent twenty hours staying alive, breath by breath, without knowing enough to desire it; saved not because she'd held out long enough; because there was nothing to say what was long enough, saved because she was saved, saved because they threw down a rope, but she couldn't reach her hand up now to take hold of it; saved because a sailor jumped off the boat, his bare white feet dangling from the legs of khaki pants, and pulled her to the ladder; saved not because her hands reached out; saved because other hands than hers reached down and saved her. (218)

The description of her rescue denies every interpretation that might attribute Marie's survival to her own will. There is no Manifest Destiny; there is no self-determination. History does not save her and she is not saved because she represents the history of a particular group or nation. Salvation—or Allah—reaches out to touch her. Her survival is literally a gift from above. The iterative quality of the narrative also denies the office of having been her savior to those who found her, reached out to her, and returned her to safety. Grammatically, the sentence has no subject—as if the name of the authorizing agent of her salvation cannot be spoken. No one in this passage, neither the rescuers nor the rescued, has any agency except what is allowed them by the very gift of life they possess by virtue of a force that does not and never did belong to them. Having reached bottom, having been emptied of her ego, Marie is saved because she has become an empty vessel prepared to receive divine grace. She is the twin to the survivor from the Koran story and she becomes another narrative model for understanding the role that Fiskadoro will play for the next civilization. In this single episode Marie has gone through all that Fiskadoro

264 Denis Johnson's Fiskadoro

will go through. Like Fiskadoro, Marie is a holy figure whose holiness is not intrinsic to herself.

The key phrase for what happens to Marie is that she is saved "because there was nothing left of her to determine anything." Marie survives the Vietnam War so that she may later be the last survivor of the American holocaust, a single self saved. Her story, taken more largely, is a denial of the sense of exceptionalism that has driven all canonical accounts of American history. She is not exceptional and for her being saved involves an act of forgetting, of letting go of the past in precisely the way her son will not be able to do. Neither Mr. Cheung nor Fiskadoro is quite a model for the reader to emulate. Marie is truly the one figure in the book with whom the reader may identify as one who would carry the reader from the doomed present to a possible future. In this way Marie's story becomes a part of Fiskadoro's future—or the force through which humankind is allowed to continue. "The world is repeating itself," one character remarks. "The story of the world is happening again" (165). So history is written and endlessly rewritten.

Marie's memories of her near death in the Pacific Ocean take place while she sits on the beach awaiting the arrival of the white boat that the Israelites have prophesied will come to end the Quarantine. As purveyors of "voodoo," they are linked to the swamp people, and it may be that they arrive to complete the task that has been attributed to the swamp people. The thoughts of presubincision Fiskadoro reveal how those outside their community view the swamp-people: "They fermented things back there in the swamps. They drank the fermented potions and danced inside the fires and were never burned. They had eaten all the white people back there. They had drunk up all the blood" (67). Voodoo in this novel relates to particular cultures, cultures that are or have been created by black people. Sammy, "a white bodyguard" to the black profiteer-prophet, Cassius Clay Sugar Ray, says that the subincision ritual is the province "of a load of niggers" (162–3). Yet these "niggers" become instrumens that help save the world. It is as if the old world's destruction cannot be complete until those who were dispossessed to build it are returned to a rightful position of authority. Having taught others the hymn about seizing the time, the Israelites presage an imminent but necessarily unnamed cultural transformation. In the same way that the swamp people initiate Fiskadoro into his proper role as savior, the Israelites administer the rites that usher in the next civilization. Their status as the novel's "chosen people" is affirmed by the fact that they are the only ones who know that the Quarantine is ending.

The rite that they perform is the "depachu" (departure) for which Flying Man has recruited Mr. Cheung and his orchestra. Mr. Cheung must bring his pupil, Fiskadoro, whose clarinet playing has become sublime since the subincision. He has forgotten how not to play; his music is Pan-like, of the spheres, and wholly appropriate for bridging civilizations. To make this point clear, the narrative states that Mr. Cheung and Fiskadoro were "standing, as a matter of fact, between two civilizations" when "ship or shape, it came in slowly with the tide" (218). What arrives is a version of the white boat that the Israelites have been "ceremoniously building" throughout the book. "It was just like a little ship... with every piece blessed by Flying Man before it was attached to the vessel. Just the same, it would never float. Everyone could see that. But they all understood that floating wasn't the point. This wasn't about sailing anywhere on a ship three meters long: it was about magic, about religion, about Jah" (116). The boat need not float because it stands for the boat that soon arrives that truly will make possible their "depachu." The boat is a vessel of faith not merely of travel. Preparing the boat is the Israelites' way of preparing themselves for their next journey, their next river to cross.[13]

True to the Israelites' understanding, the "depachu" ship arrives "to seize the day," as Mr. Cheung, Marie, and Fiskadoro await it without fully comprehending its significance:

Now the white boat, or was it a cloud, came for the Israelites out of the fog of their belief. In all likelihood it was a ghost ship, and the Israelites were ghosts, and the man standing at the bow was a ghost who had come for them, it was clear in the draw of this white, white vessel—unless the light happened to be playing tricks, it wasn't touching the water at all—clear from the majesty of it, the sense that it floats in the air and not in the waters of the world, floats in the heart of Allah, the Compassionate, the Merciful. (220)

Allah's boat comes for the Israelites because their belief compels its arrival. If the Israelites are ghosts, then they have been sent by Allah to retrieve the dying Marie and the living Fiskadoro. The death to which Marie seemed to awaken in the ocean ninety years earlier lands in the form of the Israelites' white boat. Before, "she woke up drowning," and now we are told that "in her state of waking, she jerked awake. And from that waking, she woke up" (221). Awaiting the arrival of the ghost ship, she herself is a ghost of the old world that the new world saves—saves for the final time. Her soul, existing in an eternal state of readiness, is preserved as an example to those who read and hear the narrative by which the future civilization represents itself. The last survivor of the old world, stranded between civilizations, survives until the next world arrives. As long as she was alive, the memory of the old world's destruction remained. Since the end of the old world stays inside her mind, the end of the old world ends with her. "Grandmother lives and lives," Cheung had said. "Just by surviving, she's turned into the most important personin the world" (51). Although the novel's end suggests that death is not final, her literal death is the last act before the symbolic recovery of the world initiated by Fiskadoro. It is worth noting that Johnson does not endorse the typical patriarchal history that venerates the Founding Fathers as the guiding spirits of American history. In a way that is true to the rejection of history that the book offers, Johnson underlines for us that Marie's son, the Founding Father–seeking Mr. Cheung, does not inherit what she knows. The girl Marie, who is not yet American, becomes the grandmother for the future unnamed empire that is overtaking America's past and present whether we readers of *Fiskadoro* know it or not.

V

Fiskadoro's American reader is framed either as one among the unwakeable dead or as a version of Marie reaching out to be saved. The novel promises to save the reader if the reader accepts that the conflicts of American history—our racism and our endless false claims of freedom and equality—will be resolved only with the destruction of American history, a destruction that must include everything the reader knows about herself or himself and whatever she or he understands her or his history to mean. The conflicting and essentially irreconcilable versions of American history that William Faulkner, Toni Morrison, Cormac McCarthy, Thomas Pynchon, Joan Didion, and Don DeLillo present disappear into *Fiskadoro*'s nameless future where Allah is history's only truth Johnson's vision is millennial and apocalyptic, and it is easy to attribute it to a clarity that comes from being a fundamentalist Christian. But this view would make the work more time-bound than *Fiskadoro* itself would seem to allow. The work's greatest strength—one that is explicitly religious in orientation—is to reveal history in its most powerful form to be a ritual for the expression of communal belief and aspiration. Johnson portrays the power of narrative to reinvent the world and then claims the process of that invention as the truth that holds us together. The other writers I have discussed critique a particular version of history and then hope to replace the version they critique with their own preferred history. Only Johnson shows how history as a practice endures neither as an academic argument about whether the past can be known nor as one group fighting with another for control of the past and thus the present. If *Blood Meridian* presents history as the knowable form that violence takes, then *Fiskadoro* says that the human will to tell and remember stories supersedes even the will to violence. History is the endless re-creation of the remembered world made in the image of the ones speaking and listening at a particular moment in their time. Only to those who are telling the story to themselves does that moment in time consume the perceivable world. *Fiskadoro*'s ultimate lesson is that postmodern history, no less than any understanding of history that precedes it, seeks its own transcendence.

Notes

Introduction

1. As this list suggests, one of the consequences of identity politics has been to subsume difference through a kind of nominalism of renaming identity categories. Throughout this study, however, I have followed the examples of the authors and characters I discuss, expressing identity categories as they understand them. Thus, for instance, in my discussions of Pynchon and Faulkner I have used the term "Indian," rather than "Native American," since at stake in such a langauge choice is precisely the relationship between identity and history that this word carries. In my discussion of *Blood Meridian*, I have followed, where possible, McCarthy's example of using the name of the Indian tribe. "I used to stare at the Indian in the mirror," begins Richard Rodriguez's second autobiography, *Days of Obligation* (1). In different ways, the authors I discuss all "stare at the Indian in the mirror" that is also an ineradicable component of American history.

2. The strength of Berkhofer's study is indicated by the fact that two historians who disagree sharply about the relevance of postmodern theory to the practice of history agree on the importance of Berkhofer's work. Richard J. Evans says, "Berkhofer's account of the various postmodernist positions is cool and judicious and linked to a real knowledge of how historians actually go about their business" (261). For Keith Jenkins, Berkhofer's critique of the professional, academic form of history—what Jenkins calls "lower case history"—is "devastating and unanswerable" (226). In the *American Quarterly* symposium discussion of Berkhofer's book, Saul Cornell comments, "When a future generation of intellectual historians evaluates the impact of postmodernism on the writing of American history and American Studies, Robert Berkhofer's *Beyond the Great Story* will undoubtedly occupy a central place in their story" (351).

3. In *The Greeks and Greek Civilization* (1998), Burckhardt defines his method in terms of its subjectivity. He asserts, "It will, in the end, be quite impossible to avoid a great deal of subjectivity in the selection of material. I lay no claim to be 'scientific' and have no method, at least none shared with other scholars. Given the same studies on which I have based my course, taking care in this subjective procedure to be guided by the relative importance of the material, another person would have made quite another selection, arranged it quite differently, and arrived at different conclusions" (7). Burckhardt preferred literary narratives to historical data. His historical method involved relying first on "narrative authors" regardless of whether what they narrate what "really happened," since they convey "a knowledge of the Greeks" unmatched by factual accounts (8).

4. Important critiques of "the linguistic turn" in the study of history include Perez Zagorin's "Historiography and Postmodernism" (1990), Lloyd S. Kramer's "Litera-

ture, Criticism, and Historical Imagination" (1989), John Toews's "Intellectual History after the Linguistic Turn" (1987), Bryan Palmer's *The Descent into Discourse* (1991), Eric Hobsbawm's *On History* (1997), Alan B. Spitzer's *Historical Truth and Lies about the Past* (1996), and Gertrude Himmelfarb's *On Looking into the Abyss* (1994). The 1989 debate on the merits of postmodernist approaches to the practice of history held between David Harlan ("Intellectual History") and David Hollinger ("Return"), which took place in the pages of the *American Historical Review*, remains an important critical touchstone. For an overview of the issues involved, see Evans's bibliographic essay (253–72). One may not always agree with Evans, but he is an invaluable source.

5. Geoffrey Elton, for instance, says that any "uncertainty around historical truth and a true view of the past arises from the deficiencies of the evidence and problems it poses." To say otherwise "leads to frivolous nihilism which allows any historian to say whatever he likes" (179).

6. He discusses Simon Schama's *Citizens* (1989), Orlando Figes's *A People's Tragedy* (1997), Natalie Zemon Davis's controversial *The Return of Martin Guerre* (1984), Robert Darnton's *The Great Cat Massacre* (1984), and Stuart Clark's *Thinking with Demons* (1997) as important postmodernist contributions to the study of history. He dismisses Schama's *Dead Certainties* for exemplifying "the worst" aspects of postmodernism's influence on historical writing (271).

7. See Evans's discussion (16).

8. In his brilliant work *The Progressive Historians*, Hofstadter wrote of Bancroft and Parkman, "For them the purpose of historical writing was to establish an imaginative relation with the past, not to analyze it but to re-create it" (13). The same holds true of today's popular historians.

9. Had McCullough, who is described in the blurbs for the book as "an artist," marketed the book as a novel, as Gore Vidal did with *Lincoln* (1984) or as Edmund Morris basically did with his fictional memoir of Reagan, *Dutch* (1999), his book would not have been so successful. Both Vidal and Morris were severely rebuked by readers and professional historians for confusing "their" subjects, Abraham Lincoln and Ronald Reagan, with the "real" Lincoln and Reagan. Vidal and Morris employed conventional realist strategies in the service of history, but they would not let their readers forget that historical figures are creations before they are history. The examples of Vidal and Morris show how popular biographies of the Founding Fathers, Civil War heroes, World War II heroes, and "great" charismatic presidents such as Theodore Roosevelt and Ronald Reagan satisfy an unexamined desire for "history" as a form of entertainment.

10. See White's essay "The Value of Narrativity in the Representation of Reality."

11. Hutcheon notes that "history and fiction have always been notoriously porous genres" and observes that "Defoe's works made claims to veracity and actually convinced some readers that they were factual, but most readers today (and many then) had the pleasure of a double awareness of both fictiveness and a basis in the 'real'—as do

readers of contemporary historiographic metafiction" (*Poetics* 107). Here, her argument acknowledges without pursuing it the fact that the epistemological concerns that she identifies as "historiographic metafiction" have been part of the novel's form since its birth with Miguel de Cervantes, Denis Diderot, and Daniel Defoe. Only realism, a nineteenth-century aberration in the history of the form, pretends to be true and then forgets that it is pretending.

12. See Brian McHale's "Introduction to *Postmodernist Fiction*."

13. For instance, Richard Levesque suggests that DeLillo "could be criticized for depicting the erosion of stability (authorial and otherwise) without offering solutions to this postmodern condition" (85).

14. Skip Willman notes that DeLillo emphasizes "the illusion of control and mastery that supports the social effectiveness of the CIA" and suggests that in the face of failures such as the Bay of Pigs "the CIA must preserve the illusion of control" (414, 415). Although this is, of course, true, the more disturbing point that DeLillo raises is how effectively even the seeming loss of control and authority can be recuperated by a narrative strategy that cherishes potential revelations of ambiguity and uncertainty.

15. For further discussions of Roth's understanding of history and identity, see my *Cambridge Companion to Philip Roth*.

1. *Absalom, Absalom!*

1. Poirier, like most subsequent readers, attested to Faulkner's modernist mastery, in particular the way he made Quentin into a kind of narrative-artist responsible for the coherence of the family history being told. For another well-known study that addresses Faulkner's understanding of history in the context of the Civil War generally and Abraham Lincoln specifically, see Sundquist (96–130).

2. "Faulkner's America" is the title of one of Porter's chapters on Faulkner in *Seeing and Being* (1981). She remarks that Brooks "has done more than any other to penetrate the enigma of Sutpen" (211). Her argument challenges Brooks's reading that Sutpen "is certainly not typically Southern" in part because he "embodies the calculating, rationalist temperament we associate with Weber's Protestant Ethic" (208). By Brooks's logic, Sutpen must be anathema to Quentin. Porter, by contrast, argues that Quentin sees that he is a symbolic child of Sutpen's and thus cannot deny an intimate relationship with him. Porter's Marxist critique insists that so-called southern plantation paternalism and so-called northern mercantilism were both "the product of capitalist expansion" (227). Moreover, she sees Faulkner engaged in the same kinds of narrative questions that concerned Ralph Waldo Emerson and Henry James. Thus, readers "must recognize Faulkner as a novelist whose scope encompasses an American and not simply a southern terrain" (211–12). Neither Faulkner's literary forebears nor the overlapping economic interests of the North and South, however, obligate us to see *Absalom* as a work about "Faulkner's America," except to note that Faulkner's America

272 Notes to Pages 47–60

has little to do with the United States or its generally accepted historical premises. In this context, Porter is right to use the ideas of the overlooked but brilliant American historian Louis Hartz to frame her discussion of Faulkner. No less than Hartz, Faulkner rejected the social efficacy of what Hartz identified as the central premise of U.S. history: "the reality of atomistic social freedom" (18).

3. As a practice, the novel clearly anticipates the kinds of "postmodern" claims made by Hayden White and Linda Hutcheon, who argue that the line between history and fiction is at best a convention. See Hutcheon's *The Poetics of Postmodernism*.

4. Michaels restricts his discussion of American modernism to works from the 1920s, but I see it as no stretch to include *Absalom* as part of his implied argument. At any rate, whatever is said about *The Sound and the Fury*, it is not primarily a book that is concerned with the plight of immigrant Jews.

5. Faulkner's recent biographer Frederick R. Karl gives the definitive expression of the view of Faulkner as the great American modernist. He writes, "*Absalom* is the peak of Faulkner's fictional achievement. . . . When we speak of the great novels of modernism, Faulkner's is the sole American fiction which can be discussed with those by Proust, Mann, Kafka, Conrad, Musil, Broch, Woolf, and Joyce." Comparing *Absalom* to *Moby Dick* as a work "which links all the great American themes and calling it "very much a product of the American imagination," Karl notes that "Faulkner had, if anything, a greater theme in the American Civil War and its aftermath" and that Faulkner "had caught the full glory of American failure." Throughout Karl's excellent biography, he is at pains to celebrate Faulkner as "an American writer," which Faulkner certainly was, and thus we might wonder why his "Americanness" must be so aggressively asserted. *Absalom* is not an American novel in that it celebrates the progression of American history; rather, *Absalom* laments the passing of a community destroyed by American history.

6. I refer to Godden's excellent essay "*Absalom, Absalom!* Haiti and Black Labor History: Reading Unreadable Revolutions"; I discuss this essay further in the pages that follow.

7. Baldwin would describe this tendency in terms of Faulkner's willingness to concede "the madness and moral wrongness of the South." Yet "at the same time he raises it to a level of a mystique which makes it somehow unjust to discuss Southern society in the same terms in which one would discuss any other society" (209–10). The "mystique" that Baldwin identifies is often what critics mean when they speak of the Southerner's special "sense of place."

8. As Faulkner told one interviewer after the U.S. Supreme Court decision to integrate the schools, "I will go on saying that Southerners are wrong and their position is untenable, but if I have to make the same choice Robert E. Lee made then I'll make it" (qtd. in Blotner 2: 1591).

9. Godden points out that Faulkner must have been well aware of L'Ouverture's revolu-

tion and the true history of slave revolt in Haiti. Sutpen's version of his story takes place four years after Nat Turner's slave revolt. Godden notes, therefore, that in having Sutpen tell the story of his own Haitian slave suppression to General Compson, Faulkner establishes a context in which "two planters of similar social origin talking in 1835, four years after the Turner rising, combine to construct a story that affirms their interest in clear cut racial mastery, albeit an authority tempered in rebellious fires" (687). For another discussion of Faulkner's use of Haiti in *Absalom, Absalom!* see Ladd.

10. Warren suggests that Faulkner's vision recalls that of Theodore Dreiser's *American Tragedy* in that Faulkner, like Dreiser, "gives a mythic and root drama of the rebuke of values implicit in American society, in the worship of the 'bitch goddess' Success, and the admiration of Horatio Alger" ("Faulkner: The South" 255).

11. In a letter to Albert Murray, Ellison gives an account of his introduction to Faulkner. After Faulkner acknowledged having received a copy of *Invisible Man*, Ellison commented, "You know, you have children all around now. You won't be proud of all of them, just the same they're all around" (Ellison and Murray 45). Although Faulkner always allows his black characters to project a certain nobility, he refuses to acknowledge that the white characters are at odds with them. Thus, the freed slaves are seen less as winners than as other Southerners who have also lost "their" country. Warren notes of Faulkner, "If he is aware of the romantic pull of the past, he is also aware that submission to the romance of the past is a form of death" ("Faulkner" 269). Still, Warren, writing the year after the enactment of the 1964 Civil Rights Bill, will not portray Faulkner as one who is sympathetic to post-Reconstruction African American possibility. Much of the Faulkner criticism has involved a kind of "aesthetic turn" whereby the artistry of Faulkner is praised so that the reader may accept without questioning the roles that Faulkner assigns to blacks in Southern society. More recently, Richard Gray replicates Warren's logic: "To the white Southerner, that is, and to the white Southern writer: it is worth emphasizing that writers like Faulkner have had some experience of the guilt they are talking about in their books. That guilt is part of their structure and feeling as Southerners of a particular race, and so it invariably becomes ingrained in the texture of their work. When they come to explore evil, in fact, that exploration becomes a peculiarly self-conscious activity, which is to say self-aware, self-dramatizing, and self-critical" (403). One wants to add narcissistic as well. In Gray's account, which is so much less subtle than that of either Brooks or Warren, white guilt is not only celebrated as a kind of Southern exceptionalism; more disturbingly, it is celebrated as an aesthetic achievement. Offering what he refers to as "a family systems theory approach," Gary Storhoff goes so far as to suggest that Faulkner's central obsession was not with race or history but with the "dysfunctional family." He argues, "Faulkner exposes the conservative myths that cluster about the family as ideological constructions concealing the pain and suffering of the most vulnerable

beings—children, women, the elderly" (235). Were one to substitute "race" for "family" and "African American slaves and servants" for "children, women, the elderly," the argument would be, I think, more compelling.

12. In addition to the essay included in the Warren anthology *Faulkner: A Collection of Critical Essays*, Brooks wrote two books about Faulkner, *William Faulkner: Toward Yoknapatawpha and Beyond* (1978) and *William Faulkner: First Encounters* (1983). In his latter book, which is directed at novice Faulkner readers, Brooks flatly states, "We are not to conclude that Quentin's and Shreve's final account of the story is a fiction merely" (218). Brooks was a brilliant critic generally and an insightful reader of Faulkner specifically; still, it is unlikely that his reading of Faulkner can be separated from his sense of himself as a Southerner.

13. In *Doubling and Incest/Repetition and Revenge* (1975), Irwin gives the most powerful reading of Quentin's relationship to Henry that I know. He says that ultimately for Quentin "narration does not achieve mastery over time; rather it traps the narrator more surely within the coils of time." I would say that this is not a trap that Quentin falls into but the expression of his desire. This is because Quentin writes history devoid of art. Irwin also suggests that Quentin is able to escape this moment of paralyzing self-recognition: "What Quentin realizes is that the solution he seeks must be one that frees him from time and generation, from fate and revenge: he must die childless, he must free himself from time without having passed on the self-perpetuating affront of sonship" (91). On my view, Quentin's refusal to enter the future is a self-willed repetition of Sutpen's own failure to replicate his design. It is not an act of expiation but of memorialization. The narrative of *Absalom, Absalom!* is his tombstone.

14. Faulkner's 1940 funeral sermon for Faulkner family servant Mammy Caroline Barr indicates as much (*Essays* 117–18).

15. In Faulkner's *Intruder in the Dust* (1948), the white lawyer-intellectual Gavin Stevens resists calls for immediate desegregation in terms reminiscent of those of Faulkner in his public pronouncements of the time: "We are defending not actually our politics or beliefs or even our way of life but our homogeneity [since] only from homogeneity comes anything of a people or for a people of durable and lasting value" (155). Clearly inconsistent with traditionally American invocations of *e pluribus unum*, this statement is completely of a piece with the more "poetic" *Absalom, Absalom!* which derives its power from its furious appeal to racial homogeneity.

16. Faulkner's remarks, which he later attributed to drink, were made to London *Sunday Times* reporter Russell Warren Howe: "As long as there is a middle road, all right, I'll be on it. But if it came to fighting I'd fight for Mississippi against the United States even it meant going out to the street and shooting Negroes" (qtd. in Blotner 2: 1591). Faulkner's stance on integration was complex, and it may have been that—since he was so sensitive to the views of his less-progressive Southern friends and family—even he did not know exactly what he wanted or believed. To his Scandinavian friend Else

Jonsson, he wrote, "There are people in Mississippi who will go to any length, even violence, to prevent [integration]. I am doing what I can. I can see the possible time when I shall have to leave my native state, something as the Jew had to flee Germany during Hitler" (qtd. in Blotner 2: 1539). Faulkner's imprecise comparison reveals the extent to which he felt that moderate white people like him were under attack and risked as much as outspoken black leaders did. After writing in the Memphis Press Scimitar that it was absurd for a poor state like Mississippi to waste so much of its tax dollars ensuring that its schools remain segregated, he received hate mail and threatening phone calls. Indeed, Faulkner's own family sent letters opposing his views. Yet, at the same time that Faulkner was writing letters to various newspaper editors addressing the integration question, he was also serving as a kind of cultural ambassador for the U.S. government. Faulkner was quite proud to serve his country, a representative American. Once, in Japan, when Faulkner's drinking had gotten out of hand, his behavior prompted some U.S. officials to suggest that he be sent back home to prevent an international incident. Faulkner responded, "The U.S. Government commissioned me to do a job and I'll do it" (qtd. in Blotner 2: 1546). Faulkner was uncomfortable, though, being perceived as a representative of the U.S. government in Mississippi, or what he often named his "native country." By the time he told Howe that he would take to the streets to shoot Negroes, he was speaking out of bitter disillusionment at the idiosyncrasy of his position. Without doubt, as he wrote in one letter, Faulkner felt keenly the absurdity of limiting educational prospects according "to an emotional state concerning the color of human skin" (qtd. in Blotner 2: 1534). Moreover, when Faulkner made his infamous remarks to Howe, he was speaking out because he was afraid for the life of Autherine Lucy, an African American woman who had been admitted to the University of Alabama. Faulkner feared that if she were allowed to attend, she would be murdered. He wanted to prevent her death and the more general violence that he feared would erupt if the most regressive forces in the South were allowed free expression. Hence, there is perhaps more despair than militancy in his assertion that, if pressed, he would make the same stand as Robert E. Lee.

17. Let me be clear and say directly that I am not indulging in the game in which the present condemns the past for not being modern. Faulkner was no ex-klansman—no Donald Davidson. There is no doubt that Faulkner understood himself to be for some version of equality between blacks and whites. Still, Faulkner was very reluctant to see this equality as anything but a distant, future prospect. Edmund Wilson was probably right to suggest, despite Faulkner's protests to the contrary, that outsiders made a difference in how Faulkner viewed the race problem (224). For a recent, thorough discussion of Faulkner's public positions on race that is sympathetic to Faulkner as a "liberal," see Theresa M. Towner (119–44). For a view that suggests that "the grandiloquent cadences of Absalom, Absalom!" came "to sound out of key" as Faulkner's career progressed, see Elizabeth Hardwick (226–30).

18. I agree with Michael Grimwood that Faulkner's novels after *Absalom*—*Go Down, Moses* (1942), *Intruder in the Dust*, and even *The Reivers* (1962)—represent an attempt by Faulkner to do justice to the Negro question. Indeed, following Grimwood, one can argue that Ike McCaslin's choice to relinquish his inheritance is a version of Faulkner's wanting to lay down his pen and relinquish the distortions of black identity that his artist's role required of him. From this perspective, Faulkner's position also mirrors Quentin in that after *Absalom*, he backed away from the glorification of the past Southern ideal portrayed there. Where Quentin remained in the past, Faulkner bravely, if not altogether successfully, confronted the historical injustice that made blacks suffer and gave Faulkner both his social place and the material for his art. See Grimwood's excellent "Faulkner and the Vocal Liabilities of Black Characterization."

19. Of course African American authors before Morrison critiqued Faulkner's vision. I would argue that Ellison's unfinished second novel was clearly an attempt to unseat Faulkner. Certainly, both Ellison and Baldwin took issue with Faulkner. Other African American authors who clearly respond to Faulkner's work include Ernest Gaines, Leon Forrest, David Bradley, Melvin B. Tolson, Gayl Jones, and Gloria Naylor. Morrison's *Beloved*, however, is the most successful rewriting of Faulkner, in part because it so brilliantly redeploys Faulkner's own narrative strategies and does so in the service of an African American rendering of Faulknerian themes. For an excellent account of how African American authors have answered Faulkner, see Craig Werner's illuminating essay. One important point that Werner makes is that in terms of literary history, black, not white, authors have been most influenced by Faulkner and most interested in rewriting him.

20. According to Faulkner, Quentin kills himself because of his sister. Two years before the novel was published, Faulkner wrote Harrison Smith that *Absalom*'s central narrator was "Quentin Compson, of the Sound & the Fury, [who] tells it, or ties it together; he is the protagonist so it is not complete apocrypha. I use him because he is just about to commit suicide because of his sister, and I use his bitterness which he has projected onto the South in the form of hatred of it and its people to get more out of the story than a historical novel would" (*Selected Letters* 79). Here Faulkner suggests that Quentin's implied hatred of the South is a consequence of his own private psychology rather than any reasoned historical critique.

21. As people began to express dismay and then anger over his remarks, Lott initially said he had been "winging it." Then a whole history of similar remarks began to emerge. It is important to note that the accounts of Lott's remarks were portrayed as if they were only just being unearthed, when, in point of fact, they had been clear as day all along. What had changed was that suddenly a public context for placing them in historical perspective had emerged—and now has disappeared. See Carl Hulse's November 11, 2002, *New York Times* article "Divisive Words: The Overview; Lott Fails to Quell Furor

and Quits Top Senate Post; Frist Emerges as Successor" and Peter Applebome's December 13, 2002, *New York Times* article "Devisive Words: The Record; Lott's Walk near the Incendiary Edge of Southern History."

22. This shocking burst of historicity, for a lack of a better word, disappeared quickly when the Bush administration capitalized on Lott's misfortune by replacing him with Tennessee Senator Bill Frist.

23. See Adam Clymer's June 27, 2003, *New York Times* article "Strom Thurmond, Foe of Integration, Dies at 100."

24. The Lott–Thurmond controversy received another turn of the screw when it was revealed that Thurmond was the father of an African American daughter, a fact that apparently had been an open secret even during the time Thurmond was opposing the Civil Rights movement.

2. Cormac McCarthy's *Blood Meridian*

1. Dana Phillips divides McCarthy readers into two groups. The first group consists of readers whose interest in McCarthy begins with his Tennessee novels and whose critical orientation is to view violence as a form of redemption. Edwin T. Arnold ("Naming"), Leo Daughtery, and Fred Hobson are examples of this approach. These readers are interested in McCarthy as a Southern writer and are more likely to compare him with Flannery O'Connor than with William Faulkner. The second group finds McCarthy's deepest themes in his western novels and consists of readers who are interested in violence as a type of nihilism (19–20). Vereen Bell (*Achievement*), Steven Shaviro, and John Lewis Longley Jr. represent this critical perspective. I would also single out Denis Donoghue's long, perceptive piece in the *New York Review of Books*. Donoghue says of McCarthy's work that it "issues in violence, hatred, bloodshed, to which McCarthy gives not moral consent but imaginative credence" (6). I agree for the most part, but I would also add that McCarthy is not terribly interested in moral consent, except where it is thoughtlessly given. Bell's helpful chapter on *Blood Meridian* emphasizes McCarthy's use of language and his glorification of the natural world. Daughtery offers a persuasive gnostic reading of the novel.

2. See Wallach ("From *Beowulf*").

3. See Parrish ("The Killer") and Parrish and Spiller ("A Flute").

4. Here Phillips is using Georg Lukács's definition of the historical novel. For Lukács, characters had to have "an awareness of historical conflict and its determining effect on their lives" (qtd. in D. Phillips 25). Phillips does not believe that any of the characters in *Blood Meridian* meet that description. The judge does, although Phillips says that the judge is incomprehensible. The judge's point, though, is that history defines you whether you know it or not. The problem here is that Lukács valorized the realist nineteenth-century novel, and thus does not provide an appropriate model for under-

standing a postmodern one such as *Blood Meridian*. Phillips misses that McCarthy is knowingly and ironically parodying the the conventions of the nineteenth-century novel. Destroying "character" is not the same as destroying "history."

5. Acknowledging Phillips's argument that *Blood Meridian* "is committed to an egalitarian aesthetic of 'optical democracy,'" Georg Guillemin similarly comments, "The novel ventures no ethical or historiographic tenets" (100).

6. Not unlike Phillips, Bell sees the book as "a critique of our culture's anthropocentrism" (124). According to Bell, though, "The non-human world in this novel seems to be competing on every page in every natural detail for a standing equivalent to the human" (129).

7. This is the lesson that Ike McCaslin learns in "The Bear," from *Go Down Moses*.

8. See Greenblatt for a discussion of Christian anxiety about cannibalism.

9. Parkes comments that "in McCarthy's hands, this phrase suggests a self divorced from the Romantic notion of an organic, developing consciousness" (104).

10. Or, in Leo Bersani's brilliant formulation of the nineteenth-century European novel (see *A Future for Astyanax*), the hero is made into a scapegoat for the sins of society.

11. He goes so far as to suggest that Catholicism, insofar as most of its adherents are situated in Latin America, has been transmogrified into an "Indian" religion.

12. See my discussion of Rorty and Michaels in Chapter 3.

13. See Panofsky. See also Daughtery (162–63).

14. In her consistently insightful and challenging essay "The Sacred Hunter and the Eucharist of the Wilderness," Sara Spurgeon argues that this parable shows that "in destroying the sacred power of nature and the myth that tied humankind to it, the father has robbed these sons to come of their right to take part in that myth and of the regeneration and rebirth to be had from it" (91). My consistent claim, by contrast, is that there is no killing without rebirth and that one type of killing is not better, or more morally regenerative, than another type of killing.

15. Hobson has also observed that in McCarthy's fiction the narrative voice "is often, by intent, devoid of any point of view at all" (81).

3. Off Faulkner's Plantation

1. The basic narrative strategy of Morrison's *Beloved* is Faulknerian in that it will give the reader more information and more narrative lines at any given moment than can be comprehended at that point in the story. The famous opening paragraph is a case in point. The novel proceeds by deferral and, as it progresses, yields to the attentive reader the structure of its multiple plots and perspectives. Morrison does not tie everything together, though. We do not know for certain why Halle's escape went bad, although a good guess is that after seeing his wife raped, he did not want to go on. Thus, *Beloved* is like *Absalom* in that the reader is left to choose—to "re-member"—which plots fit and how. In my view *Beloved* is more open-ended than *Absalom*, because it does not

have a narrator within the story who is putting the many points of view into a kind of order.

2. Before a gathering of Faulkner scholars in Oxford, Mississippi, Morrison all but denied any significant Faulkner influence on her work and the clear similarities of plot between Faulkner's novels and hers. Nonetheless, the subject of Faulkner often creeps—I use this word thinking of the mysterious creeping woman in her Faulknerian *Jazz*—into her public comments about her understanding of literature: "It is that business of being universal, a word hopelessly stripped of meaning for me. Faulkner wrote what I suppose could be called regional literature and had it published all over the world" (qtd. in Duvall, "Toni" 6). Morrison's remarks here might be seen as somewhat disingenuous. Faulkner may have written "regional literature," but, even taking that on its own limited terms, the region that Faulkner wrote about included, and politically dominated, the "region" that Morrison takes for her territory. Even if one says that Faulkner wrote from a white male southerner's perspective and Morrison from a female African American's, it is hard to distinguish Faulkner's region completely from Morrison's. "All over the world" people read Faulkner's "regional" literature. Her words betray her recognition of the dominance of Faulkner's works—his "regional" view dominates how others perceive a region that is also hers. In her *Paris Review* interview, though, she notes that "Faulkner in *Absalom, Absalom!* spends the entire book tracing race, and you can't find it. No one can see it, even the character who is black can't see it" ("Art" 101). She then describes a lecture that she gave in which she tried to track "all the moments of withheld, partial or disinformation, when a racial fact or clue *sort* of comes out but doesn't quite arrive. . . . Do you know how hard it is to withhold that kind of information but hinting, pointing all the time? And then to reveal it and say that is not the point anyway? It is technically just astonishing. As a reader you have been forced to hunt for a drop of black blood that means everything and nothing. The insanity of racism" (101). Although clearly she regards Faulkner's artistry with awe, as a kind of miracle, her historical point of view ultimately cannot be sympathetic with how Faulkner seems to make race disappear.

3. Morrison is deeply sympathetic to Faulkner's art—arguably, she is the strongest reader and interpreter of Faulkner in the American literary tradition. I do not think that Morrison's aesthetic vision or achievement (or that of any other American writer) is as powerful as Faulkner's. Duvall's fine essay on *Song of Solomon* mostly proves how indebted *Song of Solomon* was to Faulkner ("Doe"). In my view, Weinstein's excellent work on Morrison and Faulkner leads us to a similar conclusion. Morrison's best strategy for resisting Faulkner is to rescue her vision of African American identity from Faulkner's very powerful vision. In other words, she has to separate Faulkner's vision from the novel that expresses it. From a strictly novelistic (as opposed to historical) perspective, Morrison's work is so intricately involved with Faulkner's that it really cannot be separated from Faulkner's. The plain literary truth is that without Faulkner

we would not know Morrison as we do. Her aim, as ambitious as any in the American literary tradition, is to change how we read Faulkner. Previous criticism on this subject, while generally excellent, shows how difficult this objective is.

4. Given that Morrison and Ellison are, arguably, the two most significant African American writers, it is strange that their authorial relationship has not been discussed in greater detail. See Bloom ("Two"). When asked to comment on Morrison in 1977, Ellison stated, "She's a good novelist" (*Conversations* 374). Morrison has acknowledged her authorial kinship with Ellison with her frequent references to him as a "grandfather."

5. The full quotation is "You go to William Faulkner and Robert Penn Warren"; Warren was with Ellison that evening on the dais (*Conversations* 149).

6. Perhaps we should say that Ellison's public appraisal of Faulkner focuses on Faulkner's invention and use of characters as part of a specific aesthetic pattern. When Faulkner wrote in *Life* magazine that the Civil Rights movement needed to slow down and that integration must "wait-a-while," however, Ellison was furious. "Faulkner has delusions of grandeur because he really believes that he invented these characteristics which he ascribes to characters in his fiction and now he thinks he can end this great historical action just as he ends a dramatic action in one of his novels with Joe Christmas dead and his balls cut off by a man not nearly as worthy as himself.... Nuts! He thinks that Negroes exist simply to give ironic overtone to the viciousness of white folks, when he should know very well that we're trying hard as hell to free ourselves; thoroughly and completely, so that when we got the crackers off our back we can discover what we (Moses) really are and what we really wish to preserve out of the experience that made us" (Ellison and Murray 117). It is one thing to write novels about reactionary, nostalgic white Southerners and their uneasy relationship with "Negroes"; it is quite another to emerge as a reactionary, nostalgic white Southerner as a more refined version yourself. This gesture could suggest only that although Faulkner might read Ellison's work and even appreciate Ellison's artistry (he did write a blurb for *Invisible Man*), Faulkner would not necessarily accept Ellison as a social equal or be inclined to merge his history with Ellison's in a way that Ellison could accept.

7. See Trudier Harris for another articulation of the African Americanist argument (85–115). See also Wahneema Lubiano for an insightful discussion of how Morrison successfully blends postmodernist skepticism with the expression of an authentic African American historical presence.

8. The important recent work of psychoanalytically oriented critics has effectively argued against those who say that postmodern fiction has jettisoned history. Rothberg's compelling discussion of *Beloved* observes "that diagnoses of the waning of historical consciousness in contemporary culture may have missed the locations where it has continued to flourish—in depictions of the aftermath of traumatic events" (502). Clifton Spargo notes that novels such as *Beloved* "figure the recovery of history as an

involuntary or traumatic phenomenon" (113). See also Joseph Flanagan, who comments that "conceiving of History as traumatic is thus an attempt not to do away with the referential truth-claims of traditional historiography but, in fact, to move those claims away from suspect figurative and narrative conventions to a more stable and reliable source: the 'Real' of the nonrepresentational" (388).

9. See Margaret Atwood's "Haunted by Their Nightmares," in the September 13, 1987, *New York Times Book Review*, a review of *Beloved* that noted that the book portrays white people in an unfavorable light. It is no coincidence, then, that Sethe rents the house at 124 Bluestone Road from the Bodwins, the "good" white people, whose life work has been helping the slaves to free themselves. Just as Morrison must renounce Faulkner's white patriarchal history, so must Sethe overcome the ways in which even good-hearted white people have created her.

10. The critical consensus is that *Song of Solomon* suggests the extent to which Morrison's work can be accommodated within a framework that seeks rather then rejects a historical consciousness. Linda Krumholz's discussion of *Song* in terms of the work of anthropologist Victor Turner is especially illuminating.

11. Morrison's arguments here vividly echo similar arguments frequently made by Ellison. In "Twentieth Century Fiction" Ellison remarked that "it is unfortunate for the Negro that the most powerful formulations of modern American fictional words have been so slanted against him that when he approaches for a glimpse of himself he discovers an image drained of humanity" (*Collected* 81–82). He adds that white writers' portrayals of Negroes seem to him a strange kind of "group frenzy" in which "the white American prepares himself emotionally to perform a social role" (84). Thus, "we see that the Negro stereotype is really an image of the unorganized, irrational forces of American life, forces through which, by projecting them in forms of images of an easily dominated minority, the white individual seeks to be at home in the vast unknown world of America. Perhaps the object of the stereotype is not so much to crush the Negro as to console the white man" (97). Or, as Morrison suggests of *Huckleberry Finn*, "Freedom has no meaning to Huck or the text without the specter of enslavement" (*Collected* 56).

12. Recognizing this quality of Morrison's work, Bill Moyers once asked her when she was going to write about white people. Recalling Moyers's question, Morrison told Schappel that to be asked, " 'Are you ever going to write a book about white people?' is likely 'a kind of a compliment' since it means 'you write well enough, I would even let you write about me' " (Morrison, "Art" 119). She maintains that these questions were not put to James Joyce or Leo Tolstoy. For Morrison, Joyce is an Irishman before he is a modernist and Tolstoy a Russian before he is a realist. This is not to say that Morrison or anyone else cannot benefit from reading their works but that those novels do have cultural contexts and thus historical possibilities that are not available to all readers.

13. Morrison is no doubt aware of LeRoi Jones's (Amiri Baraka) argument—one that Ellison criticized—throughout *Blues People* (1964) that a slave could not be a man.

282 Notes to Pages 135–142

14. Valerie Smith, among others, has pointed out how different Harriet Jacobs's story is from Frederick Douglass's, since she had to withstand sexual exploitation—a point crucial in the discussion of *Beloved* as well. Sethe's story involves more than sexual exploitation; it involves (re)creating the community that Douglass abandoned. See Valerie Smith ("Circling").

15. This scene may actually be based on stories that Ellison published during the 1960s and that would eventually become Chapter 8 of *Juneteenth* (see "The Roof," "Juneteenth," and "Night-Talk"). Morrison's metaphorical "Clearing," with its vision of communal healing, is precisely what Ellison envisions in Chapter 8 of *Juneteenth*. See my discussion in "The Fight to Be a Negro Leader" (137–56).

16. For a perspective on how Morrison tries to recapture the past without romanticizing slavery, see Mobley.

17. Carolyn Jones similarly notes that "the mark becomes a sign of community, identity, and wholeness" (625).

18. The recovery of history is tied together through the meaning of *Beloved*, memories of the Middle Passage, and the novel's various mother-daughter relationships. For insightful readings that, in varying ways, trace these interconnections, see Deborah Horvitz, Elizabeth B. House, Linda Krumholz, Barbara Hill Rigney, Caroline Rody, Shirley A. Stave, and Jean Wyatt.

19. In a brilliant reading of *The Sound and the Fury*, Ellison allows readers to imagine a single moment in Faulkner where Faulkner acknowledged a future for black people. Ellison notes that Quentin's last gesture at communication before his suicide is to Deacon, a black servant from the South who reminds Quentin of someone he had known growing up. Ellison surmises that Deacon has gone North to escape the role of servility that remaining in the South required of him. "Thus Deacon, who has rejected the role assigned to him by his native South, ends up playing not the traditional black fool but, all unknowingly, the death-messenger for an apathetic Southern aristocrat who is driven to self-destruction by the same prideful confusion of values from which, as Southerners, both suffer. Having tried to live in the South, both had come north dragging the past behind them, but while Deacon used his Southern craftiness to play upon life's possibilities, the past-haunted Quentin destroyed himself because he was unable to reconcile the mythical South he loved with that which sent Deacon packing" (*Collected* 643). Appropriately, Deacon becomes the bearer of Quentin's message. When Quentin gives him a sealed envelope, Deacon suspects that he may be part of a practical joke. Quentin asks Deacon whether he was ever the victim of such a joke, only to receive an ambiguous response. "You're right," Deacon says, "they're fine folks. But you can't live with them" (643). Thus, Deacon gets to tell Quentin why he left the South—because of white folks like Quentin, while becoming the fitting bearer of Quentin's last message. Quentin and the class that he represents die, whereas

Deacon lives on for another day—largely because he was able to abandon the South, even though it was once his home.

20. Valerie Smith comments that by the end of the novel "Milkman bursts the bonds of the Western, individualistic conception of self, accepting in its place the richness of a collective sense of identity" ("Quest" 40).

21. For a strong discussion of how Morrison "privileges oral culture and memory over written culture, see see Middleton.

4. Thomas Pynchon's *Mason & Dixon*

1. In his definitive essay on *Gravity's Rainbow*, Edward Mendelson describes how Pynchon's 1973 novel renders "the full range of knowledge and beliefs of a national culture, while identifying the ideological perspectives from which the culture shapes and interprets its knowledge" (30). *Mason & Dixon* is not encyclopedic. First, it is set "near the immediate present but not in it" (30). More important, it is not really a national story, although obviously one is implied. If anything, its scope is greater than what Mendelson identifies as "encyclopedic," since it defines the point at which Europe, and in particular England, was consolidating the cultural achievements and scientific insights of the Renaissance and Reformation and reformulating them as the creation of a world empire. Arguably, this period lasted until the era of *Gravity's Rainbow*, at which point the technologies of Euro-America began to transform the world again. Without question, *Mason & Dixon* should be read as a companion to *Gravity's Rainbow*—the two bookends to the history of the West as it relates to the invention of America. Beyond *Mason & Dixon* and *Gravity's Rainbow*, no English-speaking author in any discipline has better defined and portrayed the West (Euro-America and its various national offshoots) from the time of the so-called discovery of America.

2. See the discussion in Chapter 1.

3. To be fair, one should acknowledge that its dizzying blend of intellectual disciplines and brilliant writing makes the book an unmatchable model. No one but Thomas Pynchon could have written it.

4. For an account of how Pynchon uses and often alters Mason's logs, see Clerc (57–87). For a recent history of the drawing of the Mason-Dixon Line, see Danson.

5. See, for instance, Milan Kundera's discussion of *Don Quixote* in *The Art of the Novel* (3–23).

6. Pynchon actually sets the novel at the earliest moment at which a novel of facts could be written—the time when facts were invented.

7. Strandberg may be right to say that Pynchon's mode in *Mason* "is the mock-epic" (104). Most critics, however, have emphasized the fact that Pynchon critiques received versions of American exceptionalism, which he surely does. Early reviewers such as Anthony Lane, Louis Menand, and Michael Wood all focused on Pynchon as

an ingenious novelist who happens to be a critic of U.S. history. Drawing on literary theorists such as Jacques Lacan and Dominick LaCapra, Christy L. Burns offers a more sophisticated view. Burns quite nicely describes Pynchon's "parallactic method," by which she means Pynchon's ability to maintain "a full and yet contentiously dialectical representation of America as it was in the mid- to late eighteenth century and as it is now" (paragraph 1). Rather than understand Pynchon to be writing a true (albeit contingent) version of U.S. history, Burns understands him to be practicing a form of postmodern critique. I do not disagree with this claim, but I see the book as aspiring to be more than a critique of history. Baker, for instance, argues that Pynchon both critiques and hopes for a true struggle for democracy, but I believe that Pynchon is not very optimistic about it and that he therefore writes for the future as much as he does for the present (see "A Democratic Pynchon"). In addition to the works of Lane, Menand, and Wood, see Olster's fine essay "A 'Patch of England, at a Three-Thousand-Mile Off-set'?" which places Mason & Dixon in the context of the emerging modern nation-state.

8. In "The Sound of One Man Mapping," Joseph Dewey argues that Mason & Dixon should be read as a religious book.

9. Tanner, Pynchon's best critic, calls Cherrycoke "an amiable, eighteenth-century proto-Pynchon" (223–24).

10. This is not to say that Pynchon is not playing on the recently well-documented—this in itself a reaction to the Starbucks phenomenon, I would hazard—coffee tavern boom of the eighteenth century.

11. See also Landes.

12. For an excellent discussion of this issue, see Spiller.

13. Dixon also recalls with bitterness the events of 1745: "'Twas the only time in my life I have felt that Surrender to Power, upon which, as I have learned after, to my Sorrow, all Government is founded" (312). The Weaver Rebellion was crushed by the same General Wolfe who fought against the Indians in the New World in 1763. The Weavers are often thought of as early Luddites—resisting technological developments that seemed to threaten their way of life.

14. That Pynchon renders Mason and the beetle as equals, sharing a similar experience, suggests the appropriateness of some readers' environmentalist readings of the novel (see Cowart).

15. In part, Pynchon's portrayal of Franklin pays homage to Herman Melville's portrayal in Israel Potter (1854).

16. Pynchon's strategy recalls the strategy in Gravity's Rainbow, an encyclopedic study of World War II that never mentions Adolf Hitler, Joseph Stalin, Winston Churchill, Franklin Delano Roosevelt, or any of the other figures who are usually considered principal actors in that conflict. In Pynchon's account the main actors are the scientists and the multinational corporations that trade on the scientists' discoveries.

17. Pynchon explores subsequent versions of white exploitation of the black population in South Africa in "Mondaugen's Story" (in Chapter 9 of V) and in the episodes concerning Lt. Weissmann among the Herero in *Gravity's Rainbow*.

18. The Dixon of Pynchon's history would certainly view Washington's political ascendancy and even the U.S. Constitution, rigged to prolong slavery for as long as possible, as morally dubious. See Gary Wills's *Negro President* (2003) for an account of the crucial role that slavery played in the early American republic. Of Jefferson, the key focus of the book, Wills writes, "Though everyone recognizes that Jefferson depended on slaves for his economic existence, fewer reflect that he depended on them for his political existence" (xiii).

19. As Michael Rogin argues, "Both blacks and Indians, in racialist thought, posed primitive threats to the [American] social order. But those threats differed, in keeping with the contrasting white desires for Indian land and black labor. Indians, on the margins of white settlement, posed the subversive threat of freedom; that threat was met by the displacement, elimination or confinement of the tribes. Blacks, upon whose labor whites depended, posed the subversive threat of reversing the relations of dependence. Indians offered escape from political, social, and familial institutions; blacks threatened social and sexual upheaval" (51).

5. History after Henry Adams and Ronald Reagan

1. For an excellent analysis of Pynchon's use of Adams in V, see Slade (48–89).

2. Hutcheon notes that "Baudrillard's model has come under attack for the metaphysical idealism of its view of the 'real,' for its nostalgia for a pre-mass-media authenticity, and for its apocalyptic nihilism" (31).

3. See my Introduction.

4. The climax of Adams's novel occurs when Madeleine refuses a senator's offer of marriage and repudiates Washington politics by traveling abroad; the climax of Didion's novel occurs when Inez renounces her senator husband and repudiates Washington politics by moving abroad.

5. Alan Nadel describes *Democracy* as being "steeped . . . in the conventions of postmodern meta-fiction" (98). Examining Didion's first three novels, *Run River* (1963), *Play It as It Lays* (1971), and *A Book of Common Prayer* (1977), Thomas Mallon explores "the limits of historical explanation" and in particular the gap in Didion's fiction between history and her characters' inability to articulate it (44). Michael Tager offers a sympathetic, insightful account of how Didion explores democracy's decline in the postmodern era, noting also that *Democracy* seemed to predict the 1987 Iran–Contra crisis that plagued the Reagan–Bush administration. For Didion and postmodernism, see also Levesque and Beauvais.

6. In "Nuclear Blue," an uncollected essay, Didion suggests that her close affinity with Adams has become a part of her thought process. She refers to her "Modern Library

copy of *The Education of Henry Adams*, a book [she] first read and scored at Berkeley in 1964." She singles out his "famous passage on the dynamo" and wonders what Adams would have made of "the TRIGA Mark III reactor in the basement of Etchverry Hall" with its "intense blue of the Cerenkov radiation around the fuel rods" (77–78).

7. Even if, in time, bloggers' accusations are proven to have basis, by then the beneficiaries of the scripted 9/11 drama will already have served two terms in office and will have established the logic for keeping their party in control for perhaps many more to follow.

8. In interviews DeLillo has acknowledged Didion as a writer whose work he reads avidly—along with, among others, the work of Thomas Pynchon and Cormac McCarthy.

9. Frank Lentricchia also notes that film in DeLillo's fiction "is the culturally inevitable form of our self-consciousness" (446).

10. DeLillo employs a similar strategy in *Running Dog* (1978), which hinges on the author's account of a home movie that was allegedly shot by Adolf Hitler only hours before his death.

11. See Benjamin's "The Work of Art in the Age of Mechancial Reproduction," in *Illuminations*.

12. Benjamin's classic and by now well-known definition of aura is in "The Work of Art in the Age of Mechanical Reproduction." For two different, but highly engaging, discussions of DeLillo's relationship to Benjamin see Duvall ("Baseball") and Lentricchia.

13. Baudrillard is the postmodern theorist who many critics see as most relevant to DeLillo's work. See Carmichael, Frow, and Wilcox.

14. Duvall notes that Hodges is "DeLillo's ironized self-figuration," adding that "Hodges's participation in the mythologizing of baseball parallels President Reagan's use of a mythological American past" ("Baseball" 303). DeLillo is not equating Reagan with Hodges as much as he is transforming Hodges's medium of communication into a reconsideration of how the past is packaged as nostalgia.

15. See Didion's *Salvador* for this argument.

16. See Kevin Phillips's "Armaments and Men: The Bush Dynasty and the National Security State" for a convincing account of the likely Bush family involvement in secret negotiations with the Iranians over the release of the American hostages at the end of Jimmy Carter's administration (*American* 178–210).

17. DeLillo expects his readers to know that Reagan began his career as a simulator of baseball games. As president, Reagan was able to enact—simulate—the official meaning of the Cold War. As Duvall suggests, "It is through the figure of Hoover that [DeLillo] suggests how global politics become aestheticized, so much so that the history of the Cold War nearly disappears from American consciousness" ("Baseball" 293).

18. DeLillo is happy to assume that his work will repel most readers. He describes his relationship with potential readers this way: "The writer is driven by his conviction that some truths aren't arrived at so easily, that life is still full of mystery, that it might better for you, Dear Reader, if you went back to the Living section of your newspaper because this is the dying section and you don't really want to be here. This writer is working against the age and so he feels some satisfaction at not being widely read. He is diminished by an audience" (qtd. in LeClair 87).

19. A January 7, 2004, New York Times piece provides a typical example of "the process" that Didion describes. Under the headline "A Partner in Shaping an Assertive Foreign Policy," an article by Elizabeth Bumiller describes the allegedly highly charged "partner" relationship between President George W. Bush and National Security Adviser Condoleeza Rice. The story is not about their foreign policy decisions or the likely consequences of those decisions; it is about the "partnership" that creates them. What interests the reporter—and presumably the audience—is the "closely guarded" nature of "Ms. Rice's relationship with President Bush." The rhetoric and perspective of the article would not be out of place on the celebrity gossip page. Why the "closely guarded" nature of their "relationship" is more important than the very public consequences of their public policy decisions Bumiller declines to indicate. Instead, the Times shows President Bush, one of the most unpopular presidents among African Americans in U.S. history, in a front-page publicity shot walking one step in front of his trusted "partner," the African American woman he calls "Condi" (A1, A6.).

20. Mark Royden Winchell observes, "Jack Lovett is probably the most admirable" male character in Didion's fiction (130).

21. Didion's most recent novel, The Last Thing He Wanted (1996), has a Jack Lovett–like character as its protagonist and deals with, among other conspiracies, the JFK assassination.

6. Denis Johnson's *Fiskadoro*

1. Turner's influence and his focus on liminality are especially evident. In The Forest of Symbols Turner speaks of rites de passage that "indicate and constitute the transition between states" occurring "where change is bound up with biological and meteorological rhythms and recurrences rather than technological innovations" (93). Fiskadoro presents the end of American history as its readers know it as if it were one such rite de passage; it portrays "a time between civilizations and a place ignored by authority" (12) as a liminal state leading to the next great civilization. For a discussion of Johnson and Campbell, see Lenz ("Danger").

2. Bloom does not actually discuss Johnson. A handful of critics have discussed his poetry, and his book of stories, Jesus' Son (1992), has attracted some critical attention. See Lenz ("Reinventing"), Parrish ("Denis"), Reitenbach, and R. Smith.

3. Johnson is an avowed born-again Christian. His book of essays, Seek (2001), acknowl-

edges and explores how his affinity with born-again Christianity influences his political and historical perspective.

4. The Koran provides a sort of monomyth of its own as it incorporates the teachings of the Old and New Testaments into its narrative.

5. In this sense, *Fiskadoro* is the only text I know that might claim to represent "the new imaginary" that Keith Jenkins hopes will be emblematic postmodern history; if so, however, it does so to return us to a pre-postmodern world.

6. Octavio Paz in *The Labyrinth of Solitude* and Richard Rodriguez in *Days of Obligation* have argued that Latin America remains an Indian culture—that Catholicism in the New World is an Indian religion.

7. Mr. Cheung himself can embody this truth without being aware of it. A clarinet player of some ability, Mr. Cheung is the manager of the Miami Symphony Orchestra, a ragtag collection of musicians who do not deserve, in Mr. Cheung's mind, the name under which they play. Cheung's fellow players regard him as one who possesses "the Spirit" and is "perhaps a great artist among all the clarinetists who ... ever lived" (34). However, Mr. Cheung has learned to play by studying a copy of *Sydney Bechet's Clarinet Method*. Bechet, of course, was a great New Orleans jazz clarinet player of the early twentieth century, one of many people who were responsible for the invention of jazz. Yet Mr. Cheung's debt to Bechet, who played a significant role in transforming European music into "American" music—jazz—suggests the inseparability of his identity as a musician and would-be civilized person from those forces. Earlier, reflecting on how his preference for Cornelli has been outstripped by the people's desire for other music, Mr. Cheung admits that, in order to survive, his orchestra "must do the blues, and we must do the Voodoo" (35). Mr. Cheung becomes an instance of Johnson's sense that history speaks through an individual, regardless of the individual's understanding.

8. Johnson's use of Hendrix as a cultural legacy is informed and brilliant. As great a guitar player as Hendrix was, his gifts were made apparent through his inventive use of electricity. Sonic distortion, electronic feedback—a guitar in his hands became a machine that made noise as loud and as earsplitting as any airplane engine or any jackhammer tearing up the street and he made that sound into music.

9. After Fiskadoro's father, Jimmy, has died, Mr. Cheung tells the boy, "I am an American. You, too. Jimmy was an American" (94). Fiskadoro's putative American identity is no comfort from his grief.

10. Joseph Campbell says for the mythical hero "the aim is not to *see*, but to realize that one *is*." At that point, however it occurs, "one is free to wander as that essence in the world. The essence of oneself and the essence of the world: these two are one" (*Hero* 386).

11. That the pill becomes part of the ceremony suggests that the swamp people have been able to fuse elements of the destroyed society into their own rituals.

12. The fate the Koran promises to the unfaithful is the one these past Americans receive in *Fiskadoro*: "They shall abide long ages; there they shall taste neither refreshment nor any drink, save scalding water and decaying filth, a fitting recompense" (416). What Fiskadoro witnesses is prophecy from the Koran come to life, or death. Thus, in the Koran unbelievers are said to mock the doomsday warnings of the faithful: "When we are turned to hollow bones, shall we be restored to life? A fruitless transformation! But with one blast they shall return to the earth's surface" (417).

13. Mr. Cheung is given some insight into the process that the Israelites enact when he thinks that "every thing we have, all we are, will meet its end, will be overcome, taken up, washed away. But everything came to an end before. Now it will happen again. Many times. Again and again" (219). Earlier, Mr. Cheung had scoffed at Park-Smith's notion that "some of that Voodoo may be a helpful thing" (156). Although it is unclear by the novel's end that Mr. Cheung's heart has been moved to accept voodoo as a means for bringing about his salvation, he nonetheless receives a portion of the "depachu's" healing possibilities. He sees himself in the seagulls "who walked back and forth at the border of the water, all bellies and beaks, throwing out their chests with the flat assumption like small professors" (219). He recognizes at least his own arrogance in trying to hold on to a history that has failed.

Works Cited

Adams, Henry. *The Degradation of the Democratic Dogma*. New York: Smith, 1949.

———. *Henry Adams: Novels, Mont Saint Michel and Chartres, and The Education of Henry Adams*. New York: Library of America, 1983.

Anderson, Linda. "The Re-imagining of History in Contemporary Women's Fiction." *Plotting Change: Contemporary Women's Fiction*. Ed. Linda Anderson. London: Arnold, 1990. 129–41.

Andrews, Roy Chapman. *All about Dinosaurs*. New York: Random, 1952.

Appleby, Joyce, Lynn Hunt, and Margaret Jacob. *Telling the Truth about History*. New York: Norton, 1994.

Arnold, Edwin T., and Diane Luce. "Naming, Knowing and Nothingness: McCarthy's Moral Parables." Arnold and Luce, *Perspectives on Cormac McCarthy* 43–68.

———, eds. *Perspectives on Cormac McCarthy*. Jackson: UP of Mississippi, 1993.

Awkward, Michael. " 'Unruly and Let Loose': Myth, Ideology, and Gender in *Song of Solomon*." *Toni Morrison's Song of Solomon: A Casebook* Ed. Jan Furman. Oxford: Oxford UP, 2003. 67–94.

Backman, Melvin. "Sutpen and Southern History." Kinney 121–29.

Baker, Jeff. "Plucking the American Albatross: Pynchon's Irrealism in *Mason & Dixon*." Horvath and Malin 167–88.

Baker, Jeffrey S. "A Democratic Pynchon: Counterculture, Counterforce, and Participatory Democracy." *Pynchon Notes* 32–33 (1993): 99–131.

Baldwin, James. "Faulkner and Desegregation." *James Baldwin: Collected Essays*. Ed. Toni Morrison. New York: Library of America, 1998. 209–14.

Beauvais, Paul Jude. "Postmodernism and the Ideology of Form: Narrativity and the Logic of Joan Didion's *Democracy*." *Journal of Narrative Critique* 23.1 (1993): 16–30.

Becker, Ernest. *The Structure of Evil: An Essay on the Unification of the Science of Man*. New York: George Braziller, 1968.

Bell, Vereen. *The Achievement of Cormac McCarthy*. Baton Rouge: Louisiana State UP, 1988.

Benjamin, Walter. *Illuminations*. Trans. Harry Zohn. New York: Schocken, 1969.

Berkhofer, Robert. *Beyond the Great Story*. Cambridge: Harvard UP, 1995.

Bersani, Leo. *A Future for Astyanax*. Boston: Little, Brown, 1976.

Bettelheim, Bruno. *Symbolic Wounds*. Glencoe, Ill.: Free, 1954.

Bloom, Harold, ed. *Toni Morrison*. New York: Chelsea, 1990.

———. "Two African-American Masters of the American Novel." *Journal of Blacks in Higher Education* 28 (Summer 2000): 89–93.

———. *The Western Canon*. New York: Harcourt Brace, 1994.

Blotner, Joseph. *Faulkner: A Biography*. 2 vols. New York: Random, 1974.

Brodhead, Richard C., ed. *Faulkner*. Englewood Cliffs, N.J.: Prentice, 1983.

Brooks, Cleanth. "History and the Sense of the Tragic: *Absalom, Absalom!*" Warren, *Faulkner* 186–203.

———. *William Faulkner: First Encounters.* New Haven, Conn.: Yale UP, 1983.

———. *William Faulkner: Toward Yoknapatawpha and Beyond.* New Haven, Conn.: Yale UP, 1978.

Bumiller, Elizabeth. "A Partner in Shaping an Assertive Foreign Policy." *New York Times* 7 Jan. 2004: A1, 6.

Burckhardt, Jacob. *The Greeks and Greek Civilization.* New York: St. Martin's, 1998.

Burns, Christy L. "Postmodern Historiography: Politics and the Parallactic Method in Thomas Pynchon's *Mason & Dixon.*" *Postmodern Culture* 14.1 (Sept. 2003). http://www3 .iath.virginia.edu/pmc/issue.903/14.1contents.html.

Campbell, Joseph. *The Hero with a Thousand Faces.* New York: MJF, 1949.

Campbell, Neil. "Liberty Beyond Its Proper Bounds: Cormac McCarthy's History of the West in *Blood Meridian.*" Wallach, *Myth, Legend, Dust* 217–26.

Carmichael, Thomas. "Lee Harvey Oswald and the Postmodern Subject: History and Intertextuality in Don DeLillo's *Libra, The Names,* and *Mao II.*" *Contemporary Literature* 34.2 (1993): 204–18.

Cash, W. J. *The Mind of the South.* New York: Knopf, 1941.

Chinnock, Frank. *Nagasaki: The Forgotten Bomb.* New York: World, 1969.

Civello, Paul. "Undoing the Naturalistic Novel: Don DeLillo's *Libra.*" *Arizona Quarterly* 48.2 (Summer 1992): 33–56.

Clark, Stuart. *Thinking with Demons: The Idea of Witchcraft in Early Modern Europe.* Oxford: Clarendon P, 1997.

Clerc, Charles. *Mason & Dixon & Pynchon.* New York: UP of America, 2000.

Cornell, Saul. "Moving beyond the Great Story: Postmodern Possibilities, Postmodern Problems." *American Quarterly* 50.2 (1998): 349–57.

Cowart, David. "The Luddite Vision: *Mason & Dixon.*" *American Literature* 71.2 (1999): 341–63.

Danson, Edwin. *Drawing the Line: How Mason and Dixon Surveyed the Most Famous Border in America.* New York: Wiley, 2000.

Darnton, Robert. *The Great Cat Massacre.* New York: Basic, 1984.

Daughtery, Leo. "Gravers False and True: *Blood Meridian* as Gnostic Tragedy." Arnold and Luce, *Perspectives on Cormac McCarthy* 157–72.

Davidson, Sara. "A Visit with Joan Didion." Ed. Ellen Friedman. *Joan Didion: Essays and Conversations.* Princeton: Ontario Review P, 1984. 13–21.

Davis, Kimberly Chabot. " 'Postmodern Blackness': Toni Morrison's *Beloved* and the End of History." *Productive Postmodernism: Consuming Histories and Cultural Studies.* Ed. John N. Duvall. Albany: State U of New York P, 2002. 75–92.

Davis, Natalie Zemon. *The Return of Martin Guerre.* 1983. Ed. Ellen G. Friedman. Princeton, N.J.: Ontario Review, 1984.

Davis, Thadious. "The Signifying Abstraction: Reading 'the Negro' in *Absalom, Absalom!*"
  William Faulkner's Absalom, Absalom! A Casebook. Ed. Fred Hobson. Oxford, Eng.: Oxford
  UP, 2003. 69–106.

Dawood, N. J., trans. *The Koran.* 1956. London: Penguin, 1999.

DeCurtis, Anthony. " 'An Outsider in This Society': An Interview with Don DeLillo."
  Lentricchia, *Introducing Don DeLillo* 43–66.

DeLillo, Don. "American Blood: A Journey through the Labyrinth of Dallas and JFK."
  Rolling Stone 8 Dec. 1983: 21+.

———. *Great Jones Street.* New York: Vintage-Random, 1973.

———. *Libra.* New York: Viking, 1988.

———. *Running Dog.* New York: Knopf, 1978.

———. *Underworld.* New York: Scribner, 1997.

———. *White Noise.* New York: Viking, 1985.

Dewey, Joseph. "The Sound of One Man Mapping: Wicks Cherrycoke and the Eastern
  (Re)solution." Horvath and Malin 112–21.

Didion, Joan. *After Henry.* New York: Simon, 1992.

———. *Democracy.* New York: Simon, 1984.

———. *The Last Thing He Wanted.* New York: Knopf, 1996.

———. *Miami.* New York: Simon, 1987.

———. "Nuclear Blue." *New West* 5 Nov. 1979: 77–78.

———. *Political Fictions.* New York: Knopf, 2001.

———. *Salvador.* New York: Simon, 1982.

Diggins, Keith, and Alun Munslow, eds. *The Nature of History Reader.* London: Routledge,
  2004.

Donoghue, Denis. "Dream Work." *New York Review of Books* 24 June 1993: 5–10.

DuBois, W. E. B. *The Souls of Black Folk.* 1903. New York: Library of America, 1990.

Duvall, John N. "Baseball as Aesthetic Ideology: Cold War History, Race, and Delillo's
  'Pafko at the Wall.' " *Modern Fiction Studies* 41.2 (Summer 1995): 285–313.

———. "Doe Hunting and Masculinity: *Song of Solomon* and *Go Down, Moses*" *Arizona
  Quarterly* 47.1 (Spring 1991): 95–115.

———. "Toni Morrison and the Anxiety of Faulknerian Influence." *Unflinching Gaze:
  Morrison and Faulkner Re-envisioned.* Ed. Carol A. Kolmerten, Stephen M. Ross, and
  Judith Bryant Wittenberg. Jackson: UP of Mississippi, 1997. 3–16.

Duvall, John N., and Ann J. Abadie, eds. *Faulkner and Postmodernism.* Jackson: UP of
  Mississippi, 1999.

Eliade, Mircea. *Rites and Symbols of Initiation: The Mysteries of Birth and Rebirth.* New York:
  Harper & Row, 1958.

Ellis, Joseph J. *Founding Brothers.* New York: Knopf, 2000.

Ellison, Ralph. *Collected Essays of Ralph Ellison.* New York: Modern Library, 1994.

———. *Conversations.* Jackson: UP of Mississippi, 1995.

———. *Invisible Man*. New York: Random, 1952.

———. *Juneteenth*. Ed. John Callahan. New York: Random, 1999.

Ellison, Ralph, and Albert Murray. *Trading Twelves: The Selected Letters of Ralph Ellison and Albert Murray*. Ed. Albert Murray and John Callahan. New York: Modern Library, 2000.

Elton, Geoffrey. "Return to Essentials." *The Postmodern History Reader*. Ed. Keith Jenkins. London: Routledge, 1997. 175–179.

Emerson, Ralph Waldo. *Essays*. New York: Library of America, 1983.

Erkkila, Betsy. "Critical History." *American Quarterly* 50.2 (1998): 358–64.

Evans, Richard J. *In Defense of History*. New York: Norton, 1997.

Faulkner, William. *Absalom, Absalom! The Corrected Text*. 1936. New York: Vintage-Random, 1990.

———. *Essays, Speeches and Public Letters*. Ed. James B. Meriwether. New York: Modern Library, 2004.

———. *Go Down, Moses*. 1942. New York: Vintage-Random, 1990.

———. *Intruder in the Dust*. New York: Random, 1948.

———. *Novels 1930–35*. Ed. Joseph Blotner and Noel Polk. New York: Library of America, 1985.

———. *The Reivers*. *Novels 1957–62*. Ed. Joseph Blotner and Noel Polk. 1962. New York: Library of America, 1999. 723–974.

———. *Selected Letters of William Faulkner*. Ed. Joseph Blotner. New York: Random, 1977.

———. *The Sound and the Fury: The Corrected Text*. 1929. New York: Vintage-Random, 1990.

Figes, Orlando. *A People's Tragedy: A History of the Russian Revolution*. New York: Viking, 1997.

Flanagan, Joseph. "The Seduction of History: Trauma, Re-memory, and the Ethics of the Real." *Clio* 31.4 (Summer 2002): 387–402.

Foertsch, Jaqueline. *Enemies Within*. Urbana: U of Illinois P, 2001.

Fowler, Doreen, and Ann J. Abadie, eds. *Faulkner and Race*. Jackson: UP of Mississippi, 1987.

Frow, John. "The Last Things before the Last: Notes on *White Noise*." Lentricchia, *Introducing Don DeLillo* 175–91.

Girard, Rene. *Violence and the Sacred*. Trans. Patrick Gregory. Baltimore: Johns Hopkins UP, 1977.

Glisssant, Edouard. *Faulkner, Mississippi*. Trans. Barbara Lewis and Thomas C. Spear. New York: Farrar, 1999.

Godden, Richard. "*Absalom, Absalom!* Haiti and Black Labor History: Reading Unreadable Revolutions." *ELH* 61.3 (1994): 685–720.

Gray, Richard. "From Oxford: The Novels of William Faulkner." *William Faulkner: Six Decades of Criticism*. Ed. Linda Wagner-Martin. East Lansing: Michigan State UP, 2002. 397–414.

Greenblatt, Stephen. "The Eating of the Soul." *Representations* 48 (Fall 1994): 97–116.

Grimwood, Michael. "Faulkner and the Vocal Liabilities of Black Characterization." Fowler and Abadie 255–271.

Guillemin, Georg. *The Pastoral Vision of Cormac McCarthy*. College Station: Texas A&M UP, 2004.

Hardwick, Elizabeth. "Faulkner and the South Today." Warren, *Faulkner* 225–30.

Harlan, David. *The Degradation of American History*. Chicago: U of Chicago P, 1997.

———. "Intellectual History and the Return of Literature." *American Historical Review* 94.3 (1989): 581–609.

Harris, Trudier. *Fiction and Folklore: The Novels of Toni Morrison*. Knoxville: U of Tennessee P, 1991.

Himmelfarb, Gertrude. *On Looking into the Abyss*. New York: Knopf, 1994.

Hite, Molly. "Modernist Design, Postmodernist Paranoia: Reading *Absalom, Absalom!* with *Gravity's Rainbow*." Duvall and Abadie 57–80.

Hobsbawm, Eric J. *On History*. New York: Norton, 1997.

Hobson, Fred. *The Southern Writer in the Postmodern World*. Athens: U of Georgia P, 1991.

Hofstadter, Richard. *The American Political Tradition*. 1948. New York: Vintage-Random, 1989.

———. *The Progressive Historians*. Chicago: U of Chicago P, 1968.

Hollinger, David. "The Return of the Prodigal. . . ." *American Historical Review* 94.3 (1989): 610–21.

Holloway, David. *The Late Modernism of Cormac McCarthy*. Westport, Conn.: Greenwood, 2002.

Horvath, Brooke, and Irving Malin, eds. *Pynchon and Mason & Dixon*. Newark, N.J.: U of Delaware P, 2000.

Horvitz, Deborah. "Nameless Ghosts: Possession and Dispossession in *Beloved*." *Studies in American Fiction* 17 (1989): 157–67.

House, Elizabeth B. "Toni Morrison's Ghost: The Beloved Who Is Not Beloved." *Studies in American Fiction* 18 (1990): 17–26.

Hulse, Carl. "Divisive Words: The Overview; Lott Fails to Quell Furor and Quits Top Senate Post; Frist Emerges as Successor." *New York Times*, 11 Nov. 2002. nytimes.com.

Hutcheon, Linda. *A Poetics of Postmodernism: History, Theory, Fiction*. New York: Routledge, 1988.

———. *The Politics of Postmodernism*. New York: Routledge, 1989.

Irwin, John T. *Doubling and Incest/Repetition and Revenge*. Baltimore: Johns Hopkins UP, 1975.

Isaacson, Walter. *Benjamin Franklin: A Life*. New York: Simon, 2003.

Jackson, Blyden. "Faulkner's Negroes Twain." Fowler and Abadie 58–69.

James, William. *The Will to Believe*. 1898. New York: Dover, 1956.

Jenkins, Keith. *Why History? Ethics and Postmodernity*. London: Routledge, 1999.

Johnson, Denis. *Angels*. New York: Knopf, 1983.

———. *Fiskadoro.* New York: Knopf, 1985.

———. *Jesus' Son.* New York: Farrar, 1992.

———. *Seek: Reports from the Edges of America and Beyond.* New York: Harper, 2001.

Jones, Carolyn. "Sula and Beloved: Images of Cain in the Novels of Toni Morrison." *African American Review* 27.4 (1993): 615–26.

Karl, Frederick R. *William Faulkner: American Writer.* New York: Weidenfeld, 1989.

Kartiganer, Donald M. *The Fragile Thread: The Meaning of Form in Faulkner's Novels.* Amherst: U of Massachusetts P, 1979.

Kenner, Hugh. "Faulkner and the Avante-Garde." *Faulkner: New Perspectives.* Ed. Richard Broadhead. Englewood Cliffs, N.J.: Prentice, 1983. 62–73.

Kinney, Arthur, ed. *Critical Essays on William Faulkner: The Sutpen Family.* New York: Hall, 1996

Knight, Peter. "Everything Is Connected: *Underworld*'s Secret History of Paranoia." *Modern Fiction Studies* 45.3 (Fall 1999): 811–36.

Kramer, Lloyd. "Literature, Criticism, and Historical Imagination: The Literary Challenge of Hayden White and Dominick LaCapra." *The New Cultural History.* Ed. Linda Hunt. Berkeley: U of California P, 1989. 122–24.

Kronick, Joseph. "*Libra* and the Assassination of JFK: A Textbook Operation." *Arizona Quarterly* 50.1 (Spring 1994): 109–32.

Krumholz, Linda. "The Ghosts of Slavery: Historical Recovery in Toni Morrison's *Beloved.*" *African American Review* 26 (1992): 395–408.

Kundera, Milan. *The Art of the Novel.* Trans. Linda Asher. New York: Grove. 1986.

Ladd, Barbara. " 'The Direction of the Howling': Nationalism and the Color Line in *Absalom, Absalom!*" *American Literature* 66.3 (Sept. 1994): 525–51.

Landes, David. *Revolution in Time: Clocks and the Making of the World.* Rev ed. Cambridge, Mass.: Belknap P, 2000.

Lane, Anthony. "Then, Voyager." Rev. of *Mason & Dixon. New Yorker* 12 May 1997: 97–98, 100.

LeClair, Tom. *In the Loop: Don DeLillo and the Systems Novel.* Urbana: U of Illinois P, 1992.

Lentricchia, Frank, ed. *Introducing Don DeLillo.* Durham, N.C.: Duke UP, 1991.

———. "*Libra* as Postmodern Critique." *South Atlantic Quarterly* 89.2 (Spring 1990): 431–53.

Lenz, Millicent. "*Danger Quotient*, *Fiskadoro*, *Ridley Walker*, and the Failure of the Campbellian Monomyth." *Science Fiction for Young Readers.* Ed. C. W. Sullivan. Westport, Conn.: Greenwood, 1993. 113–19.

———. "Reinventing a World: Myth in Denis Johnson's *Fiskadoro.*" *The Nightmare Considered: Critical Essays on Nuclear War Literature.* Ed. Nancy Anisfield. Bowling Green, Ohio: Popular, 1991. 114–22.

Levesque, Richard. "Telling Postmodern Tales: Absent Authorities in Didion's *Democracy* and DeLillo's *Mao II.*" *Arizona Quarterly* 54. 3 (1998): 69–87.

Lilley, James. D., ed. *Cormac McCarthy: New Directions*. Albuquerque: U of New Mexico P, 2002.

Lincoln, Abraham. *Speeches and Writings: 1859–1865*. Ed. Don E. Fehrenbacher. New York: Library of America, 1989.

Longley, John Lewis, Jr. "The Nuclear Winter of Cormac Mccarthy." *The Virginia Quarterly Review* 62 (Autumn 1986): 746–50.

Lubiano, Wahneema. "The Postmodernist Rag: Political Identity and the Vernacular in *Song of Solomon*." Smith, *New Essays on* Song of Solomon 93–116.

Mailer, Norman. *The Armies of the Night: History as Novel, the Novel as History*. New York: New American Library, 1968.

Mallon, Thomas. "The Limits of History in the Novels of Joan Didion." *Critique* 21.3 (1980): 43–52.

McCarthy, Cormac. *Blood Meridian: Or, the Evening Redness in the West*. New York: Knopf, 1985.

McCullough, C. Behan. *The Truth of History*. London: Routledge, 1998.

McCullough, David G. *John Adams*. New York: Simon, 2001.

McHale, Brian. "*Mason & Dixon* in the Zone, or, a Brief Poetics of Pynchon-Space." Horvath and Malin 43–62.

———. *Postmodernist Fiction*. New York: Methuen, 1987.

Menand, Louis. "Entropology." *New York Review of Books* 12 June 1997: 22, 24–25.

Mendelson, Edward. "Pynchon's Gravity." *Thomas Pynchon*. Ed. Harold Bloom. New York: Chelsea, 1986. 15–22.

Michaels, Walter Benn. *Our America*. Durham, N.C.: Duke UP, 1995.

———. *The Shape of the Signifier*. Princeton, N.J.: Princeton UP, 2004.

Middleton, Joyce Irene. "From Orality to Literacy: Oral Memory in Toni Morrison's *Song of Solomon*." Smith, *New Essays on* Song of Solomon 19–39.

Mobley, Marilyn Sanders. "A Different Remembering: Memory, History, and Meaning in *Beloved*." *Toni Morrison*. Ed. Harold Bloom. New York: Chelsea, 1990. 189–99.

Morris, Edmund. *Dutch: A Memoir of Ronald Reagan*. New York: Random, 1999.

Morrison, Toni. "The Art of Fiction CXXXIV." Interview with Elissa Schappel. *Paris Review* 129 (1993): 83–125.

———. *Beloved*. New York: Knopf, 1987.

———. "Interview with Gloria Naylor." *Southern Review* 21 (1985): 567–93.

———. *Playing in the Dark*. Cambridge, Mass.: Harvard UP, 1992.

———. "Rootedness: The Ancestor as Foundation." *Black Women Writers (1950–80): A Critical Evaluation*. Ed. Mari Evans. Garden City, N.Y.: Anchor-Doubleday, 1984. 339–45.

———. *Song of Solomon*. New York: Knopf, 1977.

Nadel, Alan. "Postwar America and the Story of Democracy." *National Identities and Post-Americanist Narratives*. Ed. Donald Pease. Durham, N.C.: Duke UP, 1994. 95–120.

O'Donnell, Patrick. "Faulkner in Light of Morrison." *Unflinching Gaze: Morrison and Faulkner Re-envisioned.* Ed. Carol A. Kolmerten, Stephen M. Ross, and Judith Bryant Wittenberg. Jackson: UP of Mississippi, 1997. 219–27.

Olster, Stacey. "A 'Patch of England, at a Three-Thousand-Mile Off-set'? Representing America in *Mason & Dixon.*" *MFS: Modern Fiction Studies* 50.2 (Summer 2004): 283–302.

Owens, Barclay. *Cormac McCarthy's Western Novels.* Tucson: U of Arizona P, 2000.

Palmer, Bryan D. *The Descent into Discourse: The Reification of Language and the Writing of Social History.* Philadelphia: Temple UP, 1991.

Panofsky, Erwin. *Meaning in the Visual Arts.* Chicago: U of Chicago P, 1955.

Parker, Hershel. "What Quentin Saw Out There." Kinney 275–78.

Parkes, Adam. "History, Bloodshed, and the Spectacle of American Identity in *Blood Meridian.*" Lilley 103–22.

Parrish, Timothy, ed. *The Cambridge Companion to Philip Roth.* Cambridge: Cambridge UP, 2007.

———."Denis Johnson's *Jesus' Son:* To Kingdom Come." *Critique* 43.1 (Fall 2001): 17–29.

———. "The Fight to Be a Negro Leader." *The Cambridge Companion to Ralph Ellison.* Ed. Ross Posnock. Cambridge: Cambridge UP, 2005. 137–56.

———. "The Killer Wears the Halo: Cormac McCarthy, Flannery O'Connor, and the American Religion." *Sacred Violence: A Reader's Companion to Cormac McCarthy.*" El Paso: Texas Western P, 1995.

Parrish, Timothy, and Elizabeth Spiller. "A Flute Made of Human Bone: *Blood Meridan* and the Survivors of American History." *Prospects* 23 (1998): 461–81.

Paz, Octavio. *The Labyrinth of Solitude: Life and Thought in Mexico.* Trans. Lysander Kamp. New York: Grove, 1961.

Phillips, Dana M. "History and the Ugly Facts of *Blood Meridian.*" Lilley 17–46.

Phillips, Kevin P. *American Dynasty: Aristocracy, Fortune, and the Politics of Deceit in the House of Bush.* New York: Viking, 2004.

Poirier, Richard. "The Importance of Thomas Pynchon." *Thomas Pynchon.* Ed. Harold Bloom. New York: Chelsea, 1986. 47–58.

———. " 'Strange Gods' in Jefferson, Mississippi: Analysis of *Absalom, Absalom!*" *William Faulkner's Absalom, Absalom! A Critical Casebook.* Ed. Elisabeth Muhlenfield. New York: Garland, 1984. 1–22.

Porter, Carolyn. *Seeing & Being.* Middletown, Conn.: Wesleyan UP, 1981.

Pynchon, Thomas. *The Crying of Lot 49.* Cutchogue, N.Y.: Buccaneer, 1966.

———. *Gravity's Rainbow.* New York: 1973.

———. *Mason & Dixon.* New York: Holt, 1997.

———. *V: A Novel.* Philadelphia: Lippincott, 1963.

Rahv, Philip. "Review, *New Masses,* November 1936." *William Faulkner: The Critical Heritage.* Ed. John Basset. London: Routledge, 1975. 208–10.

Reitenbach, Gail. "Foreign Exchange in Denis Johnson's *The Stars at Noon*." *Arizona Quarterly* 47.4 (Winter 1991): 27–47.

Rigney, Barbara Hill. " 'A Story to Pass On': Ghosts and the Significance of History in Toni Morrison's *Beloved*." *Haunting the House of Fiction: Feminist Perspectives on Ghost Stories Written by American Women*. Ed. Lynette Carpenter and Wendy Kolmar. Knoxville: U of Tennessee P, 1991. 229–35.

Rodriguez, Richard. *Brown: The Last Discovery of America*. New York: Viking, 2002.

———. *Days of Obligation*. New York: Viking, 1992.

Rody, Caroline. "Toni Morrison's *Beloved*: History, 'Rememory,' and a 'Clamor for a Kiss.' " *American Literary History* 7.1 (1995): 92–119.

Rogin, Michael Paul. *Ronald Reagan, the Movie, and Other Episodes in Political Demonology*. Berkeley: U of California P, 1987.

Rorty, Richard. *Achieving Our Country*. Cambridge, Mass.: Harvard UP, 1999.

———. *Consequences of Pragmatism*. Minneapolis: U of Minnesota P, 1982.

———. *Objectivity, Relatavism, and Truth: Philosophical Papers, Vol. 1*. Cambridge: Cambridge UP, 1991.

Rothberg, Michael. "Dead Letter Office: Conspriacy, Trauma, and *Song of Solomon*'s Posthumous Communication." *African American Review* 37.4 (Winter 2003): 501–16.

Saltzman, Arthur. " 'Cranks of Ev'ry Radius': Romancing the Line in *Mason & Dixon*. Horvath and Malin 63–72.

Sartre, Jean-Paul. "On *The Sound and the Fury*: Time in the Works of William Faulkner." Warren, *Faulkner* 87–93.

Schama, Simon. *Citizens: A Chronicle of the French Revolution*. New York, Knopf, 1989.

———. *Dead Certainties: Unwarranted Speculations*. New York: Vintage-Random, 1992.

Schaub, Thomas H. "Plot, Ideology, and Compassion in *Mason & Dixon*." Horvath and Malin 189–202.

Schwartz, Delmore. "The Fiction of William Faulkner." *William Faulkner: The Critical Heritage*. Ed. John Basset. London: Routledge, 1975. 276–89.

Seed, David. "Mapping the Course of Empire in the New World." Horvath and Malin 84–99.

Shaviro, Steven. " 'The Very Life of Darkness': A Reading of *Blood Meridian*." Arnold and Luce, *Perspectives on Cormac McCarthy* 143–52.

Slade, Joseph W. *Thomas Pynchon*. New York: Warner, 1974.

Smith, Robert McClure. "Addiction and Recovery in Denis Johnson's *Jesus' Son*." *Critique* 42.2 (Winter 2001): 180–91.

Smith, Valerie. " 'Circling the Subject': History and Narrative in *Beloved*." *Toni Morrison: Critical Perspectives, Past and Present*. Ed. Henry Louis Gates, Jr., and K. Anthony Appiah. New York: Amistad, 1993. 342–55.

———, ed. *New Essays on Song of Solomon*. Cambridge, Eng.: Cambridge UP, 1995.

———. "The Quest for and Discovery of Identity in Toni Morrison's *Song of Solomon*. Ed. Jane Furman. Toni Morrison's *Song of Solomon: A Casebook*. Oxford, Oxford UP, 2003. 27–40.

Sobel, Dava. *Longitude*. New York: Walker, 1995.

Spargo, R. Clifton. "Trauma and the Specters of Enslavement in Morrison's *Beloved*." *Mosaic* 35 (Mar. 2002): 113–19.

Spiller, Elizabeth. *Science, Reading, and Renaissance Literature*. Cambridge, Eng.: Cambridge UP, 2004.

Spitzer, Alan B. *Historical Truth and Lies about the Past*. Chapel Hill: U of North Carolina P, 1996.

Spurgeon, Sara. "The Sacred Hunter and the Eucharist of the Wilderness: Mythic Reconstruction in *Blood Meridian*." Lilley 75–102.

Stave, Shirley A. "Toni Morrison's *Beloved* and the Vindication of Lilith." *South Atlantic Review* 58 (1993): 49–56.

Storhoff, Gary. "Faulkner's Family Dilemma: Quentin's Crucible." *William Faulkner: Six Decades of Criticism*. Ed. Linda Wagner-Martin. East Lansing: Michigan State UP, 2002. 236–52.

Strandberg, Victor. "Dimming the Enlightenment: Thomas Pynchon's *Mason & Dixon*." Horvath and Malin 100–111.

Sundquist, Eric J. *Faulkner: The House Divided*. Baltimore: Johns Hopkins UP, 1983.

Suskind, Ron. "Without a Doubt." *New York Times Sunday Magazine* 17 Oct. 2004. http://www.nytimes.com/2004/10/17/magazine/17BUSH.html,

Tager, Michael. "The Political Vision of Joan Didion's *Democracy*." *Critique* 31.3 (1990): 173–84.

Tanner, Tony. *The American Mystery*. Cambridge, Eng.: Cambridge UP, 2000.

Toews, John E. "Intellectual History after the Linguistic Turn: The Autonomy of Meaning and the Irreducibility of Experience." *American Historical Review* 92.4 (1987): 879–907.

Tompkins, Jane. *West of Everything*. New York: Oxford UP, 1992.

Towner, Theresa M. *Faulkner on the Color Line*. Jackson: UP of Mississippi, 2000.

Turner, Victor. *The Forest of Symbols*. Ithaca, N.Y.: Cornell UP, 1967.

Vidal, Gore. *Lincoln*. New York: Random, 1984.

Waggoner, Hyatt. "Past as Present: *Absalom, Absalom!*" Warren, *Faulkner* 163–74.

Wallach, Rick. "From *Beowulf* to *Blood Meridian*: Cormac McCarthy's Demysticification of the Martial Code." In Lilley, 199–214.

———. ed. *Myth, Legend, Dust: Critical Responses to Cormac McCarthy*. Manchester, Eng.: Manchester UP, 2000.

Warren, Robert Penn, ed. *Faulkner: A Collection of Critical Essays*. Englewood Cliffs, N.J.: Prentice, 1966.

———. "Faulkner: The South, the Negro, and Time." Warren, *Faulkner* 251–71.

Weinstein, Philip M. *What Else but Love? The Ordeal of Race in Faulkner and Morrison.* New York: Columbia UP, 1996.

Werner, Craig. "Minstrel Nightmares: Black Dreams of Faulkner's Dream of Blacks." Fowler and Abadie 35–57.

White, Hayden. "Interview with Ewa Domanska: The Image of Self-presentation." *Diacritics* 24.1 (Spring 1994): 91–100.

———. *Tropics of Discourse.* Baltimore: Johns Hopkins UP, 1978.

———. "The Value of Narrativity in the Representation of Reality." *The Content and the Form: Narrative Discourse and Historical Representation.* Baltimore: Johns Hopkins UP, 1989. 1–10.

Wilcox, Leonard. "Baudrillard, DeLillo's *White Noise,* and the End of Heroic Narrative." *Contemporary Literature* 32.3 (1991): 346–55.

Willman, Skip. "Traversing the Fantasies of the JFK Assassination: Conspiracy and Contingency in Don DeLillo's *Libra.*" *Contemporary Literature* 39.3 (1998): 405–33.

Wills, Gary. *Negro President.* Boston: Houghton, 2003.

Wilson, Edmund. "William Faulkner's Reply to the Civil Rights Program." Warren, *Faulkner* 219–25.

Winchell, Mark Royden. *Joan Didion.* Rev. ed. Boston: Twayne, 1989.

Wood, Michael. "Pynchon's *Mason & Dixon.*" Rev. of *Mason & Dixon,* by Thomas Pynchon. *Raritan* 17:4 (Spring 1998): 120–30.

Wyatt, Jean. "Giving Body to the Word: The Maternal Symbolic in Toni Morrison's *Beloved.*" *PMLA* 108 (1993): 474–88.

Zagorin, Perez. "Historiography and Postmodernism: Reconsiderations." *History and Theory: Studies in the Philosophy of History* 29.3 (1990): 263–74.

Index

multiculturalism, 2, 22, 41, 85, 98–101,
241–47, 255
Murray, Albert, 123, 273n10

Nadel, Alan, 203, 285n5
Naylor, Gloria, 118, 276n18
New Science, the (empiricism), 40, 151,
160, 170, 189
New World, 85, 115, 153; European
conquest of, 39, 95–116, 240–47
New York Times Book Review list, 33–36
Newton, Isaac, 160–62, 166–67
Nietzsche, Friedrich, 9, 81, 89
9/11, 2, 41, 210–11, 219, 233–34
Nixon, Richard, 34
Norris, Frank, 20
North, Oliver, 205
nuclear holocaust, 233, 237–38, 247–48,
254–55, 260

O'Donnell, Patrick, 121
Old World, 85, 93. *See also* Europe
Olster, Stacey, 154, 284n7
Orwell, George, 226
Oswald, Lee Harvey, 26–31

Pafko, Andy, 214
Palmer, Bryan, 16, 196, 270n4
Palmerston, Henry, 202
Panofsky, Erwin, 105, 278n13
Parker, Hershel, 67–68
Parkes, Adam, 82, 278n9
Parkman, Francis, 16–17, 270n8
Parrish, Timothy, 271n15, 277n3, 287n2
Partner, Nancy F., 151
Patriot Act, 187, 211
Paz, Octavio, 288n6
Penn, William, 151
Phillips, Dana, 82–83, 277n1, 277n4
Phillips, Kevin, 286n16
Plame, Valerie, 224
Poirier, Richard, 44, 153, 271n1
Porter, Carolyn, 43, 45, 79, 271–72n2
postmodernism, 2, 13, 126, 151; and
multiculturalism, 3, 255
postmodernist critiques of history, 2, 12,
16, 23–31, 150–92, 240
post-postmodernism, 8, 156, 260

Prince, 251–52; "Purple Rain," 251–52
Proust, Marcel, 16, 21, 76, 208, 235
Pynchon, Thomas, 4, 22, 33–34, 38, 40,
118, 193, 197, 204, 266; *The Crying of
Lot 49*, 176–77; *Gravity's Rainbow*, 153,
175–77, 193–44, 214, 283n1, 284n16,
285n17; "Is It OK to Be a Luddite?" 155;
Mason & Dixon, 150–92, 194; *V* 153, 193,
227; version of American Indian history,
153, 156–60, 173, 176, 190–92, 269n1

Quetzalcoatl, 240–47

Rahv, Philip, 48
Ranke, Leopold von, 12–14, 42, 179
Reagan, Nancy, 199–201
Reagan, Ronald, 6, 194, 199–201, 204–5,
209–19, 286n17
"relativism," 1, 6, 11–12
Republican Party, 63, 77–79, 199–201
Revolutionary War, 183
Rodriguez, Richard, 189, 269n1, 288n6;
"India," 97–99
Rogin, Michael, 199–201, 217–18, 285n19
Roosevelt, Franklin Delano, 35, 284n16
Rorty, Richard, 10–11, 13, 32–33, 98, 118,
123–26, 278n12
Roth, Philip, 34–36
Rothberg, Michael, 119, 280n8
Rove, Karl, 204, 213, 231
Russert, Tim, 224

Sachs, Oliver, 232
Saltzman, Arthur, 154
Santayana, George, 76
Sappho, 167
Sartre, Jean-Paul, 76
Saussure, Ferdinand de, 9
Schama, Simon, 11, 270n6
Schappel, Elissa, 127
Schaub, Thomas, 154
Schwartz, Delmore, 48
science: and empire, 164–66, 168, 171, 180,
188–90; and historical narrative, 151–56,
189, 195, 236, 241, 244–47, 259
Scott, Walter, 14
Seed, David, 154
Shakespeare, William, 105